Crosscurrents in American C

Crosscurrents in American Culture

A READER IN UNITED STATES HISTORY

VOLUME I: TO 1877

Bruce Dorsey
Swarthmore College

Woody Register
Sewanee: The University of the South

HOUGHTON MIFFLIN HARCOURT PUBLISHING COMPANY
Boston   New York

For Sophie and Tim

Publisher: Suzanne Jeans
Senior Sponsoring Editor: Ann West
Senior Marketing Manager: Katherine Bates
Senior Discipline Product Manager: Lynn Baldridge
Senior Development Editor: Lisa Kalner Williams
Senior Project Editor: Bob Greiner
Senior Media Producer: Lisa Ciccolo
Senior Content Manager: Janet Edmonds
Art and Design Manager: Jill Haber
Cover Design Director: Anthony L. Saizon
Senior Photo Editor: Jennifer Meyer Dare
Senior Composition Buyer: Chuck Dutton
Project Manager: Susan Peltier
Marketing Associate: Lauren Bussard
Editorial Production Assistant: Laura Collins

Cover Art: *Interior of the Park Theatre, New York City*, 1822 by John Searle Collection of the New-York Historical Society/The Bridgeman Art Library

Text Credits: Credits appear on page 336, which constitutes an extension of the copyright page.

Printed in the U.S.A.

Library of Congress Catalog Number: 2007941740

Instructor's exam copy:
ISBN-10: 0-618-73229-2
ISBN-13: 978-0-618-73229-6

For orders, use student text ISBNs:
ISBN-10: 0-618-07738-3
ISBN-13: 978-0-618-07738-0

1 2 3 4 5 6 7 8 9 –EB– 12 11 10 09 08

Contents

CHAPTER 6
The Southern Culture of Slavery and a Slave Culture:
1790–1860 171

Double Consciousness as a Slave:
An African American Culture Amidst Slavery 172

Saddles and Spurs: Creating a Proslavery Ideology 185

CHAPTER 7
Reforming America: 1820–1860 200

Meeting the Spirit: Cultural Disputes Over Revivalist Religion 201

CHAPTER 9
Sectional Conflict and Civil War: 1850–1865   272

Uncle Tom's Cabin *and Anti-Uncle Tom Novels*   273

John Brown's Body: Symbols and Meanings of the Civil War   281

Preface

Crosscurrents in American Culture offers an innovative approach to the study of U.S. history that conforms to the new directions of historians' research and students' interests. The idea for this project arose from our own classroom experiences as college teachers. With all the readers available, we have been unable to find a comprehensive collection of historical documents that supported the cultural approach and sensibility that we used in our classes. We have designed this collection to solve this problem. This U.S. history reader is the first devoted to primary-source cultural history texts, images, and documents. Many of the materials in these volumes are those that we ourselves have collected and used in our American history classes. From experience, we know them to be effective not only in teaching the subject of U.S. history, but also in exciting students' interest in the study of history.

Crosscurrents explores a broad range of themes and topics, some familiar and some unfamiliar to surveys of U.S. history. Our aim is not to be novel, but to incorporate sources that represent various and alternative voices and perspectives: women, people of color, residents of cities and the countryside, artists and novelists, people in business, entertainment, advertising, and sports. At the same time, the significant events in the history of the United States, from the American Revolution to Reconstruction to the late twentieth-century culture wars, are all addressed with the fresh and new perspectives made possible through a critical reading of cultural documents. These materials raise the kinds of questions that many historians today are directing at the American past. Social conflicts can be examined in accounts of the popular violence provoked over the question of how to perform Shakespearean drama in antebellum America; shifts in the political understandings of citizenship rights can be plotted in the letters ordinary women wrote to the First Lady pleading, during the era of the Great Depression, for help in adopting a child so that they, too, could be mothers. Questions about economics and the family are posed by the comical stories of wily pre–Civil War Yankee peddlers suckering rural families into purchasing their overpriced wares; for a later era, the same questions can be explored in Ruth Handler's autobiographical account of the keen stratagems she used to override the objections of men to give birth to her creation, the *Barbie* doll.

As these examples suggest, we define "culture" broadly to encompass many of the various segments of expression between which scholars usually have drawn boundaries: the material artifacts and fashions of everyday life that are categorized as "consumer" or "mass culture"; the arts and other modes of expression that are popular among ordinary working people and their families, and are categorized as "folk" or "popular culture"; celebrated examples of "high culture," like the Hudson River

School paintings of the mid-nineteenth century, as well as the often ignored categories of low culture, from the pulp novels of antebellum America to late-twentieth-century rock 'n' roll music and video games. Moreover, we present the literary, visual, and aural materials in an integrated fashion. We hope this approach will discourage students from regarding images or music as mere "illustrations" of themes that are more legitimately investigated in written primary texts. On the contrary, we encourage students to treat all of these cultural forms as historical evidence for significant questions about the past.

This reader is also the first in step with today's generation of college students, who are already accustomed to think with and about culture. *Crosscurrents* taps into students' orientation toward images, sounds, and visual texts, but does so in a manner that deepens their sense and appreciation of the degree to which their world has been made by the past. It challenges students and teachers alike to think critically about the importance and power of culture in shaping lives in the pasts as well as in our own times.

Crosscurrents follows the contours of general surveys of American history. The chapters are organized in chronological order, and each chapter is divided into thematic sections. In addition to the editors' introductions to each section, the documents are preceded by "Problems to Consider," questions designed to stimulate thoughtful reflection on and possible discussion of the historical significance of that text. With the "problems" in the study of American history included in *Crosscurrents*, we try to open up discussion and inquiry, not to close them off by directing students toward a particular answer or solution. The "problems" approach of these volumes reflects our position that studying the past is less about coming to final answers to questions than about wrestling with the problems posed by the evidence.

᎒ ACKNOWLEDGMENTS

We would like to thank our own students who have helped us to refine our own critical assessment of American culture. We are especially grateful for the assistance of student research assistants Sarah Yahm, Timothy Stewart-Winter, Peter Wirzbicki, Margaret Hughes, and Katherine Rogers. We are also grateful for the assistance of the many librarians who guided us, including the staff of the Library Company of Philadelphia, the Friends Historical Library, Swarthmore College Library, and Sewanee's du Pont Library. Kevin Reynolds and the interlibrary loan staff at Sewanee deserve special mention and thanks. This project relied on the guidance, perseverance, and patience of Terri Wise, Margaret Manos, and Lisa Kalner Williams at Houghton Mifflin. As our respective spouses, Martha Hodes and Julie Berebitsky, well know, we are most deeply indebted to them. Both are talented historians and generous partners who have shaped how we think about history and how we imagined and constructed this reader. The collection itself we dedicate to Tim Dorsey and Sophie Register. Anyone who knows them will understand how they have inspired and taught us to be better teachers and human beings.

Instructors from around the country provided us with valuable feedback on the various drafts of *Crosscurrents*. We heartily thank the following reviewers for their comments: Scott E. Casper, University of Nevada at Reno; Lyde Cullen Sizer, Sarah Lawrence College; Nancy Davis, DePaul University; Kathleen DuVal, University of North Carolina at Chapel Hill; Christopher Johnson, Palomar College; Carol A. Keller, San Antonio College; Carolyn J. Lawes, Old Dominion University; Scott Miltenberger, University of California, Davis; Krystyn R. Moon, Georgia State University; Janet Moore Lindman, Rowan University; Richard Moss, Purdue University; Jonathan Nashel, Indiana University South Bend; Scott A. Sandage, Carnegie Mellon University; Lisa C. Tolbert, University of North Carolina at Greensboro; and Daniel Wickberg, University of Texas at Dallas.

Bruce Dorsey
Woody Register

Introduction:
Reading Culture

IN NOVEMBER 2004, in the midst of the U.S. war in Iraq, the *Los Angeles Times* published a photograph of a young, unnamed Marine resting "after more than twelve hours of nearly nonstop deadly combat." Within days, the unknown soldier's face—smeared with dirt and camouflage paint, a bloody scrape on his nose, and, dangling from his lips, a legibly labeled Marlboro cigarette—had appeared on network television and in more than a hundred newspapers. The tabloid *New York Post* made the image its front-page cover, under the banner headline "SMOKIN'." CBS News anchorman Dan Rather showcased the image on the evening news. "This," he told viewers, "is a warrior with his eyes on the far horizon, scanning for danger. See it, study it, absorb it. Think about it. Then take a deep breath of pride." By that point, the soldier had been identified as Lance Corporal James Blake Miller, and the attention he was receiving because of the photo had become a story in itself. In his rural Kentucky hometown, Miller was a local hero, and his mother was thrilled by her son's fame. Elsewhere, women wrote to the *Los Angeles Times* asking for the mailing address of the soldier whose "gaze [was] warm but deadly." The newspaper boasted that the image of "the Marlboro Man" (as he was called) had "moved into the realm of the iconic."

That assessment seems fairly straightforward, but is it? What gave an image of a battle-weary man smoking a cigarette such significance? What made it work? An "iconic" photograph, as the newspaper used that word, is more than a popularly recognized image that generates a lot of positive emotional response. An iconic image expresses recognizable and agreed-upon truths and values that seem to be eternal, essential, and natural dimensions of the human experience. It stands for something universal. To accomplish this task, the image has to fit into or remind us of a story that we all know and that tells us something about ourselves as a people.

1

A major source of this image's explanatory power appears in the name assigned to the soldier before his actual identity was established. He was not just any American man, but the world's best-known cowboy: "the Marlboro Man," the globally advertised emblem of the Philip Morris cigarette. If we are to understand what makes this photograph work—why it makes some people swell with pride—we have to follow some of Dan Rather's advice. We have to look at "the Marlboro Man" image, study it, and think about it. We have to break it down, examine its parts, and ask questions: Would it have worked in the same way or as well if the soldier had been a woman or an African American man? What if he were smoking Camels or Virginia Slims? What if he were not smoking at all? In other words, how do our expectations about gender, race, and class shape what we see in this photograph? These are the kinds of questions that cultural historians bring to historical materials from America's past. They also are the types of questions that we hope you will ask of the documents and images in this book as you seek to wrestle with the problems of understanding American history.

Marine Lance Corporal James Blake Miller on the front page of the *New York Post*, November 10, 2004.

Studying history is often thought of as a matter of mastering information about what happened and when. That kind of factual record is important, but we believe it is insufficient by itself. *Crosscurrents in American Culture* encourages students of American history to engage in a lively, critical, and analytical examination of the cultural record of the American past. "Culture," in this sense, refers to the many forms of expression that surround people in their everyday lives: stories, plays, movies, songs, art, political rituals, cartoons, propaganda, dance steps, amusement park rides, billboards, TV marketing pitches. The list could go on indefinitely. Professionally trained scholars often have written off these dimensions of life as unworthy of their or anyone else's serious attention. We, however, regard such materials as the very "stuff" of history. When we use the word "culture," then, we mean not just things but also the ideas, values, behaviors, and meanings that any given people share. How is it that they come to share these cultural constructs? This is accomplished through the forms of expression that we have begun to list here. These cultural materials communicate meaning and represent reality for that group.

Historians are always interested in discovering the meaning and significance of any evidence from the past. To understand *meaning*, we try to reconstruct what a document might have meant in its own time, to its creator or author, and to its viewers or readers. To ascertain its *significance*, we use our critical judgments and our store of knowledge about the past to determine why this document was important and how it related to other texts or events and concerns in that era. To borrow the words of the historian James Axtell, we seek "to imagine the imaginations" of people who lived in the past. Because something is imagined does not mean we should dismiss it. On the contrary, many historians today treat people's imaginations as the "solid facts" of history. People in the past—no less than ourselves today—were predisposed to see the world in particular, although often conflicting, ways. Reflecting on the European "discovery" of America beginning in the fifteenth century, the historian Richard White reminds us that, in a cultural sense, there is no such thing as *terra incognita*, or "unknown land," even for those shiploads of Europeans who saw the fauna and flora of the New World for the first time. The new, White observes, "always arrives to the eye fully stocked with expectations, fears, rumors, desires, and meanings." Those expectations influence how people see the landscape, explain the world and its human relations, and defend or resist the social changes and conflicts that are enacted in their everyday lives. That is why we treat all cultural materials, whether those documents are words in print or visual images on canvas, film, or video, as "texts"—that is, as virtual transcripts from the past that we can read. Such documents are the evidence of how people thought and acted in the past.

The emphasis on *action* is worth repeating. Cultural history should do more than explain what people in the past thought, believed, and feared, or the meaning of the things with which they surrounded themselves. It also should help us examine how cultural texts shape actions, and how actions take the form of cultural texts. Cultural history should enable us to see how people put ideas to work to justify, to preserve, or, as often was the case, to resist particular social orders or arrangements. For instance, when English Puritans cleared the woodlands of New England to build villages in the 1630s and 1640s, their actions were guided by culturally specific ideas about the landscape and its appropriate uses. These ideas determined the shape of their fields and the architecture of their houses. These beliefs also bolstered the colonists' claims to their rightful ownership of the land, since in their minds, native inhabitants were not using the land in a legitimate way. The Puritans did more than settle a new land; they sought to impose their "story," with all its meanings, on the land itself, despite the resistance of native peoples who had their own, very different stories about the land and its use. Cultural history helps us see how military, political, diplomatic, and economic conflicts took the form of conflicting stories and that they were, in fact, cultural conflicts.

Culture, as we use the word, also defines what is normal, moral, appropriate, and natural, as well as what is abnormal, strange, barbarous, and unnatural. Culture gives meaning to concepts such as "the nation" and "the enemy," civilization and wilderness, "a man's work" or "a woman's place." In doing so, it sets the stage for conflict as well as harmony because such sharply drawn opposites always are subject to being challenged or defended. We want you to reflect on the ways people put ideas—stories—into action in their daily lives and in many of the most important moments of conflict and of unity that have shaped the history of the United States.

Crosscurrents in American Culture presents a cultural history of the United States through the lens of a diverse collection of documents from the past. You will find familiar topics in American history—slavery, industrialization, the Civil War and Reconstruction, the Great Depression, the environmental movement—but you will learn about these topics through less conventional sources. Novelty, however, is not our sole aim. We wish to incorporate materials and perspectives that raise the kinds of questions that many historians today are directing at the American past. We use popular entertainment, advertising, Shakespearean plays and pulp fiction, the words of founding fathers such as Thomas Jefferson and of innovative mothers such as Ruth Handler (inventor of the Barbie doll). To investigate antebellum slavery, we look at folktales told by slaves and proslavery fiction written by their masters. To explore how Americans made sense of the

Great Depression, we examine the era's best-selling self-help book, stories from America's leading pulp magazines, and episodes from the decade's most popular radio program.

To make this approach clearer, let's briefly put it to use in investigating more closely the artifact and question we started with: what makes "the Marlboro Man" work? The answer is not as obvious as it seems. Most Americans living a century ago, when a self-respecting man smoked nothing but a "lusty pipe or cigar," would have read Miller's cigarette as a sign of weakness, even effeminacy and degeneracy. Such danger signs were on the mind of Ernest Thompson Seton, the founder of the American Boy Scouts, when he worried that modern life was turning the nation's "robust manly, self-reliant boyhood into a lot of flat-chested cigarette smokers with shaky nerves and doubtful vitality." America's entry into World War I (1917–1918) did more to change that message (and tobacco history) than anything else. At that point, tobacco companies had the technology to mass-produce cigarettes, but there was very little demand for them. When war came, these companies gave away tons of ready-made cigarettes, cigarette tobacco, and wrapping papers to U.S. forces. Besides becoming addicted, American doughboys found that cigarettes, which are easily lit and quickly enjoyed, were more convenient to smoke than cigars or pipes. Industrial technology and smart marketing tactics, in combination with the circumstances of modern warfare, invigorated the cigarette-smoking American man. By the late 1920s, he seemed manfully modern compared with men who indulged in the "lazy" cigar. The point here is that cigarettes (or any other cultural artifact) are not in themselves masculine or feminine. They acquire these meanings, which are unstable and impermanent, in culture. Thus, cigarettes did not lose their gender signification. They still said something about the men who smoked them. However, gender distinctions were redrawn, and in ways that made "the Marlboro Man" conceivable.

But other changes had to occur first. For one, the Marlboro cigarette is much older than the Marlboro Man. Philip Morris introduced it in the 1920s for the stylish woman. By the early 1950s, when it sported a red filter tip to hide lipstick stains, hardly anyone was buying it, least of all men. In 1954, Philip Morris hired Chicago adman Leo Burnett to reinvent the brand. Burnett called it a "sissy smoke" and determined to change its image. "What is the most masculine figure in America?" he asked his ad writers. When someone suggested "cowboy," the Marlboro Man was born.

To symbolize the brand, Burnett wanted an authentic man, like the "cowboy" whose rugged close-up he remembered from the cover of *Life* magazine back in 1949. The photo was of C. H. Long, the foreman of a big Texas ranch

"Cowboy" C. H. Long from the cover of *Life* Magazine (1949).
(Leonard McCombe/Time Life Pictures/Getty Images.)

whom *Life* described as one of a dying breed of uniquely American types: "undiluted individuals clinging with some ferocity" to the rough life of the frontier West. *Life* observed that, in modern America, these men were being replaced by a "feebler" breed who worked in offices and tended suburban home fires at night. Burnett's ad campaign identified Marlboro's "man-size flavor of honest tobacco" as the choice of men who did not mind getting their hands dirty. But Marlboro was aimed at city-dwelling men who envied the cowboy's "freedom," not at rural or working-class men. Overnight, Marlboro became a man's smoke and was well on its way to becoming the most popular brand on earth. The Marlboro Man was crafted to represent qualities that seem uniquely American: manly independence; honest, productive work performed close to the soil; and, to quote a Marlboro poster, the "strength of self-confidence."

But does he epitomize those qualities? A cigarette or a cowboy does not mean anything until we imagine those meanings. History and cultural influences prepare us to imagine what we see in certain ways, although what people imagine often proves hard to control. That observation brings us back to Corporal Miller. Everyone, it seemed, recognized in his photograph the text of "the Marlboro Man." More important, they also knew that this text told a story about the United States that explained what Americans were trying to achieve in Iraq. For the *New York Post*, the story explained military success in terms of American machismo: "Marlboro men kick butt in Fallujah." The picture "motivated the heck out of me all day," said a Marine recruiter in Long Island, New York. But the image did not make everyone swell with pride. Some objected that the image was misused to rally support for an unpopular and wrongheaded war. Even worse, in some people's minds, "the Marlboro Man" made smoking cigarettes look really cool. "Lots of children, particularly boys, play 'army' and like to imitate this young man," a writer complained to the *Houston Chronicle*. "The clear message of the photo is that the way to relax after a battle is with a cigarette." Even Miller's mother, who relished her son's celebrity, imagined something else when she saw the photo. She wished he would stop smoking. The story of both Miller and the photograph, however, did not end there. He returned from Iraq and was medically discharged from the Marines exactly one year after his face first appeared in newspapers and on television screens around the world. Now suffering from post-traumatic stress disorder, Miller has struggled to rebuild his life after combat and to reconcile his own pain and personal loss with the famous image of him. The photograph of the "Marlboro Marine" has still retained its power to move Americans. Viewed through the context of Miller's circumstances and faltering public support for the Iraq War, it now poignantly suggests to many observers not what has been won in Iraq, but what has been lost. Cultural symbols, then, are open to numerous interpretations, and these interpretations may change dramatically over time. They also inspire conflicting responses and actions, including those their creators did not intend or imagine. One of the strengths of cultural history is its sensitivity to this ambiguity. In studying the various ways in which the meanings of things have been imagined, we can achieve a richer and more complicated understanding of the past.

CHAPTER I

New Worlds and Old Worlds: 1490–1640

HISTORIANS NO LONGER write that Europe discovered America when Columbus "sailed the ocean blue in 1492." Those continents had already been inhabited for at least 10,000 years, and other Europeans might well have made contact with them before Columbus. How could Europeans claim to have discovered America in 1492, when at the time Columbus thought he had reached islands off the coast of Asia? Still, the encounter with the Americas that Columbus initiated, and which continued unabated for centuries, ushered in a new mental universe forged by the discovery that different plants, animals, diseases, technologies, cultures, and peoples existed elsewhere in the world. It was a "new world" for both Europeans and Americans, although for each it would become new in different ways.

It takes an act of historical imagination to contemplate what it must have been like for Europeans and Americans to come face-to-face with a new world. There is nothing in our mental universe to which we can compare that encounter. Yes, we are avid consumers of popular fiction and movies that depict extraterrestrial life, but we have never been suddenly told that these stories are actually true and that it is possible to journey to these alien lands beginning tomorrow. The questions provoked by the New World were enormous: How big is the earth? Where are its oceans and landmasses in relation to home? Who are these newly encountered peoples? Where do they come from, and are they like us? Can their existence be explained in sacred texts or traditions? Why were the ancient sources of wisdom and knowledge ignorant of new peoples and places?

The mental discovery of the New World unleashed extraordinary imaginative energies. Europeans did not "invent" America, but the America that captured European consciousness was a long-term work of imagination. Fortunately, a new technology allowed Europeans to share in that process. The encounter with the New World coincided with the invention and proliferation of the printing press. News, tales, pictures, and maps of the New World spread with unprecedented speed through western Europe in the decades after 1492.

The encounter between Europeans and Americans profoundly transformed both "old worlds." Native Americans marveled at the bearded strangers who first set foot on their shores and who apparently "drank blood and ate wood," as they thought when they first witnessed the communion custom of consuming bread and wine. In different ways, Europeans marveled and wondered at the things and peoples of the New World. Royal courts presented elaborate pageants and court masques in which Indian customs and costumes, and occasionally real Indians, were displayed for public consumption. The Americas also contributed a treasure-trove of things for Europeans to wonder at, collect, and display in personal "cabinets of curiosities" or in collections so large that they resembled museums.

Tradition, however, is a powerful cultural force, and people prefer not to disrupt the beliefs of their old world as they confront the new. Many European thinkers at the time of the encounter hoped to fit new information about the natural world into models inherited from the past. Renaissance humanists were slow in abandoning ancient texts on science even when observations of the New World contradicted them. Because Europeans had also developed systems of thought regarding encounters with non-Europeans over the centuries, it became easy for them to explain the native peoples of the Americas within a framework of ideas about civilization and barbarism inherited from the ancient Greeks. Native Americans were no less willing to abandon their traditional beliefs. Anthropologists have discovered that although items like copper kettles were eagerly embraced by Algonquian Indians in North America, native peoples frequently sliced up those kettles and transformed the copper into ceremonial jewelry, producing items that conveyed greater status in their traditional cultures.

This tension between the new and the old—be it sacred or scientific, curiosity or close-mindedness, objects or people—is the focus of this chapter. The documents explore the imagined space of land and peoples, and the understandings of origins and creation, that reveal the creative ways Europeans and Americans came to understand the meaning of their new worlds.

ᛜ *Colonial Dreams: Imagining the "New World"* ᛜ

The German artist Albrecht Dürer was in a state of rapturous joy after he visited Brussels in 1520 to witness an exhibit of Mexican artifacts sent by Hernán Cortés to the court of Charles V. "I saw things which had been brought to the King from the new land of gold (Mexico), a sun of all gold a whole fathom broad, and a moon all of silver of the same size, also two rooms full of the armour of the people there, and all manner of wondrous weapons . . . and all kinds of wondrous objects of human use. . . . All the days of my life I have seen nothing that rejoiced my heart so much as these things, for I saw amongst them wonderful works of art, and I marvelled at the subtle Ingenia of men in foreign lands." Apparently Charles V and his court did not share Dürer's appreciation for the intrinsic value of these "wonderful works of art," for they extracted the precious stones and melted down the gold and silver for the imperial treasury.

The encounter between Americans and Europeans was filled with acts of wonder and exhibits of the imagination. This section examines how the European understanding of a "new world" was exhibited for audiences through the popularity of curiosities, maps, and a theater of fools, and how this "new world" for Native Americans required their own acts of imagining Europeans.

ᔭ CABINETS OF CURIOSITY

Europeans expressed their wonder at the New World by collecting and displaying rare objects from the Americas. In both continental Europe and the British Isles, numerous collectors amassed material objects associated with the New World — hammocks, axes, featherworks, and the wonders of nature, including countless plants, animals, birds, and insects. They then exhibited these items to friends and neighbors, or even charged admission to the general public. These collections, called "cabinets of curiosities" in England or *wunderkammern* in Germany, were often too vast to be confined to the small space we might associate with a cabinet. A Swiss visitor to London in 1599 reported that he visited Sir Walter Cope's collection, displayed in "an apartment, stuffed with queer foreign objects in every corner," including Virginia fire-flies and an "Indian canoe." Decades later, Cope pressed a group of real Indians brought over to England from Virginia to exhibit their skills in his canoe on the Thames. The discovery of the New World elicited a seemingly insatiable curiosity for the exotic and foreign, and made Europeans avid consumers of a world of new things.

John Tradescant's Collection (1638)

One of the most extensive European collections of curiosities was amassed by John Tradescant and his son. The Tradescants were gardeners who traveled extensively in the employ of various English aristocrats in the early 1600s. Their collecting began by gathering exotic plants from around the globe but then expanded to include artifacts and material objects. When the elder Tradescant moved his family to London, he converted his house into a private museum, known throughout Europe as "The Ark." Crowds of ordinary people paid a fee of sixpence to gawk at the oddities in the collection, which included items from the Americas as well as the rest of the world. In 1638, a traveling German-speaking student recorded an account of Tradescant's curiosities, reproduced here. Tradescant's collection eventually became the foundation for the Ashmolean Museum at Oxford University, Britain's first public museum.

PROBLEMS TO CONSIDER

1. What possible meanings might European visitors have taken from surveying this diverse collection?
2. Is there a thread that holds all of these items together as a whole, and how is it related to the "New World"?

In the museum of Mr. John Tradescant are the following things: . . . a salamander, a chameleon, a pelican, a remora, a lanhado from Africa, a white partridge, a goose which has grown in Scotland on a tree, a flying squirrel, another squirrel like a fish, all kinds of bright coloured birds from India, a number of things changed into stone, amongst others a piece of human flesh on a bone, gourds, olives, a piece of wood, an ape's head, a cheese etc.; all kinds of shells, the hand of a mermaid, the hand of a mummy, a very natural wax hand under glass, all kinds of precious stones, coins, a picture wrought in feathers, a small piece of wood from the cross of Christ, pictures in perspective of Henry IV and Louis XIII of France, . . . two cups of "rinocerode," a cup of an E. Indian alcedo which is a kind of unicorn, many Turkish and other foreign shoes and boots, a sea parrot, a toad-fish, an elk's hoof with three claws, a bat as large as a pigeon, a human bone weighing 42 lbs, Indian arrows such as are used by the executioners in the West Indies—when a man is condemned to death, they lay open his back with them and he dies of it—an instrument used by the Jews in circumcision, some very light wood from Africa, the robe of the King of Virginia, a few goblets of agate, a girdle such as the Turks wear in Jerusalem, the passion of Christ carved very daintily on a plumstone, a large magnet stone, a S. Francis in wax under glass, as also a S. Jerome, the Pater Noster of Pope Gregory XV, pipes from the East and West Indies, a stone found in the West Indies in the water, whereon are graven Jesus, Mary and Joseph. . . .

Tradescant's Rarities: Essays on the Foundation of the Ashmolean Museum, 1683, with a Catalogue of the Surviving Early Collections, edited by Arthur MacGregor (Oxford: Clarendon Press, 1983), 21.

ᴈ

America (c. 1664–1666)

JAN VAN KESSEL

Jan Van Kessel, a seventeenth-century Flemish painter, captured the essence of European collections of exotica in his painting America *(c. 1664–1666). Kessel's painting depicts a room filled with all of the types of items commonly found in European* wunderkammern, *from fishes, insects, and animals to golden plates, jewelry, and weaponry. Kessel also figuratively opens the door for European eyes to see the peoples of the New World, or at least how Europeans imagined them. Much as Tradescant's curiosities overflowed with items from several different continents, Kessel blurred the distinctions between people and objects of the New World and exotic people and places from the past and present.*

Yet Kessel intended to depict something more than just a room full of collectibles; he wished to convey a story that connected these items to prevailing ideas about the New World. On the right side hang three tableaus portraying Native American life; the top one emphasizes the nakedness of natives, the tableau in the middle portrays their cannibalism, and the bottom one presents a human sacrifice.

PROBLEMS TO CONSIDER

1. What messages was Kessel trying to communicate in this painting? What is the relationship between the hodgepodge of items and the people in the painting, or the tableau images on the right side?
2. Make a list of the associations that Europeans likely made when they viewed this painting. When they thought about the New World, what immediately came to mind?

America (c. 1664–1666) by Jan Van Kessel.

(Bayerische Staatsgemaldesmmlungen, Alte Pinakothek Munchen.)

∾ MAPPING THE NEW WORLD

The European encounter with the New World represented a convergence of several significant developments in European life, and perhaps the most important of these was the rapid spread of a print culture after Johannes Gutenberg first printed the Bible in 1454. Within decades, hundreds of printers were working in Europe's largest cities, producing works in Latin and modern languages that circulated across national boundaries. Maps of the world became an important part of this print explosion. Even the naming of the New World "America" reflected the international scope of this new print culture. In 1507, Martin Waldseemüller, a German-speaking resident of Lorraine (bordering France), named the new landmasses after an Italian who sailed under the flags of the Spanish and Portuguese Crowns.

Maps are representations that can evoke significant meaning for a culture. They are not just scientific representations of the geography of locales or the world as a whole. Often maps are also texts, intended to communicate stories, values, and judgments. We are familiar with this process: during the Cold War, the United States was situated right in the center of most world maps hanging in elementary school classrooms, even if that meant that the world's largest continent, Asia, had to be divided on either side of the map. European maps during the age of "discovery" communicated cultural values through visual texts in much the same way. Maps can often tell us much more about the mapmaker than they can about the places the map depicts.

Cordiform (Heart-Shaped) Map of the World (1530)
PETER APIAN

Fool's Cap (c. 1590)
ANONYMOUS

European maps made a theater of the world. As dramatic stories, the symbols and images that surrounded maps, even their shapes, became far more important than the geographic information they contained. Most mapmakers were artists, not scientists, and the European public examined maps for the messages they contained, not to get from one place to another. The first work examining the geometric science of map projections was not published until 1590, while world maps continued to proliferate at the hands of artists, engravers, and printers. The printing of maps democratized and secularized images of the world. And maps became one of the many new consumer items generated by New World enterprises, much like sugar and tobacco in later centuries.

European artists recognized the relationship of maps to the wealth and luxury that sprang from the "discovery" of America. By the early seventeenth century, Dutch and English painters had produced a slew of still-life paintings around the theme of vanitas, which represented the fragility of life's pleasure and the folly of the pursuit of happiness in material objects. These paintings often juxtaposed maps and globes alongside images of sated Europeans at a feast or a house full of other luxury items, such as musical instruments and books. The maps reproduced here reflect these artistic themes of the map as theater and folly. The first is Peter Apian's cordiform (heart-shaped) map, an experiment with projecting a globe on a flat surface. Although Europeans would not understand the physiological function of the heart for another century, they already associated the heart with the seat of emotions. The second image is an anonymous artist's rendition of a world map inside a fool's cap. The map itself was a completely up-to-date depiction of the world's landmasses, but the artist wished to communicate something else as well.

PROBLEMS TO CONSIDER

1. What is the significance of depicting a map of the world, including the New World, in the shape of a heart?
2. What message did the artist of the fool's cap map wish to communicate? At what was he directing his critique?

Cordiform (Heart-Shaped) Map of the World (1530) by Peter Apian.
(The Granger Collection, New York.)

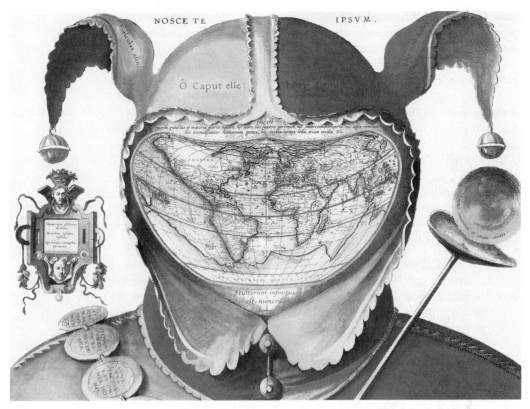

Fool's Cap (c. 1590).

(The Granger Collection, New York.)

ᢒ

A New Voyage to Carolina (1709)

JOHN LAWSON

Catawba Deerskin Map (c. 1721)

Europeans were not the only ones to map their worlds (old and new). Native Americans had traditions of communicating a map's information, even though they did not possess European printing presses. In fact, much of European knowledge of New World geography was acquired through a two-way flow of information exchanged between native peoples and European explorers and colonizers. Baron de Lahontan, a French traveler in the late 1600s, observed that Indians "are as ignorant of Geography as of the other Sciences, and yet they draw the most exact Maps imaginable of the Countries they're acquainted with." Europeans usually missed the fact that maps were lived experiences for Native Americans, composed of stories and traditions about the names and meanings of places, learned with one's feet or canoe, long before being depicted on a flat surface. And

Native Americans misunderstood the full consequences of what maps meant for European ideas of property ownership until conflicts over land and its uses became the ground for European-American encounters (as we will see in the next section of this chapter).

John Lawson was a traveler, explorer, surveyor, and naturalist who surveyed the backcountry of the Carolinas in the early 1700s. His account of his travels reveals the exchange of mapping information that characterized European encounters with North American Indians. Following Lawson's journal is a map drawn on a deerskin by the Catawba Indians in Carolina in the 1720s. The Catawbas themselves were a new confederation of native peoples whose original tribes had been decimated by disease and war. Their map represents the various neighboring Siouan-speaking tribes as circles, with their trading relationships marked as paths connecting the circles in a series of networks. Virginia is depicted as the square off to the right, and Charleston appears to the left as lines at right angles.

PROBLEMS TO CONSIDER

1. What does Lawson's account reveal about the practices of mapping in Native American culture? Was that culture maintained, protected, and preserved?
2. What information did the Catawba map provide for its native viewers? Do the symbols on this map differ from the symbols Europeans used? How would English colonists have understood it?

They are expert Travellers, and though they have not the Use of our artificial Compass, yet they understand the North-point exactly, let them be in never so great a Wilderness. One Guide is a short Moss, that grows upon some Trees, exactly on the North-Side thereof.

Besides, they have Names for eight of the thirty two Points, and call the Winds by their several Names, as we do; but indeed more properly, for the North-West Wind is called the cold Wind; the North-East the wet Wind; the South the warm Wind; and so agreeably of the rest. Sometimes it happens, that they have a large River or Lake to pass over, and the Weather is very foggy, as it often happens in the Spring and Fall of the Leaf; so that they cannot see which Course to steer: In such a Case, they being on one side of the River, or Lake, they know well enough what Course such a Place (which they intend for) bears from them. Therefore, they get a great many Sticks and Chunks of Wood in their Canoe, and then set off directly for their Port, and now and then throw over a Piece of Wood, which directs them, by seeing how the Stick bears from the Canoes Stern, which they always observe to keep right aft; and this is the *Indian* Compass by which they will go over a broad Water of ten or twenty Leagues wide. They will find the Head of any River, though it is five, six or seven hundred miles off, and they never were there, in their Lives before; as is often prov'd, by their appointing to meet on the Head of such a River, where perhaps, none of them ever was before, but where they shall rendezvous exactly at the prefixt time; and if they meet with any Obstruction, they leave certain Marks in the Way, where they that come after will understand how many have pass'd by already, and which way they are gone. . . . Yet there was never found any Letters amongst the Savages of *Carolina*; nor, I believe, among any other Natives in *America*, that were possess'd with any manner of Writing or Learning throughout all the Discoveries of the New-

World. They will draw Maps, very exactly, of all the Rivers, Towns, Mountains, and Roads, or what you shall enquire of them, which you may draw by their Directions, and come to a small matter of Latitude, reckoning by their Days Journeys. These Maps they will draw in the Ashes of the Fire, and sometimes upon a Mat or Piece of Bark. I have put a Pen and Ink into a Savage's Hand, and he has drawn me the Rivers, Bays, and other Parts of a Country, which afterwards I have found to agree with a great deal of Nicety: But you must be very much in their Favour, otherwise they will never make these Discoveries to you; especially, if it be in their own Quarters.

John Lawson, *A New Voyage to Carolina* . . . (London, 1709), 204–5.

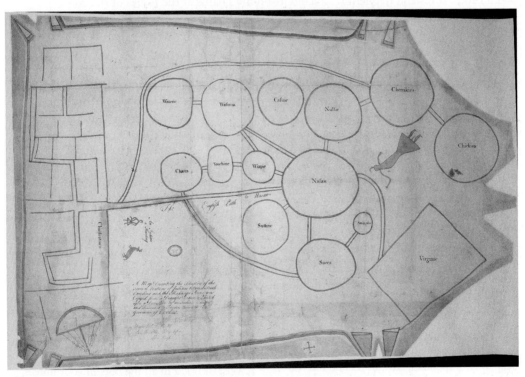

Catawba Deerskin Map (c. 1721).
(The National Archives of the UK, reference C0700/North American Colonies General 6 (1).)

〜 THEATER OF THE FOOL'S ERRAND

In 1494, just two years after Columbus's famous voyage, a German author named Sebastian Brant published a satire on the follies and sins of European society entitled *Das Narrenschiff*, or *The Ship of Fools*. Brant crafted tales of one hundred different fools who all boarded a ship bound for Narragonia, the island of fools. *Das*

Narrenschiff was the first in a genre of allegorical satires of human folly popular in Europe from the late fifteenth until the seventeenth century. That this "fool's literature" began at the moment of the discovery of the New World should not escape our attention. The fool's cap world map reminds us that not all Europeans were at ease with the wonderment and curiosity, the new consumer tastes, or the greed that seemed to fuel colonization. A fool's literature was already well rooted in English culture when England finally joined the circle of European colonizing nations. At that moment, Englishmen and -women not only shelled out their pennies to see curiosities and real Indians but also flocked to theaters to be entertained by Shakespeare and his peers. Elizabethan theater exposed English folk of all ranks to news about exotic lands and frequently directed its pointed barbs at the follies of the colonizing enterprise in Virginia.

Eastward Ho! (1605)
GEORGE CHAPMAN, BEN JONSON, AND JOHN MARSTON

One of the first plays to address the Virginia colony was George Chapman's Eastward Ho!, *a comedy produced in 1605. Chapman would later stage* masques *(elaborate pageants) for the court of King James I, in which the participants donned feathers as Indian costumes and imitated the work of "Virginia priests." But in* Eastward Ho! *Chapman gave voice to the male fantasy of colonial adventures, articulated by three fools over drinks in a tavern.*

PROBLEMS TO CONSIDER

1. What was the promise of the New World for these adventurers? What meanings did the playwright suggest by giving these names to his characters?
2. What role did sexuality play in this fantasy of colonial adventure?

Dramatis Personae:
Seagull, a sea captain
Scapethrift, Spendall, adventurers bound for
    Virginia

ACT III, SCENE 3
Enter Seagull, Spendall, and Scapethrift in the tavern, with a Drawer.

SEAGULL: Come, Drawer, pierce your neatest hogsheads, and let's have cheer, not fit for your Billingsgate tavern, but for our Virginian colonel; he will be here instantly.

DRAWER: You shall have all things fit, sir; please you have any more wine?

SPENDALL: More wine, slave? Whether we drink it or no, spill it, and draw more.

SCAPETHRIFT: Fill all the pots in your house with all sorts of liquor, and let 'em wait on us here like soldiers in their pewter coats; and though we do not employ them now, yet we will maintain 'em till we do.

DRAWER: Said like an honourable captain; you shall have all you can command, sir. *Exit* Drawer.

SEAGULL: Come, boys, Virginia longs till we share the rest of her maidenhead.

SPENDALL: Why, is she inhabited already with any English?

SEAGULL: A whole country of English is there, man, bred of those that were left there in '79. They have married with the Indians, and make 'em bring forth as beautiful faces as any we have in England; and therefore the Indians are so in love with 'em, that all the treasure they have, they lay at their feet.

SCAPETHRIFT: But is there such treasure there, captain, as I have heard?

SEAGULL: I tell thee, gold is more plentiful there than copper is with us; and for as much red copper as I can bring, I'll have thrice the weight in gold. Why, man, all their dripping pans and their chamber pots are pure gold; and all the chains, with which they chain up their streets, are massy [*solid*] gold; all the prisoners they take are fettered in gold; and for rubies and diamonds, they go forth on holidays and gather 'em by the seashore, to hang on their children's coats, and stick in their children's caps, as commonly as our children wear saffron-gilt brooches and groats with holes in 'em.

SCAPETHRIFT: And is it a pleasant country withal?

SEAGULL: As ever the sun shined on, temperate and full of all sorts of excellent viands: wild boar is as common there as our tamest bacon is here; venison, as mutton. And then you shall live freely there, without sergeants, or courtiers, or lawyers, or intelligencers— Then for your means to advancement there, it is simple, and not preposterously mixed. You may be an alderman there, and never be [a] scavenger; you may be any other officer, and never a slave; you may come to preferment enough, and never be a pander; to riches and fortune enough and have never the more villainy, nor the less wit. . . .

SPENDALL: God's me! and how far is it thither?

SEAGULL: Some six weeks' sail, no more, with any indifferent good wind. And if I get to any part of the coast of Africa, I'll sail thither with any wind. Or when I come to Cape Finisterre, there's a foreright wind continually wafts us till we come to Virginia. See, our colonel's come.

George Chapman, Ben Jonson, and John Marston, *Eastward Ho!: As It Was Played in the Black-friers* (London: William Aspley, 1605) [no page numbers].

♜

The Tempest (1611)
WILLIAM SHAKESPEARE

England became a successful colonizer of the New World during the age of Shakespeare. Unfortunately, literary purists for a long time could not see past the Mediterranean setting and characters to acknowledge what English theater audiences certainly recognized in Shakespeare's play The Tempest *(1611). One scholar even declared, "There is not a word in* The Tempest *about America." Playgoing audiences in England, however, would have set their minds westward when they heard Miranda's exclamation, "O brave new world / That has such people in 't!" Shakespeare and his audience were clearly influenced by the spectacular news of the shipwreck and survival of the* Sea-Venture — *bound with new colonists and governors for Virginia — which became a sensation in July 1610 with the publication of William Strachey's account,* The True Reportory of the Wracke.*

The following selections include the opening scene, portraying the "tempest" and shipwreck; a scene in which the characters reflect on building a plantation on the island on which they have been marooned; and, finally, Shakespeare's undeniable allusion to

American colonizing: the description of the one native inhabitant, Caliban, whom Shakespeare introduces as "a savage and deformed Slave." Hence, Shakespeare's Caliban serves as a transition from considering the dreams of colonial enterprises to exploring the imaginings of the people colonized.

PROBLEMS TO CONSIDER

1. What would English theater audiences have thought about England's colonizing in Virginia as they witnessed this play performed? How did Shakespeare exploit the idea of *vanitas* in this play?

2. As you read the next section, consider how Shakespeare's Caliban fit into the discourse on native peoples and "savagery" in the Americas. What meaning might his name connote?

Dramatis Personae:
Alonso, King of Naples.
Sebastian, his brother.
Prospero, the rightful Duke of Milan.
Antonio, his brother, the usurping Duke of Milan.
Ferdinand, son of the King of Naples.
Gonzalo, an honest old Counsellor of Naples. . . .
Caliban, a savage and deformed Slave.
Trinculo, a jester. . . .
Master of a Ship, Boatswain, and Mariners.

ACT I, SCENE I
On a ship at sea: a tempestuous noise of thunder and lightning heard.

Enter a Shipmaster and a Boatswain.

MASTER: Boatswain!

BOATSWAIN: Here, master; what cheer?

MASTER: Good, speak to the mariners: fall to 't yarely, or we run ourselves aground; bestir, bestir. *[Exit]*

Enter Mariners.

BOATSWAIN: Heigh, my hearts! cheerly, cheerly, my hearts! yare, yare! Take in the topsail. Tend to the master's whistle. Blow till thou burst thy wind, if room enough!

Enter Alonso, Sebastian, Antonio, Ferdinand, Gonzalo, and others.

ALONSO: Good boatswain, have care. Where's the master? Play the men.

BOATSWAIN: I pray now, keep below.

ANTONIO: Where is the master, boatswain?

BOATSWAIN: Do you not hear him? You mar our labour; keep your cabins; you do assist the storm.

GONZALO: Nay, good, be patient.

BOATSWAIN: When the sea is. Hence! What cares these roarers for the name of king? To cabin! Silence! trouble us not.

GONZALO: Good, yet remember whom thou hast aboard.

BOATSWAIN: None that I love more than myself. You are a counsellor; if you can command these elements to silence, and work the peace of the present, we will not hand a rope more; use your authority. If you cannot, give thanks you have lived so long, and make yourself ready in your cabin for the mischance of the hour, if it so hap. Cheerly, good hearts! Out of our way, I say. *[Exit]*

GONZALO: I have great comfort from this fellow. Methinks he hath no drowning mark upon him; his complexion is perfect gallows. Stand fast, good Fate, to his hanging! Make the rope of his destiny our cable, for our own doth little advantage. If he be not born to be hanged, our case is miserable. *[Exeunt]* . . .

Enter Mariners, wet.

MARINERS: All lost! to prayers, to prayers! all
lost! [*Exeunt*]

BOATSWAIN: What, must our mouths be cold?

GONZALO: The king and prince at prayers! Let's
assist them, for our case is as theirs.

SEBASTIAN: I'm out of patience.

ANTONIO: We are merely cheated of our lives
by drunkards. This wide-chapp'd rascal —
would thou mightst lie drowning,
The washing of ten tides!

GONZALO: He'll be hanged yet;
Though every drop of water swear against it,
And gape at widest to glut him.

[*A confused noise within:* Mercy on us! —
We split, we split! Farewell, my wife and
children!
Farewell, brother! — We split, we split,
we split!]

ANTONIO: Let's all sink with the king.

SEBASTIAN: Let's take leave of him. [*Exeunt*
Antonio and Sebastian]

GONZALO: Now would I give a thousand fur-
longs of sea for an acre of barren ground,
long heath, brown furze, any thing. The wills
above be done! But I would fain die a dry
death. [*Exeunt*] . . .

ACT II, SCENE I

GONZALO: Had I plantation of this isle, my
lord, —

ANTONIO: He'd sow 't with nettle-seed.

SEBASTIAN: Or docks, or mallows.

GONZALO: And were the king on 't, what would
I do?

SEBASTIAN: 'Scape being drunk for want of wine.

GONZALO: I' the commonwealth I would by
contraries
Execute all things; for no kind of traffic
Would I admit; no name of magistrate;
Letters should not be known; riches, poverty,
And use of service, none; contract, succession,
Bourn, bound of land, tilth, vineyard, none;
No use of metal, corn, or wine, or oil;
No occupation; all men idle, all:
And women too, but innocent and pure;
No sovereignty, —

SEBASTIAN: Yet he would be king on 't.

ANTONIO: The latter end of his commonwealth
forgets the beginning.

GONZALO: All things in common nature should
produce
Without sweat or endeavour. Treason, felony,
Sword, pike, knife, gun, or need of any engine,
Would I not have; but nature should bring
forth,
Of it own kind, all foison, all abundance,
To feed my innocent people.

SEBASTIAN: No marrying 'mong his subjects?

ANTONIO: None, man: all idle; whores and
knaves.

GONZALO: I would with such perfection govern,
sir,
To excel the golden age.

SEBASTIAN: Save his Majesty!

ANTONIO: Long live Gonzalo! . . .

ACT II, SCENE 2
Another part of the island.

Enter Caliban, with a burden of wood. A noise
of thunder heard. . . .

Enter Trinculo [*a jester*]

CALIBAN: Lo, now, lo!
Here comes a spirit of his [*Prospero's*], and to
torment me
For bringing wood in slowly. I'll fall flat;
Perchance he will not mind me.

TRINCULO: . . . What have we here? a man or a
fish? dead or alive? A fish: he smells like a
fish; a very ancient and fish-like smell; a
kind of not-of-the-newest Poor-John. A
strange fish! Were I in England now, as once
I was, and had but this fish painted, not a

holiday fool there but would give a piece of silver. There would this monster make a man; any strange beast there makes a man: when they will not give a doit to relieve a lame beggar, they will lay out ten to see a dead Indian. Legged like a man, and his fins like arms! Warm, o' my troth! I do now let loose my opinion; hold it no longer: this is no fish, but an islander, that hath lately suffered by thunderbolt. *[Thunder]* Alas, the storm is come again!

William Shakespeare, *The Works of William Shakespeare*, 10 vols., edited by C. H. Herford (London: Macmillan, 1902), 4:409–12, 439–40, 447–48.

ᛒ

ᛒ Picturing New Peoples and Retaining Old Notions ᛒ

For all the plants and objects that stirred Europeans' fancies, nothing could match their curiosity about the peoples who inhabited the New World. With little else to frame their knowledge, Europeans relied on centuries-old notions about non-European peoples to craft their images of Native Americans. The contrast between civilization and barbarism had a long history, coursing its way from the classical era through the medieval period. By invoking that discourse, western Europeans distanced themselves from non-Europeans, creating a categorical "other," against whom Europeans by comparison appeared superior in material, intellectual, and cultural development. It was simultaneously an act of self-congratulation and an act of cultural aggression or imperialism. Barbarians (or, later, "savages") were people depicted as sharing certain characteristics, among them a resemblance to animals (in either appearance or behavior), an absence of religion, and the practices of human sacrifice and cannibalism. In the European imagination, these characteristics placed barbarians outside the pale of civilization.

ᛒ BODIES AND CANNIBALISM

When imagining the peoples of the New World nothing fascinated Europeans more than stories of alleged cannibalism. Reports of cannibalism can be traced to the very earliest contact with the Americas; Columbus even coined the word "cannibal" in his private journal. Columbus's international fame, and the legend of cannibals, can be traced to the publication in 1493 of his letter to Luis de Santangel, trumpeting his feats for the Spanish Crown. The letter was republished twelve times in five countries in three different languages within the first few months of Columbus's return. In the letter, Columbus wrote:

> So I have found no monsters, nor heard of any except on an island here . . . which is inhabited by people who are held in all the islands to be very ferocious and who eat human flesh. These people have many canoes in which they sail around all the islands of India robbing and stealing whatever they want. . . . They are ferocious with these other people who are excessively cowardly, but I take no more account of them than of the rest.

Let's consider this letter for a moment. For Columbus and other Europeans, a belief in New World cannibalism was based almost entirely on hearsay evidence. He did not actually witness people eating human flesh; he had simply been told by the Arawak Indians that their enemies, the Caribs, were man-eaters. So how was Columbus told this when he did not speak their language? Most likely, the Arawaks and Columbus communicated using awkward signs or pantomime—not the best means for relating the subtleties of culture. And Columbus had a tendency for misunderstandings, not the least of which was his assumption that he had found a route to India, leading him to call these people Indians. That Europeans were primed to believe these stories, that they initiated the idea, tells us much more about European culture than it does about the lives of pre-Columbian Americans. The question of whether anyone in the past ever exhibited cannibalism is actually much less significant than the prominent place this idea held in the European imagination of the New World.

The documents in this section reveal the Europeans' imaginative invention of the Indian cannibal during the first century of the encounter. That image justified ideologies of conquest and sparked misunderstandings of culture that continued for centuries of encounters in the New World. An alternative image of the Indian as "the noble savage" eventually emerged from the imagination of Europeans who criticized the discourse on cannibalism. As we will see, cannibalism was a recurring theme in American history, returning again (and even being turned on its head in several ways) when Africa and the slave trade entered the imagination of the Atlantic world in the eighteenth century (see chapters 3 and 6).

Mundus Novus (Letter from the New World) (1503)
AMERIGO VESPUCCI

The People of the Islands Recently Discovered (c. 1505)

The idea of cannibals in the New World got a kick-start from Amerigo Vespucci, the man for whom nearly one-third of the earth is named. He did even more than Columbus to spread the image of New World cannibalism. Vespucci hailed from Florence at the time of Machiavelli and Botticelli and was a civil servant for the powerful Medici family before he moved to Spain in 1492. He quickly learned astronomy and became a navigator on two voyages to the New World, one each for the Spanish and Portuguese Crowns. Vespucci was a self-promoter, claiming he took two other voyages and was the first to sight the mainland of a new continent. Vespucci's fame grew when he published letters about these spurious voyages, entitled Mundus Novus *(New World). The letters excited European readers with fantastic tales of strange new peoples. In the early years of the printing press, Vespucci's* Mundus Novus *was a runaway bestseller. Fourteen editions in Latin had been printed by 1505; ten years later, there were thirty more editions in modern languages. We do not know how much of Vespucci's lurid prose was the invention of enterprising printers eager to satisfy European imaginations.*

Recently, a journalist offered a humorous take on Vespucci's fame. Vespucci, he argued, gave the folks back home in Europe what they wanted to believe in, "the imaginary world they were certain had to exist somewhere. It's a tabloid rendition of the New World, starring the usual cast: hot naked girls, cannibals, dragons, pigmies, and an island of giant women." Vespucci's account drew upon far-fetched imaginings of exotic travel that preceded his New World explorations, particularly The Voyages and Travels of Sir John Mandeville, *first published in 1356. Pretending to have traveled half the globe, Mandeville spun wildly imagined tales of monstrous races, including dog-faced men who appear as illustrations in various editions of Mandeville's and Marco Polo's travels published on the eve of Columbus's voyages. These extravagant fables are the reason that Columbus wrote, "I have found no monsters"; he expected to see doglike men in the Indies. Mandeville's influence on the European imagination of the Americas, however, appears most dramatically in the close parallels between Vespucci's descriptions of New World peoples and Mandeville's imaginary account of Asians living on islands that he called Lamary. As you read Vespucci's letter, remember that he had read the following words from Mandeville:*

> The custom there is for men and women to go completely naked. . . . In that land there is no marriage between man and woman; all the women of that land are common to every man. . . . And in the same way the land is common property. . . . Nothing is locked up, and every man is as rich as another. . . . But they have an evil custom among them, for they will eat human flesh more gladly than any other.

Europeans were not satisfied with these stories alone. Soon, illustrations accompanied editions of Vespucci's letters. The woodcut reproduced here was the first published artistic rendering of Native Americans as cannibals. In the next century, such images became commonplace in European books and maps on the New World.

PROBLEMS TO CONSIDER

1. How did cannibalism fit into Vespucci's overall description of native bodies and culture? What ties all of these images together? What effect would Vespucci's depictions of the sexual proclivities of native peoples have had on European readers?
2. How does the woodcut correspond to Vespucci's account? What message might illiterate viewers have taken from seeing the print but not reading Vespucci's letters?

As regards the people: we have found such a multitude in those countries that no one could enumerate them, as we read in the Apocalypse. They are people gentle and tractable, and all of both sexes go naked, not covering any part of their bodies, just as they came from their mothers' wombs, and so they go until their deaths. They have large, square-built bodies, and well proportioned. Their colour reddish, which I think is caused by their going naked and exposed to the sun. Their hair is plentiful and black. They are agile in walking, and of quick sight. They are of a free and good-looking expression of countenance, which they themselves destroy by boring

The People of the Islands Recently Discovered (c. 1505).
(The Granger Collection, New York.)

the nostrils and lips, the nose and ears. . . . Another custom among them is sufficiently shameful, and beyond all human credibility. Their women, being very libidinous, make the penis of their husbands swell to such a size as to appear deformed; and this is accomplished by a certain artifice, being the bite of some poisonous animal, and by reason of this many lose their virile organ and remain eunuchs.

They have no cloth, either of wool, flax, or cotton, because they have no need of it; nor have they any private property, everything being in common. They live amongst themselves without a king or ruler, each man being his own master, and having as many wives as they please. The children cohabit with the mothers, the brothers with the sisters, the male cousins with the female, and each one with the first he meets. They have

no temples and no laws, nor are they idolaters. What more can I say! They live according to nature, and are more inclined to be Epicurean than Stoic. They have no commerce among each other, and they wage war without art or order. The old men make the youths do what they please, and incite them to fights, in which they mutually kill with great cruelty. They slaughter those who are captured, and the victors eat the vanquished; for human flesh is an ordinary article of food among them. You may be the more certain of this, because I have seen a man eat his children and wife; and I knew a man who was popularly credited to have eaten 300 human bodies. I was once in a certain city for twenty-seven days, where human flesh was hung up near the houses, in the same way as we expose butcher's meat. I say further that they were surprised that we did not eat our enemies, and use their flesh as food, for they say it is excellent. Their arms are bows and arrows, and when they go to war they cover no part of their bodies, being in this like beasts. We did all we could to persuade them to desist from their evil habits, and they promised us to leave off. The women, as I have said, go naked, and are very libidinous, yet their bodies are comely; but they are as wild as can be imagined.

They live for 150 years, and are rarely sick. If they are attacked by a disease they cure themselves with the roots of some herbs. These are the most noteworthy things I know about them.

The Letters of Amerigo Vespucci and Other Documents Illustrative of His Career, translated by Clements R. Markham (London: The Hakluyt Society, 1894), 45–47.

☙

On the Cannibals (1580)
MICHEL DE MONTAIGNE

The imagined Native American, and the discourse of civilization and barbarism, were powerful cultural constructs that sometimes worked in diametrically opposing ways. On some occasions, Europeans confronted the differences of Native Americans and chose to present them in a more positive light. Some Europeans looked at the peoples of the New World and thought they saw themselves as they once were in simpler times, or as they hoped they might become in a better world. Peter Martyr, in his book De novo ordo *(1511), insisted that Indians "seem to live in that golden world of which the old writers speak so much, wherein men lived simply and innocently without enforcement of laws, without quarreling, judges and libels." Rather than the exotic, animal-like barbarians portrayed by Vespucci, Native Americans became "noble savages" — living in a state of nature more pure than civilization itself and offering moral lessons for the supposedly civilized. Michel de Montaigne, a French humanist and essayist during the Renaissance, voiced those ideas in his essay "Of Cannibals" (1580). Montaigne was an avid collector of New World artifacts; his home was cluttered with hammocks, weapons, bracelets, and dance sticks. He also made a point of speaking with the Tupinamba Indians from Brazil, who visited Rouen in 1562. All of these factors influenced his imaginings of Native Americans. Readers of Montaigne's essay, however, encountered no lurid depictions of cannibal feasts but instead found a critique of French civilization after the nearly thirty-year-long Wars of Religion between Catholics and Protestants.*

PROBLEMS TO CONSIDER

1. How did Montaigne convert cannibalism into one of the virtues of the noble savage? Are there any similarities between Montaigne's opinions and those displayed in Vespucci's letter and illustration?
2. What were the French to learn from the example of native peoples in America? How would you interpret the last line in Montaigne's essay?

I find (from what has been told me) that there is nothing savage or barbarous about those peoples, but that every man calls barbarous anything he is not accustomed to; it is indeed the case that we have no other criterion of truth or right-reason than the example and form of the opinions and customs of our own country. There we always find the perfect religion, the perfect polity, the most developed and perfect way of doing anything! Those "savages" are only wild in the sense that we call fruits wild when they are produced by Nature in her ordinary course: whereas it is fruit which we have artificially perverted and misled from the common order which we ought to call savage. . . .

Those peoples, then, seem to me to be barbarous only in that they have been hardly fashioned by the mind of man, still remaining close neighbours to their original state of nature. They are still governed by the laws of Nature and are only very slightly bastardized by ours; but their purity is such that I am sometimes seized with irritation at their not having been discovered earlier, in times when there were men who could have appreciated them better than we do. . . . I would tell Plato that those people have no trade of any kind, no acquaintance with writing, no knowledge of numbers, no terms for governor or political superior, no practice of subordination or of riches or poverty, no contracts, no inheritances, no divided estates, no occupation but leisure, no concern for kinship—except such as is common to them all—no clothing, no agriculture, no metals, no use of wine or corn. Among them you hear no words for treachery, lying, cheating, avarice, envy, backbiting or forgiveness. How remote from such perfection would Plato find that Republic which he thought up. . . .

They spend the whole day dancing; the younger men go off hunting with bow and arrow. Meanwhile some of the women-folk are occupied in warming up their drink: that is their main task. . . . They believe in the immortality of the soul: souls which deserve well of the gods dwell in the sky where the sun rises; souls which are accursed dwell where it sets. They have some priests and prophets or other, but they rarely appear among the people since they live in the mountains. When they do appear they hold a great festival and a solemn meeting of several villages. . . . The prophet then addresses them in public, exhorting them to be virtuous and dutiful, but their entire system of ethics contains only the same two articles: resoluteness in battle and love for their wives. . . .

These peoples have their wars against others further inland beyond their mountains. . . . Their steadfastness in battle is astonishing and always ends in killing and bloodshed: they do not even know the meaning of fear or flight. Each man brings back the head of the enemy he has slain and sets it as a trophy over the door of his dwelling. For a long period they treat captives well and provide them with all the comforts which they can devise; afterwards the master of each captive summons a great assembly of his acquaintances; he ties a rope to one of the arms of his prisoner and holds him by it, standing a few feet away for fear of being caught in the blows, and allows his dearest friend to hold the prisoner the same way by the other arm: then, before the whole assembly, they both hack at him with their swords and kill him. This done, they roast him and make a common meal of him, sending chunks of his flesh to absent friends. This is not as some think done for food—as the Scythians used to do in antiquity—but to symbolize ultimate revenge. As a proof of this, when they noted that the Portuguese who were allied to their enemies practiced a different kind of execution on them when taken prisoner—which was to bury them up to the waist, to shoot showers of arrows at their exposed parts and then to hang them—they thought that these men from the Other World, who had scattered a knowledge of many a vice throughout their neighbourhood and who were greater masters than they were of every kind of revenge, which must be more severe than their own; so they began to abandon their ancient method and adopted that one. It does not sadden me that we should note the horrible barbarity in a practice such as theirs: what does sadden me is that, while judging correctly of their wrong-doings we should be so blind to our own. I think there is more barbarity in eating a man alive than in eating him dead; more barbarity in lacerating by rack and torture a body still fully able to feel things, in roasting him little by little and having him bruised and bitten by pigs and dogs . . . than in roasting him and eating him after his death. . . .

And our medical men do not flinch from using corpses in many ways, both internally and externally, to cure us. Yet no opinion has ever been so unruly as to justify treachery, disloyalty, tyranny and cruelty, which are everyday vices in us. So we can indeed call those folk barbarians by the rules of reason but not in comparison with ourselves, who surpass them in every kind of barbarism. . . . They are not striving to conquer new lands, since without toil or travail they still enjoy that bounteous Nature who furnishes them abundantly with all they need, so that they have no concern to push back their frontiers. They are still in that blessed state of desiring nothing beyond what is ordained by their natural necessities: for them anything further is merely superfluous. . . .

It is no lie to say that these men are indeed savages—by our standards; for either they must be or we must be: there is an amazing gulf between their souls and ours. . . .

Not at all bad, that.—Ah! But they wear no breeches . . .

Michel de Montaigne, "On the Cannibals," in *The Essays of Michel de Montaigne,* translated and edited by M. A. Screech (London: Penguin Press, 1991), 231–36, 239, 241.

↝

↢ LAND AND PROPERTY

In 1638, the Englishman John Winthrop, governor of the Massachusetts Bay Colony, ran into a dispute with a group of colonists led by the Reverend John Wheelwright, who had been banished from the colony for supporting Anne Hutchinson, his sister-in-law and an accused heretic. Wheelwright's followers had moved to a place called Winicowett (present-day Exeter, New Hampshire), where they claimed an exclusive title to that land because they had purchased it from the local native population. Winthrop and the leaders of the Massachusetts colony accused Wheelwright of acting "against good neighborhood, religion, and common honesty," since he knew that the colony claimed a right to that land either by grant from the king or because it was vacant land. To further emphasize his position, Winthrop argued that the "Indians having only a natural right to so much land as they had or could improve, so as the rest of the country lay open to any that could and would improve it." Here in a nutshell was an ideology justifying conquest. Yet it also illustrates the misunderstandings and conflicts that occurred between Europeans and Native Americans concerning the meaning of land and property during their earliest years of cultural encounter.

Colonizing European nations performed their own distinct ceremonies to establish their indisputable authority over the lands in the New World when they first began to lay claim to them. The Spanish ritual of possession involved reading a speech to the natives demanding their submission to the Crown. The French acted out a royal procession, ending with the planting of a large cross within eyesight of the local natives. The Portuguese displayed some of their astronomical technology, and the Dutch proceeded to draw a map. The English, however, pitched a dwelling as their ceremony of possession. This was more than mere spectacle. English colonists defended their right to possess the lands of Native Americans based on their acts of building houses, erecting fences, marking boundaries, and planting gardens. If the inhabitants did not construct these "improvements" on the land, they could claim no right to possess it.

How European colonists and Native Americans understood the meaning of property and wealth in different ways is the focus of this section. These dissimilar cultural perspectives on the value, use, and meaning of land led them to misunderstand each other's actions. Because Native Americans left behind no written accounts, we need to scrutinize the places where their voices or perspectives enter the documents left by European colonists.

Arthur Barlowe (Roanoke) (1584)

Robert Cushman (Plymouth) (1621)

English colonists were fascinated by the landscape they witnessed when they first set eyes on the North American continent. They wrote jaw-dropping descriptions of the abundant plant and animal life they encountered. At a time when most of England's forests had been cut down for fuel, they were amazed by the plenitude of the forests. English observers frequently noted that the woods in North America were open and clear and resembled parks. This was not, however, the product of a different continent but instead the imprint of Indian land use. Native Americans regularly burned the underbrush in the woods, thus quickly recycling forest nutrients into the soil, creating favorable conditions for berries, and leaving the woods ideal for deer hunting.

Descriptions of land and its value and uses were never strictly factual observations. Therefore, we need to read these documents critically and to consider what the Europeans saw as well as what they meant by those descriptions. For example, when colonists noted the abundance of fish off the coast, or specific species of trees in the forest, they were not only leaving a record for science but were also informing their countrymen of the "merchantable commodities" that the New World offered. The following selections show how some of England's earliest colonists thought about the land and about Englishmen's right to claim it as their own. Arthur Barlowe co-captained the earliest voyage to Sir Walter Raleigh's colony of Roanoke in 1584, soon after Raleigh was granted a patent by Queen Elizabeth I. Robert Cushman was a minister in Plymouth; he preached the following sermon in 1621, just one year after the Pilgrims landed in the New World.

PROBLEMS TO CONSIDER

1. List all the reasons Englishmen gave for their right to claim the natives' land as their own. For English colonizers, what was the relationship between religious and economic ideas?

2. What do these documents reveal about the differences in English and Indian attitudes about building wealth and using land? How did English culture prevent the colonists from seeing what was valuable or successful in Indian patterns of existence?

ARTHUR BARLOWE

The 27 day of April, in the year of our redemption, 1584 we departed the West of England, with two barkes *[small ships]* well furnished with men and victuals. . . .

The second of July . . . we entered [an inlet], though not without some difficulty, & cast anchor about three harquebus *[gun]*-shot within the havens mouth, on the left hand of the same: and after thanks given to God for our safe arrival thither, we manned our boats, and went to view the land next adjoining, and to take possession of the same, in the right of the Queen's most excellent Majesty, as rightful Queen, and Princess of the same, and after delivered the same over to your use, according to her Majesty's grant, and letters patent, under her Highness great Seal. . . .

This Island had many goodly woods full of Deer, Conies *[rabbits]*, Hares, and Fowle, even in the midst of Summer in incredible abundance. The woods are . . . the highest and reddest Cedars in the world, far bettering the Cedars of the Azores. . . .

The next day there came unto us divers boats, and in one of them the Kings brother, accompanied with forty or fifty men, very handsome and goodly people, and in their behavior as mannerly and civil as any in Europe. His name was Granganimeo, and the king is called Wingina, the country Wingandacoa, and now by her Majesty Virginia. . . .

The King is greatly obeyed, and his brothers and children reverenced: the King himself in person was at our being there, sore wounded in a fight which he had with the King of the next country. . . . A day or two after this, we fell to trading with them, exchanging some things that we had, for Chamoys, Buffe, and Deer skins: when we showed him all our packet of merchandise, of all things that he saw, a bright tin dish most pleased him, which he presently took up and clapt it before his breast, and after made a hole in the brim thereof and hung it about his neck, making signs that it would defend him against his enemies arrows: for those people maintain a deadly and terrible war, with the people and King adjoining. We exchanged our tin dish for twenty skins, worth twenty Crowns, or twenty Nobles: and a copper kettle for fifty skins worth fifty Crowns. They offered us good exchange for our hatchets, and axes, and for knives, and would have given anything for swords: but we would not depart with any. . . .

We were entertained with all love and kindness, and with as much bounty (after their manner) as they could possibly devise. We found the people most gentle, loving, and faithful, void of all guile and treason, and such as live after the manner of the golden age. . . .

And whereas we have above certified you of the country taken in possession by us, to her Majesty's use, and so to yours by her Majesty's grant, we thought good for the better assurance thereof, to record some of the particular Gentlemen, & men of account, who then were present, as witnesses of the same. . . .

We brought home also two of the Savages being lusty men, whose names were Wanchese and Manteo.

Richard Hakluyt, *The Principall Voyages, Traffiques, and Discourses of the English Nations* (London, 1599–1600). Reprinted in *American History Told by Contemporaries*, 5 vols., edited by Albert Bushnell Hart (New York: Macmillan, 1896), 1:89–95.

ROBERT CUSHMAN

Objection: But some will say, What right have I to go and live in the heathens' country?

Answer: Letting pass the ancient discoveries, contracts and agreements which our Englishmen have long since made in those parts, together with the acknowledgment of the histories and chronicles of other nations, who profess the land of America from the Cape de Florida unto the Bay of Canada . . . is proper to the king of England. . . .

And first, seeing we daily pray for the conversion of the heathens, . . . Now it seemeth unto me that we ought also to endeavor and use the means to convert them; and the means cannot be used unless we go to them, or they come to us. To us they cannot come, our land is full; to them we may go, their land is empty.

This then is a sufficient reason to prove our going thither to live, lawful. Their land is spacious and void, and there are few, and do but run over the grass, as do also the foxes and wild beasts. They are not industrious, neither have art, science, skill or faculty to use either the land or the commodities of it; but all spoils, rots, and is marred for want of manuring, gathering, ordering, &c. As the ancient patriarchs, therefore, removed from straiter places into more roomy, where the land lay idle and waste, and none used it, though there dwelt inhabitants by them, as Gen. 13:6, 11, 12, and 34:21, and 41:20, so is it lawful now to take a land which none useth, and make use of it.

And as it is common land, or unused and undressed country, so we have it by common consent, composition and agreement; which agreement is double. First, the imperial governor, Massasoit, whose circuits, in likelihood, are larger than England and Scotland, hath acknowledged the King's Majesty of England to be his master and commander, . . . Neither hath this been accomplished by threats and blows, or shaking of sword and sound of trumpet; for as our faculty that way is small, and our strength less, so our warring with them is after another manner, namely, by friendly usage, love, peace, honest and just carriages, good counsel, &c., that so we and they may not only live in peace in that land, and they yield subjection to an earthly prince, but that as voluntaries they may be persuaded at length to embrace the Prince of Peace, Christ Jesus, and rest in peace with him forever. . . .

The country is yet raw; the land untilled; the cities not builded; the cattle not settled. We are compassed about with a helpless and idle people, the natives of the country, which cannot, in any comely or comfortable manner, help themselves, much less us. We also have been very chargeable to many of our loving friends, which helped us hither, and now again supplied us; so that before we think of gathering riches, we must even in conscience think of requiting their charge, love, and labor; and cursed be that profit and gain which aimeth not at this. . . .

Robert Cushman, *Reasons and Considerations Touching the Lawfulness of Removing Out of England into the Parts of America* (1621) and *The Sin and Danger of Self-Love* (London, 1622). Reprinted in Alexander Young, *Chronicles of the Pilgrim Fathers of the Colony of Plymouth, from 1602 to 1625* (Boston: Charles C. Little and James Brown, 1841), 242–44, 265.

✣

Roger Williams versus John Cotton (Massachusetts) (1647)

Native American ideas of landownership were communal rather than individual. What Indian families and tribes possessed in a field, woods, or river was the use they derived from it, and hence they named the landscape based on its use ("where the deer are hunted" or "where blueberries grow"). Europeans, however, viewed land as the property of individuals. Even so, not every colonist ran roughshod over Indian land rights. Those rare instances in which English colonists disagreed—such as the exchange between two New England clergymen, Roger Williams and John Cotton—are illuminating. Williams is best known for his advocacy of the separation of church and state (a position that led to his banishment from the Massachusetts colony), but he also tussled with the colony's leaders over Indian landownership. At one point, Williams wrote: "The Natives are very exact and punctuall in the bounds of their Lands, belonging to this or that Prince or People. . . . And I have knowne them make a bargaine and sale amongst themselves for a small piece, or quantity of Ground: notwithstanding a sinfull opinion amongst many that Christians have right to Heathen Lands." In the following document, Williams's dispute with the colony is recalled by the Reverend John Cotton, the preeminent defender of Puritan orthodoxy.

PROBLEMS TO CONSIDER

1. How could two men of similar faith come to such different conclusions about the rightness of laying claim to Indian lands?
2. How did Cotton or Williams define what was *just* or *right* about land use and ownership?

  . . . Two things there were, which (to my best observation, and remembrance) caused the Sentence of his *[Williams's]* Banishment: and two others fell in, that hastened it.

1. His violent and tumultuous carriage against the Patent.

By the Patent it is, that we received allowance from the King to depart his Kingdome, and to carry our goods with us, without offence to his Officers, and without paying custome to himselfe. . . .

By the Patent we have Power to erect such a Government of the Church, as is most agreeable to the Word, to the estate of the People, and to the gaining of Natives (in Gods time) first to Civility, and then to Christianity. . . .

This Patent, Mr. *Williams* publickly, and vehemently preached against, as containing matter of falsehood, and injustice: Falsehood in making

the King the first Christian Prince who had discovered these parts: and injustice, in giving the Countrey to his *English* Subjects, which belonged to the Native *Indians*. This therefore he pressed upon the Magistrates and People, to be humbled for from time to time in dayes of solemne Humiliation, and to returne the Patent back againe to the King. It was answered to him, first, That it was neither the Kings intendement, nor the *English* Planters to take possession of the Countrey by murder of the Natives, or by robbery: but either to take possession of the void places of the Countrey by the Law of Nature, . . . or if we tooke any Lands from the Natives, it was by way of purchase, and free consent.

A little before our coming, God had by pestilence, and other contagious diseases, swept away many thousands of the Natives, who had inhabited the Bay of *Massachusets*, for which the Patent was granted. Such few of them as survived were glad of the coming of the *English*, who might preserve them from the oppression of the *Nahargansets*. For it is the manner of the Natives, the stronger Nations to oppress the weaker.

This answer did not satisfy Mr. *Williams*, who pleaded, the Natives, though they did not, nor could subdue the Countrey, . . . yet they hunted all the Countrey over, and for the expedition of their hunting voyages, they burnt up all the underwoods in the Countrey, once or twice a yeare, and therefore as Noble men in *England* possessed great Parkes, and the King, great Forrests in *England* only for their game, and no man might lawfully invade their Propriety: So might the Natives challenge the like Propriety of the Countrey here.

It was replyed unto him. 1. That the King, and Noble men in *England*, as they possessed greater Territories than other men, so they did greater service to Church, and Common-wealth.

2. That they employed their Parkes, and Forrests, not for hunting only, but for Timber, and for the nourishment of tame beasts, as well as wild, and also for habitation to sundry Tenants.

3. That our Townes here did not disturb the huntings of the Natives, but did rather keepe their Game fitter for their taking; for they take their Deer by Traps, and not by Hounds.

4. That if they complained of any straites wee put upon them, wee gave satisfaction in some payments, or other, to their content.

5. We did not conceive that it is a just Title to so vast a Continent, to make no other improvement of millions of Acres in it, but only to burne it up for pastime.

But these Answers not satisfying him, this was still pressed by him as a Nationall sin, to hold to the Patent, yea, and a Nationall duty to renounce the Patent: which to have done, had subverted the fundamentall State, and Government of the Countrey. . . .

These were (as I tooke it) the causes of his Banishment. . . .

"Master John Cotton's Answer to Master Roger Williams," in *Complete Writings of Roger Williams*, vol. 2 (New York: Russell & Russell, 1963), 44–47, 50.

ᴈ

A Micmac Chief (New France) (1691)

Despite European misinterpretations, native peoples did possess land and maintained important cultural connections to it. Mobility, however, was central to the way of life of many North American Indian peoples. They moved with the seasons. When they had exhausted the potential for food and fuel in one place, they literally picked up their homes (mats and wooden frames) and carried them on their backs to a new locale. In addition, agriculture was usually performed by women, giving mothers of families a direct link to (if not implied ownership of) the land. A wonderful account of a North American Indian's response to European attitudes about land, property, and wealth was recorded by Chrestien Le Clercq, a French Recollet (Franciscan) priest. Le Clercq labored as a missionary near Gaspé, on the Gaspé Peninsula, at the mouth of the St. Lawrence River (present-day eastern Quebec). Unlike Jesuit missionaries who dominated French missions during the early seventeenth century, and who allowed Indians to retain many beliefs and practices and still be baptized into Christianity, Recollet missionaries (like English Protestants) thought Indian conversions were not genuine until they abandoned their traditional ("savage") culture. Nonetheless, Le Clercq was fascinated with Indian reactions to Europeans and recorded the following speech by a Micmac chief.

PROBLEMS TO CONSIDER

1. Explain how this speech is a defense not just of land use but of an entire way of life. What makes a person rich in this chief's eyes?
2. How do you think a French colonist would have responded to this speech?

I am greatly astonished that the French . . . have so little cleverness, as they seem to exhibit in the matter of which thou hast just told me on their behalf, in the effort to persuade us to convert our poles, our barks, and our wigwams into those houses of stone and of wood which are tall and lofty, according to their account, as these trees. Very well! But why now . . . do men of five to six feet in height need houses which are sixty to eighty? For, in fact, as thou knowest very well thyself, Patriarch—do we not find in our own all the conveniences and the advantages that you have with yours, such as reposing, drinking, sleeping, eating, and amusing ourselves with our friends when we wish? This is not all, . . . my brother, hast thou as much ingenuity and cleverness as the Indians, who carry their houses and their wigwams with them so that they may lodge wheresoever they please, independently of any seignior *[lord]* whatsoever? Thou art not as bold nor as stout as we, because when thou goest on a voyage thou canst not carry upon thy shoulders thy buildings and thy edifices. Therefore it is necessary that thou preparest as many lodgings as thou makest changes of residence, or else thou lodgest in a hired house which does not belong to thee. As for us, we find ourselves secure from all these inconveniences, and we can always say, more truly than thou, that we are at home everywhere, because we set up our wigwams with ease wheresoever we go, and without asking permission of anybody. Thou reproachest us, very inappropriately, that our country is a little hell in contrast with France, which thou comparest to a terrestrial paradise, inasmuch as it yields thee, so thou sayest, every kind of provision in abundance.

Thou sayest of us also that we are the most miserable and most unhappy of all men, living without religion, without manners, without honour, without social order, and, in a word, without any rules, like the beasts in our woods and our forests, lacking bread, wine, and a thousand other comforts which thou hast in superfluity in Europe. Well, my brother, if thou dost not yet know the real feelings which our Indians have towards thy country and towards all thy nation, it is proper that I inform thee at once. I beg thee now to believe that, all miserable as we seem in thine eyes, we consider ourselves nevertheless much happier than thou in this, that we are very content with the little that we have; and believe also once for all, I pray, that thou deceivest thyself greatly if thou thinkest to persuade us that thy country is better than ours. For if France, as thou sayest, is a little terrestrial paradise, art thou sensible to leave it? And why abandon wives, children, relatives, and friends? Why risk thy life and thy property every year, and why venture thyself with such risk, in any season whatsoever, to the storms and tempests of the sea in order to come to a strange and barbarous country which thou considerest the poorest and least fortunate of the world? Besides, since we are wholly convinced of the contrary, we scarcely take the trouble to go to France, because we fear, with good reason, lest we find little satisfaction there, seeing, in our own experience, that those who are natives thereof leave it every year in order to enrich themselves on our shores. We believe, further, that you are also incomparably poorer than we, and that you are only simple journeymen, valets, servants, and slaves, all masters and grand captains though you may appear, seeing that you glory in our old rags and in our miserable suits of beaver which can no longer be of use to us, and that you find among us, in the fishery for cod which you make in these parts, the wherewithal to comfort your misery and the poverty which oppresses you. As to us, we find all our riches and all our conveniences among ourselves, without trouble and without exposing our lives to the dangers in which you find yourselves constantly through your long voyages. . . . Now tell me this one little thing, if thou hast any sense: Which of these two is the wisest and happiest—he who labours without ceasing and only obtains, and that with great trouble, enough to live on, or he who rests in comfort and finds all that he needs in the pleasure of hunting and fishing? It is true . . . that we have not always had the use of bread and of wine which your France produces; but, in fact, before the arrival of the French in these parts, did not the Gaspesans live much longer than now? And if we have not any longer among us any of those old men of a hundred and thirty to forty years, it is only because we are gradually adopting your manner of living, for experience is making it very plain that those of us live longest who, despising your bread, your wine, and your brandy, are content with their natural food of beaver, of moose, of waterfowl, and fish, in accord with the custom of our ancestors and of all the Gaspesian nation. Learn now, my brother, once for all, because I must open to thee my heart: there is no Indian who does not consider himself infinitely more happy and more powerful than the French. . . .

Father Chrestien Le Clercq, *New Relation of Gaspesia, with the Customs and Religion of the Gaspesian Indians*, edited and translated by William F. Ganong (Toronto: Champlain Society, 1910), 103–6.

ॐ

⌐: Cosmology: Creation Stories from American Indian, West African, and European Cultures :~

All three groups of people (American Indian, West African, and European) who interacted in the New World maintained beliefs in creation or origin stories. Origin legends reveal a great deal about the core cultural ideas and meaningful values of a culture. Not only do these stories attempt to account for the origin of the cosmos and the earth, but they also explain relationships among people, including gender roles, and the establishment of a society's most significant social institutions. Hence, origin stories offer historians intriguing sources for comparing cultures.

European colonists set out on their colonizing ventures during the same era when the printed book began to proliferate; hence their attachment to a written text of origins in the book of Genesis in the Bible. In contrast, both American Indian and West African peoples disseminated their origin narratives as part of oral literatures that were performed in the presence of others. Unfortunately, European colonists did not value these stories enough to record them for posterity. The earliest accounts we have of American Indian and African origin legends were first reproduced as texts in the nineteenth century.

Hopi Creation Story (Spanish America)

Mande Creation Narrative (West Africa)

Genesis (King James Version of the Bible)

Two types of origin stories were common among Native Americans. One involved Earth-Diver stories in which an animal (often a turtle) brings enough mud from the floor of the waters to create the landmass of earth. The other common legend was an emergence tale, in which the first humans emerge from the underworld to the earth's surface. The creation story of the Hopi (who lived in lands colonized by Spain, or present-day Arizona) is a variation on an emergence tale. Because this story was not recorded in print until the twentieth century, it reveals the ability of oral traditions to adapt to new knowledge, such as the existence of Europeans. The Mande creation legend comes from the peoples originating at the source of the Niger River in West Africa, a culture that influenced the peoples of Senegal, Sudan, Ivory Coast, Guinea, and other African nations. The European creation narrative is from the first two chapters of Genesis, in the King James version (1611) of the Bible.

PROBLEMS TO CONSIDER

1. What cultural values are reinforced in each of these origin stories, and what do these values reveal about the most cherished qualities and characteristics of life among American Indian, West African, and European peoples?
2. What do each of these stories suggest about the status of men and women, and what influence would you expect these stories to have on the construction of gender in each society?

HOPI CREATION STORY

A very long time ago there was nothing but water. In the east Hurúing Wuhti, the deity of all hard substances, lived in the ocean. Her house was a kiva like the kivas of the Hopi of today. *[Among Pueblo Indians, a kiva is a ceremonial room, partly or completely underground, that is entered by a ladder through a hole in the center of the ceiling.]* To the ladder leading into the kiva were usually tied a skin of a gray fox and one of a yellow fox. Another Hurúing Wuhti lived in the ocean in the west in a similar kiva, but to her ladder was attached a turtle-shell rattle.

The Sun also existed at that time. Shortly before rising in the east the Sun would dress up in the skin of the gray fox, whereupon it would begin to dawn—the so-called white dawn of the Hopi. After a little while the Sun would lay off the gray skin and put on the yellow fox skin, whereupon the bright dawn of the morning—the so-called yellow dawn of the Hopi—would appear. The Sun would then rise, that is, emerge from an opening in the north end of the kiva in which Hurúing Wuhti lived. . . .

By and by these two deities caused some dry land to appear in the midst of the water, the waters receding eastward and westward. The Sun passing over this dry land constantly took notice of the fact, that no living being of any kind could be seen anywhere, and mentioned this fact to the two deities. So one time the

Hurúing Wuhti of the west sent word through the Sun to the Hurúing Wuhti in the east to come over to her as she wanted to talk over this matter. The Hurúing Wuhti of the east complied with this request and proceeded to the west over a rainbow. After consulting each other on this point the two concluded that they would create a little bird; so the deity of the east made a wren of clay, and . . . they sang a song over it, and after a little while the little bird showed signs of life. . . . "Yes," they said, "we want you to fly all over this dry place and see whether you can find anything living." They thought that as the Sun always passed over the middle of the earth, he might have failed to notice any living beings that might exist in the north or the south. So the little Wren flew all over the earth, but upon its return reported that no living being existed anywhere. Tradition says, however, that by this time Spider Woman (Kóhkang Wuhti), lived somewhere in the south-west at the edge of the water, also in a kiva, but this the little bird had failed to notice. . . .

Hereupon the Hurúing Wuhti of the west made of clay all different kinds of animals, and they were brought to life in the same manner as the birds. They also asked the same question: "Why do you want us so quickly?" "We want you to inhabit this earth," was the reply given them, whereupon they were taught by their creators their different sounds or languages, after which they proceeded forth to inhabit the different parts of the earth. They now concluded that they would create man. The deity of the east made of clay first a woman and then a man, who were brought to life in exactly the same manner as the birds and animals before them. They asked the same question, and were told that they should live upon this earth and should understand everything. Hereupon the Hurúing Wuhti of the east made two tablets of some hard substance, whether stone or clay tradition does not say, and drew upon them with the wooden stick certain characters, handing these tablets to the newly created man and woman,

who looked at them, but did not know what they meant. So the deity of the east rubbed the palms of her hands, first the palms of the woman and then the palms of the man, by which they were enlightened so that they understood the writing on the tablets. Hereupon the deities taught these two a language. [Some Hopi say that these two people were the ancestors of what are now called the White Man, and the people say that they believe this language taught to these two people was the language of the present White Man.] . . . By this time Spider Woman had heard about all this matter and she concluded to anticipate the others and also create some beings. So she also made a man and woman of clay, covered them up, sang over them, and brought to life her handiwork. But these two proved to be Spaniards. She taught them the Spanish language, also giving them similar tablets and imparting knowledge to them by rubbing their hands in the same manner as the woman of the East had done with the "White Men." . . .

These were the kind of people that Spider Woman had created. The Hurúing Wuhti of the west heard about this and commenced to meditate upon it. Soon she called the goddess from the east to come over again, which the latter did. "I do not want to live here alone," the deity of the west said, "I also want some good people to live here." So she also created a number of other people, but always a man and a wife. They were created in the same manner as the deity of the east had created hers. They lived in the west. Only wherever the people that Spider Woman had created came in contact with these good people there was trouble. The people at that time led a nomadic life, living mostly on game. Wherever they found rabbits or antelope or deer they would kill the game and eat it. This led to a good many contentions among the people. Finally the Woman of the west said to her people: "You remain here; I am going to live, after this, in the midst of the ocean in the west. When you want anything from me, you pray to me there."

Her people regretted this very much, but she left them. The Hurúing Wuhti of the east did exactly the same thing, and that is the reason why at the present day the places where these two live are never seen.

H. R. Voth, *The Traditions of the Hopi* (Chicago: Field Columbian Museum, 1905), 1–4.

MANDE CREATION NARRATIVE

God, *Mangala*, first created the *balāzā* (*Acacia albida*) seed *[a tree native to Africa]*, which was, however, a failure. So he abandoned it in order to create twin varieties of eleusine seed *[a grain]*, *fani berere* and *fani ba*; thus, as the Keita say, he "made the egg of the world in two twin parts which were to procreate." God then created six more seeds and associated with this group of eight seeds the four elements and the "cardinal points" in order to mark out the organization of the world and its expansion. Thus there was: in the west (*klebi*): *fani berere* and *fani ba*; in the east (*koro*): *sañō* and *keninge*; in the north (*kañanga*): *so* and *kende*; in the south (*worodugu*): *kaba* and *malo*. Finally the whole was enfolded in a hibiscus seed.

The seeds are thus conceived as twins of opposite sex in the "egg of God" which is also called "egg of the world" or "placenta of the world." They are often represented in drawings as an open flower with four petals which are also sometimes called the four "clavicles" of God.

In the same egg, according to the myth, there were in addition two pairs of twins, each consisting of one male and one female, archetypes of the future men. One of the males, Pemba, desiring to dominate the creation, emerged prematurely, before gestation was complete, tearing away a piece of his placenta as he did so. He came down through empty space; the piece of placenta became the earth, but it was dry and barren and he could do nothing with it. Seeing this, he went back to heaven and tried to resume his place in the placenta and find his twin. In this he could not succeed, for God had changed the remaining part of his placenta into the sun. So Pemba then stole from one of God's clavicles the eight male seeds which he carried down in a calabash flask (*bara*).

He sowed these seeds in the place of placenta which had become the earth. In this first field, which the Keita locate near Bounan (a village not far from Lake Debo), only the *fani berere*—one of the eleusine seeds—germinated in the blood of the placenta; the other seeds died for want of water. Because of Pemba's theft and his incestuous act (for Pemba had put the seed in his own placenta, that is, in his mother's womb) the earth became impure and the eleusine seed turned red as it is today.

The other male twin, Faro, assumed, while in heaven, the form of twin *mannogo* fishes, which are represented in the Niger river today by the *mannogo ble* and the *mannogo fi*. The first represented his strength and his life, the second his body. In order to atone for Pemba's sin and purify the earth, Faro was sacrificed in heaven and his body was cut into sixty pieces which were scattered throughout space. They fell on the earth where they became trees, symbols of vegetal resurrection. God then brought Faro back to life in heaven and, giving him human shape, sent him down to earth on an ark made of his celestial placenta. . . .

The first human beings, like Faro himself, had a common vital force (*nyama*) and complementary spiritual forces *ni* and *dya*, each of which had both a male and a female form. Also, in their clavicles were deposited the symbols of the eight seeds created by God. Emerging from the ark they watched, for the first time, the rising of the sun. . . .

Faro's Journey

Faro now traveled east in order to flood all the places where Mousso Koroni dropped eleusine seeds and he finally reached Bounan and flooded Pemba's field. He was able to recover all the seeds that had been stolen, for he sent the *mannogo ble* everywhere to eat the seeds and it was followed by all the other fishes.

Thus the River Niger, which has been formed from this series of floods, represents Faro's body; and it is said that "Faro lies face downward in the Niger." His head is Lake Debo, his right arm is the Bani, while his body is the Niger itself. The Bani and Niger are also called *bala*, which is male, and *bogolo*, which is female; the river from its source to Sama is Faro's single leg and Sama itself is his genitals. But on the opposite bank Faro, who was androgynous (or a twin), took the opposite sex; thus between Tamani and Sama, from being male on the right bank he became female on the left bank. All along the river a series of *faro tyn* marks the place where he halted: the place where he drowned Mousso Koroni's seeds which the *mannogo ble* had eaten; the place where he left his seeds in the shape of silurian fish for the future birth of men. For Faro is said to be unique and ubiquitous, and procreative.

Germaine Dieterlen, "The Mande Creation Myth," in *Africa: Journal of the International African Institute* 27 (1957): 126–27, 130–31.

GENESIS

Genesis 1

In the beginning God created the heaven and the earth. And the earth was without form, and void; and darkness was upon the face of the deep. And the Spirit of God moved upon the face of the waters. And God said, Let there be light: and there was light. And God saw the light, that it was good: and God divided the light from the darkness. And God called the light Day, and the darkness he called Night. And the evening and the morning were the first day.

And God said, Let there be a firmament in the midst of the waters, and let it divide the waters from the waters. And God made the firmament, and divided the waters which were under the firmament from the waters which were above the firmament: and it was so. And God called the firmament Heaven. And the evening and the morning were the second day.

And God said, Let the waters under the heaven be gathered together unto one place and let the dry land appear: and it was so. And God called the dry land Earth; and the gathering together of the waters called he Seas: and God saw that it was good. And God said, Let the earth bring forth grass, the herb yielding seed, and the fruit tree yielding fruit after his kind, whose seed is in itself, upon the earth: and it was so. And the earth brought forth grass, and herb yielding seed after his kind, and the tree yielding fruit, whose seed was in itself, after his kind: and God saw that it was good. And the evening and the morning were the third day.

And God said, Let there be lights in the firmament of the heaven to divide the day from the night; and let them be for signs, and for seasons, and for days, and years. . . . And God made two great lights; the greater light to rule the day, and the lesser light to rule the night: he made the stars also. And God set them in the firmament of the heaven to give light upon the earth, and to rule over the day and over the night, and to divide the light from the darkness: and God saw that it was good. And the evening and the morning were the fourth day.

And God said, Let the waters bring forth abundantly the moving creature that hath life, and fowl that may fly above the earth in the open firmament of heaven. And God created great whales, and every living creature that moveth, which the waters brought forth abundantly, after their kind, and every winged fowl after his kind: and God saw that it was good. And God blessed them, saying, Be fruitful, and multiply, and fill the waters in the seas, and let fowl multiply in the earth. And the evening and the morning were the fifth day.

And God said, Let the earth bring forth the living creature after his kind, cattle, and creeping thing, and beast of the earth after his kind:

and it was so. And God made the beast of the earth after his kind, and cattle after their kind, and every thing that creepeth upon the earth after his kind: and God saw that it was good. And God said, Let us make man in our image, after our likeness: and let them have dominion over the fish of the sea, and over the fowl of the air, and over the cattle, and over all the earth, and over every creeping thing that creepeth upon the earth. So God created man in his own image, in the image of God created he him; male and female created he them. And God blessed them, and God said unto them, Be fruitful, and multiply, and replenish the earth, and subdue it: and have dominion over the fish of the sea, and over the fowl of the air, and over every living thing that moveth upon the earth. . . . And God saw every thing that he had made, and, behold, it was very good. And the evening and the morning were the sixth day.

Genesis 2

Thus the heavens and the earth were finished, and all the host of them. And on the seventh day God ended his work he had made; and he rested on the seventh day from all his work which he had made. And God blessed the seventh day, and sanctified it: because that in it he had rested from all his work which God created and made. . . .

And the LORD God said, It is not good that the man should be alone; I will make him an help meet for him. . . . And the LORD God caused a deep sleep to fall upon Adam and he slept: and he took one of his ribs, and closed up the flesh instead thereof; and the rib, which the LORD God had taken from man, made he a woman, and brought her unto the man. And Adam said, This is now bone of my bones, and flesh of my flesh: she shall be called Woman, because she was taken out of Man. Therefore shall a man leave his father and his mother, and shall cleave unto his wife: and they shall be one flesh. And they were both naked, the man and his wife, and were not ashamed.

Holy Bible, Authorized King James Version (1611), Genesis 1–2. Electronic Text Center, University of Virginia Library, http://etext.lib.virginia.edu.

ᔐ

CHAPTER 2

Cross-Cultural Encounters: 1607–1690

WHEN EUROPEANS finally succeeded in sustaining long-term colonies in North America, neither European migrants nor Native Americans were fully prepared for the types of intimate, and often violent, intersections of vastly different cultures they would experience in the first century of colonization. European and Indian peoples brought to this convergence traditional customs and beliefs as well as new uncertainties brought on by social changes. For instance, English migrants came from a society where the patriarchal family was a metaphor for a stable social and political order. Robert Filmer expressed this correspondence in *Patriarcha* (1642): "as the Father over one family, so the king, as Father over many families, extends his care to preserve, feed, clothe, instruct and defend the whole commonwealth." English discourses on gender thus provided a way of naturalizing power and inequality within that society. Native American societies also had a system of gender roles and identities, and rituals of social integration through family relationships, although their worlds were often organized along matrilineal lines.

When cultures collide, new languages, meanings, and customs are born. Recently, an important change has taken place in the way historians think about European colonization in North America. No longer does anyone view the colonial era as the inevitable precursor to the founding of the United States, as did nineteenth-century historian George Bancroft, who titled his chapter on the colonial period "England Discovers the United States." Historians now supplement concepts such as invasion and conquest, which imply an overwhelming dominance by Europeans, with interpretations that emphasize the metaphor of an encounter, or the creation of a "middle ground." A middle ground suggests that the encounter between European colonists and Native Americans can best be understood as an ongoing struggle between two alien cultures, an uneasy (and often violent) interaction usually built on a foundation of mutual misunderstanding. But speaking of an encounter or a middle ground does not mean equal degrees of power or dominance, since American Indians were devastated by epidemic diseases and were eventually outnumbered by centuries of European immigration. These metaphors, however, do more accurately reflect the full complexity of the interaction between Europeans and Native Americans. They also change the vantage point of the historian, forcing a recognition that native peoples were important historical actors rather than merely victims. Recently, one historian has challenged us to examine the encounter by "facing east," from the vantage point of Native Americans rather than Europeans.

This chapter investigates this middle ground of the encounter by exploring instances of individuals who crossed the cultural frontier that separated Europeans from Indians in colonial North America. Indians who lived with Europeans, and Europeans who lived among Indians, became (often unwillingly) brokers for the transmission of new knowledge. And their identities, stories, and performances became the principal ways by which each culture interpreted and explained New World encounters. In the cross-cultural experiences of Pocahontas, Englishmen John Smith and John Rolfe, and Europeans and Indians held captive by the other, we can glimpse a colonial world confronted with different approaches to gender, family, war, religion, and power.

∽ Pocahontas: Race and Gender in England's Colonization of Virginia ∾

Virginians, in fact all English colonists, had an origin legend all their own. It was not the tale of a primordial creation, but rather the narrative of a romantic and sexual relationship between an Indian maiden and an English male colonist. This sexual and racial boundary crossing grew in mythic stature by the time the United States was founded. In fact, of all the artistic renditions that line the Rotunda of the U.S. Capitol depicting the seminal events of the discovery, colonization, and nation-building history of the United States, the only individuals represented more than once are Christopher Columbus, George Washington, and an "Indian princess" known as Pocahontas. What gives Pocahontas a mythic power rivaled only by Columbus or Washington? And what does it mean for her to be depicted as a half-naked Indian in one Rotunda tableau and a traditionally clothed newly Christian and English woman in the other?

By the beginning of the nineteenth century, both a French and a British traveler had popularized erotic fantasies of the relationship between Captain John Smith and Pocahontas. John Davis published several versions of this fantasy, including *Captain Smith and Princess Pocahontas* (1805). Davis portrayed Pocahontas with long black hair that would "riot down her comely" back, shading "but not hiding the protuberance of her bosom," implying that "conjugal endearments" and "passionate embraces" led to a sexual liaison between Smith and Pocahontas. So the Disney film *Pocahontas* (1995) was not the first to transform a twelve-year-old girl into a nubile and full-bosomed young woman who lusted after English men.

The trouble with this romantic fantasy is that Smith, who invented the myth of Pocahontas in his story of how she rescued him from an execution, never suggested a sexual relationship between himself (age twenty-seven) and the young daughter of Powhatan, the powerful overlord of a coalition of Chesapeake Algonquian peoples. More troubles plague this myth: Pocahontas was not even her real name, merely a nickname meaning "mischievous one." Her formal name was Amonute, her personal name was Matoaka, and she gained celebrity in England by assuming a Christian name, Rebecca, upon her baptism and marriage to the Virginia colonist John Rolfe.

For the English, Pocahontas personified their God-ordained colonial enterprise. Her iconic status reveals that English ways of imagining their New World colonization were buttressed by ideas about race and gender, as well as by religion and culture. In the process, a two-sided image of the mythical Pocahontas emerged: as forest maiden (noble savage) and Christian lady (convert). Missing from that mythology was a deeper understanding of the types of diplomatic and cross-cultural actions that Pocahontas, Rolfe, and Smith performed in the making of a middle ground, and the ways the Algonquian peoples interpreted Pocahontas's role as an intermediary between cultures.

Captain John Smith's Narrative of His Captivity and Rescue (1624)

The myth of Pocahontas begins with the writings of Captain John Smith. And here the controversy blazes. Smith has been characterized as a notorious braggart, never at a loss for embellishing his manly adventures or trumpeting his ferocity as a warrior. For more than a century, historians have debated the truthfulness of Smith's account of how Pocahontas saved him from execution at the hands of his native captors. His detractors emphasize that Smith never mentioned his rescue by Pocahontas in his first narrative of Virginia, A True Relation *(1608). In that account, he wrote that Powhatan "kindly welcomed me with good wordes, and great Platters of sundrie Victuals, assuring mee his friendship, and my libertie within foure dayes." Only after Pocahontas had become a celebrity in England as a Christian convert married to an English gentleman, and only after the deaths of Pocahontas, Powhatan, and John Rolfe, did Smith publish the adventurous tale of his capture and rescue by the Indian king's daughter in* The Generall Historie of Virginia *(1624). But other historians have pointed to the accuracy of Smith's accounts in all other details and have noted Smith's earlier references to Pocahontas's rescue in his 1616 letter to Queen Anne, casting doubt on the theory that Smith entirely fabricated this tale. For the foreseeable future, then, the pendulum is likely to swing back and forth between those who think Smith described an actual experience and those who insist that he invented the story.*

But even if these events did occur, does that mean that Smith understood their mean-ing for Powhatan's people? Whereas Smith perceived that his life was being threatened by savages, who, in his mind, might be either cannibals or cruel barbarians, several histori-ans have suggested that Smith was probably participating unknowingly in an adoption ritual, in which Powhatan tried to situate the English as a subordinate people by making Smith his fictive son. The documents that follow are Smith's account of his rescue in The Generall Historie; *his 1616 letter to the Queen, which exists only in that publication; and the artist Robert Vaughan's illustration of Smith's story.*

PROBLEMS TO CONSIDER

1. What did Captain Smith intend to convey in these accounts about himself, as well as about the "salvages" who captured him? How would his contemporaries have regarded his self-presentation?
2. In what ways do these three versions of Smith's narrative differ? How does the image of a half-naked Pocahontas correspond with the tone and content of Smith's narrative of his rescue?

Smith little dreaming of that accident, being got to the marshes at the rivers head, twentie miles in the desert, had his two men slaine (as is supposed) sleeping by the Canoe, whilst him-selfe by fowling sought them victuall, who find-ing he was beset with 200 Salvages, two of them hee slew, still defending himselfe with the aid of a Salvage his guide, whom he bound to his arm with his garters, and used him as a buckler [*shield*], yet he was shot in his thigh a little, and had many arrowes that stucke in his cloathes but no great hurt, till at last they tooke him prisoner. When this newes came to James towne, much was their sorrow for his losse, fewe expecting what ensued.

Sixe or seven weekes those Barbarians kept him prisoner, many strange triumphes and con-jurations [*sorcery*] they made of him, yet hee so demeaned himselfe amongst them, as he not only diverted them from surprising the Fort, but procured his own libertie, and got himselfe and his company such estimation amongst them, that those Salvages admired him more than their owne Quiyouckosucks [*gods*].

The manner how they used and delivered him, is as followeth. . . .

Their order in conducting him was thus: Drawing themselves all in file, the King [*Pow-hatan*] in the middest had all their Pieces and Swords borne before him. Captaine Smith was led after him by three great Salvages, holding him fast by each arm: and on each side six went in file with their Arrowes nocked. . . . A good time they continued this exercise, and then cast themselves in a ring, dancing in such severall Postures, and singing and yelling out such hell-ish notes and screeches; being strangely painted, every one his quiver of Arrowes, and at his backe a club; on his arm a Fox or an Otters skinne, or some such matter for his vambrace [*armor*]; their heads and shoulders painted red. . . . All this while Smith and the King stood in the middest guarded, as before is said, and after three dances they all departed. Smith they conducted to a long house, where thirtie or fortie tall fellowes did guard him, and ere long more bread and venison was brought him than would have served twentie men. I thinke his stomacke at that time was not very good; what he left they put in baskets and tied over his head. [*Smith de-scribes other ceremonies and feasts over the next days and weeks.*] . . .

At last they brought him to Werowocomoco, where was Powhatan their Emperor. Here more than two hundred of those grim Courtiers stood wondering at him, as [if] he had beene a monster; till Powhatan and his train had put themselves in their greatest braveries *[i.e., finest attire]*. Before a fire upon a seat like a bedsted, he sat covered with a great robe, made of Rarowcun *[raccoon]* skins, and all the tails hanging by. . . .

At his entrance before the King, all the people gave a great shout. The Queene of Appamatuck was appointed to bring him water to wash his hands, and another brought him a bunch of feathers, in stead of a Towell to dry them: having feasted him after their best barbarous manner they could, a long consultation was held, but the conclusion was, two great stones were brought before Powhatan: then as many as could laid hands on him, dragged him to them, and thereon laid his head, and being ready with their clubs, to beate out his braines, Pocahontas, the Kings dearest daughter, when no entreaty could prevaile, got his head in her arms, and laid her owne upon his to save him from death: whereat the Emperor was contented he should live to make him hatchets, and her bells, beads, and copper; for they thought him as well of all occupations as themselves. . . .

Two dayes after, Powhatan having disguised himselfe in the most fearfullest manner he could, . . . more like a devil than a man, with some two hundred more as blacke as himself, came unto him *[Smith]* and told him now they were friends, and presently he should goe to James towne, to send him two great guns, and a grindstone, for which he would give him the Countrey of Capahowosick, and for ever esteeme him as his son Nantaquoud.

So to James towne with 12 guides Powhatan sent him. That night they quartered in the woods, he still expecting (as he had done all this long time of his imprisonment) every houre to be put to one death or other: for all their feasting. But almightie God (by his divine providence) had mollified the hearts of those sterne Barbarians with compassion. The next morning betimes they came to the Fort, where Smith having used the Salvages with what kindnesse he could. . . . But at last we . . . sent to Powhatan, his women, and children such presents, as gave them in generall full content.

Now in James towne they were all in combustion, the strongest preparing once more to run away with the Pinnace *[small boat]*: . . . Smith forced now the third time to stay or sinke.

Some no better than they should be, had plotted with the President, the next day to have put him to death by the Leviticall law, for the lives of Robinson and Emry *[the two Virginians killed when Smith was captured]*; pretending the fault was his that had led them to their ends: but he quickly took such order with such Lawyers, that he laid them by the heels till he sent some of them prisoners for England.

Now ever[y] one in foure or five dayes, Pocahontas with her attendants, brought him so much provision, that saved many of their lives, that else for all this had starved with hunger.

[Letter to Queen Anne, after Pocahontas's arrival in England, 1617]

To the most high and vertuous Princesse, Queene Anne of Great Brittanie.

Most admired Queene,

. . . Some ten yeeres agoe being in Virginia, and taken prisoner by the power of Powhatan their chiefe King, I received from this great Salvage exceeding great courtesie, especially from his son Nantaquaus, the most manliest, comeliest, boldest spirit, I ever saw in a Salvage, and his sister Pocahontas, the Kings most deare and well-beloved daughter, being but a childe of twelve or thirteene years of age, whose compassionate pitifull heart, of my desperate estate, gave me much cause to respect her: I being the first Christian this proud King and his grim attendants ever saw: and thus enthralled in their barbarous power, I cannot say I felt the least occasion of want that was in the power of those

Robert Vaughan's Engraving of Pocahantas Rescuing Captain John Smith, from
Captain John Smith, *Generall Historie of Virginia . . .* (1624): Caption reads: "Powhatan
comands C. Smith to be slayne, his daughter Pokahontas beggs his life . . ."
(Photo by MPI/Getty Images.)

my mortall foes to prevent, notwithstanding
all their threats. After some six weeks fatting
amongst those Salvage Courtiers, at the minute
of my execution, she hazarded the beating out of
her owne braines to save mine, and not only
that, but so prevailed with her father, that I was
safely conducted to James towne, where I found
about eight and thirtie miserable poore and
sicke creatures, to keepe possession of all those
large territories of Virginia, such was the weak-
nesse of this poore Commonwealth, as had the
Salvages not fed us, we directly had starved.

And this reliefe, most gracious Queene, was commonly brought us by this Lady Pocahontas.

Notwithstanding all these passages, when inconstant Fortune turned our peace to war, this tender Virgin would still not spare to dare to visit us, and by her our jars have beene oft appeased, and our wants still supplyed; were it the policie of her father thus to employ her, or the ordinance of God thus to make her his instrument, or her extraordinarie affection to our Nation, I know not: but of this I am sure; when her father with the utmost of his policie and power, sought to surprize mee, having but eighteene with mee, the darke night could not affright her from comming through the irkesome woods, and with watered eyes gave me intelligence, with her best advice to escape his fury; which had hee knowne, hee had surely slaine her. . . .

Since then, this businesse having beene turned and varied by many accidents from that I left it at: it is most certaine, after a long and troublesome war after my departure, betwixt her father and our Colonie, all which time shee was not heard of.

About two years after shee her selfe was taken prisoner, being so detained near two years longer, the Colonie by that meanes was relieved, peace concluded, and at last rejecting her barbarous condition, was married to an English Gentleman, with whom at this present she is in England; the first Christian ever of that Nation, the first Virginian ever spake English, or had a childe in marriage by an Englishman, a matter surely, if my meaning bee truly considered and well understood, worthy a Princes understanding.

Captain John Smith, *The Generall Historie of Virginia . . .* (1624), in Captain John Smith, *Works: 1608–1631*, edited by Edward Arber (Birmingham: [Editor], 1884) 395–401, 530–32.

ᔤ

Pocahontas's Kidnapping (1615)

Native Americans and Europeans frequently encountered each other's culture through episodes of captivity. Aside from premature death from disease, there was no more common New World experience than capture. Captivity even became one of the most prominent literary devices in European writings on the encounter (see the next section, "Captives"). However, the myth of Pocahontas as princess of the forest or as Lady Rebecca, the Christian convert, routinely skips an important detail: Virginia's military leaders used trickery and deceit to kidnap her in 1613. She was held hostage and was bartered for ransom for more than a year, in an effort to regain eight Englishmen as well as guns, swords, and tools taken by Powhatan's warriors. The following account — detailing Pocahontas's kidnapping, the ransom attempt, and the English retribution after a breakdown in negotiations — was published in London in 1615 by Ralph Hamor, secretary of the Virginia colony.

PROBLEMS TO CONSIDER

1. How does the kidnapping and ransoming of Pocahontas affect the mythical stories of her as the Indian princess who saves the Virginia colony? How would you characterize the tactics of the English in this episode?
2. Describe the ways in which gender, either womanhood or manhood, influenced this story of the kidnapping of Pocahontas.

It chanced Powhatans delight and darling, . . . his daughter Pocahuntas (whose fame hath even been spread in England by the title of Non-parella of Virginia), in her princely progresse, if I may so terme it, tooke some pleasure (in the absence of Captaine Argall) to be among her friends at Pataomecke . . . employed thither, as shopkeepers to a Fare, to exchange some of her fathers commodities for theirs, where residing some three months longer, it fortuned upon occasion either of promise or profit, Captaine Argall to arrive there, whom Pocahuntas, desirous to renew her familiaritie with the English, and delighting to see them, as unknowne, fearefull perhaps to be surprised, would gladly visit, as she did, of whom no sooner had Captaine Argall intelligence, but he dealt with an old friend, and adopted brother of his Iapazeus [Powhatan consolidated his power by creating kinship relationships (marriages and adoptions) throughout the region, making Iapazeus an adoptive uncle to Pocahuntas], how and by what means he might procure her captive, . . . in ransome of her he might redeeme some of our English men and arms, now in the possession of her Father, promising to use her withall faire and gentle entreaty: Iapazeus . . . promised his best endeavors and secrecy to accomplish his desire, and thus wrought it, making his wife an instrument (which sex have ever been most powerfull in beguiling enticements) to effect his plot which hee had thus laid, he agreed that himselfe, his wife, and Pocahuntas, would accompanie his brother to the water side, whether come, his wife should feign a great and longing desire to goe aboard, and see the shippe [i.e., Argall's ship], . . . which deniall she taking unkindely, must feign to weepe, (as who knows not that women can command teares) whereupon her husband seeming to pity those counterfeit teares, gave her leave to goe aboard, so that it would please Pocahuntas to accompany her: . . . so forthwith aboard they went, . . . to supper they went, merry on all hands, especially Iapazeus and his wife. . . . Supper ended, Pocahuntas was lodged in the Gunners roome, but Iapazeus and his wife desired to have some conference with their brother, which was only to acquaint him by what stratagem they had betrayed his prisoner, . . . after which discourse to sleepe they went, Pocahuntas nothing mistrusting this policy, who nevertheles being most possessed with feare, and desire of returne, was first up, and hastened [to find] Iapazeus to be gone. Capt. Argall having secretly well rewarded him, with a small Copper kettle, and some other less valuable toys so highly by him esteemed, that doubtless he would have betrayed his owne father for them, . . . his father [i.e., Powhatan] had then eight of our English men, many swords, pieces [guns], and other tooles, which he had at severall times by treacherous murdering our men, taken from them which though of no use to him, he would not rediliver. . . . And so to James towne [Pocahontas] was brought, a messenger to her father forthwith dispatched to advertise him, that his only daughter was in the hands and possession of the English: there to be kept til such time as he would ransom her with our men, swords, pieces, & other tools treacherously taken from us: the news was unwelcome, and troublesome unto him, partly for the love he bare to his daughter, and partly for the love he bare to our men his prisoners, of whom . . . he made great use: and those swords, and pieces of ours (which though of no use to him), it delighted him to view, and looke upon.

[Argall kept Pocahontas a captive for three months before Powhatan sent back seven of the Englishmen, each with a no-longer-functioning musket. But the English colonists refused to believe that the rest of the arms had been broken or stolen from Powhatan and refused to return their captive. Months passed before they heard from Powhatan again, and by this time Sir Thomas Dale decided to take a ship with 150 men up the river to demand the ransom in return for the deliverance of Pocahontas. The Indians fired on the English; Hamor's narrative continues at this point.]

Being thus justly provoked, we presently manned our boates, went ashore, and burned in that very place some forty houses, and of the things we found therein, made freeboote and pillage, and as themselves afterward confessed unto us, hurt and killed five or sixe of their men, with this revenge satisfying our selves, for that their presumption in shooting at us, and so the next day proceeded higher up the River, the Indians calling unto us, and demanding why we went ashore, burnt their houses, killed and hurt their men, and tooke away their goods. We replied that though we came to them in peaceable manner, and would have beene glad to have received our demands with love and peace, yet we had hearts and power to take revenge, and punish where wrongs should be offered, which having now done ... we rested content therewith and are ready to embrace peace with them if they pleased.

Ralphe Hamor, *A True Discourse of the Present Estate of Virginia* (London: John Beale, 1615; facsimile, New York: Da Capo Press, 1971), 4–6, 8.

⌘

John Rolfe's Letter on Marrying Pocahontas (1614)

If the kidnapping of Pocahontas revealed the unstable relationship between militant English colonists and Algonquian natives, her marriage to John Rolfe, a Virginia planter, became perhaps the most strategic moment in England's earliest colonization of North America. Rolfe had wedded himself to the Virginia project from its beginning. Indeed, he was tied to nearly every important moment in the colony's first fifteen years. He sailed with his expectant English wife on the supply ships that wrecked off Bermuda in 1609, an event that inspired Shakespeare to write The Tempest. *(For Rolfe, that voyage brought personal tragedy as well: his newborn daughter did not survive, and his wife died shortly after their arrival in Virginia.) By 1612, Rolfe had become the first Englishman to export tobacco from Virginia, an achievement that led to his appointment as the colony's recorder and to a seat in the first House of Burgesses. Yet Rolfe was also a widower in a colony where there were practically no marriageable English women. So when Pocahontas remained a captive under the tutelage of an Anglican minister, Rolfe resolved to marry her.*

For an Englishman to marry a "savage" was no small matter, and Rolfe knew it. In the following letter to the deputy governor, Sir Thomas Dale, Rolfe pleaded for advice while revealing the dilemmas he faced. It was no coincidence that Rolfe appealed to this official. Dale had recently imposed martial law, with severe penalties (including death) for colonists who failed to live an orderly and outwardly Christian life. Two years earlier, when several colonists had run away to live with the Indians, Dale ordered their execution: "some he apointed to be hanged Some burned Some to be broken upon wheels, others to be staked and some to be shott to death." The intent of these measures was "to terrefy the reste" of the colonists from following their path. Cohabitating with Indians, or "going savage," could be a fatal mistake. So Rolfe was probably not the first Englishman to marry and father children with an Algonquian Indian woman; rather, he was the first to do it under the banner of Christianity.

Much like his previous actions, Rolfe may have planned his marriage to Pocahontas with the success of the Virginia colony in mind. Rolfe's letter reveals his many-sided motivations, as well as the importance of Pocahontas's conversion for Virginia colonists and their supporters in England. But before he could accomplish his mission, Rolfe needed to wrestle with the dilemmas of marrying across the cultural and racial boundaries of the new colonial world.

PROBLEMS TO CONSIDER

1. Describe all of Rolfe's conflicting "passions of [his] troubled soule": in other words, what different forces were tugging at Rolfe's conscience as he contemplated and sought permission for this marriage?
2. What does this letter indicate about early English understandings of race? In the eyes of the colonial leaders, which mattered more: that Pocahontas was an Indian or that she was a non-Christian?

John Rolfe, to Sir Thomas Dale, 1614

Honourable Sir, and most worthy Governor:

. . . But (my case standing as it doth) what better worldly refuge can I here seeke, than to shelter my selfe under the safety of your favourable protection? And did not my ease proceede from an unspotted conscience, I should not dare to offer to your view and approved judgement, these passions of my troubled soule. . . .

Let therefore this my well advised protestation, which here I make betweene God and my own conscience, be a sufficient witnesse, at the dreadfull day of judgement (when the secret of all mens harts shall be opened) to condemne me herein, if my chiefest intent and purpose be not, to strive with all my power of body and minde, in the undertaking of so mightie a matter, no way led (so far forth as mans weakenesse may permit) with the unbridled desire of carnall affection: but for the good of this plantation, for the honour of our countrie, for the glory of God, for my owne salvation, and for the converting to the true knowledge of God and Jesus Christ, an unbeleeving creature, namely Pokahuntas. To whom my hearty and best thoughts are, and have a long time been so entangled, and enthralled in so intricate a labyrinth that I was even awearied to unwinde my selfe thereout. But almighty God, who never faileth his, . . . led me by the hand that I might plainely see and discerne the safe paths wherein to tread.

. . . Nor was I ignorant of the heavie displeasure which almightie God conceived against the sons of Levie and Israel for marrying strange wives, nor of the inconveniences which may thereby arise, with other the like good motions which made me looke about warily and with

good circumspection, into the grounds and principall agitations, which thus should provoke me to be in love with one whose education hath been rude, her manners barbarous, her generation accursed, and so discrepant in all nurtriture from myselfe, that oftentimes with feare and trembling, I have ended my private controversie with this: surely these are wicked instigations, hatched by him who seeketh and delighteth in mans destruction; and so with fervent prayers to be ever preserved from such diabolical assaults (as I tooke those to be) I have taken some rest.

Thus when I had thought I had obtained my peace and quietnesse, beholde another, but more gracious temptation had made breaches into my holiest and strongest meditations; . . . for besides the many passions and sufferings which I have daily, hourely, yea and in my sleepe endured, even awaking mee to astonishment, taxing mee with remisnesse, and carelesnesse, refusing and neglecting to performe the duty of a good Christian, pulling me by the eare, and crying: why dost not thou endeavour to make her a Christian? And these have happened to my greater wonder, even when she hath been furthest seperated from me, which in common reason (were it not an undoubted worke of God) might breede forgetfulnesse of a far more worthie creature. Besides, I say the holy spirit of God hath often demanded of me, why I was created? If not for transitory pleasures and worldly vanities, but to labour in the Lords vineyard, there to sow and plant, to nourish and increase the fruites thereof, daily adding with the good husband in the Gospell, somewhat to the talent, that in the end the fruites may be reaped, to the comfort of the laborer in this life, and his salvation in the world to come? . . . Likewise, adding hereunto her great appearance of love to me, her desire to be taught and instructed in the knowledge of God, her capablenesse of understanding, her aptnesse and willingnesse to receive any good impression, and also the spirituall, besides her owne incitements stirring me up hereunto.

What should I doe? shall I be of so untoward a disposition, as to refuse to leade the blind into the right way? . . . Shall I despise to actuate these pious duties of a Christian? Shall the base feare of displeasing the world, overpower and withhold mee from revealing unto man these spirituall workes of the Lord, which in my meditations and prayers, I have daily made knowne unto him? God forbid. . . .

But I doubt not these [words] shall be sufficient, both to certifie you of my true intents, in discharging of my dutie to God, and to your selfe, to whose gracious providence I humbly submit my selfe, for his glory, your honour, our Countreys good, the benefit of this Plantation, and for the converting of one unregenerate, to regeneration; which I beseech God to grant, for his dear Son Christ Jesus his sake.

Now if the vulgar sort, who square *[measure]* all mens actions by the base rule of their own filthinesse, shall taxe or taunt me in this my godly labour: let them know, it is not any hungry appetite, to gorge my selfe with incontinency; sure (if I would, and were so sensually inclined) I might satisfie such desire, though not without a seared conscience, yet with Christians more pleasing to the eye, and lesse fearefull in the offence unlawfully committed. . . .

But shall it please God thus to dispose of me (which I earnestly desire to fulfill my ends before set down) I will heartely accept of it as a godly taxe appointed me, and I will never cease (God assisting me), untill I have accomplished, and brought to perfection so holy a worke, in which I will daily pray God to blesse me, to mine, and her eternall happines. . . .

At your command most willing to be disposed of

JOHN ROLFE.

John Rolfe to Sir Thomas Dale, 1614, in *Narratives of Early Virginia, 1606–1625*, edited by Lyon Gardiner Tyler (New York: Charles Scribner's Sons, 1907), 239–44.

ᴓ

Portrait of Pocahontas (1617)

By the time Pocahontas arrived in England in 1616, her transformation under the watchful eye of John Rolfe and the Virginia Company was nearly complete. Rolfe certainly brought Pocahontas to England to demonstrate the moral triumph of England's colonizing in the New World. Various English aristocrats (investors in the Virginia enterprise) welcomed her, and King James I and Queen Anne invited her to a court masque. At some point, she sat for a portrait engraved by the artist Simon van de Passe. The caption below the portrait reads "Matoaka, alias Rebecca, daughter of the mighty Prince Powhatan, Emperor of Attanoughkomouck, alias Virginia, converted and baptized in the Christian faith, and wife of the worshipful Mr. John Rolff." That Pocahontas took Rebecca as her new Christian name was filled with irony. In Genesis 26, translated in the Geneva Bible, Rebecca, the bride of Isaac (Abraham's son), was told: "Two nations are in thy womb, and two manner of people shall be divided out of thy bowels; and the one people shall be mightier than the other, and the elder shall serve the younger. . . . So he that came out first was red . . . and they called his name Esau." Not everyone in English society, however, seemed convinced of Pocahontas's metamorphosis from Indian savage to Christian lady. A tone of sarcasm can be heard in John Chamberlain's description of her portrait as "a fine picture of no fayre Lady and yet with her tricking up and high stile and titles you might thinke her and her worshipfull husband to be somebody."

PROBLEMS TO CONSIDER

1. Reading both the visual image and the caption of this portrait, what did this image of Pocahontas convey about the project of English colonization? How did she embody England's colonial designs?
2. What vestiges of her Indian identity did the artist wish to portray, and what did they represent?

Engraving of Pocahontas by Simon Van de Passe (1616).

(Photo by Time Life Pictures/Mansell/Time Life Pictures/Getty Images.)

Pocahontas's Last Conversation with John Smith (1624)

John Smith had not seen Pocahontas in nearly eight years when she arrived in England as the Christian lady Rebecca Rolfe. And despite the later mythical story of his rescue, Smith had apparently not spent much time or energy writing or talking about his encounter with Pocahontas. So when he arranged a meeting with Pocahontas during her stay in England, he left behind a glimpse of the real nature of his relationship with Powhatan and Pocahontas. Smith's description of that last conversation provides a rare opportunity to discern the conflicting ways that the English and Native Americans understood the encounter between their cultures in America.

PROBLEMS TO CONSIDER

1. Read carefully these last recorded words of Pocahontas: What do they reveal about the cultural values of her people compared with those of the English? What do they reveal about the different meanings that Algonquian Indians and the English attached to the encounter between their cultures?
2. Compare Pocahontas's last conversation with the words of her Algonquian brother-in-law, Uttamatomakkin. Did they share the same concerns when encountering the English across the Atlantic from America?

Being about this time preparing to set saile for New-England, I could not stay to doe [Pocahontas] that service I desired, and she well deserved; but hearing shee was at Branford with divers of my friends, I went to see her: After a modest salutation, without any word, she turned about, obscured her face, as not seeming well contented; and in that humor her husband, with divers others, we all left her two or three houres, repenting my selfe to have written she could speake English. But not long after, she began to talke, and remembred mee well what courtesies shee had done: saying,

> You did promise Powhatan what was yours should bee his, and he the like to you; you called him father being in his land a stranger, and by the same reason so must I doe you:

which though I would have excused, I durst not allow of that title, because she was a Kings daughter; with a well set countenance she said,

> Were you not afraid to come into my fathers Countrie, and caused feare in him and all his people (but mee) and feare you here I should call you father; I tell you then I will, and you shall call mee childe, and so I will bee for ever and ever your Countrieman. They did tell us always you were dead, and I knew no other till I came to Plimoth; yet Powhatan did command Uttamatomakkin to seeke you, and know the truth, because your Countriemen will lie much.

This Salvage *[Uttamatomakkin, husband of Pocahontas's sister]*, one of Powhatans Councell, being amongst them held an understanding fellow; the King purposely sent him, as they say, to number the people here, and informe him well what wee were and our state. Arriving at Plimoth, according to his directions, he got a long sticke, whereon by notches hee did thinke to have kept the number of all the men hee could see, but he was quickly wearie of that taske.

Comming to London, where by chance I met him, having renewed our acquaintance, where many were desirous to heare and see his behaviour, hee told me

Powhatan did bid him to finde me out, to shew him our God, the King, Queene, and Prince, I so much had told them of.

Concerning God, I told him the best I could, the King I heard he had seene, and the rest hee should see when he would; he denied ever to have seene the King, till by circumstances he was satisfied he had: Then he replyed very sadly,

You gave Powhatan a white Dog, which Powhatan fed as himselfe, but your King gave me nothing, and I am better than your white Dog.

The small time I staid in London, divers Courtiers and others, my acquaintances, hath gone with mee to see her, that generally concluded, they did thinke God had a great hand in her conversion, and they have seene many English Ladies worse favored, proportioned and behaviored, and as since I have heard, it pleased both the King and Queenes Majestie honorably to esteeme her, accompanied with that honorable Lady the Lady De la Ware, and that honorable Lord her husband, and divers other persons of good qualities, both publicly at the maskes and otherwise, to her great satisfaction and content, which doubtlesse she would have deserved, had she lived to arrive in Virginia.

. . . The Lady Pocahontas alias Rebecca, . . . it pleased God at Gravesend to take this young Lady to his mercie, where shee made not more sorrow for her unexpected death, than joy to the beholders, to heare and see her make so religious and godly an end. Her little childe Thomas Rolfe therefore was left at Plimoth with Sir Lewis Stukly, that desired the keeping of it.

Captain John Smith, *The Generall Historie of Virginia* . . . (1624), in Captain John Smith, *Works: 1608–1631*, edited by Edward Arber (Birmingham: [Editor], 1884), 533–35.

ᴔ

ᴔ Captives: Puritans and Narratives of Crossing Cultures in the Colonial World ᴔ

Besides Pocahontas, the other tale that generations of schoolchildren have learned about colonial America features the role of Squanto, a lone Indian who befriended the Pilgrims, taught them how to grow corn, saved them from starvation, and mediated peace with neighboring Indians. Like Pocahontas, the other details of Squanto's life story have been omitted from this mythic tale of a "good Indian." Missing from this tale is an explanation of how a single Indian, who could already speak English, happened to be living nearby when the Pilgrims landed at Plymouth. The real story was that six years earlier Squanto and twenty other Pawtuxets were kidnapped by marauding English fur traders and sold into slavery in Spain; somehow Squanto escaped and returned to London. After three years in England, he convinced English would-be colonizers to return him to New England as a guide. Yet when Squanto returned in 1619, he found his village had been completely devastated by a smallpox epidemic, introduced by contact with the same English traders who had kidnapped him. Squanto's full story leads us away from the mythic Thanksgiving story and reveals instead a cross-cultural encounter between Indians and Europeans that was marked by devastating epidemics, volatile trading relationships, and the ever-present experience of capture.

Captivity was a centuries-old custom practiced everywhere in the Atlantic world by Americans, Europeans, and Africans. Often it was the first step toward enslavement. But for many Native Americans, capturing people was an important strategy of warfare and social integration. Northeastern Indians, such as the Iroquois, practiced a form of "mourning war," whereby they compensated grieving families for the physical and psychological loss of their own kin in wars by either subjecting captives to rituals of torture and execution (usually adult male captives) or adopting them (usually women and children). In either case, women played an important role in captivities, as bereaved native women assuaged their grief and replenished their family groups in a matrilineal society (organized by the mother's, not the father's, family). Europeans interpreted the native practice of capture as an act of savagery, beyond the pale of civilization, despite their own practice of enslaving Indians and kidnapping them for ransom or for public display to satisfy European curiosities about the New World. Although a sentimental trope of forced imprisonment, separation from families, or the death of children did not become a cultural staple of Anglo-American literature until the eighteenth century, seventeenth-century tales of Europeans captured by American Indians still resonated with those same themes. From this, they created a new cultural form, the *captivity narrative*, a new literary style and product that exposed the emerging gender and racial thinking central to the English colonizing enterprise in America.

Captivity sparked an intersection of cultures: American Indians and Europeans were forced to confront their differences and similarities in the most bare and first-hand experiences of living with each other. Because captivity narratives featured warriors and warfare, women as captives and mothers, adoption rituals and family conventions, they offer a principal site for examining the interaction between the gender systems of European and Indian peoples. Gender was often the means by which Englishmen and -women expressed their conceptions of the naturalness of their own cultural practices, while also revealing their anxieties about the disruptive possibilities inherent in their chosen self-exile in the New World.

It was no coincidence that the captivity narrative originated among the Puritans of New England. Their very worldview mirrored the classic struggle of the captive: an exiled soul buffeted by outward forces of evil and inward temptations, contending with the bondage to sin and the flesh, and hoping for the hand of redemption. When Mary Rowlandson, who was taken captive in 1675, refers to herself as "in this Wilderness-condition," it is never clear whether she is alluding to her captivity, the state of her soul, or a metaphor for Puritan fears about their godly errand in the New World. New England Puritans found expression for their deepest anxieties in tales of captivity and redemption that created meaning out of cross-cultural encounters with Indians. This section begins by exploring the mindset of New England's Puritan men and women.

A Model of Christian Charity (1630)

JOHN WINTHROP

Puritanism was an Old World rather than a New World invention. It was at once a commitment to zealous piety; a reform movement of church, state, and society; and an appealing set of values for England's anxious "middling sort" during an era of social upheaval. Puritans longed for a completed Reformation in England, one in which the Anglican church would be stripped of any vestiges of Catholicism and, like the original church of Jesus and his apostles, local congregations would be communities for true believers only, bound together by close adherence to the Bible and a Calvinist theology that emphasized God's complete control over grace and salvation. When there seemed little hope of realizing this reformation in England by the 1620s and 1630s, tens of thousands of English Puritans migrated to the New England colonies to try to make that dream a reality. Whereas Puritan clergymen trumpeted an almost utopian vision of their biblical commonwealth in the New World, many Puritan colonists could not help but be swayed by Captain John Smith's alluring description of New England as a place where "every man may be master of his own labour and land . . . and by industry grow rich." And Puritan parents wondered aloud whether they could pass on their own intense zeal to live godly lives to their children's generation, which possessed no memories of the tribulations that they had endured. For many Puritans, the best hope of achieving that balance lay in a commitment to a particular type of community and in a special understanding of the ties that bound them to God and to their fellow colonists—what Puritans called a "covenant" relationship. On board the ship The Arabella, *which carried their royal charter to establish the colony of Massachusetts, soon-to-be governor John Winthrop delivered a sermon that challenged the earliest Puritan migrants to establish these types of godly communities.*

PROBLEMS TO CONSIDER

1. What exactly was Winthrop's greatest fear for this new colony? How did Puritans such as Winthrop understand their relationship with God and with one another, and how were these two related?
2. The most quoted phrase from this sermon is Winthrop's assertion that "we shall be as a city upon a hill, the eyes of all people are upon us." What does this mean? What does it reveal about the mindset of New England Puritans at the onset of colonization?

God Almighty in his most holy and wise providence hath so disposed of the condition of mankind, as in all times some must be rich, some poor, some high and eminent in power and dignity; others mean and in subjection.

THE REASON HEREOF

First, to hold conformity with the rest of his works, being delighted to show forth the glory of his wisdom in the variety and difference of the creatures and the glory of his power, in ordering all these differences for the preservation and good of the whole, and the glory of his greatness that as it is the glory of princes to have many officers, so this great King will have many stewards counting himself more honored in dispensing his gifts to man by man, than if he did it by his own immediate hand.

Secondly, that he might have the more occasion to manifest the work of his Spirit: first, upon the wicked in moderating and restraining them: so that the rich and mighty should not eat up the poor, nor the poor and despised rise up against their superiors, and shake off their yoke; secondly in the regenerate in exercising his graces in them, as in the great ones, their love, mercy, gentleness, temperance, etc.; in the poor and inferior sort, their faith, patience, obedience, etc.

Thirdly, that every man might have need of other, and from hence they might be all knit more nearly together in the bond of brotherly affection: from hence it appears plainly that no man is made more honorable than another or more wealthy, etc., out of any particular and singular respect to himself, but for the glory of his Creator and the common good of the creature, Man. . . . All men being thus (by divine providence) ranked into two sorts, rich and poor; under the first, are comprehended all such as are able to live comfortably by their own means duly improved; and all others are poor according to the former distribution. There are two rules whereby we are to walk one towards another: JUSTICE and MERCY. These are always distinguished in their act and in their object, yet may they both concur in the same subject in each respect; as sometimes there may be an occasion of showing mercy to a rich man, in some sudden danger of distress, and also doing of mere justice to a poor man in regard of some particular contract, etc. . . .

From the former considerations ariseth these conclusions.

First, This love among Christians is a real thing not imaginary.

Secondly, This love is as absolutely necessary to the being of the body of Christ, as the sinews and other ligaments of a natural body are to the being of that body.

Thirdly, This love is a divine spiritual nature, free, active, strong, courageous, permanent, under valuing all things beneath its proper object, and of all the graces this makes us nearer to resemble the virtues of our heavenly father. . . .

Thus stands the cause between God and us, we are entered into Covenant with him for this work, we have taken out a Commission, the Lord hath given us leave to draw our own articles we have professed to enterprise these actions upon these and these ends, we have hereupon besought him of favor and blessing: Now if the Lord shall please to hear us, and bring us in peace to the place we desire, then hath he ratified this Covenant and sealed our Commission, [and] will expect a strict performance of the articles contained in it, but if we shall neglect the observation of these articles which are the ends we have propounded, and dissembling with our God, shall fall to embrace this present world and prosecute our carnal intentions, seeking great things for ourselves and our posterity, the Lord will surely break out in wrath against us, be revenged of such a perjured people, and make us know the price of the breach of such a Covenant.

Now the only way to avoid this shipwreck and to provide for our posterity is to follow the counsel of Micah, to do justly, to love mercy, to walk humbly with our God: for this end, we must be knit together in this work as one man, we must entertain each other in brotherly affection, we must be willing to abridge ourselves of our superfluities, for the supply of others' necessities, we must uphold a familiar commerce together in all meekness, gentleness, patience and liberality, we must delight in each other, make others' conditions our own, rejoice together, mourn together, labor, and suffer together; always having before our eyes our commission and community in the work, our community as members of the same body, so shall we keep the unity of the spirit in the bond of peace, the Lord will be our God and delight to dwell among us, as his own people and will command a blessing upon us in all our ways, so that we shall see much more of his wisdom, power, goodness, and truth than formerly we have been acquainted with, we shall find that the God of Israel is among us, when ten of us shall be able to resist a thousand of our enemies, when he shall make us a praise and glory, that men shall say of succeeding plantations: the Lord make it like that of New England: for we must consider that we shall be as a city upon a hill, the eyes of all people are upon us; so that if we shall deal falsely with our God in this work we have undertaken and so cause him to withdraw his present help from us, we shall be made a story and a by-word through the world, we shall open the mouths of enemies to speak evil of the ways of God and all professors for God's sake; we shall shame the faces of many of God's worthy servants, and cause their prayers to be turned into curses upon us till we be consumed out of the good land whither we are going: And to shut up this discourse with that exhortation of Moses that faithful servant of the Lord in his last farewell to Israel, Deut. 30. Beloved there is now set before us life, and good, death and evil in that we are commanded this day to love the Lord our God, and to love one another to walk in his ways and to keep his commandments and his ordinance, and his laws, and the articles of our Covenant with him that we may live and be multiplied, and that the Lord our God may bless us in the land whither we go to possess it: But if our hearts shall turn away so that we will not obey, but shall be seduced and worship other Gods, our pleasures, and profits, and serve them; it is propounded unto us this day, we shall surely perish out of the good land whither we pass over this vast sea to possess it.

Winthrop Papers, vol. 2: 1623–1630 (Boston: Massachusetts Historical Society, 1931), 282–83, 292, 294–95.

ᴧ

Of the Vanity of All Worldly Creatures (1650)

ANNE BRADSTREET

By the beginning of the twentieth century, Puritanism suffered from a bad reputation. Newspaperman H. L. Mencken defined it as "the haunting fear that someone, somewhere may be happy." Although Mencken's criticism was actually lampooning the prudish Victorian-era mores of the nineteenth century, the tag stuck. For all the efforts to characterize the Puritans as typical Elizabethan-era English folk—a people who loved to drink, read books, write love poems, and enjoy sex as well as the pleasures of good food— there were still Puritans like Michael Wigglesworth to remind us that Mencken's caricature of Puritans was not entirely off the mark. Because Puritans believed that they were God's new Israel, in a special covenant relationship with God and with their community, they had reason to be nosy about one another's affairs. Puritan ministers developed a formulaic sermon, known as a jeremiad, to remind the faithful that current misfortunes—warfare with Indians, diseases, droughts, or Crown interference with their charter—might signal God's disfavor for their sins or their diminishing piety. Wigglesworth, a minister from Malden, Massachusetts, wrote a hundred-page poem entitled

The Day of Doom *(1666), a vivid depiction of the Day of Judgment. It was the most popular book in New England during his lifetime.*

Not all Puritans, however, were like Wigglesworth. Anne Bradstreet, the first woman in colonial America to be a published writer, gave voice to female piety within a moderate vein of Puritanism, stressing the love of wives and husbands and pointing to the parallels between conjugal love and the love of Christ for the redeemed. Bradstreet belonged to a Puritan ruling family (both her father and husband served as governors of Massachusetts), so she disapproved of public challenges to orthodoxy or to the male hierarchy in the church and the colony. She kept her distance from her contemporary, Anne Hutchinson, who was banished from the colony for her theological beliefs and her threats to male authority. Bradstreet's poem, "Of the Vanity of All Worldly Creatures," reveals a softer edge to the jeremiads spoken by men such as Wigglesworth, but it indicates nonetheless the sober earnestness of Puritan spirituality.

PROBLEMS TO CONSIDER

1. What does Bradstreet's poem say about the priorities of Puritan life?
2. From Bradstreet's perspective, where does the source of life's happiness reside?

As he said vanity, so vain say I,
O vanity, O vain all under skie,
Where is the man can say, lo, I have found
On brittle earth, a consolation sound?
What is't in honour, to be set on high?
No, they like beasts, and sons of men shall die,
And whilst they live, how oft doth turn their
    State?
He's now a slave, that was a Prince of late.
What is't in wealth, great treasures for to gain?
No, that's but labour anxious, care and pain.
He heaps up riches, and he heaps up sorrow,
Its his to day, but who's his heire to morrow?
What then? content in pleasures canst thou find?
More vain than all, that's but to grasp the wind.
The sensuall senses for a time they please,
Mean while the conscience rage, who shall
    appease?
What is't in beauty? no, that's but a snare,
They'r foul enough to day, that once was fair,
What, Is't in flowring youth, or manly age?
The first is prone to vice, the last to rage.
Where is it then? in wisdome, learning, arts?
Sure if on earth, it must be in those parts;
Yet these, the wisest man of men did find,
But vanity, vexation of the mind,

And he that knows the most doth still bemoan,
He knows not all, that here is to be known,
What is it then? to do as Stoicks tell,
Nor laugh, nor weep, let things go ill or well:
Such stoicks are but stocks, such teaching vain:
While man is man, he shall have ease or pain.
If not in honor, beauty, age, nor treasure,
Nor yet in learning, wisdome, youth nor
    pleasure,
Where shall I climbe, sound, seek, search or
    find,
That *summum Bonum* which may stay my
    mind?
There is a path, no vultures eye hath seen.
Where lions fierce, nor lions whelps hath been,
Which leads unto that living Christall fount,
Who drinks thereof, the world doth naught
    account.
The depth, and sea, hath said its not in me,
With pearl and gold it shall not valued be:
For *Saphyre, Onix, Topas,* who will change,
Its hid from eyes of men, they count it strange,
Death and destruction, the fame hath heard,
But where, and what it is, from heaven's
    declar'd,
It brings to honour, which shall not decay,

It steeres with wealth, which time cann't wear
 away.
It yeeldeth pleasures, farre beyond conceit,
And truly beautifies without deceit.
Nor strength nor wisdome, nor fresh youth
 shall fade,
Nor death shall see, but are immortal made,
This pearl of price, this tree of life, this spring,
Who is possessed of, shall reign a King.

Nor change of state, nor cares shall ever see,
But wear his Crown unto eternitie,
This satiates the soul, this stayes the mind,
The rest's but vanity, and vain we find.

————

Anne Bradstreet, *The Tenth Muse* (London: Stephen Bow-
tell, 1650; facsimile, Gainesville, Fla.: Scholars' Facsimiles &
Reprints, 1965), 206–7.

ꜱ

The Soveraignty and Goodness of God (1682)
MARY ROWLANDSON

*Mary Rowlandson was steeped in the culture of New England Puritanism. Her parents
and seven siblings joined the 20,000 other English migrants to New England in the
1630s, and by the 1650s they had moved out to western Massachusetts, aspiring to pass
along larger landed inheritances to their teeming families. Mary eventually married a
Puritan minister, Joseph Rowlandson, and settled in the town of Lancaster. In February
1676, a party of Nipmuc, Narragansett, and Wampanoag Indians attacked Lancaster and
seized Rowlandson, three of her children, and nineteen other English colonists. Her capture
was not a product of first contact between Europeans and American Indians. New England's Puritans and various Algonquian peoples had been living in close proximity for
more than fifty years when Metacom's (or King Philip's) War began. Metacom's War
proved to be the bloodiest war (per capita) in American history. Nearly 5,000 Indian
deaths along with 2,500 English casualties represented about 40 percent and 5 percent of
their total populations, respectively. The extensive bloodshed and brutality revealed the
festering hostility that had been building between the two neighboring societies for decades.*

*Rowlandson spent the next three months as a captive of these Indian peoples as they
moved throughout western Massachusetts fighting the colonists. Near the end of the war,
she was ransomed and reunited with her husband and family. Rowlandson organized her
narrative around the various moves (or "removes") she encountered during her three-month
captivity. It is a rich document that reveals the mindset of a Puritan woman forced into
a cross-cultural encounter, who crafted her experience into a tale of faith, trial, and
redemption and yet also unmasked the gender and racial thinking of English colonists.*

*Mary Rowlandson's account of her captivity became the first instance of a cultural
form whose immense appeal would have an enduring influence in English-speaking
America. Rowlandson's narrative was reproduced in thirty editions and inspired hundreds of subsequent narratives. Before novels became Anglo America's most popular literary form, captivity narratives were the bestsellers of their day. Such tales have retained
their popular appeal ever since: they can be found in the writings of nineteenth-century
novelists such as James Fenimore Cooper and Mark Twain, in the countless "dime novels"
published after the Civil War, and in popular films of the twentieth century, from* The
Birth of a Nation *(1915) to Kevin Costner's Academy Award–winning film* Dances
with Wolves *(1990).*

PROBLEMS TO CONSIDER

1. How did Puritanism shape Rowlandson's narrative? In other words, how did she use her captivity and redemption to express her religious beliefs?
2. Rowlandson was not only a Puritan but also a woman. What gender constraints—or lack of constraints—shaped her captivity experience? Did she interact differently with her male and female captors? What does her narrative tell us about these particular Indian societies and cultures?

On the tenth of February 1675, Came the Indians with great numbers upon Lancaster. Their first coming was about Sun-rising; hearing the noise of some Guns, we looked out; several Houses were burning, and the Smoke ascending to Heaven. There were five persons taken in one house, the Father, and the Mother and a sucking Child, they knockt on the head; the other two they took and carried away alive. . . . There were three others belonging to the same Garison who were killed; the Indians getting up upon the roof of the Barn, had advantage to shoot down upon them over their Fortification. Thus these murtherous wretches went on, burning, and destroying before them.

At length they came and beset our own house, and quickly it was the dolefullest day that ever mine eyes saw. . . .

I had often before this said, that if the Indians should come, I should chuse rather to be killed by them than be taken alive, but when it came to the trial my mind changed; their glittering weapons so daunted my spirit, that I chose rather to go along with those (as I may say) ravenous Beasts, than that moment to end my dayes; and that I may the better declare what happened to me during that grievous Captivity, I shall particularly speak of the severall Removes we had up and down the Wilderness.

THE FIRST REMOVE

Now away we must go with those Barbarous Creatures, with our bodies wounded and bleeding, and our hearts no less than our bodies. About a mile we went that night, up upon a hill within sight of the Town, where they intended to lodge. . . . This was the dolefullest night that ever my eyes saw. Oh the roaring, and singing and dancing, and yelling of those black creatures in the night, which made the place a lively resemblance of hell. And as miserable was the waste that was there made, of Horses, Cattle, Sheep, Swine, Calves, Lambs, Roasting Pigs, and Fowls (which they had plundered in the Town) some roasting, some lying and burning, and some boyling to feed our merciless Enemies; who were joyfull enough though we were disconsolate. To add to the dolefulness of the former day, and the dismalness of the present night: my thoughts ran upon my losses and sad bereaved condition. All was gone, my Husband gone (at least separated from me, he being in the Bay; and to add to my grief, the Indians told me they would kill him as he came homeward) my Children gone, my Relations and Friends gone, our House and home and all our comforts within door, and without, all was gone (except my life), and I knew not but the next moment that might go too. There remained nothing to me but one poor wounded Babe, and it seemed at present worse than death that it was in such a pitiful condition, bespeaking Compassion. . . . Little do many think what is the savageness and brutishness of this barbarous Enemy! even those that seem to profess more than others *[i.e., "Praying Indians"]* among them, when the English have fallen into their hands. . . .

THE THIRD REMOVE

The morning being come, they prepared to go on their way. One of the Indians got up upon a horse, and they set me up behind him, with my poor sick Babe in my lap. A very wearisome and tedious day I had of it; what with my own wound, and my Childs being so exceedingly sick, and in a lamentable condition with her wound. It may be easily judged what a poor feeble condition we were in, there being not the least crumb of refreshing that came within either of our mouths, from Wednesday night to Saturday night, except a little cold water. . . . The next day was the Sabbath; I then remembered how careless I had been of Gods holy time: how many Sabbaths I had lost and misspent, and how evily I had walked in Gods sight; which lay so close unto my spirit, that it was easie for me to see how righteous it was with God to cut off the thread of my life, and cast me out of his presence forever. Yet the Lord still shewed mercy to me, and upheld me; and as he wounded me with one hand, so he healed me with the other. . . . I sat much alone with a poor wounded Child in my lap, which moaned night and day, having nothing to revive the body, or cheer the spirit of her, but in stead of that, sometimes one Indian would come and tell me in one hour, that your Master will knock your Child in the head, and then a second, and then a third, your Master will quickly knock your Child in the head.

This was the comfort I had from them, *miserable comforters are ye all, as he said.* [Job 16:2] Thus nine days I sat upon my knees, with my Babe in my lap, till my flesh was raw again; my Child being even ready to depart this sorrowful world, they bade me carry it out to another Wigwam (I suppose because they would not be troubled with such spectacles) Whither I went with a very heavy heart, and down I sat with the picture of death in my lap. About two houres in the night, my sweet Babe, like a lamb departed this life, on Feb. 18. 1675, It being about six yeares, and five months old. . . . I have thought since of the wonderfull goodness of God to me, in preserving me in the use of my reason and senses, in that distressed time, that I did not use wicked and violent means to end my own miserable life. In the morning, when they understood that my

child was dead they sent for me home to my Masters Wigwam: (by my Master in this writing, must be understood Quanopin, who was a Saggamore *[a political leader]*, and married King Philips wives Sister; not that he first took me, but I was sold to him by another Narhaganset Indian, who took me when first I came out of the Garison). . . . Whereupon I earnestly entreated the Lord, that he would consider my low estate, and shew me a token for good, and if it were his blessed will, some sign and hope of some relief. And indeed quickly the Lord answered, in some measure, my poor prayers: for as I was going up and down mourning and lamenting my condition, my Son came to me, and asked me how I did; I had not seen him before, since the destruction of the Town, and I knew not where he was, till I was informed by himself, that he was amongst a smaller parcel of Indians, whose place was about six miles off. . . . I cannot but take notice of the wonderfull mercy of God to me in those afflictions, in sending me a Bible. . . . So I took the Bible, and in that melancholy time, it came into my mind to read first the 28. Chap. of Deut. which I did, and when I had read it, my dark heart wrought on this manner, *That there was no mercy for me, that the blessings were gone, and the curses come in their room, and that I had lost my opportunity.* But the Lord helped me still to go on reading till I came to Chap. 30 the seven first verses, where I found, *There was mercy promised again, if we would return to him by repentance; and though we were scattered from one end of the Earth to the other, yet the Lord would gather us together, and turn all those curses upon our Enemies.* I do not desire to live to forget this Scripture, and what comfort it was to me. . . .

THE FIFTH REMOVE

. . . The first week of my being among them, I hardly ate any thing; the second week, I found my stomach grow very faint for want of something; and yet it was very hard to get down their filthy trash: but the third week, though I could think how formerly my stomach would turn against this or that, and I could starve and die before I could eat such things, yet they were sweet and savory to my taste. I was at this time knitting a pair of white cotton stockins for my mistriss: and had not yet wrought upon a Sabbath day; when the Sabbath came they bade me go to work; I told them it was the Sabbath-day, and desired them to let me rest, and told them I would do as much more tomorrow; to which they answered me, they would break my face. And here I cannot but take notice of the strange providence of God in preserving the heathen: They were many hundreds, old and young, some sick, and some lame, many had Papooses at their backs, the greatest number at this time with us, were Squaws, and they travelled with all they had, bag and baggage, and yet they got over this River aforesaid; and on Monday they set their Wigwams on fire, and away they went: On that very day came the English Army after them to this River, and saw the smoke of their Wigwams, and yet this River put a stop to them. God did not give them courage or activity to go over after us; we were not ready for so great a mercy as victory and deliverance; if we had been, God would have found out a way for the English to have passed this River, as well as for the Indians with their Squaws and Children, and all their Luggage: *Oh, that my People had hearkened to me, and* Israel *had walked in my ways, I should soon have subdued their Enemies, and turned my hand against their Adversaries,* Psal. 81.13, 14. . . .

THE EIGHTH REMOVE

. . . Then I went to see King Philip, he bade me come in and sit down, and asked me whether I would smoke (a usual Complement now adayes amongst Saints and Sinners) but this no way suited me. For though I had formerly used Tobacco, yet I had left it ever since I was first taken. It seems to be a bait, the Devil lays to make men loose their precious time: I remember with shame, how formerly, when I had taken two or three pipes, I was presently ready for an-

other, such a bewitching thing it is: But I thank God, he has now given me power over it; surely there are many who may be better imployed than to lie sucking a stinking Tobacco-pipe.

. . . During my abode in this place, Philip spake to me to make a shirt for his boy, which I did, for which he gave me a shilling: I offered the money to my master, but he bade me keep it: and with it I bought a piece of Horse flesh. Afterwards he asked me to make a Cap for his boy, for which he invited me to Dinner. I went, and he gave me a Pancake, about as big as two fingers; it was made of parched wheat, beaten, and fryed in Bears grease, but I thought I never tasted pleasanter meat in my life. . . .

THE NINTH REMOVE

. . . And I cannot but admire at the wonderfull power and goodness of God to me, in that, though I was gone from home, and met with all sorts of Indians, and those I had no knowledge of, and there being no Christian soul near me; yet not one of them offered the least imaginable miscarriage to me. . . . And my spirit was ready to sink, with the thoughts of my poor Children: my Son was ill, and I could not but think of his mournfull looks, and no Christian Friend was near him, to do any office of love for him, either for Soul or Body. . . . I repaired under these thoughts to my Bible (my great comfort in that time) and that Scripture came to my hand, *Cast thy burden upon the Lord, and He shall sustain thee,* Psal. 55.22.

But I was fain to go and look after something to satisfie my hunger, and going among the Wigwams, I went into one, and there found a Squaw who shewed herself very kind to me, and gave me a piece of Bear. I put it into my pocket, and came home, but could not find an opportunity to broil it, for fear they would get it from me, and there it lay all that day and night in my stinking pocket. In the morning I went to the same Squaw, who had a Kettle of Ground-nuts boyling: I asked her to let me boyle my piece of

Bear in her Kettle, which she did, and gave me some Ground-nuts to eat with it: and I cannot but think how pleasant it was to me. . . .

THE TWELFTH REMOVE

It was upon a Sabbath-day morning, that they prepared for their Travel. This morning I asked my master whither he would sell me to my husband; he answered me Nux *[yes]*, which did much rejoyce my spirit. My mistriss, before we went, was gone to the burial of a Papoos, and returning, she found me sitting and reading in my Bible; she snatched it hastily out of my hand, and threw it out of doors; I ran out and caught it up, and put it into my pocket, and never let her see it afterward. Then they packed up their things to be gone, and gave me my load: I complained it was too heavy, whereupon she gave me a slap in the face, and bade me go; I lifted up my heart to God, hoping the Redemption was not far off: and the rather because their insolency grew worse and worse.

But the thoughts of my going homeward (for so we bent our course) much cheared my Spirit, [but] . . . on a sudden my mistriss gives out, she would go no further, but turn back again, and said, I must go back again with her. . . . My Spirit was upon this, I confess, very impatient, and almost outragious. I thought I could as well have dyed as went back: I cannot declare the trouble that I was in about it; but yet back again I must go. As soon as I had an opportunity, I took my Bible to read, and that quieting Scripture came to my hand, Psal. 46.10. *Be still, and know that I am God.* Which stilled my spirit for the present. . . .

THE THIRTEENTH REMOVE

. . . About this time I began to think that all my hopes of Restoration would come to nothing. I thought of the English Army, and hoped for their coming, and being taken by them, but that failed. . . . I thought of being sold to my Hus-

band, as my master spake, but in stead of that, my master himself was gone, and I left behind, so that my Spirit was now quite ready to sink. I asked them to let me go out and pick up some sticks, that I might get alone, And poure out my heart unto the Lord. Then also I took my Bible to read, but I found no comfort here neither, which many times I was wont to find: So easie a thing it is with God to dry up the Streames of Scripture comfort from us. Yet I can say, that in all my sorrows and afflictions, God did not leave me to have my impatience work towards himself, as if his ways were unrighteous. But I knew that he laid upon me less than I deserved. Afterward, before this dolefull time ended with me, I was turning the leaves of my Bible, and the Lord brought to me some Scriptures, which did a little revive me, as that Isai. 55.8. *For my thoughts are not your thoughts, neither are your wayes my ways, saith the Lord.* And also that, Psal. 37.5. *Commit thy way unto the Lord, trust also in him, and he shall bring it to pass.* . . .

Hearing that my Son was come to this place, I went to see him, and told him his Father was well, but very melancholly. . . . He told me also, that a while before, his Master (together with other Indians) were going to the French for Powder; but by the way the Mohawks met with them, and killed four of their Company which made the rest turn back again, for which I desired that my self and he may bless the Lord; for it might have been worse with him, had he been sold to the French, than it proved to be in his remaining with the Indians. . . .

That night they bade me go out of the Wigwam again: my Mistrisses Papoos was sick, and it died that night, and there was one benefit in it, that there was more room. I went to a Wigwam, and they bade me come in, and gave me a skin to lie upon, and a mess of Venison and Ground-nuts, which was a choice Dish among them. On the morrow they buried the Papoos, and afterward, both morning and evening, there came a company to mourn and howle with her: though I confess, I could not much console with them. Many sorrowfull dayes I had in this place. . . . Now had I time to examine all my wayes: my Conscience did not accuse me of unrighteousness toward one or other: yet I saw how in my walk with God, I had been a careless creature. . . . On the Sabbath-dayes, I could look upon the Sun and think how People were going to the house of God, to have their Souls refresht; and then home, and their bodies also: but I was destitute of both. . . .

THE TWENTIETH REMOVE

. . . But before I go any further, I would take leave to mention a few remarkable passages of providence, which I took special notice of in my afflicted time.

. . . It was thought, if their Corn were cut down, they would starve and die with hunger: and all their Corn that could be found, was destroyed, and they driven from that little they had in store, into the Woods in the midst of Winter; and yet how to admiration did the Lord preserve them for his Holy ends, and the destruction of many still amongst the English! Strangely did the Lord provide for them; that I did not see (all the time I was among them) one Man, Woman, or Child, die with hunger.

Though many times they would eat that, that a Hog or a Dog would hardly touch; yet by that God strengthened them to be a scourge to His People. . . .

I can but stand in admiration to see the wonderful power of God, in providing for such a vast number of our Enemies in the Wilderness, where there was nothing to be seen, but from hand to mouth. . . . It is said, Psal. 81.13, 14. *Oh, that my People had hearkened to me, and* Israel *had walked in my wayes, I should soon have subdued their Enemies, and turned my hand against their Adversaries.* But now our perverse and evil carriages in the sight of the Lord, have so offended him, that instead of turning his hand against

them, the Lord feeds and nourishes them up to be a scourge to the whole Land.

Another thing that I would observe is, the strange providence of God, in turning things about when the Indians were at the highest, and the English at the lowest. . . . Now the Heathen begins to think all is their own, & the poor Christians hopes to fail (as to man) and now their eyes are more to God, and their hearts sigh heaven-ward: and to say in good earnest, Help Lord, or we perish: When the Lord had brought his people to this, that they saw no help in any thing but himself, then he takes the quarrel into his own hand: and though they had made a pit, in their own imaginations, as deep as hell for the Christians that Summer, yet the Lord hurll'd themselves into it. And the Lord had not so many wayes before to preserve them, but now he hath as many to destroy them.

But to return again to my going home, where we may see a remarkable change of Providence. . . . O the wonderfull power of God that I have seen, and the experience that I have had. . . . Gods power is as great now, and as sufficient to save, as when he preserved Daniel in the Lions den; or the three Children in the fiery Furnace. I may well say as his Psal. 107.12, *Oh give thanks unto the Lord for He is good, for his mercy endureth for ever.* Let the Redeemed of the Lord say so, whom He hath redeemed from the hand of the Enemy, especially that I should come away in the midst of so many hundreds of Enemies quietly and peacably, and not a Dog moving his tongue. So I took my leave of them, and in coming along my heart melted into tears, more than all the while I was with them, and I was almost swallowed up with the thoughts that ever I should go home again.

Mary Rowlandson, *The Soveraignty and Goodness of God, Together with the Faithfulness of His Promises Displayed; Being a Narrative of the Captivity and Restauration of Mrs. Mary Rowlandson* (Cambridge, Mass.: Samuel Green, 1682), 1–2, 5–7, 8–14, 19–20, 24–25, 27–28, 30–31, 34–36, 39–40, 59–64.

✌

Indian Captives on Display in Europe

Rowlandson was not the only captive produced by the Indian–European encounter. Europeans captured Native Americans from the very first moment of contact. It began with Columbus, who carried away nine "Indians" and brought them back to Spain on his first voyage. From that moment, European explorers saw humans as prized treasures to be taken from the New World. At first, Indian captives were spirited away as curiosities to be displayed before royal courts and to bolster investments in colonizing ventures. Over time, capturing natives became a preferred way for English colonizers to learn the language. Thus, Indian captives were retained as cultural intermediaries to bridge the misunderstandings at the heart of the colonial encounter. The experience of Pocahontas showed this practice at work. The next two documents reveal some of the earliest descriptions of European captivity practices. The first is a European account of Martin Frobisher's abduction of Inuits in 1576 along the coast of Baffin Island, north of Labrador; the second is a Micmac tale of an Indian named Silmoodawa, who was carried away to France.

PROBLEMS TO CONSIDER

1. Consider how each of these documents uses the idea of predator and prey, hunter and hunted. How did such references convey the meanings and purposes of captivity and colonial expansion for Europeans?
2. Analyze the importance of theatrical performance in these captivity documents. Were such spectacles a product of Europeans' political objectives? Do these examples suggest that natives were powerless objects of European designs or instead were capable of resisting the power of their captors?

MARTIN FROBISHER'S CAPTURED INUIT

The captain, notwithstanding, desirous to bring some token from thence of his being there, was greatly discontented that he had not before apprehended some of them. And therefore to deceive the deceivers he wrought a pretty policy, for knowing well how they delighted in our toys, and especially in bells, he rang a pretty low bell, making wise that he would give him the same that would come and fetch it. . . . And to make them more greedy of the matter he rang a louder bell, so that in the end one of them came near the ship side to receive the bell, which when he thought to take at the captain's hand he was thereby taken himself. . . . Whereupon, when he found himself in captivity . . . he bit his tongue in twain *[two]* within his mouth: notwithstanding, he died not thereof, but lived until he came to England, and then he died of [a] cold which he had taken at sea.

Now with this new prey (which was a sufficient witness of the captain's far and tedious travel towards the unknown parts of the world, as did well appear by this strange infidel, whose like was never seen, read, nor heard of before, and whose language was neither known nor understood of any) the said Captain Frobisher returned homeward, and arrived in England in August following, 1576. . . .

George Best, *True Discourse of the Late Voyages of Discoverie . . . Under the Conduct of Martin Frobisher Generall* (London, 1578). Reprinted in *Old South Leaflets*, vol. 5 (Boston: Old South Meeting House, 1902), 344.

And so came to London with their Ship Gabriel the 9th day of October & there were joyfully received with the great Admiration of the People, bringing with them their strannge man & his boat, which was such a wonder unto th[e] whole City, & to the rest of the Realm that heard of it, as seemed never to have happened the like great matter to any mans knowledge. . . . He was very [ ] good sh[ape] . . . he . . . [fay]re & [s]trongly pight *[i.e., pitched or colored]* & made, . . . his Neck, his Brest . . . very broad face, & very fat & full [about] his Body. . . . His hair color Black, & long hanging & tyed [up] [a]bove hiss fore head. His Eyes little and a . . . black Beard. His color of Skyn all over his Bo[dy & f]ace was of a dark Sallow, much like to the tawny Mores; [or ra]ther to the Tartar Nation, whereof I think he was.

———

Michael Lok, [Account of Frobisher's First Voyage], ms. British Library, London, 1577. Reprinted in William C. Sturtevant and David Beers Quinn, "This New Prey: Eskimos in Europe in 1567, 1576, and 1577," in *Indians and Europe: An Interdisciplinary Collection of Essays*, edited by Christian F. Feest (Lincoln: University of Nebraska Press, 1999), 71–72.

SILMOODAWA (MICMAC)

Shortly after the country was discovered by the French, an Indian named Sĭlmoodāwā' was taken to Plâncheân' (France) as a curiosity. Among other curious adventures, he was prevailed upon to exhibit the Indian mode of killing and curing game. A fat ox or deer was brought out of a beautiful park and handed over to the Indian; he was provided with all the necessary implements, and placed within an enclosure of ropes, through which no person was allowed to pass, but around which multitudes were gathered to witness the butchering operations of the savage.

He shot the animal with a bow, bled him, skinned and dressed him, sliced up the meat, and spread it out on flakes to dry; he then cooked a portion and ate it, and in order to exhibit the whole process, and to take a mischievous revenge upon them for making an exhibition of him, he went into a corner of the yard and eased himself before them all.

———

Silas T. Rand, *Legends of the Micmac* (New York: Longmans, Green, and Co., 1894), 279.

✌

Indian Captives from Metacom's War (1676)

Even as Mary Rowlandson trekked through the New England countryside with her captives, her fellow New England colonists were taking captives of their own. Yet the English had no equivalent to Native American practices of ritual adoption or cultural assimilation of different races or religions. And in the midst of the violent hatreds of Indian wars, colonists rarely exercised any mercy on native enemies, or even friendly Indians. Following the Pequot War in 1637, Massachusetts authorities enslaved forty-eight captured women and children and sold the most fierce captive Pequot warriors to the West Indies in exchange for the first black slaves brought into New England. During Metacom's War, however, even the "Praying Indians" (natives who had agreed to live in English towns under Christian laws) were rounded up and placed in captivity on Deer Island in Boston Harbor, where they lived out the duration of the war in near-starving conditions. The hundreds of hostile Indians captured while fighting for Metacom were also destined for sale as slaves, including Metacom's wife and son. Reprinted here is Governor John Leverett's order authorizing the enslavement of Indian captives, as well as the seal of the Massachusetts Bay Colony that Leverett affixed to his order, depicting an Indian saying "Come over and help us."

PROBLEMS TO CONSIDER

1. What does a comparison of the treatment of Rowlandson with that of the Indians captured by New England colonists indicate about the similarities and differences in the two cultures' understanding of captivity and its purposes?
2. Does the seal that Governor Leverett attached to his order contradict the sentiments expressed in his letter? Or could Leverett have perceived both sentiments as being complementary?

BOSTON IN THE MATTACHUSETTS COLONY OF NEW-ENGLAND

To all People unto whome these prsente may come, John Leverett Esq. Governor, greeting &r: Bee it known, and manifest that whereas Philip an heathen Sachem inhabiting this Continent of New-England, with others his wicked complices and abettors have treacherously and perfidiously rebelled against and revolted from theire obedience unto the Government our Sovereign Lord his Majesty of England Scotland ffrance and Ireland, here Established in and other of our confederate Colonies, unto which they had willingly Subjected themselves & have been protected by and enjoyed this priviledge of the English Laws, having entred into a solemn League and Covenant with the Authority of the said Respective Colonies, and have without any just cause, or provocation given them, broken their League and Covenant, which they had often renewed, and contrary thereunto have taken up arms, used many acts of hostility, and have perpetrated many notorious barbarous and execrable murthers, villanies and outrages both upon the persons and Estates of many of his said Ma[jes]ties Subjects in all the said Colonies; without giving any account of their controversys and refusing (according to the manner of civill nations) an open decision of the same by Treaty or the Sword: and Whereas many of the said Heathen have of late been captivated by the Arms of his said Ma[jest]ties Subjects, and been duly convicted of being actors and Abettors of said Philip with said inhumane and barbarous crueltys murder, outrages and vilainies. Wherefore by due and legall procedure the said heathen Malefactors men, women, and Children have been Sentenced & condemned to perpetuall Servitude and by speciall License Seventy of the said Malefactors are transported in this Ship—Sea-fflower–Thomas Smith Comander to be made Sale of in any of his said Majesties Dominions or the Dominions of any other Christian Prince. In Testimony whereof I the said Gov[erno]r have Signed this prsent with my hand and caused them to be Sealed with the publique Seal of the above written Colony this twelfth day of Septembr . . . Annos Dm. 1676.

—JOHN LEVERETT,
September 12, 1676

John Leverett to All People, September 12, 1676, bound ms., Massachusetts Historical Society. Reprinted in Jill Lepore, *The Name of War: King Philip's War and the Origin of American Identity* (New York: Alfred A. Knopf, 1998), 162–63.

Seal of the Massachusetts Bay Colony.
(The Granger Collection, New York.)

Eunice Williams, the "Unredeemed Captive" (1713)

Mary Rowlandson always looked toward her eventual redemption, never thinking for a moment that she would be permanently incorporated into Narragansett society. But not all European captives chose to return to colonial society. Of the more than fifteen hundred colonists taken captive by Indians in New England during wars that continued from 1675 to 1763, more than two hundred voluntarily remained with their adopted Indian families. They joined native communities and married Indian spouses; many converted to Roman Catholicism, the religion of the Indians' French allies. Eunice Williams was one of those "white Indians" who refused to return to English colonial life. Ironically, she was the daughter of the minister John Williams from Deerfield, Massachusetts, who penned a best-selling captivity narrative, The Redeemed Captive, *in which he depicted captivity as a religious trial for the salvation of the soul. In his desperate efforts to achieve Eunice's return, Williams accepted the aid of New York fur trader John Schuyler, who traveled to Canada to plead with Eunice to return to her father and her former home. Schuyler's account of "Margarett Williams" (Eunice had converted to Catholicism and assumed the name Margaret at her baptism) is a fascinating document of the cross-cultural encounter prompted by a captivity, one that includes a Dutch trader, a French governor, French priests, English Puritans, and Mohawk Iroquois Indians.*

PROBLEMS TO CONSIDER

1. Analyze Eunice Williams's actions toward Schuyler in this narrative. How would you characterize her response? Does she come across as a woman who controlled her own choices and destiny?
2. Discuss the gender and family dynamics revealed in this document, including Schuyler's role as redeemer and the roles played by Eunice's father, Eunice, her husband, and even celibate Catholic priests.

A true and perfect Memoriall of my proceedings in behalf of Margarett Williams now Captive amongst ye Indians at the fort of Caghenewaga in Canada, insisting upon her Reliese and to persuade her to go home to her father and Native Countrey, it being upon the instant and earnest desire of her father now Minister at Dearfeild in New England. I arrived from Albany at Mont Reall on ye 15th of April last, 1713, Where I understood that Monsieur de Vaudruille, Governor and chief of Canada, was expected then every day from Quebeck. Upon which I thought proper not to mention anything touching the aforesaid Captive, untill his Excellency should be here himself: and accordingly when he arrived here I propos'd the matter to him, who gave me all the Encouragement I could immagine for her to go home, he also permitted me to go to her at the fort, where she was, to prepare if I could persuade her to go home. Moreover, his Excellency said, that with all his heart, he would give a hundred Crowns out of his own pockett, if that she might be persuaded to go to her Native Countrey: I observing all this, then was in hopes I should prevaile with her to go home. Accordingly I went to the fort at Caghenewaga, being accompanied by one of the King's Officers and a french Interpreter, likewise another of the Indian Language Being upon the 26 Day of May. Entring at the Indian fort I thought fitt first to apply myself to the priests; As I did, Being two in Company, And was informed before that this infant (As I may say) was married to a young Indian, I therefore proposed to know the Reason why this poor Captive should be Married to an Indian, being a Christian Born (tho neerly taken from the Mother's Breast and such like Instances &c) Whereupon the priest Sett forth to me Such good Reasons with Witnesses that mySelf, or any other person (as I believe) could fairly make Objection against their Marriage; (First, said he they came to me to Marry them) very often which I always refus'd with good words and persuasions to the Contrary, But both continuing in their former resolution to Such a Degree that I was constrained to be absent from ye fort three Severall times, because not Satisfyed myself in their Marriage; Untill at last after Some days past they both came to me, and Said that they were joined together, And if he would not marry them they matter'd not, for they were resolved never to leave one the other. But live together heathen like; Upon which I thought proper to join them in Matrimony and Such like Reasons as aforesaid the priest did plainly Sett forth and after some further discourse, I desired the priest, to let me see her at his house, for I knew not where to find her upon which he sent for her, who presently came with the Indian she was Married to both together. She looking very poor in body, bashfull in the face but proved harder than Steel in her breast, at her first Entrance into the Room I desired her to sitt down, which she did, I first Spoke to her in English, Upon which she did not Answer me; And I believe She did not understand me, she being very Young when she was taken, And liveing always amongst the Indians afterwards, I Imployed my Indian Languister *[interpreter]* to talk to her; informing him first by the french Interpreter, who understood the English Language, What he should tell her and what Questions he should Ask her. Accordingly he did I understood almost all what he said to her; And found that he Spoke according to my Order, but could not gett one word from her. Upon which I desired the priest To Speak to her, And if I could not prevaile with her to go home to Stay there, that She might only go to see her father, And directly return hither again, The priest made a long Speech to her and endeavored to persuade her to go, but after almost half an hours discourse—could not get one word from her; And afterwards when he

found She did not Speak, he again Endeavored to persuade her to go and see her father. And I seeing She continued impersuadable to speak; I promised upon my Word and honor, if she would go only to see her father, I would convey her to New England and give her Assureance of liberty to return if she pleased—the priest asked her Severall times for answer upon this, my earnest request And fair offers which was after long Solicitations *zaghte oghte* which words being translated into the English Tongue, their Signifycation is *may be not*; but the meaning thereof amongst the Indians is a plain denial, and these words were all we could gett from her; in allmost two hours time that we talked with her. Upon this my eyes being allmost filled with tears, I said to her myself. Had I made such proposalls and prayings to the worst of Indians I did not doubt but have had a reasonable Answere and consent to what I had said. Upon which her husband seeing I was so much concerned about her replyed had her father not Married againe She would have gone and Seen him long Ere this time, But gave no further reason and the time growing late and I being very Sorrowfull that I could not prevail upon nor get one word more from her, I took her by the hand and left her in the priest's house.

JOHN SCHUYLER

C. Alice Baker, *True Stories of New England Captives* (Cambridge: [Author], 1897), 144–46.

❧

CHAPTER 3

Colonial Cultures
in an Atlantic World:
1690–1760

IN APRIL 1712, colonists in the city of New York awakened to the violent carnage of a slave revolt the night before. Nine European men had been killed and six seriously wounded. By the time the authorities were finished, the bloodshed had escalated further, since New York's magistrates had determined that these murders were part of a conspiracy, a "Negro plot." Within two weeks, they had convicted and executed seventeen African men and women. Perhaps the most revealing aspect of this alleged slave conspiracy was the geographic diversity of its participants. The Europeans included three Englishmen, three French Protestants, two Dutchmen, a French-speaking Walloon (Belgian), and a German; the Africans probably hailed from even more distant nations and cultures, spanning thousands of miles along the western coast of Africa.

This tragedy reminds us that colonial North America was something more than just the "English colonies." Colonists (free and slave) lived in an Atlantic world, making them part of a larger network of exchanges of goods, peoples, ideas, and practices that traversed back and forth throughout the ocean basin that gave birth to a "new world" for Europeans, Native Americans and Africans. New York was a trading center for an economy and a social order that were never exclusively local. And like all North American colonies, the city's history was shaped by several different cultures at any given moment. This Atlantic perspective has begun to revolutionize the way that we conceive of the history of colonial America.

This chapter examines three different transatlantic phenomena — slavery, witchcraft, and the relationship between amusements and religious revivalism — each of which illuminates the connections and interactions of the cultural world of the American colonies with a much larger cultural universe of the Atlantic.

What does it mean to find at the center of the Salem witch trials a South American native woman who had lived as a slave among Africans on the Caribbean sugar colony of Barbados before being transported to a New England Puritan village ravaged by decades of wars with local Indians and living uneasily in the shadow of a seaport that prospered from trading routes throughout the Atlantic? Her story mirrors the Atlantic world connections that shaped the cultural history of the American colonies.

৵ *Confirming Difference and Inventing Race: The Origins of Slavery in the Americas* ৵

Captivity, as we have seen, often defined the intersection of different cultures throughout the Atlantic, nowhere more so than in the proliferation of slavery as the principal form of labor in the New World. Slavery was a long-standing, worldwide phenomenon. Early modern Europeans did not invent it; Africans and Americans practiced slavery even before the Columbian encounter. Yet Europeans did broaden the institution's scale and intensity. Never before had an international, transoceanic market for slave labor reached this scale, and not since ancient Greece and Rome had societies been organized so that slave labor was as central to production and the social order as it was in the slave societies established in Brazil, the Caribbean, and the American South. "Surely, this is a new refinement in cruelty," lamented Olaudah Equiano in the narrative of his enslavement.

Historians have wrestled for decades over the relationship between racism and slavery: did race thinking cause slavery, or did slavery lead to racism? This debate has refined our understanding of how economic factors principally fueled the transition to slave labor; but beyond that, the debate has proved to be misguided. Perhaps what demands an explanation is not why Europeans felt they could bind, transport, and enslave Africans (and Indians) and their children for their lifetimes, but rather, why they did not take that step toward other Europeans. For an answer to that question, one has to look to the ideological and cultural constructions of race in the Atlantic world. Such a search will expose the uneven and often contradictory developments that constituted the history of race in America.

৵ MIDDLE PASSAGE: TALES OF THE ATLANTIC SLAVE TRADE

The Portuguese were the first Europeans to sail successfully to West Africa, where they initiated the Atlantic slave trade in the mid-fifteenth century and monopolized it for the next century and a half. By the time English traders horned in on Dutch, French, and Portuguese slave traders in the mid-seventeenth century, a profitable network of the exchange of goods for slaves spanned the Atlantic. It was called the "triangular trade" because it had three segments: European textiles or New England rum was shipped to Africa in exchange for African slaves, who were transported to the Americas in exchange for sugar, tobacco, or rice, which was then shipped back to Europe. The Middle Passage was the notorious voyage that brought Africans to the New World. With the formation of the Royal African Company in 1672, the English displaced the Dutch and Portuguese as the dominant force in the Atlantic slave trade. For the next century (1680s–1780s), more Africans were forcibly transported to the Americas on English vessels than on those of any other European power.

A Journal of the Voyage Made in the Hannibal of London, Ann. 1693–1694 (1732)

THOMAS PHILLIPS

The following narrative is the unpublished account of Thomas Phillips, ship's captain and part owner of the 450-ton vessel Hannibal. *The account reveals the mindset of one English slave trader as well as the experiences of African slaves during the Middle Passage. Note that the practice of branding slaves with a hot iron was ironically the first exposure many West Africans had to the English alphabet. Slave masters in the Americas used the force of law to keep slaves illiterate for centuries after that.*

PROBLEMS TO CONSIDER

1. How do you reconcile Phillips's matter-of-fact treatment of slaves as commodities with his assertion that he considered them "the works of God's hands" who should not be "despis'd for their colour"?
2. What insights does this account give for understanding how West Africans understood the Middle Passage? Can Phillips be trusted as a source for this?

M*ay the 21st.* This morning I went ashore at Whidaw, accompany'd by my doctor and purser, Mr. Clay, the present Capt. of the *East-India Merchant*, his doctor and purser, and about a dozen of our seamen for our guard, arm'd, in order here to reside till we could purchase 1300 negro slaves, which was the number we both wanted, to compleat 700 for the *Hannibal*, and 650 for the *East-India Merchant*, according to our agreement in our charter-parties with the royal African company; in procuring which quantity of slaves we spent about nine weeks. . . .

Our factory *[a factory was a trading outpost—in this case, an outpost for trade in slaves]* lies about three miles from the sea-side, . . . [and] stands low near the marshes, which renders it a very unhealthy place to live in; the white men the African company send there, seldom returning to tell their tale. . . .

When we had selected from the rest *[of the slaves]* such as we liked, we agreed in what goods to pay for them, the prices being already stated before the king, how much of each sort of merchandize we were to give for a man, woman, and child, which gave us much ease, and saved abundance of disputes and wranglings, and gave the owner a note, signifying our agreement of the sorts of goods; upon delivery of which the next day he receiv'd them; then we mark'd the slaves we had bought in the breast, or shoulder, with a hot iron, having the letter of the ship's name on it, the place being before anointed with a little palm oil, which caus'd but little pain, the mark being usually well in four or five days, appearing very plain and white after. . . .

The negroes are so wilful and loathe to leave their own country, that they have often leap'd out of the canoes, boat and ship, into the sea, and kept under water till they were drowned, to avoid being taken up and saved by our boats, which pursued them; they having a more dreadful apprehension of Barbadoes than we can have of hell, tho' in reality they live much better there than in their own country; but home is home, etc: we have likewise seen divers of them eaten by the sharks, of which a prodigious number kept about the ships in this place. . . .

We had about 12 negroes did willfully drown themselves, and others starv'd themselves to death; for 'tis their belief that when they die they return home to their own country and friends again.

I have been inform'd that some commanders have cut off the legs and arms of the most wilful, to terrify the rest, for they believe if they lose a member, they cannot return home again: I was advis'd by some of my officers to do the same, but I could not be perswaded to entertain the least thought of it, much less put in practice such barbarity and cruelty to poor creatures, who, excepting their want of christianity and true religion (their misfortune more than fault) are as much the works of God's hands, and no doubt as dear to him as ourselves; nor can I imagine why they should be despis'd for their colour, being what they cannot help, and the effect of the climate it has pleas'd God to appoint them. I can't think there is any intrinsick value

in one colour more than another, nor that white is better than black, only we think so because we are so, and are prone to judge favorably in our own case, as well as the blacks, who in odium of the colour, say, the devil is white, and so paint him. . . .

Having bought my compliment of 700 slaves, *viz.* 480 men and 220 women, and finish'd all my business at Whidaw, I took my leave of the old king, and his cappasheirs *[attendants]*, and parted. . . . I set sail the 27th of July in the morning, accompany'd with the *East-India Merchant*, who had bought 650 slaves, for the island of St. Thomas, with the wind at W.S.W. . . .

We spent in our passage from St. Thomas to Barbadoes two months eleven days, from the 25th of August to the 4th of November following: in which time there happen'd much sickness and mortality among my poor men and negroes, that of the first we buried 14, and of the last 320, which was a great detriment to our voyage, the royal African company losing ten pounds by every slave that died, and the owners of the ship ten pounds ten shillings, being the freight agreed on to be paid them by the charter-party for every negroe deliver'd alive ashore to the African company's agents at Barbadoes; whereby the loss in all amounted to near 6560 pounds sterling. . . .

I deliver'd alive at Barbadoes to the company's factors 372, which being sold, came out at about nineteen pounds per head one with another.

"A Journal of the Voyage Made in the Hannibal of London, Ann. 1693–1694 . . . ," in Awnsham Churchill, *Collection of Voyages and Travels* (1732), vol. 6, 173–239. Reprinted in *Documents Illustrative of the History of the Slave Trade to America*, 4 vols., edited by Elizabeth Donnan (Washington, D.C.: Carnegie Institution of Washington, 1930) 1:398–99, 401–3, 408–10.

ᔕ

The Interesting Narrative of the Life of Olaudah Equiano (1791)
OLAUDAH EQUIANO

What we know about the Atlantic slave trade, and the horrific Middle Passage, is almost entirely derived from the testimony of former slave traders and their crews. By the late 1780s, a slew of antislavery writings prompted members of Britain's Parliament to stage a bitter and protracted debate over abolishing the slave trade. That antislavery literature was deeply indebted to several important eighteenth-century cultural developments, including evangelicalism, sentimentalism, and the humanitarian (anticruelty) sensibilities of the Enlightenment. Perhaps the most famous advocate in Britain's antislavery debate was a former slave ship captain, John Newton, who converted to Christianity, became convinced of the immorality of the slave trade, and is best known for penning the sentimental evangelical hymn "Amazing Grace." In antislavery tracts and slave trader memoirs, writers did not merely state the facts of the horrors of the Middle Passage but also crafted their narratives of these voyages in order to touch the "feelings" of readers familiar with the devices of sentimental texts.

One of the only firsthand accounts we have of the Middle Passage from a person of African descent is the self-titled Interesting Narrative of the Life of Olaudah Equiano. *This text has recently been the subject of scholarly controversy, with one historian suggesting that Equiano might have never lived in Africa or experienced the terrors of slave transport that he describes. We cannot know for certain, but what we can do is read Equiano's narrative for what it does reveal. We can surmise that Equiano would have been well versed in antislavery writings, including the indictments of the Middle Passage that had circulated during Parliament's debate over the slave trade, and that Equiano was familiar with evangelical sentiments since he devoted a substantial portion of his autobiography to describing his conversion under the influence of the revivalist George Whitefield.*

PROBLEMS TO CONSIDER

1. How did Equiano hope to touch the emotions of his readers, and what devices did he employ for that purpose? How does his narrative differ in tone and substance from Thomas Phillips's account of the Middle Passage?
2. How is Equiano's text similar to a captivity narrative (see chapter 2)? What is the significance of Equiano's inverting the cannibalism imagery of the early encounter in his narrative?

One day, when all our people were gone . . . out to their works as usual, and only I and my dear sister were left to mind the house, two men and a woman got over the walls, and in a moment seized us both, and, without giving us time to cry out, or make resistance, they stopped our mouths, and ran off with us into the nearest wood. . . . For a long time we had kept [to] the woods, but at last we came into a road which I believed I knew. I had now some hopes of being delivered; for we had advanced but a little way before I discovered some people at a distance, on which I began to cry out for their assistance; but my cries had no other effect than to make them tie me faster and stop my mouth, and then they put me into a large sack. They also stopped my sister's mouth, and tied her hands; and in this manner we proceeded till we were out of sight of these people. . . .

The first object which saluted my eyes when I arrived on the coast was the sea, and a slave ship, which was then riding at anchor, and waiting for its cargo. These filled me with astonishment, which was soon converted into terror, when I was carried on board. I was immediately handled, and tossed up to see if I were sound, by some of the crew; and I was now persuaded that I had gotten into a world of bad spirits, and that they were going to kill me. Their complexions, too, differing so much from ours, their long hair, and the language they spoke (which was very different from any I had ever heard) united to confirm me in this belief. Indeed, such were the horrors of my views and fears at the moment, that, if ten thousand worlds had been my own, I would have freely parted with them all to have exchanged my condition with that of the meanest slave in my own country. When I looked round the ship too and saw a large furnace of copper boiling, and a multitude of black people of every description chained together, every one of their countenances expressing dejection and sorrow, I no longer doubted of my fate; and, quite overpowered with horror and anguish, I fell motionless on the deck and fainted. When I recovered a little I found some black people about me. . . . I asked them if we were not to be eaten by those white men with horrible looks, red faces, and long hair. They told me I was not. . . . Soon after this, the blacks who brought me on board went off, and left me abandoned to despair.

I now saw myself deprived of all chance of returning to my native country, or even the least glimpse of hope of gaining the shore, which I now considered as friendly; and I even wished for my former slavery in preference to my present situation, which was filled with horrors of every kind, still heightened by my ignorance of what I was to undergo. I was not long suffered to indulge my grief; I was soon put down under the decks, and there I received such a salutation in my nostrils as I had never experienced in my life: so that with the loathsomeness of the stench, and crying together, I became so sick and low that I was not able to eat, nor had I the least desire to taste any thing. I now wished for the last friend, death, to relieve me; but soon, to my grief, two of the white men offered me eatables; and, on my refusing to eat, one of them held me fast by the hands, and laid me across, I think, the windlass, and tied my feet, while the other flogged me severely. I had never experienced any thing of this kind before: and although not being used to the water, I naturally feared that element the first time I saw it, yet nevertheless, could I have got over the nettings, I would have jumped over the side, but I could not. . . .

In a little time after, amongst the poor chained men, I found some of my own nation, which in a small degree gave ease to my mind. I inquired of these what was to be done with us? They gave me to understand we were to be carried to these white people's country to work for them. I then was a little revived, and thought, if it were no worse than working, my situation was not so desperate; but still I feared I should be put to death, the white people looked and acted, as I thought, in so savage a manner; for I had never seen among any people such instances of brutal cruelty; and this not only shown towards us blacks, but also to some of the whites themselves. . . .

At last, when the ship we were in, had got in all her cargo, they made ready with many fearful noises, and we were all put under deck, so that we could not see how they managed the vessel. But this disappointment was the least of my sorrow. The stench of the hold while we were on the coast was so intolerably loathsome, that it was dangerous to remain there for any time, and some of us had been permitted to stay on the deck for the fresh air; but now that the whole ship's cargo were confined together, it became absolutely pestilential. The closeness of the place, and the heat of the climate, added to the number in the ship, which was so crowded that each had scarcely room to turn himself, almost suffocated us. This produced copious perspirations, so that the air soon became unfit for respiration, from a variety of loathsome smells, and brought on a sickness among the slaves, of which many died, thus falling victims to the improvident avarice, as I may call it, of their purchasers. . . . The shrieks of the women, and the groans of the dying, rendered the whole a scene of horror almost inconceivable. . . . Every circumstance I met with served only to render my state more painful, and heightened my apprehensions, and my opinion of the cruelty of the whites. . . .

One day, when we had a smooth sea and moderate wind, two of my wearied countrymen who were chained together (I was near them at the time), preferring death to such a life of misery, somehow made through the nettings and jumped into the sea: immediately another quite dejected fellow, who, on account of his illness, was suffered to be out of irons, also followed their example; and I believe many more would very soon have done the same if they had not been prevented by the ship's crew who were instantly alarmed. Those of us that were the most active were in a moment put down under the deck, and there was such a noise and confusion amongst the people of the ship as I never heard

before, to stop her, and get the boat out to go after the slaves. However, two of the wretches were drowned, but they got the other, and afterwards flogged him unmercifully for thus attempting to prefer death to slavery. . . .

At last we came in sight of the island of Barbadoes, at which the whites on board gave a great shout, and made many signs of joy to us. . . . Many merchants and planters now came on board, though it was in the evening. They put us in separate parcels, and examined us attentively. They also made us jump, and pointed to the land, signifying we were to go there. We thought by this we should be eaten by these ugly men, as they appeared to us; and, when soon after we were all put down under the deck again, there was much dread and trembling among us, and nothing but bitter cries to be heard all the night from these apprehensions, insomuch that at last the white people got some old slaves from the land to pacify us. They told us we were not to be eaten, but to work, and were soon to go on land, where we should see many of our country people. This report eased us much; and sure enough, soon after we were landed, there came to us Africans of all languages.

[Olaudah Equiano], *The Interesting Narrative of the Life of Olaudah Equiano, or Gustavus Vassa, The African. Written by Himself* (New York: W. Durell, 1791), 34–35, 49–53, 55–60.

ᔰ

ᔰ PLANTATIONS BEFORE AND AFTER SLAVES

English colonists brought to the Americas very loosely defined ideas about both race and slavery. Although they knew and expected inequality and servitude in society, no one from England had any previous experience with slavery. So the English system of colonizing and slavery developed in fits and spurts and took decades, in some places nearly a century, to be fully established. Once England's colonies discovered the marketable commodities that made their colonizing profitable, they looked first to the surplus labor of the English countryside and urban centers to populate and work on their plantations. White indentured servitude modified traditional forms of bound labor for New World purposes. In exchange for passage to

America, and the hope of landownership at the end of their labors, poor English-men and -women contracted ("indentured") themselves to Chesapeake or Carib-bean planters for a period of usually four years.

The reasons for the transition from European servants to African slaves had little to do with the failures of indentured servitude and more to do with declining surplus population and Atlantic economic and imperial developments that made African slaves more readily available and more affordable to English planters. Moving from a social order in which some amount of slavery existed to a society dependent on slave labor required that the colonists develop a legal system that rationalized slavery as well as a racial ideology that justified and sustained that slave system.

When the first people of African ancestry arrived in Virginia in 1619, they were not unseasoned slaves brought directly from their homes on the coast of West Africa. Instead, they embodied a new type of people created all along the periphery of the Atlantic, whom one historian has aptly called "Atlantic creoles." Such creoles were the product of centuries of interaction between Europeans (especially Por-tuguese and Spaniards) and West Africans. Intermarriage and other forms of inter-cultural exchange produced scores of individuals who spoke African as well as European languages (and a form of pidgin language known as "Guinea speech") and who served as cultural brokers for the cross-fertilization of African and Euro-pean practices. Communities of creoles dotted the rim of the Atlantic. Ten percent of Lisbon's population was black, thousands of Angolans were converts to Catholi-cism, and men of color accompanied Columbus, Balboa, Cortés, de Soto, and Pizarro on their explorations and conquests. So when the first Africans were sold by a Dutch warship to John Rolfe in Virginia, they possessed names such as Antonio and Fernando, a reflection of their cross-cultural identity. No evidence exists that English colonists saw Africans and immediately concluded that they and their chil-dren should be perpetually enslaved.

Court Action Involving Anthony Johnson and His Servant (1655)

Testimony Concerning Anthony Longo (1654)

Like English indentured servants who survived their term of servitude and could then become property owners and small planters, some of the first generation of Africans in the Chesapeake acquired farms, married and created families, baptized their children, and left landed estates for their heirs. Some of them, such as Anthony Johnson, even came to own slaves of their own. Johnson arrived on Virginia's eastern shore as Antonio the Negro, labored on an Englishman's plantation, and was rewarded for his hard labor and loyalty to the colony during the 1622 Indian war. By the 1650s, Johnson and his wife, Mary, had earned a 250-acre tract of land by sponsoring new indentured servants, and their sons owned estates of 550 and 100 acres each. Still, evolving racial distinctions de-fined Mary and their daughters as "taxables" (agricultural workers) and hence different

from white women, who were exempted from field labor. The first two documents repro-
duced here reveal a dispute between Johnson and other white planters over the status of
one of Johnson's black slaves. The experiences of another Afro-Virginian planter, Anthony
Longo, seems to parallel Johnson's. When an English neighbor, John Neele, was sent to
deliver a court summons to Longo, the Afro-Virginian Longo responded with the kind of
contempt for authority that any white Virginia colonist might have commonly displayed.

PROBLEMS TO CONSIDER

1. Do these documents reveal anything about the attitudes of white Virginians regarding a black man who owned landed property and slaves? What does the court's ruling and Samuel Goldsmith's testimony say about Johnson's place in the social order of mid-seventeenth-century Virginia?
2. How would you characterize Longo's attitudes and values, as expressed in this deposition?

COURT ACTION INVOLVING ANTHONY JOHNSON AND HIS SERVANT

The deposition of Captain Samuel Goldsmith taken (in open court) 8th of March Sayth, That beinge at the house of Anthony Johnson Negro (about the beginninge of November last to receive a hogshead *[barrel]* of tobacco) a Negro called John Casar came to this Deponent, and told him that hee came into Virginia for seven or Eight years (per Indenture) And that hee had demanded his freedome of his master Anthony Johnson; And further said that Johnson had kept him his servant seven years longer than hee ought, And desired that this deponent would see that hee might have noe wronge, whereupon your Deponent demanded of Anthony Johnson his Indenture, hee answered, hee never sawe any; The said Negro (John Casor) replyed, hee came for a certain time and had an Indenture Anthony Johnson said hee never did see any But that hee had him for his life; Further this deponent saith That mr. Robert Parker and George Parker they knew that the said Negro had an Indenture . . . And the[y] said [if] Anthony Johnson did not tell the negro goe free The said John Casor would recover most of his

Cowes of him; Then Anthony Johnson (as this deponent did suppose) was in a feare. Upon this his Son in lawe, his wife and his 2 sons persuaded the said Anthony Johnson to sett the said John Casor free. more saith not

Samuel Goldsmith

This daye Anthony Johnson Negro made his complaint to the Court against mr. Robert Parker and declared that hee detained his servant John Casor negro (under pretence that the said Negro is a free man.) The Court seriously consideringe and maturely weighing the premises, doe find that the said Mr. Robert Parker most unjustly keepeth the said Negro from Anthony Johnson his master as appeareth by the deposition of Captain Samuel Goldsmith and many probable circumstances. It is therefore the judgment of the Court and ordered That the said John Casor Negro forthwith returne unto the service of his said master Anthony Johnson, And that mr. Robert Parker make payment of all charge in the suit.

Reprinted in *The Old Dominion in the Seventeenth Century: A Documentary History of Virginia, 1606–1689*, edited by Warren M. Billings (Chapel Hill: University of North Carolina Press, 1975), 155–56.

TESTIMONY CONCERNING
ANTHONY LONGO

Sayth that coming to Tony Llongo his house
with a warrant of Major Walkers your Deponent
asked him whether hee would goe alonge to Mr.
Walkers with mee. his answere was what shall I
goe to Mr. Walkers for: goe about your business
you idle Rascall: Upon those slighting terms, I
told him I had a warrant for him saying, will you
goe with that, hee made mee answer, s--t of your
warrant have I (said hee) nothinge to doe but goe
to Mr. Walker, goe about your business you idle
Rascall as did likewise his wife, with such noise
that I could hardly heare my owne words, reading the warrant to them, which when I had done
reading, the said Tony stroke att mee, and gave
mee some blowes, soe preceiving it was to little
purpose to staye with him, I went to Mr. Little-
ton's house and requested Daniel Baker to goe to
Tony Longos with mee only to testifie that I had
a warrant from Mr. Walker for his appearance
before him; Daniel Baker att my request went
with mee which when wee came, I desired him

to read it to him which he did his answers were
that hee would not goe, hee must gather his
corne. Nowe it beinge about the sun settinge (or
somethinge after) I told him wee might goe to
night and neither hinder himselfe much nor
mee. But his answer was thats a good one nowe I
have bine att worke shall goe to Mr. Walkers I
your said deponent requested him to go alonge
with mee. And as I could not make my debt appear I could give him for his payment 20 lb of tobacco. Well said hee I cannot goe, why when
shall I attend you said your deponent tomorrowe
or next daye, or next week I'll goe with you att
any time his answer was in generall, well, well,
Ile goe when my corne is in whereupon I bade
him goodnight, and left him, and on the morning returned the warrant. All which to the best of
my remembrance were his very words (or to the
same effect).

As reprinted in Edmund S. Morgan, *American Slavery,
American Freedom: The Ordeal of Colonial Virginia* (New
York: W. W. Norton, 1975), 156–57.

✌

A True & Exact History of the Island of Barbadoes (1657)
RICHARD LIGON

*Because the English had little previous experience with slavery or Africans, a racial ide-
ology of domination was created in the crucible of plantation labor systems and was reproduced through the representation of gendered and sexualized bodies. In 1647, Richard
Ligon, an Englishman, set sail from London to establish himself as a planter on the sugar
colony of Barbados. Along the sea journey, Ligon's ship stopped in the Cape Verde islands,
and there Ligon cast his eyes for the first time on a black woman, the mistress of the governor of the island. Ligon's lustful fixation on this woman's striking beauty dominates the
opening sections of his* True & Exact History of the Island of Barbadoes.*
    Once he arrives in Barbados and acquires a five-hundred-acre sugar plantation with
one hundred slaves, Ligon's watchful gaze shifts toward a wholly different preoccupation
with the bodies of Africans. This time he sees black women (and men) through the prism
of their productive capabilities, associating them with domestic animals and presenting
them as monstrously different rather than as objects of infatuation. We must not think of
these two depictions as incompatible. Concepts of racial difference acquired their rhetorical power as their inventors connected them with other power relationships defined as*

natural, such as animal behavior, gender conventions, and sexuality. Slave masters in the English colonies repeatedly constructed their ideas of racial difference upon representations of a black woman's irresistible sexuality, or her ease of both productive and reproductive labor, all of which made her different from white women.

PROBLEMS TO CONSIDER

1. In what ways is Ligon's sexualized depiction of African women still present in his description of his slaves on Barbados? Did racial difference negate his sexual attraction?
2. What advantages might slave masters gain from a rhetoric that associated African slaves with animals?

Dinner being ended, and the Padre well near weary of his waiting, we rose, and made room for better Company; for now the Padre, and his black Mistress were to take their turns; A Negro of the greatest beauty and majesty together: that ever I saw in one woman. Her stature large, and excellently shap'd, well favour'd, full eye'd, and admirably grac'd. . . . But her eyes were her richest Jewels, for they were the largest, and most oriental that I have ever seen.

Seeing all these perfections in her only at passage, but not yet heard her Speak; I was resolv'd after dinner, to make an Essay what a present rich silver, silk, and gold Ribbon would do, to persuade her to open her lips: Partly out of a Curiosity, to see whether her teeth were exactly white, and clean, as I hop'd they were; for 'tis a general opinion, that all Negroes have white teeth, but that is a Common error, for the black and white, being so near together, they set off one another with the greater advantage. . . . But it was not the main end of my enquiry; for there was now, but one thing more, to set her off in my opinion, the rarest black Swan that I had ever seen, and that was her language, and graceful delivery of that, which was to unite and confirm a perfection in all the rest. And to that end I took a Gentleman that spoke good Spanish with me, and awaited her coming out, which was with far greater Majesty, and gracefulness,

than I have seen Queen Anne, descend from the Chair of State, to dance the Measures with a Baron of England, at a Masque in the Banquetting house. . . . But finding her but slightly attended, and considering she was but the Padres Mistress, & therefore the more accessible, I made my addresses to her, by my interpreter; and told her I had some Trifles made by the people of England. . . . She with much gravity, and reservedness, opened the paper; but when she lookt on them, the colors pleased her so, as she put her gravity into the loveliest smile that I have ever seen. And then she shew'd her rows of pearls, so clean, white, orient, and wel shaped, as Neptunes Court was never pav'd with such as these; and to shew whether was whiter, or more Orient, those or the whites of her eyes, she turn'd them up, & gave me such a look, as was a sufficient return for a far greater present, and withall wisht, I would think of somewhat wherein she might pleasure me, and I should find her both ready & willing.

The Island [Barbados] is divided into three sorts of men, *viz.* Masters, Servants, and Slaves. . . .

When they [*slaves*] are brought to us, the Planters buy them out of the Ship, where they find them stark naked, and therefore cannot be deceived in any outward infirmity. They choose them as they do Horses in a Market; the strongest, youthfullest, and most beautiful, yield the greatest prices. . . . And we buy them so, as the sexes may be equal; for, if they have more Men than Women, the men who are unmarried will come to their Masters, and complain, that they cannot live without Wives. . . . And he tells them, that the next ship that comes, he will buy them Wives, . . . the bravest fellow is to choose first, and so in order, as they are in place, and every one of them knows his better, and gives him the precedence, as Cows to one another, in passing through a narrow gate; for, the most of them are as near-beasts as may be, setting their souls aside. . . .

I have been very strict, in observing the shapes of these people; and for the men, they are very well timber'd, that is, broad between the shoulders, full breasted, well filletted *[a term to describe a horse with plenty of flesh around the ribs]*, and clean leg'd. . . . These women are faulty; for I have seen very few of them, whose hips have been broader than their shoulders, unless they have been very fat. The young Maids have ordinarily very large breasts, which stand strutting out so hard and firm, as no leaping, jumping, or stirring, will cause them to shake any more, than the brawns of their arms. But when they come to be old, and have had five or six Children, their breasts hang down below their Navels, so that when they stoop at their common work of weeding, they hang almost down to the ground, that at a distance, you would think they had six legs: And the reason of this is, they tye the cloaths about their Children's backs, which comes upon their breasts, which by pressing very hard, causes them to hang down to that length. . . .

Richard Ligon, *A True & Exact History of the Island of Barbadoes* (London: Peter Parker, 1673; repr., London: Frank Cass, 1970), 12–13, 43, 46–47, 51.

❧

Virginia Slave Codes (1660–1705)

As Anthony and Mary Johnson's and Anthony Longo's lives make clear, the history of the origins of slavery in English America was complex and ever changing, more like a motion picture than a photographic snapshot. Concepts of gender and the racial construction of slave bodies provided one means of naturalizing dominance. Slave masters also solidified their power over their enslaved laborers by their control of the state and by enacting laws that defined the meaning of freedom and slavery, and consequently the meaning of whiteness and blackness as well. Every English colony that became a plantation slave society, in which slavery was the central economic and social relationship, enacted slave codes to invest masters with near-complete power over their slaves. Because Virginia began without a legal code for enslavement, tracing the development of its laws between 1660 and 1705 gives us a moving picture of how slavery became permanently entrenched in that colony. These slave codes coincided with the period when slaves arrived directly from West Africa, white indentured servitude decreased dramatically, and large planters consolidated their control over land resources and political power. With each passing decade, slaves were denied more and more freedoms. By 1705 Virginia's slave law included forty different sections and thoroughly denied personhood and individual rights to slaves. (Note that the 1691 law was the first time that the term "white" was used to distinguish free persons from slaves.)

PROBLEMS TO CONSIDER

1. How would you characterize the progression of these slave laws? Was there a logic to the way in which Virginia slavery systematically denied freedoms to slaves?
2. Read these documents from the perspectives of the slaves: what do they reveal about what slaves were doing in Virginia and why white planters needed to legislate against those behaviors?

March 1660/1661

Bee itt enacted that in case any English servant shall run away in company with any negroes who are incapable of making satisfaction by addition of time, *Bee itt enacted* that the English so running away in company with them shall serve for the time of the said negroes absence as they are to do for their owne by a former act.

December 1662

Whereas some doubts have arisen whether children got by any Englishman upon a negro woman should be slave or free, *Be it therefore enacted and declared by this present grand assembly*, that all children borne in this country shall be held bond or free only according to the condition of the mother, *And* that if any christian shall committ fornication with a negro man or woman, hee or shee so offending shall pay double the fines imposed by the former act.

September 1667

Whereas some doubts have risen whether children that are slaves by birth, and by the charity and piety of their owners made partakers of the blessed sacrament of baptisme, should by vertue of their baptisme be made free; *It is enacted and declared by this grand assembly, and the authority thereof,* that the conferring of baptisme doth not alter the condition of the person as to his bondage or freedome; that diverse masters, freed from this doubt, may more carefully endeavour the propagation of christianity by permitting children, though slaves, or those of greater growth if capable to be admitted to that sacrament.

October 1669

Whereas the only law in force for the punishment of refractory servants resisting their master, mistris or overseer cannot be inflicted upon negroes, nor the obstinacy of many of them by other than violent meanes supprest, *Be it enacted and declared by this grand assembly*, if any slave resist his master (or other by his masters order correcting him) and by the extremity of the correction should chance to die, that his death shall not be accounted a felony, but the master (or that other person appointed by the master to punish him) be acquit from molestation, since it cannot be presumed that prepensed *[premeditated]* malice (which alone makes murther felony) should induce any man to destroy his own estate.

June 1680

Whereas the frequent meeting of considerable numbers of negroe slaves under pretence of feasts and burialls is judged of dangerous consequence; for prevention whereof for the future, *Bee it enacted by the kings most excellent majestie by and with the consent of the general assembly . . .* it shall not be lawfull for any negroe or other slave to carry or arme himselfe with any club, staffe, gunn, sword or any other weapon of defence or offence, nor to go or depart from his masters ground without a certificate from his master, mistris, or overseer. . . . *And it is further enacted by the authority aforesaid* that if any negroe or other slave shall presume to lift up his hand in opposition against any christian, shall for every such offence, upon due proof made thereof by the oath of the party before a magistrate, have and receive thirty lashes on his bare back well laid on. *And it is hereby further enacted by the authority aforesaid* that if any negroe or other slave shall absent himself from his masters service and lie hid and lurking in obscure places, comitting injuries to the inhabitants, and shall resist any person or persons that shall by any lawful authority be employed to apprehend and take the said negroe, that then in case of such resistance, it shall be lawful for such person or persons to kill the said negroe or slave so lying out and resisting. . . .

April 1691

. . . And for the prevention of that abominable mixture and spurious issue which hereafter may encrease in this dominion, as well as by negroes, mulattoes, and Indians intermarrying with English, or other white women, as by their unlawfull accompanying with one another, *Be it enacted by the authoritie aforesaid, and it is hereby enacted,* that for the time to come, whatsoever English or other white man or woman being free shall intermarry with a negroe, mulatto, or Indian man or woman bond or free shall within three months after such marriage be banished and removed from this dominion forever. . . . *And be it further enacted* . . . That if any English woman being free shall have a bastard child by any negro or mulatto, she pay the sum of fifteen pounds sterling, within one month after such bastard child shall be born, to the Church wardens of the parish where she shall be delivered of such a child, and in default of such payment she shall be taken into the possession of the said Church wardens and disposed of for five years, and the said fine of fifteen pounds, or whatever the woman shall be disposed of for, shall be paid, . . . and that such bastard child be bound out as a servant by the said Church wardens until he or she shall attaine the age of thirty years. . . .

And forasmuch as great inconveniences may happen to this country by the setting of negroes and mulattoes free, by their either entertaining negroe slaves from their masters service, or receiving stolen goods, or being grown old bring a charge upon the country; for prevention thereof, *Be it enacted by the authority aforesaid, and it is hereby enacted,* That no negro or mulattoe be after the end of this present session of assembly set free by any person or persons whatsoever,

unless such person or persons, their heires, executors or administrators pay for the transportation of such negro or negroes out of the countrey within six months after such setting them free, upon penalty of paying ten pounds sterling to the Church wardens. . . .

October 1705

And if any slave shall be found offending herein [*i.e., possessing a gun or weapon or leaving a plantation without a written certificate from his or her master*], it shall be lawful for any person or persons to apprehend and deliver such slave to the next constable . . . who is hereby enjoined and required . . . to give such slave twenty lashes on his or her bare back, well laid on, and so send him or her home. And all horses, cattle, and hogs, now belonging, or that hereafter shall belong to any slave . . . shall be seized and sold by the church-wardens of the parish, . . . and the profit thereof applied to the use of the poor of the said parish. . . .

And whereas, many times, slaves run away and lie out, hid and lurking in swamps, woods, and other obscure places, killing hogs, and committing other injuries to the inhabitants of this her majesty's colony and dominion, *Be it therefore enacted* . . . [that] any two justices of the peace of the county wherein such slave is supposed to lurk or do mischief, shall be and are impowered to and required to issue proclamations against all such slaves. . . . And in case any slave, against whom proclamation hath been thus issued, and once published at any church or chapel, as aforesaid, stay out, and do not immediately return home, it shall be lawful for any person or persons whatsoever, to kill and destroy such slaves by such ways and means as he, she, or they shall think fit, without accusation or impeachment of any crime for the same.

The Statutes at Large; Being a Collection of All of the Laws of Virginia, 13 vols., edited by William Waller Hening (New York: R. & W. & G. Bartow, 1823), 2:26, 170, 260, 270, 481–82; 3:86–88, 459–60.

⌇

᠅ Magic and Witchcraft Within European, Indian, and African Cultures ᠅

The most enduring images of colonial life in American popular culture surround the witch trials in Salem, Massachusetts. Nathaniel Hawthorne immortalized his Puritan ancestors' intolerance in *The Scarlet Letter* (1850) and *The House of Seven Gables* (1851), and a century later, playwright Arthur Miller lambasted the conspiratorial thinking of the McCarthy era by exposing its parallels with Salem's witch-hunts in *The Crucible* (1953). But magical beliefs and practices, devils, and witch-hunts were not the exclusive province of New England's Puritans. Take, for example, Luís de Rivera. The Spanish-born Rivera spent ten years (from the age of thirteen) driving cattle throughout the Spanish colony of New Mexico and encountering witchcraft customs from three different continents. During his first year, an Indian man gave Rivera an herb charm that reputedly would attract any woman whom he sexually desired. He discarded the love potion a few days later, "seeing that it had no effect." Later that year, Rivera worked alongside an African slave, who had a figure of the Devil tattooed on his foot and who promised the Devil's loyal assistance to Rivera if he signed a special book with his own blood. Although Rivera secretly signed and kept this book for several weeks, he eventually tore it up, fearing he had sinned.

Years later, when a herd of mules and cattle stampeded under his watch, Rivera guiltily confessed his secrets and in 1630 found himself brought before the Inquisition in Mexico City, accused of becoming a slave of the Devil and severing himself from the Catholic Church. Rivera fully confessed to possessing a love herb and signing a pact with the Devil, but he denied that he had cut himself off from the Church; for Rivera, belief in magic and devils was not incompatible with his Catholic Christian faith. The Inquisition agreed and limited his punishment to a series of minor penances. Luís de Rivera might have been a confused young man, but then again, his choices reveal how the diversity of peoples, cultures, and spiritual beliefs throughout the Atlantic world shaped the history of the European colonies in the Americas.

Throughout the early modern Atlantic world, all kinds of men and women—those of power or learning, as well as the powerless and naïve, speaking many different languages and hailing from cultures in Africa, Europe, and the Americas—believed in wonders, magic, and supernatural powers. Their world was, in the words of one historian, "an enchanted universe." They believed that the mysterious, whether benign or malicious, frequently originated from human agents in league with spirits or with the divine. Witchcraft served various functions in different cultures. Folkways of healing never strayed far from sorcery; nor did the settling of personal disputes. Disgruntled or oppressed individuals (often women and children) used witchcraft and evil spirits to challenge the powerful. Conversely, accusations of witchcraft commonly served to silence dissent, discipline the disorderly, and ostracize community pariahs. Most important, witchcraft offered explanations for often inexplicable happenings in a universe filled with undiagnosed illnesses, hardships, and personal tragedies.

Beyond offering proof of Puritan intolerance, witchcraft and conjuring also allow us to examine the interplay of European, Native American, and African cultures in the

American colonies. Contemporary descriptions of witchery also expose the conflicts embedded within those cultures, as ordinary individuals' beliefs and actions frequently competed with the desires and viewpoints of their community's spiritual leaders.

Examination of Tituba, Salem Witch Trials (1692)

Even in Salem, the site of the most infamous witch trials in America, we can discover the presence of witchcraft beliefs and folk practices from European, Indian, and perhaps even African cultures. The yearlong witch terror gripped the residents of Salem Village (now Danvers), Massachusetts, in 1692. Hundreds were accused, twenty were executed, and four died while in jail. Yet the Salem trials actually were something out of a time warp. Witch crazes had subsided throughout Europe by the early 1600s. Historians have attributed the Salem Village episode to a set of extreme social pressures unique to the Massachusetts colony at that time. Community hostilities flared as settlers moved away from town centers, inciting decades of violent conflicts with Native Americans that left in their wake countless widows and orphans as well as gender discord and land disputes. At the same time, England's bloodless Glorious Revolution of 1688 had installed new monarchs at home but left unsettled the autonomy of the Puritan colony.

At the center of Salem's tumult stood a South American Indian woman, Tituba, a slave whom the town's new minister, Samuel Parris, had brought with him from the sugar island of Barbados. The troubles in Salem Village began when several young girls experimented with a crystal ball to foretell "what trade their sweet harts should be of." When Parris's daughter and niece were taken with fits and complained of being mysteriously and painfully pinched, a neighbor woman asked Tituba and her husband John Indian to make a "witchcake" out of rye meal and the girls' urine and then feed it to a dog. This countermagic was supposed to determine the name of the witch tormenting the girls. Instead, the girls' symptoms grew more severe, and they declared that they had been bewitched by Tituba and two local women—Sarah Good, a young beggar with a four-year-old daughter, and Sarah Osborne, an elderly woman who had married a younger man and denied her sons their inheritance after being widowed. These were the types of women commonly accused of witchcraft.

When Tituba confessed before the court presided over by John Hathorne (the novelist's ancestor), her testimony unleashed a torrent of accusations by persons claiming to be bewitched and tormented by specters (ghostlike representations of real persons, conjured by a devil). Tituba may have been beaten and coerced (by Parris) into making her confession, but her statement was a masterful performance nonetheless. Like the "witchcake" she had made, Tituba proved capable of drawing upon practices and ideas that satisfied many different people's notions of witchcraft. Local folks looked for malicious acts against neighborliness, but they were also firm believers in the efficacy of magic and countermagic; clergymen and judges demanded proof of a pact with the Devil for someone to be guilty of witchcraft; and all Puritans associated Native Americans and their religion with the Devil and witchcraft. Tituba walked a fine line in trying to exploit the expectations of her accusers, judges, and neighbors. In the end, her confession may have saved her life, but her property value as a slave may well have been a determining factor. She was jailed until the trials ended and then was sold away.

PROBLEMS TO CONSIDER

1. In the examination of Tituba, who seemed to be in control of the testimony—her questioner, Justice Hathorne, or Tituba? What information was Hathorne trying to extract from her? Was she a cooperative witness, or was she trying to lead him with her responses?
2. Do you think her identity as an Indian and a slave influenced how her contemporaries interpreted her testimony? Did her race and status make her more or less credible as a witness?

FIRST EXAMINATION

(H) Titibe what evil spirit have you familiarity with[?]

(T) none

(H) why do you hurt these children[?]

(T) I do not hurt them

(H) who is it then[?]

(T) the devil for ought I know

(H) did you never see the devil[?]

(T) the devil came to me and bid me serve him

(H) who have you seen[?]

(T) 4 women sometimes hurt the children

(H) who were they[?]

(T) goode *["Goody" or "goodwife" referred to a common married woman]* Osburn and Sarah good and I doe not know who the other were Sarah good and Osburne would have me hurt the children but I would not shee further saith there was a tall man of Boston that shee did see

(H) when did you see them[?]

(T) Last night at Boston

(H) what did they say to you[?]

(T) they said hurt the children

(H) and did you hurt them[?]

(T) no there is 4 women and one man they hurt the children and then lay all upon me and they tell me if I will not hurt the children they will hurt me

(H) but did you not hurt them[?]

(T) yes, but I will hurt them no more. . . .

(H) what is this appearance you see[?]

(T) sometimes it is like a hog and some times like a great dog this appearance shee saith shee did see 4 times

(H) what did it say to you[?]

(T) the black dog said serve me but I said I am a fraid he said if I did not he would doe worse to me

(H) what did you say to it[?]

(T) I will serve you no longer then he said he would hurt me and then he lookes like a man and threatens to hurt me shee said that this man had a yellow bird that keept with him and he told me he had more pretty things that he would give me if I would serve him. . . .

(H) how did you go *[to Boston]*[?]

(T) we ride upon stickes and are there presently

(H) doe you goe through the trees or over them[?]

(T) we see no thing but are there presently.
. . .

(H) what attendants hath Sarah good[?]

(T) a yellow bird and shee would have given me one

(H) what meate did she give it[?]

(T) it did suck her between her fingers. . . .

written by Ezekiell Chevers
Salem Village March the 1't 1691/[169]2

SECOND EXAMINATION, MARCH 2
1691/[169]2

Q. What Covenant did you make w'th that man that Came to you? What did he tell you[?].

A. he Tell me he god, & I must beleive him & Serve him Six years & he would give me many fine things. . . .

Q. w't did he Say you must doe more? did he Say you must write anything? did he offer you any paper?

A. yes, the Next time he Come to me & showed me some fine things, Some thing like Creatures, a little bird something like green & white.

Q. did you promiss him then when he spake to you then what did you answer him?

A. I then sayd this I told him I Could nott beleive him God, I told him I ask my maister & would have gone up but he stopt Mee & would nott lett me

Q. whatt did you promiss him?

A. the first tyme I beleive him God & then he was Glad. . . .

Q. What did this man Say to you when he took hold of you?

A. he Say goe & doe hurt to them and pinch them & then I went in, & would nott hurt them a good while, I would nott hurt Betty, I loved Betty, but they hall me & make me pinch Betty & the next Abigall & then quickly went away altogether & I pinched them. . . .

Q. and when would he come then?

A. the next friday & showed me a book in the day time betimes in the morneing. . . .

Q. did nott he make you write yo'r Name?

A. noe nott yett for mistris Called me into the other roome.

Q. whatt did he say you must doe in that book?

A. he Sayd write & sett my name to itt.

Q. did you write?

A. yes once I made a marke in the Book & made itt with red Blood.

Q. did he gett itt out of your Body?

A. he Said must gett itt out the Next time he Come againe, he give me a pin tyed in a stick to doe itt w'th, butt he noe Lett me blood w'th itt as yett butt Intended another time when he Come againe.

Q. did you See any other marks in his book?

A. yes a great many Some marks red, Some yellow, he opened his book a great many marks in itt.

Q. did he tell you the Names of them?

A. yes of two note more Good & Osburne & he Say thay make them marks in that book & he showed them mee. . . .

Q. did they write there Names?

A. thay made marks Goody Good Sayd she made hir mark, butt Goody Osburne would nott tell she was Cross to mee.

Q. when did Good tell you, She Sett hir hand to the Book?

A. the same day I Came hither to prison. . . .

Q. & what did he say to you when you made your Mark?

A. he sayd Serve mee & always Serve mee the man w'th the two women Came fro[m] Boston.

The Salem Witchcraft Papers, 3 vols., edited by Paul Boyer and Stephen Nissenbaum (New York: Da Capo Press, 1977), 3:747–49, 753–55.

ॐ

Neighbors' Testimony About a Witch:
Rachel Clinton, Ipswich, Massachusetts (1687–1693)

There was a typical pattern for witchcraft accusations in both England and New England. A middle-aged or older woman, usually with a history of irascible behavior, might pass by a neighbor's house, asking for some charity or mentioning an unsettled dispute. After being rebuffed, the woman would walk away muttering a curse under her breath. The next day the neighbor's cow mysteriously went lame, or a child became ill, or, worse still, someone in the household died. As neighbors gossiped about similar episodes, the seeds were planted for suspecting witchcraft. Most laypeople interpreted witchcraft as a malicious act (maleficium) of black magic to inflict harm on other persons or their property. Whereas clergymen and justices insisted that witchcraft required a covenant with the Devil, common folk showed little interest in this and suspected witchcraft wherever they recognized black magic.

The persons suspected of practicing witchcraft in the English colonies almost always were women. In a society where church, government, and family were dominated by men, unruly and outspoken women posed a clear threat to the social order. As historians have noted, when women retained an unexpected control over inherited land, or when they spoke in curses and slanders ("the tongue is a witch," one English minister opined), they risked the angry reprisals of their neighbors' accusations. The following selections illustrate the types of behavior that constituted witchcraft to ordinary New Englanders in the seventeenth century. Rachel Clinton was twice accused by her Ipswich, Massachusetts, neighbors, both before and after the Salem trials began.

PROBLEMS TO CONSIDER

1. Describe Rachel Clinton's crimes: what was it about her behavior that most upset her neighbors?
2. How else could a person in seventeenth-century New England have interpreted these episodes? What explanations other than witchcraft might have explained Rachel Clinton's actions and those of her neighbors?

DEPOSITION OF THOMAS KNOWLTON (1687)

The deposition of Thomas Knowlton, aged 40 years, sayeth that about three weeks ago [when] Mr. John Rogers and his wife were gone to Boston . . . Rachel, the wife of Lawrence Clinton, that is now suspected to be a witch, went to Mr. Rogers' house, and told Mr. Rogers' maid that she must have some meat and milk. And the said Rachel went into several rooms of the said house. . . . And when she saw me come in, she, the said Rachel, went away, scolding and railing, calling me . . . "hellhound" and "whoremasterly rogue," and said I was a limb of the devil. And she said she had rather see the Devil than see me. . . . (Samuel Ayers and Thomas Smith, tailor, can testify to the same language that Rachel used or called the said Knowlton.) And after this the said Rachel took up a stone and threw it toward me, and it fell short three or four yards off from me . . . and so came rolling to me, and just touched the toe of my shoe. And presently my great toe was in a great rage, as if the nail were held up by a pair of pincers. . . . And further the said Thomas Knowlton testified and saith that about three months ago my daughter Mary did wake and cried out in a dreadful manner that she was pricked of her side with pins, as she thought. Being asked who pricked her, she said she could not tell. And when she was out of her fits, I . . . asked her whether she gave Rachel any pins; and she said she gave Rachel about seven. And after this she had one fit more of being pricked.

———

"Witchcraft 1687," ms. Cornell University Library, Ithaca, N.Y., quoted in John Putnam Demos, *Entertaining Satan: Witchcraft and the Culture of Early New England* (New York: Oxford University Press, 1982), 20–21.

DEPOSITION OF MARY FULLER (1693)

The Deposition of Mary Fuller . . . aged about 41 years saith: About the 23 or fourth of Last March 1691/2 . . . Rachel Clinton came to our house and charged me with Raising Lies of her about my Daughter and Mary Thorne and while . . . Rachel was drawing, my Brother Joseph Fuller's boy came in and said their Betty was fall Down Dead. And this was as she said Rachel passed by her: [I was] coming to our house and further [I] run up to my Brother Joseph Fuller's house for the space of three hours without any motion of Life. . . . I got a hold of her hand. If said Rachel was the cause of it and she dead, and when she could speak she said the woman with a white cape passed by and struck her on the forehead.

DEPOSITION OF THOMAS BOARMAN (1693)

The Deposition of Thomas Boarman . . . aged 47. This Deponant testifieth and saith that some women of worth and quality Desired me To Aquaint the [town] men that Rachel Clinton was a great Disturber unto them in the [meeting] house in hunching them with her Elbow as they went by the said Clinton, and then the same Day I the said Boarman Desired the [town] men to take some care that Rachel Clinton might be forewarned not to come into those women's house, no more to Disturb them, and as I the said Boarman was Riding home that night after I had been [with the town men, I saw appear] Before me Like a Cat . . . and then I Looked wishfully upon it; and it seemed to be something Like a Little Dog and then I pursued it and it Kept the same Distance in the path before me. And though I Rode hard after it I could not over take it, then I Looked once [to] my right hand: and I Saw a great Turtle that moved as fast as I Rode along: and then I thought of Rachel Clinton then the Little Creature and the Turtle vanished away. . . .

———

The Salem Witchcraft Papers, 3 vols., edited by Paul Boyer and Stephen Nissenbaum (New York: Da Capo Press, 1977), 1:216–17.

✤

Customs of the American Indians (1724)
FATHER JOSEPH FRANÇOIS LAFITAU

Forms of magic, healing, and spirit communication could be found in nearly all Native American cultures. With folk healers and magic in common, one might expect colonists to have identified with aspects of Indian life. But instead, European colonizers (whether English, Dutch, French, or Spanish) without exception misinterpreted Indian belief systems as devil worship and witchcraft. This oddly reciprocal relationship between natives and Europeans can be illustrated by examining the writings of Jesuit missionaries in New France, who sought to convert to Catholicism the Iroquoian peoples of the eastern

Great Lakes region. Jesuit priests vied with Iroquois shamans by evidencing their own form of spiritual power. After all, Jesuit rituals and objects such as the Mass, rosaries, and crucifixes had magiclike qualities. (Keep in mind that the term "hocus-pocus" is an imitation of the Latin words a priest says at the moment of changing bread into the body of Christ.) And Jesuit missionaries especially wished to exploit these sacred objects and ceremonies as Iroquois shamans struggled to prove their spiritual power in the face of devastating epidemics in Indian villages following the first encounter with European diseases.

Despite their contempt for Iroquois shamans, Jesuit missionaries left behind detailed descriptions of Native American religious practices in eastern North America. Iroquoian peoples, like their Algonquian neighbors, believed that all living things possessed a spiritual power but that a dualism divided the evil power (utgon) from the good and protecting power (orenda). Witches (who could be male or female, human or nonhuman) employed the utgon to inflict harm or disease on another person, while shamans and healers mobilized the orenda to defend sufferers from the power of evil. So, rather than being devil worshipers, the Iroquois tried to use spiritual powers to counteract human suffering in ways that were strikingly similar to the kinds of countermagic practiced by common folk throughout Europe.

PROBLEMS TO CONSIDER

1. How do the two different meanings of "magical"—trickery and deception versus enchanting and marvelous—show themselves in European missionaries' accounts of Indian witchcraft and sorcery?
2. How might Iroquoian peoples have explained the spiritual power of their shamans differently from how these Jesuit missionaries depicted it?

[The Indians] have still another species of remarkable people whom they call also *Agotkon* or spirits. These are the ones who cast spells or curses. There is a great number of them of both sexes. The women especially are suspected of playing a part in this little business. Since they have no aim except to do harm and to cause it [to others], they are regarded, for this reason, with horror, forced to hide for their wicked mysteries and serve to accredit the diviners whose principal occupation is to uncover these spells, make known their authors and bring some remedy for them.

It is a work of atheists and a result of that spirit of irreligion which today is making such evident headway in the world as to impair the belief of the very people who pride themselves on being religious, that there are to be found men who have intercourse with the spirits via enchantment and magic. This belief has carried with it the implication of a certain weakness of mind so that it is no longer tolerated except among silly women and people of the lower classes, or, among priests and monks, who are supposed to have some advantage in maintaining these popular visions which an intelligent person would be ashamed to confess. . . .

Today, even the Relations of the newly discovered countries where idolatry reigns in all its force, apprise us that the demon exercises his power in them on the unfaithful in a palpable manner, that he renders oracles by the mouth of some one of these unfortunates who he makes pay dearly for the honor which he does them in using them as his organ: and the missionaries have often had the consolation of learning that simply the presence of a Christian has rendered him mute and arrested the power of the superstitions of paganism.

People have spoken in various ways on what concerns the American Indians. Those who have written Relations about South America and Mexico, all, without exception, . . . say that the devil appears to them under different forms, that they have a lively intercourse with him, that they fear him above everything that one can say, because he exercises a cruel empire over them. . . .

The greatest number of the authors, however, speak differently of the North American Indians. The missionaries of New France who have had most to suffer from those shamans who, keeping the people in their ancient superstitions, formed the greatest obstacle to their conversion, examined first very carefully whether the demon had a part in their spells and other superstitious practices; but, whatever trouble they were able to take, they could uncover nothing on which they could base an assured judgment. In this uncertainty, they, then, took the part of condemning their superstitions which are certainly undesirable and of baptising only those who would make an open profession of condemning and renouncing them. They believed, however, that they should regard what the Indians themselves said of their spells and divinations as useless and foolish and they saw, in their so-called diviners, only charlatans and very poor doctors who have always since then been called tricksters as if their art was nothing but simple charlatanism. . . .

These shamans and the men and women who cast spells [sorcerers] are regarded, as I have said, as *agotkon* or spirits because of the traffic which people think that they have with the spirits or tutelary geniuses. They differ in appearance from one another only in the motives of their actions: those who cast spells have no other aim than to harm and work harm; the shamans, on the contrary, although they may misuse their art, have as their purpose only the public good and seek to bring a remedy to the harm which others might be able to do or might have already done.

The power of doing extraordinary things stems from the same source with both groups, that is, from communication with the spirits. The esteem of the Indians for their shamans and their extreme antipathy to the sorcerers, make me believe that they make some distinction between those who they think communicate with the spirits in such a way that they think that good spirits are the cause of the miracles done by their diviners, and the evil ones, on the contrary, who are the authors of their curses and witchcraft. . . .

The Abenaqui and Algonquin are much given to pyromancy, or divination by fire. . . . Although today the Abenaqui all make profession of Christianity, they still do not fail to have recourse sometimes to this art which they have received from their fathers. They make confession of it, nevertheless, because of the horror of it which has been instilled in them. There are some of them who try to justify it as if there was nothing blameworthy in it. An Indian woman said to a missionary who tried to show her the harm in it, "I have never understood what harm there is in it and I still have great difficulty in seeing any. Listen, God has given men different gifts. To the Frenchmen, he has given the Scriptures by which you learn the things which take place far from you as if they were in front of you; to us he has given the art of knowing, by fire, things remote in time or place. Suppose then that this fire is our book, our Scriptures, thou willst not see that there is any difference or more harm in the one than in the other. My mother taught me this secret in my infancy as thy parents taught thee to read and write. I used it successfully several times before I became a Christian. I have done it sometimes with some success since. I have been tempted and yielded to temptation but without thinking that I was committing any sin."

The second thing which has struck me is the inward belief of all of them in the demon's power over them, in the efficacy of spells and the power of their shamans to know and reveal the caster of spells. Is it very probable that as, since their origin they have been bewitched by these beliefs, they would not have discovered the deceit if it had been only pure boasting? . . . But this belief is so general and deep rooted that there is not one tribe in the whole extent of America which has not its diviners or shamans, not one which does not fear spells, not one where any refuses to have recourse to the shamans, and does not willingly undergo all the tests of the initiations to be made a shaman himself.

Father Joseph François Lafitau, *Customs of the American Indians Compared with the Customs of Primitive Times*, edited and translated by William N. Fenton and Elizabeth L. Moore (Paris, 1724; repr., Toronto: The Champlain Society, 1974), 238–41, 245–46.

ᴣᴥ

The Natural History of Barbados (1750)
GRIFFITH HUGHES

European colonists proved no more successful in understanding various West African cosmologies than they had been in understanding those of Native Americans. In both cases, Europeans translated complex healing and spiritual practices into behavior that they could understand and dismiss—that is, witchcraft and devil worship. Abducted from their homelands and dispersed among other African-born slaves of different languages and cultures, African American slaves were forced to create a creole *culture that both derived from their African ancestry and emerged anew in America. This was especially true for the system of healing, spirit communication, and charms known as* obia *or* obeah, *practiced by Igbo peoples of West Africa in the English-speaking Caribbean colonies.*

Obeah practitioners (also called dibia*) were almost always men. They possessed abilities that included healing by herbs and charms, communicating with spirits to discover the source of a malicious spell or disease, and foretelling the future. Obeah men's role became even more important in African and Afro-Caribbean communities as the slave trade expanded, since dibia were responsible for discerning why evil happened and for remedying calamities and punishing transgressors. Slave masters' common fears that slaves might poison them attest to one aspect of obeah men's skillful knowledge. Unfortunately, we have little record of how slaves explained their own religious and magical practices, because they left behind few written documents. Instead, cultural historians must examine the writings of European observers in hope of glimpsing the significance and meaning of African beliefs and practices. As an Anglican clergyman on Barbados from 1735 to 1754, Griffith Hughes saw firsthand African slaves and their masters. Although his Christianity made him dismissive of obeah, Hughes's natural history of the island was embraced by early abolitionists for denouncing slave masters' cruelty and endorsing the human equality of African slaves.*

PROBLEMS TO CONSIDER

1. Despite his dismissive tone, can Hughes's descriptions of slaves' religious practices help us understand how and why such rituals thrived, especially in the context of a slaveholder culture that regarded them as foolish superstitions?
2. How do you reconcile Hughes's statement about the intellectual equality of Africans and Europeans with his criticism of slaves' beliefs in magic?

The Negroes in general are very tenaciously addicted to the Rites, Ceremonies, and Superstitions of their own Countries, particularly their Plays, Dances, Music, Marriages, and Burials. There are but few Negroes who believe that they die a natural Death, but rather that they are fascinated, or bewitched. The Bearers, in carrying the Corpse of such a one to the Grave, when they come opposite to, or in Sight of the House of the Person who is supposed to have bewitched the Deceased, pretend to stagger, and say, that the Corpse is unwilling, and will not permit them to carry it to the Grave, until it is suffered to stop near, or opposite to, that House: After this is complied with for a few Minutes, the Corpse is, as they think, appeased, and the Bearers, without Difficulty, carry it to the Grave. . . .

And even such as are born and bred here, cannot be entirely weaned from these Customs: They stand much in Awe of such as pass for *Obeah* Negroes, these being a sort of Physicians and Conjurers, who can, as they believe, not only fascinate them, but cure them when they are bewitched by others. And if once a Negro believes, that he is bewitched, the Notion is so strongly riveted in his Mind, that, Medicines seldom availing, he usually lingers till Death puts an End to his Fears.

These *Obeah* Negroes get a good Livelihood by the Folly and Ignorance of the rest of the Negroes. I shall here insert one Instance of their pretended Method of curing the Sick, which was performed upon a Negro Woman; who, being troubled with Rheumatic Pains, was persuaded by one of these *Obeah* Doctors, that she was bewitched, and that these Pains were owing to several Pieces of Glass, rusty Nails, and Splinters of sharp Stones, that were lodged in the different Parts of her Body; adding, that it was in his Power, if paid for it, to cure her, by extracting these from her through her Navel. Upon the Payment of the stipulated Præmium, he produced his Magical Apparatus, being two Earthen Basins, a Handful of different Kinds of Leaves, and a Piece of Soap. In one of these Basins he made a strong Lather, in the other he put the bruised Herbs; then clapping these with one Hand to the Navel, and pouring the Suds by Degrees upon them, he stroked the Parts most affected with the other Hand, always ending towards the Navel: In a short time after, thrusting his Finger and Thumb into the Cataplasm of Herbs, he produced several Pieces of broken Glass, Nails, and Splinters of Stones (which he had before artfully conveyed among the bruised Herbs). As such a great Number extracted, was looked upon as an extraordinary Instance of the Doctor's great Skill, he unluckily demanded a further Reward than what was stipulated: But as the Woman's Husband was one of those very few, who had no Faith in such pretended Cures, being accidentally knowing in some of their Secrets, instead of an additional Reward, he made him by Threats refund the Money he had already received, bidding him, if he was a Conjurer, find out by his Art some Means of getting it again restored to him. . . .

When these Negroes die a natural Death, or especially when they destroy themselves, they believe that they shall return to their own Country. It would be too gross to believe, that they expect to be restored and to live there in their mortal Bodies: Therefore we must conclude, that they have some Notion of the Immortality of the Soul; and what they mean by their own Country is, that they shall, after this Life, enjoy the Company of their Friends and Relations in another World.

The Capacities of their Minds in the common Affairs of Life are but little inferior, if at all, to those of the *Europeans*. If they fail in some Arts, it may be owing more to their Want of Education, and the Depression of their Spirits by Slavery, than to any Want of natural Abilities; for an higher Degree of improved Knowledge in any Occupation would not much alter their Condition for the better.

Griffith Hughes, *The Natural History of Barbados in Ten Books* (London: Griffith Hughes, 1750), 15–16.

ᢒ

ᢒ Cockfights, Horse Races, and Revivals: Colonial Amusements and the Great Awakening ᢒ

When we conjure mental images of colonists in North America, pictures of fun-loving and playful folk are probably not the first pictures to appear; instead, we tend to visualize witch-accusing Puritans dressed in black, rugged frontier farmers, or fearful slaveholders. Yet recreation and amusements were as vital to colonial life as religious services. If you think for a moment of the crowds of spectators who gravitated to both religious revivals and sporting events throughout American history, you will understand why historians look to the interaction between religion and sports when examining the dynamics of a past culture.

By the eighteenth century, fully mature colonial societies had emerged along the eastern seaboard from New Hampshire to Georgia, and colonists hailed from German, Dutch, French, Scottish, Irish, English, and African ancestry. A stable and powerful elite class in the southern colonies and eastern seaports encouraged patterns of recreation and leisure designed to reinforce their superior status through outward displays of luxury, prowess, and risk. A "gentleman" wore wigs, kept pace with London fashions, built a great house, comported himself with manners and wit, and played in conspicuous ways after the turn of the century. William Byrd II of Westover plantation was among that class of Virginia's rising elite; he wrote the following entry in his diary in June 1709:

> I rose at 5 o'clock this morning but could not read anything because of Captain Keeling, but I played at billiards with him and won half a crown of him and the Doctor. George B-th brought home my boy Eugene . . . In the evening I took a walk about the plantation. Eugene was whipped for running away and had the [bit] put on him. I said my prayers and had good health, good thought, and good humor, thanks be to God Almighty.

Byrd's chronicle of the day's events exposes the distinct features of this genteel culture of recreation in eighteenth-century America. Certainly horse racing, gambling, dancing, and court days bonded men of wealth and power, but ever present was the reminder of lower-class white men and African American slaves, without whom the performance of gentility would be impossible. And Byrd's prayer at the end reminds us that just as these forms of popular culture became firmly rooted in the colonies, other colonists challenged this gentry-based leisure culture. Their criticisms were based on new concepts of sensibility (notions such as civility, manners, and humanitarianism) or new countercultural religious ideas rooted in evangelicalism. Religion and leisure once again found their paths intersecting, but this time in the conflicts over appropriate identity in maturing American colonies.

Horse Racing in Virginia: Court Records and Newspaper Accounts (1674–1739)

Horse racing became the sport of Virginia's gentlemen. And they wished to keep it that way. When the Virginia Gazette *reported in the 1730s that a group of "merry-dispos'd gentlemen" were going to celebrate St. Andrew's Day with quarter-horse races, the newspaper noted that spectators would be permitted as long as they "behave[d] themselves with Decency and Sobriety, the Subscribers being resolv'd to discountenance all Immorality with the utmost Rigour." Horseracing mirrored the workings of gentry culture. When the eighteenth century began, Virginia's gentry class was neither long-standing nor secure. Their forefathers had been former servants and small landowners who had exploited the new labor system of slavery to create enormous new wealth. So, if a gentleman's status was unclear, he could convince his neighbors through conspicuous displays of risk, lavish spending, and masculine prowess. Who else could afford to train valuable domestic animals, necessary for plowing or transportation, into racehorses? Men also demonstrated their honor and manliness, and their wealth, by their willingness to wager their fortunes in a reckless game of chance as well as skill. Glimpses of the gentlemen's world of horse racing can be found in the courtroom disputes they provoked, as well as in the newspaper accounts of races and their prizes.*

PROBLEMS TO CONSIDER

1. What was the purpose of these elaborate legal agreements that preceded horse races in Virginia? What do they reveal about the relationships between men in this leisure activity?
2. What means did Virginia's leading men use to ensure that horse racing remained the sport of gentlemen? Why were such measures necessary, and what did the Virginia elite gain from the sport's exclusiveness?

COURT RECORDS

York County, Virginia, September 10, 1674
James Bullocke, a Taylor, having made a race for his mare to runn with a horse belonging to Mr. Mathew Slader for twoe thousand pounds of tobacco and caske, it being contrary to Law for a Labourer to make a race, being a sport only for Gentlemen, is fined for the same one hundred pounds of tobacco and caske.

Whereas Mr. Mathew Slader & James Bullocke, by condition under the hand and seale of the said Slater, that his horse should run out of the way that Bullocke's mare might win, which is an apparent cheate, is ordered to be putt in the stocks & there sitt the space of one houre.

Henrico County, Virginia, April 1, 1698
At a Court held at Varina, April 1st, 1698, Richard Ward complains against John Stewart, Jun'r, in a plea of debt for that, that is to say the said plaintiff & defendant did on the 12th day of June Last, covenant and agree in the following words:

It is Covenanted and agreed this 12th day of June, 1697, Between Mr. Richard Ward of the one part, in Henrico County, & John Steward, Jun'r, of ye other part in ye same County: Witnesseth, that the aforesaid Mr. Richard Ward doth hereby covenant, promise & agree to run a mare named Bony, belonging to Thomas Jefferson, Jun'r *[grandfather of the president]*, against a horse now belonging to Mr. John Hardiman, named Watt, the said horse & mare to Run at the race-place commonly called ye Ware, to run one quarter of a mile. . . . The said horse to give the said mare five horse lengths, Vizt: that is to say ten yards. . . . And it is further agreed upon by the parties above said that if the said mare doth come within five Lengths of the foresaid Horse, the foresaid John Steward to pay unto Mr. Richard Ward the sum of five pounds Sterling on Demand . . . It is further agreed by the parties aforesaid, that there be fair Rideing & the Riders to weigh about one hundred & thirty Weight, to the true performance of all & singular the promises, the parties above said have hereunto set their hands the day and year above written." . . .

Wherefore the aforesaid plaintiff saith that the aforesaid Mare, Bony, with fair Running & Rideing, according to agreement, Did beat the said horse Watt, and that according to the true meaning of the said agreement he, the said plaintiff, hath Won the wager, to-witt: the sum of five pounds sterling of the aforesaid John Steward. And thereupon he brings suit against the aforesaid John Steward, Jun'r, & demands

Judgement for the aforesaid sum of five pounds Sterling, with Costs, &c. . . .

Whereupon, it is ordered that a Jury be impanelled & sworn to try the issue. . . .

Who Returned this Verdict: We find for the plaintiff. Upon the motion of the plaintiffs' attorney the said Verdict is Recorded, & Judgment is awarded the said plaintiff against the Defendant for the sum of five pounds Sterling, to be paid with Costs.

Virginia Gazette (1739)
Williamsburg, Dec. 14, 1739. Last Wednesday the Fair began in this City and held three days. . . .

The prizes were all contended for. There was a Horse Race, round the Mile Course, the First Day, for a Saddle of Forty Shillings Value. Eight Horses started, by Sound of Trumpet, and Col. Chiswell's Horse, Edgcomb, came in First, and won the Saddle; Mr. Cocke's Horse, Sing'd Cat, came in Second, and won the Bridle, of 12 Shillings Value; and Mr. Drummond's Horse, ———, came in Third, and won the Whip.

The Second Day, a Silver Soup Ladle, of 45 Shillings Value, was run for, the same Ground; and was won by Mr. Coke's Horse; Mr. Gooch's Horse, Top, came in Second, and won the Bridle, of 12 Shillings Value; and Mr. Stanhope's Horse won the Whip.

The Third day, a Saddle and Bridle, of about 40 Shillings Value, were run for, the same Ground; Mr. Gooch's Horse, Top, came in First, and won the Saddle and Bridle; Mr. Drummond's Horse came in Second, and won the Bridle, of 12 Shillings value; and Mr. Booker's Horse, Tail, won the Whip.

"Racing in Colonial Virginia," *Virginia Magazine of History and Biography* 2 (1895): 294, 296–98, 300.

ᴠ

Cockfighting (1752)

VIRGINIA GAZETTE

Virginia's gentlemen could not keep all recreations exclusive to their own class; nor would they have wanted it that way. With the social and racial inequalities of the colonial South, there was a greater need for leisure activities that crossed the class divide that otherwise separated white colonists. White southerners embraced an ethic of leisure because work itself had become racially debased. As two historians of sport have argued: "Black chattel slavery made it difficult for whites to venerate work, easy for them to idealize play. How could whites value hard work unequivocally once labor was associated with degraded, servile blacks? . . . Labor was the burden of blackness; leisure, the prerogative of whiteness." One of the more popular cross-class male recreations in colonial Virginia was cockfighting. Cockfights were usually staged at a tavern or a town square, where roosters would spar in a large "cockpit," surrounded by men of all classes mingling together. The birds would be armed with sharp, steel points and inflict repeated blows until one was struck dead. Wagering was as important as the spectacle of the fight. Gentlemen made sure that recreating together with common farmers allowed them to display their superior wealth and standing. They sponsored the animals and their trainers and wagered large sums only with other gentleman — it showed no honor to challenge a lesser man. And in a society that denied them a masculine identity, slaves secretly staged cockfights outside the watchful eyes of their masters. In 1752, a Virginia planter wrote the following letter to the newspaper, criticizing the practice of cockfighting.

PROBLEMS TO CONSIDER

1. To what extent did the class dynamics of Virginia society shape this author's criticism and his suggested solutions to the problem of cockfighting?
2. What is the relationship between this planter's criticism of cockfights as cruelty and his critique of them as immorality or vice? Are they related concerns?

To the Printer
Sir,

If you'll please to communicate to the Public the following Observations on one of the reigning Diversions of this Country, you'll oblige, *Your very humble Servant.*

. . . The Domestick, or innocent Animals are not to be killed to gratify an extravagant Passion for Money, out of Wantonness, or with Circumstances of Cruelty attending such killing. Because this is a Transgression of the Laws that forbid such Crimes. For even the Law of Nature forbids Cruelty. It is grievous to see, or even to hear of an Animal in Torment. Our very Make and Constitution (if not vitiated) restrains us from being insensible of the Pains of others. . . .

This Practice will be found attended with Circumstances shockingly prophane and impious. This I can assert from my own Observation. For having casually been present at a Cock-fight, some Time ago, I could not but take Notice, with much Concern, that some Gentlemen, who, upon other Occasions, behav'd with great Decency, and as if they had been influenced with suitable Impressions of the awful and tremendous Name of GOD, did then speak and act, as if the Divine Law had been for that Time abrogated, opening their Mouths with horrid Oaths, and dreadful Imprecations. And all this when their Passions were not much inflam'd, being early in the Day, and their high Bets not yet begun. I, for my Part, was soon tir'd with the Place and Diversion, as 'tis called, and left it, with a firm Purpose, never to be present at another such. To it succeeded Drinking and Gaming, an uninterrupted Violation both of Divine, and Human Laws, for some Days and Nights.

Now admitting that the Practice of Cock-fighting were lawful in itself, which I absolutely deny; yet when 'tis attended with such Circumstances, and follow'd by such terrible Consequences, is it not a Shame that it should be allowed in a Christian Country. Were one of the primitive Christians but to revisit the Globe, and be dropt at a modern Cock-fight, he would hardly be persuaded, that he was among Christians; but upon his being assured, that he was in the purest Part of the Christian Church, how great must his Surprize and Concern be, to find such a dreadful Dissolution of Manners, among those that bear the Redeemer's Name. . . .

For I'm persuaded, that if those in eminent Stations, would shew their Dislike, not only to that, but to every other dissolute Practice, the Vulgar, who are very apt to mimick them, would soon give it up also; at least it would become so infamous, that none who regarded their Character, would be found publickly to practice it.

Virginia Gazette, January 2, 1752.

ᏹ

Dancing (1738–1747)
PENNSYLVANIA GAZETTE

The new masculine culture of genteel recreations was not limited to Virginia or the southern colonies. In the middle colonies, where much greater ethnic and religious diversity developed, colonists still experienced the tension between commoners' penchant for traditional pastimes, elite aspirations for genteel recreations, and moralists' concerns about vice and idleness. Pennsylvania is a case in point. The Quakers who founded the colony in 1682 had a mindset more in sync with their Puritan compatriots in New England than with their contemporaries in Virginia. By 1700, Quaker leaders in Philadelphia had outlawed theater, gaming, and "rude and riotous sports" and discouraged dancing as inappropriate intimacy. But Quakers were soon outnumbered by immigrants of other cultures and faiths, particularly Germans and Scotch-Irish, while a rival elite group of Anglicans and Presbyterians grew in social prominence within the fast-growing city of Philadelphia. Dancing was one of the markers of gentility that the new upper class used to distinguish itself from common folk. By the time Pennsylvania's population had become more diverse, notices of dancing instruction began to appear in Benjamin Franklin's Philadelphia newspaper, the Pennsylvania Gazette. *These* Pennsylvania Gazette *excerpts also reveal the persistence of older critiques of dancing on religious grounds as well as a hint of the new challenge to a genteel culture from the proliferation of revivalism.*

PROBLEMS TO CONSIDER

1. What did dancing instructors try to sell to Philadelphia's upper classes as the product to be derived from dancing lessons?
2. How was this urban amusement similar or different in function from the sporting culture in the colonial South?

August 31, 1738

This is to give publick Notice that Theobald Hackett, Dancing-Master, from England, has open'd a Dancing-School, at the House where Mr. Brownell, lately liv'd in Second Street, Philadelphia, where he will give due Attendance, and teach all sorts of fashionable English and French Dances, after the newest and politest manner, as practised in London, Dublin and Paris, and will give young Ladies, Gentlemen and Children (that please to learn of him) the most graceful Carriage in Dancing, and gentle Behaviour in Company, on all Occasions that possibly can be by any Dancing Master whatsoever, he will teach by the Month or Quarter, as reasonable as any good Master. N.B. If any be inclin'd to agree by the quarter, or learn privately, he will attend duly at their own Houses, or in his Room, out of School Hours, & that with the utmost Discretion.

January 27, 1747

This is to give Notice to all Gentlemen, who desire to learn the noble art and science of defence, and pursuit of the small sword; and likewise to all young Gentlemen and Ladies who are minded to acquire the accomplishment of dancing; that they may be taught the same either publickly or privately, by their humble servant, THOMAS SKILLIEN.

N.B. He is to be spoke with at the House of Mr. Richard Swan, in Market street.

March 16, 1747

Some serious REFLECTIONS on an Advertisement lately published in the Pennsylvania Gazette.

Having lately read in the Gazette of the 20th of January, 1746–7, an Advertisement, subscribed by one Thomas Skillien, in which he has published his intention of erecting a Fencing and Dancing School: I thought it necessary to make some Observations and Remarks thereon.

I was indeed surprized at the Contents of it, but more at the audacity and brasen Impudence of the Author, in giving those detestable Vices, these high Epithets, viz. "The noble Art and Science of Defence," and "Pursuit of the Small word, and the Accomplishment of Dancing:" Contrary to which Titles, they may be proved to be of infernal Race and diabolical Descent. This he is not ashamed to publish to the World to be his Calling, to teach People to spend their precious, irrevocable Moments, in the most unprofitable, profuse Manner imaginable; for besides these particular Vices above mentioned, they are accompanied with a Train of other Evils, such as Pride, Emulation, Lasciviousness, Luxury, Idleness, & c. & c. and all this covered with the specious Color of Noble Arts and Accomplishments; O HORROR! . . . Now let me make my humble Address to, and beseech the Supreme Authority of the Province of Pennsylvania, who bear the Christian Name, to consider how inconsistent with Christianity such heathenish Practises are, and provide that the free People of this City and Province may not become slaves to such impious Sensualities. But if these base corrupting Vices, so openly put in Practise, are connived at by those in Authority, it is justly to be fear'd, that they'll be accessary to the drawing down Divine Vengeance upon the land, rather than prolonging its Tranquility under so happy a political Constitution. SAMUEL FOULKE.

May 1, 1740
Philadelphia

On Sunday last the Rev. Mr. [George] WHITEFIELD preached twice at New Brunswick, to about 7000 People and collected 31£. 10 s. Currency, which is about 26£. Sterling, for the Orphans in Georgia. Mr. [Gilbert] Tennent also preached between the Sermons, and there were great Meltings in the Congregations. On Monday Mr. Whitefield was to preach at Woodbridge and Elizabeth Town; on Tuesday and every Day this Week in or about New York. . . .

Since Mr. Whitefield's Preaching here, the Dancing School Assembly and Concert Room have been shut up, as inconsistent with the Doctrine of the Gospel: And though the Gentlemen concern'd caus'd the Door to be broke open again,

we are inform'd that no Company came the last Assembly Night.

———————

Pennsylvania Gazette, August 31, 1738; January 27, 1747; March 16, 1747; May 1, 1740. Accessible Archives: http://www.accessible.com.

ᢲ

Spiritual Travels of Nathan Cole (c. 1771)

NATHAN COLE

A wave of spiritual excitement swept over communities beginning in the 1730s in the mid-Atlantic and New England colonies, and continuing for decades throughout all regions of colonial America. Labeled by historians as the Great Awakening, this phenomenon was part of a transatlantic movement of Protestant pietism that produced religious groups such as the Methodists in England, the Moravians in Germany, and the Baptists throughout North America. What these pietist movements had in common was an attachment to revivalist preaching and a shared identity based on a "new birth" conversion experience. Most ordinary people experienced this awakening as a local event, sometimes resulting in either profound transformations in an individual's self-identity or bitter disputes over social authority in local churches and communities. At the heart of this evangelical phenomenon was a divisive new perception of the self and of community. One of the best accounts of that experience by an ordinary person can be found in the handwritten memoirs of Nathan Cole, a Connecticut farmer, who wrote of his encounter with George Whitefield, the era's best-known evangelist.

PROBLEMS TO CONSIDER

1. What does Cole's description of his conversion tell us about his own perception of the self? How could this type of conversion encourage greater individualism?
2. How did his new religious experience affect his relationships with others in the broader community?

I *was born Feb 15th 1711 and born again octo 1741—*

. . . Now it pleased God to send Mr Whitefield into this land; and my hearing of his preaching at Philadelphia, like one of the Old apostles, and many thousands flocking to hear him preach the Gospel; and great numbers were converted to Christ; I felt the Spirit of God drawing me by conviction; I longed to see and

hear him, and wished he would come this way.
. . .

Then on a Sudden, in the morning about 8 or 9 of the Clock there came a messenger and said Mr Whitfield preached at Hartford and Weathersfield yesterday and is to preach at Middletown this morning at ten of the Clock, I was in my field at Work, I dropt my tool that I had in my hand and ran home to my wife telling her to make ready quickly to go and hear Mr Whitfield preach at Middletown. . . .

And when we came within about half a mile or a mile of the Road that comes down . . . to Middletown . . . I heard a noise something like a low rumbling thunder and presently found it was the noise of Horses feet coming down the Road and this Cloud was a Cloud of dust made by the Horses feet; . . . and as I drew nearer it seemed like a steady Stream of horses and their riders, scarcely a horse more than his length behind another, all of a Lather and foam with sweat, their breath rolling out of their nostrils every Jump; every horse seemed to go with all his might to carry his rider to hear news from heaven for the saving of Souls, it made me tremble to see the Sight, how the world was in a Struggle. . . .

We went down in the Stream but heard no man speak a word all the way for 3 miles but every one pressing forward in great haste and when we got to Middletown old meeting house there was a great Multitude *it was said to be 3 or 4000* of people Assembled together. . . .

When I saw Mr Whitfield come upon the Scaffold he Lookt almost angelical; a young, Slim, slender, youth before some thousands of people with a bold undaunted Countenance, and my hearing how God was with him every where as he came along it Solemnized my mind; and put me into a trembling fear before he began to preach; for he looked as if he was Cloathed with authority from the Great God; *and a sweet sollome solemnity sat upon his brow* And my hearing him preach, gave me a heart wound; By Gods blessing: my old Foundation was broken up, and I saw that my righteousness would not save me; then I was convinced of the doctrine of Election: and went right to quarrelling with God about it; because that all I could do would not save me; and he had decreed from Eternity who should be saved and who not.

I began to think I was not Elected, and that God made some for heaven and me for hell. And I thought God was not Just in so doing, I thought

I did not stand on even Ground with others, if as I thought; I was made to be damned; My heart then rose against God exceedingly, for his making me for hell; Now this distress lasted Almost two years:—Poor—Me—Miserable me. . . . It took away *most* all my Comfort of eating, drinking, Sleeping, or working. Hell fire was most always in my mind; and I have hundreds of times put my fingers into my pipe when I have been smoking to feel how fire felt: And to see how my Body could bear to lye in Hell fire for ever and ever. Now my countenance was sad so that others took notice of it. . . .

And while these thoughts were in my mind God appeared unto me and made me cringe. . . . I knew not whether I was in the body or out, I seemed to hang in open Air before God, and he seemed to Speak to me in an angry and Sovereign way what won't you trust your Soul with God; My heart answered O yes, yes, yes; before I could stir my tongue or lips. . . .

When God appeared to me every thing vanished and was gone in the twinkling of an Eye, as quick as a flash of lightning; But when God disappeared or in some measure withdrew, every thing was in its place again and I was on my Bed. My heart was broken; my burden was fallen of[f] my mind; I was set free, my distress was gone, and I was filled with a pineing desire to see Christs own words in the bible. . . .

Now I saw that I must Suffer as well as do for Christ, now I saw that I must forsake all and follow Christ; now I saw with new eyes; all things became new, A new God; new thoughts and new heart; Now I began to hope I should be converted some time or other, for I was sure that God had done some great thing for my soul. . . .

Now I began to see the Old Standing Churches were not in a gospel order. I was called a member of this old Church for 14 or 15 years; but now I saw Ichabod *[In the Bible (I Sam. 4.21) Eli's daughter-in-law named her son Ichabod, saying "the glory is departed from Israel." New England ministers had used this text to warn the people of their waning piety and God's displeasure.]* was written upon it, the Glory of the Lord was departed, for they held several things contrary to the Gospel. . . .

Now I was called to give up what the world calls a fine reputation, and to become the off-

s[c]ouring of the Earth, and to lose my own life as it were in the world, for my religion.

"The Spiritual Travels of Nathan Cole," edited by Michael J. Crawford, *William and Mary Quarterly*, 3rd ser., 33 (1976): 92–94, 96–97, 103–4.

ᔆ

The Danger of an Unconverted Ministry (1741)
GILBERT TENNENT

Besides describing his own conversion story, Cole's narrative depicted the consequences for local communities when groups of people felt they could no longer remain in churches with members and ministers who had not experienced the "new birth." George Whitefield had stirred up this controversy when he declared that "the generality of preachers talk of an unknown and unfelt Christ. The reason why congregations have been dead is, because they had dead men preaching to them." Revival supporters ("New Lights") began to encourage traveling (or "itinerant") preachers to come to villages and convert the unfaithful and denounce the resident ministers. The most caustic example was a sermon by Gilbert Tennent, a New Jersey protégé of Whitefield, entitled The Danger of an Unconverted Ministry. *Acrimonious disputes arose in communities across the colonies, with New Lights accusing traditionalists of foisting "their old, rotten, and stinking routine religion" on the people, and their opponents ("Old Lights") denouncing all of the disruptions and disorder from emotional revival preaching under the label of "enthusiasm." These conflicts also provoked local financial crises since churches and ministers in most colonies were funded by taxes on all residents. Whenever converts joined a newly formed separate congregation, either they were forced to support two ministers or they refused and thus increased the tax burden on remaining residents. Revival converts formed new churches and denominations, gathering with fellow believers in an intimate fellowship of equals and attesting to their new spiritual families by calling one another "brother" or "sister."*

PROBLEMS TO CONSIDER

1. Read this document as if it were a personal assault on you as the local clergyperson. What do you feel are Tennent's most inflammatory comments?
2. Is Tennent's sermon an act of religious intolerance or an appeal for freedom of conscience?

. . . Natural Men have no Call of GOD to the Ministerial Work under the Gospel-Dispensation.

Isn't it a principal Part of the ordinary Call of GOD to the Ministerial Work, to aim at the Glory of GOD, and, in Subordination thereto, the Good of Souls, as their chief Marks in their Undertaking that Work? And can any natural Man on Earth do this? No! no! Every Skin of them has an evil Eye; for no Cause can produce Effects above its own Power. Are not wicked Men forbid to meddle in Things sacred? . . .

Now, are not all unconverted Men wicked Men? . . . See, our LORD will not make Men Ministers, 'til they follow him. Men that do not follow Christ, may fish faithfully for a good name, and for worldly Pelf *[riches]*; but not for the Conversion of Sinners to God. Is it reasonable to suppose, that they will be earnestly concerned for others Salvation, when they slight their own? . . . For how can those Men be faithful, that have no Faith? It's true Men may put them into the Ministry, thro' Unfaithfulness, or Mistake; or Credit and Money may draw them, and the Devil may drive them into it, knowing by long Experience, of what special Service they may be to his Kingdom in that Office: But GOD sends not such hypocritical Varlets *[rascals]*. . . .

Their Conversation hath nothing of the Savour of Christ, neither is it perfumed with the Spices of Heaven. They seem to make as little Distinction in their Practice, as Preaching. They love those Unbelievers, that are kind to them, better than many Christians, and chuse them for Companions. . . . Poor Christians are stunted and starv'd, who are put to feed on such bare Pastures, and such dry Nurses. . . . It's only when the wise Virgins sleep, that they can bear with those dead Dogs, that can't bark; but when the LORD revives his People, they can't but abhor them! O! it is ready to break their very Hearts with Grief, to see how luke-warm those Pharisee-Teachers are in their publick Discourses, while Sinners are sinking into Damnation, in Multitudes! . . .

And right Reason will inform us, how unfit Instruments they are to negotiate that Work they pretend to. Is a blind Man fit to be a Guide in a very dangerous Way? Is a dead Man fit to bring others to Life? a mad Man fit to give Counsel in a Matter of Life and Death? Is a possessed Man fit to cast out Devils? . . . Isn't an unconverted Minister like a Man who would learn others to swim, before he has learn'd it himself, and so is drowned in the Act, and dies like a Fool? . . .

And isn't this the Reason, why a Work of Conviction and Conversion has been so rarely heard of, for a long Time, in the Churches, till of late, *viz.* That the Bulk of her spiritual Guides, were stone-blind, and stone-dead! . . .

If the Ministry of natural Men be as it has been represented; Then it is both lawful and expedient to go from them to hear Godly Persons; yea, it's so far from being sinful to do this, that one who lives under a pious Minister of lesser Gifts, after having honestly endeavour'd to get Benefit by his Ministry, and yet gets little or none, but doth find real Benefit and more Benefit elsewhere; I say, he may lawfully go. . . .

To bind Men to a particular Minister, against their Judgment and Inclinations, when they are more edified elsewhere, is carnal with a Witness; a cruel Oppression of tender Consciences, a compelling of Men to Sin. . . .

Besides it is an unscriptural Infringment on Christian Liberty. . . .

Gilbert Tennent, *The Danger of an Unconverted Ministry, Considered in a Sermon on Mark VI. 34* (Philadelphia: Benjamin Franklin, 1740), 7–8, 11–13, 18–19, 21.

∿

The Life of the Rev. James Ireland (1819)
JAMES IRELAND

In Virginia, the Great Awakening resulted in a battle over church authority, led by evangelical Baptists, who ultimately forged an alliance after the Revolution with rationalists such as Thomas Jefferson to establish religious freedom in the state. But initially Virginians became aware that evangelicalism meant a rejection of the gentry-dominated culture that had reigned in the colony for more than half a century. New converts aban-

doned the notion that their self-worth could be measured by displays of wealth or by tests of skill and manliness on the horse track or the dance floor. They believed that God measured them solely on their faithfulness to their new birth and that their conversion demanded that they renounce card playing, dancing, and luxuries such as fine clothing and jewelry. One man's personal journey away from amusements to the new light can be seen in the memoirs of James Ireland. However, Virginia's gentry had even more to fear from evangelicalism than an abandonment of dancing or gambling. The movement's countercultural tendencies also manifested themselves in a willingness to preach to African American slaves. Baptists and Methodists welcomed slave converts as spiritual equals into their churches and even encouraged gifted slave preachers to preach to white and black congregants alike. The values of Virginia's gentry class were indeed being turned upside down.

PROBLEMS TO CONSIDER

1. What was the new type of person that the Great Awakening produced?
2. Ireland would have interpreted his change of life as the experience of greater freedom. How could he arrive at that conclusion?

Visiting these parts repeatedly, I became tolerably well acquainted with the settlement in general. . . . A considerable number of the people of both sexes were nearly of my age; their recreations, pleasures and pastimes, were very congenial to my wishes. Balls, dancing and chanting to the sound of the violin, was the most prevailing practice in that settlement. That being my darling idol, and being esteemed by all who ever saw me perform upon the floor, a most complete dancer; which accomplishment so called, together with my other moods of address, soon acquired me the confidence and esteem of those called, now a days, young ladies. The young men through the settlement in general, appeared to be destitute of every virtuous or moral qualification, and heads of tolerably numerous families were equally as wild and dissipated as the youth. When in companies together nothing was heard, comparatively speaking, but obscene language, cursing and swearing, drinking and frolicking, horse racing and other vices, with the exception of a few characters or families in that settlement. . . .

I was then led on to a few reflections.— Having been not long before that period, at a yearly meeting of a people, to which my religious friend belonged, I recollected them calling each other brother, which appellation I knew did not belong to them by blood, otherwise than being the children of the universal family of Adam; my reflections immediately lead me to conceive they possessed a religion which united them together in affection, and called each other brother in consequence thereof.

. . . I was going that evening to visit a respectable Presbyterian family, of which the old Lady I believe possessed the grace and spirit of Jesus Christ. . . . On my way to her house, (which was a little better than a mile) I felt an unusual conflict within; the aforementioned words running through my mind, all at once I was made as it were to stand!—God was pleased to manifest light to my understanding, and brought it home to my conscience that I was the slighter and condemner of the salvation of Christ; and that the law of God was then breathing death against my soul. The impression was so forcibly brought home to my conscience, that it never became obliterated from that period until I had reason to believe that Christ was formed in my soul the hope of Glory. . . .

The news of my awakening impressions, had diffused itself through every part of the settlement and its vicinity. It became the topic in all companies that "James Ireland was going to be mighty good now, for he is going to be converted." My acquaintance had not seen me for some short period, previous to my soul's distresses. There was a dance appointed to be held the Monday following, at a wealthy neighbour's house. My country-man in company with others, hearing the remarks they were making about me, and being tolerably dissipated in language at times, swore they need not believe any thing about it, for there could not be a dance in the settlement without my being there, and if they could leave it to him, he would convert me, and that to the dance, on Monday; and they would see me lead the ball that day . . . When I viewed him riding up, I never beheld such a display of pride in any man, before or since, as I beheld in him at that juncture, arising from his deportment, attitude and jesture; he rode a lofty elegant horse, and exhibited all the affectation possible, whilst his countenance appeared to me as bold and daring as satan himself, and with a commanding authority called upon me, if I were there to come out, which I accordingly did, with a fearful and timorous heart. But O! how quickly can God level pride to the ground. . . . In a few minutes did the person, who, no doubt, made sure, as he came to visit me, of making an easy conquest of me, find, that the race is not to the swift nor the battle to the strong. For no

sooner did he behold my disconsolate looks, emaciated countenance and solemn aspect, than he instantly appeared, as if he was riveted to the beast he rode on; his passions were so powerfully impressed, that I conceived he should have fainted and dropped from his horse.

For some short space of time, he was past utterance, and did not nothing but stare at me with wild amazement. As soon as he could articulate a little his eyes fixed upon me, and his first address was this; "In the name of the Lord, what is the matter with you?" . . . I instantly took him by the hand, and with a tender heart, and tears streaming from my eyes, spoke to him as follows. "My dear friend I possess a soul that will be either happy or miserable in the world to come; and God has been pleased to give me a view of the worth of my soul, as also of the guilty and condemned state it lies by reason of sin; and I plainly see that if my soul is not converted, regenerated and born again, I will be damned." Holding my hand fast in his, and looking at me, with all the eagerness of desire, he burst out into the following words—"O! you will not leave me nor forsake me now." To which I observed that "I would not, upon condition he would renounce his former wicked ways, as I had done, and seek God through Jesus Christ, for pardon and salvation to our poor souls." To which he replied, with streaming eyes, "from that moment forward, through the strength of the Lord Jesus Christ, he would."

_____

James Ireland, *The Life of the Rev. James Ireland, who was, for many years, Pastor of the Baptist Church at Buck Marsh, Waterlick and Happy Creek, in Frederick and Shenandoah Counties, Virginia* (Winchester, Va.: J. Foster, 1819), 44–53, 66–69, 82–86, 110–11.

⁊

CHAPTER 4

Creating a Nation:
1760–1800

WHEN AMERICAN COLONISTS moved closer to independence, ready to sever the ties that bound them to the powerful British empire, they read these words of Thomas Paine in *Common Sense* (1776): "we have it in our power to begin the world over again." Neither Paine nor most of the rebel colonists were timid when it came to announcing that their struggle was not just about ending colonialism. They were creating a revolution. Looking back nearly seven years later, with a war for independence successfully won and new constitutions written in every state, Paine declared, "We see with other eyes; we hear with other ears; and think with other thoughts, than those we formerly used." The American Revolution was indeed a sea change. It established a new nation where none had existed before, championed a new vocabulary of freedom and equality, and invented a sovereign "we the people" in a world where the only sovereigns were kings. These changes led one historian to maintain that the American Revolution "was as radical and revolutionary as any other" revolution in history.

The American Revolution occurred during a period of long-term cultural reorientation in the Anglo-American world. What made the American Revolution so revolutionary was that it corresponded with and further accelerated new ways of thinking, transforming not just government and politics but the foundations of identity and authority as well. The fact that individuals went from being subjects of a monarch to being citizens in a republic represented a profound transformation. When people began to think differently about politics, they also had to rethink conceptions of family, the self, dependence, and independence, all intertwined notions in an Anglo-American culture. Something was indeed afoot when American colonists grew uncomfortable with the notion that Britain was their "mother country." John Adams would reflect back with perfect hindsight when he told his sons in 1799 that the "the source of the revolution" could be found in "a systematical dissolution of the true family authority."

This chapter begins by examining the revolution in conceptions of authority that corresponded with the crisis in the British empire and explores how various cultural forms (novels, newspapers, broadsides, and cartoons) were the transmitters of those new ideas. These materials expose the central questions of the Revolutionary era: who was capable of being a patriot and citizen, and who was included in (or excluded from) the promises of freedom and equality on which the nation was founded? And when independence had been secured, Americans turned their attention to creating the "imagined community" of a new nation with the cultural apparatus of a new modern nationalism.

❧ *A Family Drama: Patriarchy, Independence, and Colonial Rebellion* ❧

❧ FAMILY DRAMA

Since the seventeenth century, the idea that all authority, particularly the state's, rested on an analogy with family relationships was a prevailing axiom of England's political culture. King James I (r. 1603–1625) defended his divine right to rule, in part, by comparing a king to "Fathers of families; for a King is trewly *Parens patriae*, the politique father of his people." Not surprisingly, English clergymen interpreted the Fifth Commandment ("honor thy father and mother") as an obedience due all political leaders, especially the king. Robert Filmer gave this defense of the Crown's parental authority its definitive statement in his book *Patriarcha* (1680). "If we compare the natural duties of a Father with those of a King, we find them to be all one," wrote Filmer; "all the duties of a King are summed up in an universal fatherly care of his people."

For three-quarters of a century before the American Revolution, various cultural developments began to chip away at the ideal of children's dutiful obedience toward their parents. John Locke's ideas on education introduced the notion that children's minds begin as a blank slate and that their successful development depends on the example of affectionate parents. Coerced obedience, Locke maintained, only weakened a parent's authority. Locke's ideas profoundly influenced a host of British writers who produced moralistic and entertaining novels and advice books intimating that ideal families were no longer based on the unquestioned rule of a patriarch. Attitudes about families began to show signs of change.

The crisis provoked by Britain's demands for new taxes and restraints after 1763, and by the colonists' organized resistance to those measures, made the discourse of parental authority inescapable, as the colonists were repeatedly reminded that they owed a filial obedience to the "mother country." Ardent patriots offered a new critique of the family analogy as soon as they began to resist the empire. John Adams wrote in 1765: "We have been told . . . 'that Britain is the mother and we are the children, that a filial duty and submission is due from us to her.' . . . But admitting we are children, have not children a right to complain when their parents are attempting to break their limbs, to administer poison, or to sell them to the enemies for slaves?" This was part of the logic of colonial thinking: Britain was constraining the colonies' natural growth and maturation into adulthood, and the schemes of the king's ministers in Parliament represented a deep-laid plan to enslave the colonies.

The documents in this section expose how some American colonists experienced the conflict that led to their independence as a "family romance" (to borrow the phrase one historian applied to the French Revolution). We will examine what they read, thought, and wrote about parental authority at the time of their rebellion against the British empire. The documents also illustrate how categories of dependence (whether on the part of women, Indians, or slaves) rooted in other family metaphors shaped the rituals of resistance and the meaning of patriotism during the independence movement.

The Wonderful Life, and Surprising Adventures of That Renowned Hero, Robinson Crusoe (1774 and 1784)
DANIEL DEFOE

Knowing which books were popular with American readers in the 1770s can tell us much about the mindset of many colonists on the eve of the Revolution. Colonial readers consumed a heavy diet of novels and advice books that focused on the tenuous ties between parents and children. Daniel Defoe's Robinson Crusoe *was among these bestsellers. Although* Robinson Crusoe *was not a new book (it was first published in 1719), the first American edition was released in 1774 at the height of the crisis between Britain and the colonies. Defoe's novel remained popular with American readers throughout the Revolutionary era. The two American editions published during this time were abridged versions intended for young readers; the 1774 edition was just over a hundred pages, and the 1784 children's edition was only thirty-two pages. As such, Americans encountered a novel that placed even greater emphasis on the relationship between parents and children than had the original.* Robinson Crusoe *was essentially a parable of a prodigal son, yet Crusoe's story must have seemed to American readers remarkably like an allegory of their colonial experience. He leaves England in search of riches in the West African slave trade; he endures a period of captivity; he briefly owns a plantation in Brazil; and then he is shipwrecked and for twenty-eight years is marooned on an island somewhere off the North American coast, where he subdues a native population of "savages." The first selection contains Crusoe's description of his defiance of parental authority as it appeared in the popular American edition released two years before the Declaration of Independence; in the second selection, from the post-Revolutionary edition of 1784, we can see how the family drama of Crusoe's return had changed compared with the 1774 edition.*

PROBLEMS TO CONSIDER

1. How would you characterize the sentiments of child and parent depicted in these two versions of Defoe's novel? What are the consequences of rebelling against parental authority?
2. How would American readers think differently about this story than British readers? Why would a new ending become necessary after the Revolution?

I was born of a good family, in the city of York, where my father, who was a native of Bremen, had settled, after his having got a handsome estate, by merchandize. My heart began to be very early filled, with rambling thoughts, and though, when I grew up, my father often persuaded me, to settle to some business, and my mother used the tenderest entreaties, yet nothing could prevail upon me to lay aside my desire of going to sea; and I, at length, resolved to gratify my roving disposition, notwithstanding the extreme uneasiness, my father and mother always shewed, at the thoughts, of my leaving them. As if bent on my own destruction, I hardened my self against the prudent and kind advice, of the most indulgent parents; and I being one day at Hull, where I met one of my companions, who was going to sea, in his father's ship; he easily persuaded me to go with him. . . .

Had I now had the sense to return home, my father would have received me with much tenderness; but a weak and foolish shame, opposed all thoughts of it; I was afraid of being laughed at by the neighbours and should be ashamed to see, not only my father, but every body else. I had, without blushing, committed an action, which bore all the marks of folly; but was ashamed of returning, though that was the wisest step, I could have taken. I remained some time in doubt, what course to take; but having money in my pocket, I traveled to London by land.

On my arrival in that city, I happily fell into no bad company; but being well dressed, I contracted an acquaintance with the master of a ship, who had been on the coast of Guiney [*West Africa*], and having good success there, was resolved to go again; and he taking a fancy to me,

told me, if I would go the Voyage, with him, I should be at no expence; and if I would carry any thing with me, I should have the advantage of trading for myself. . . .

CRUSOE'S RETURN (1774 EDITION)

Thus I left the island, after being on it twenty-eight years.

On my arrival in England, I was as perfect a stranger as if I had never been known there; my faithful steward the widow, was become poor; my father and mother were dead; but I had two sisters, and two of the children, of one of my brothers were living. The merchant concerned in the ship I had saved, having heard the captain's story, invited me to an entertainment, and made me a present of nearly 200£. I then went to Lisbon, to see after my effects in the Brasils, and found the generous captain, who had been so much my friend, still alive, and he put me in a way of recovering the produce of my plantation. And a few months after, there arrived ships in the *[river]* Tagus, with effects for my use to the amount of 50,000£, besides 1000£ a year, which I expected to receive annually from my plantation.

The Wonderful Life, and Surprising Adventures of That Renowned Hero, Robinson Crusoe. . . (New York: Hugh Gaine, 1774), 5–6, 10–11, 110–11.

CRUSOE'S RETURN (1784 EDITION)

. . . Very fortunately an English merchant ship, homeward bound, . . . generously took us on board to Liverpool, from thence I went to York, but was greatly shocked at the news I received; my rambling disposition, I found, had bro't my dear father and mother to their graves; they both died soon after I left Hull.

I cannot express the agony it now causes in me; I consider myself entirely as the author of their deaths; and though property sufficient is left for me to live like a gentleman, I cannot have peace to enjoy it, and at this moment I re-ally believe myself the most miserable object living, and heartily I repent giving way to the restless disposition which made me leave my parents, as from that hour I date all the subsequent misfortunes of my life.

The Wonderful Life, and Surprising Adventures of That Renowned Hero, Robinson Crusoe . . . (Boston: N. Coveely, 1784), 30–32.

ఌ

A Speech to the Six Confederate Nations, Mohawks, Oneidas, Tuscaroras, Onondagas, Cayugas, Senecas, from the Twelve United Colonies, Convened in Council at Philadelphia (1775)

Once the imperial crisis had degenerated into the first armed battles at Lexington and Concord in April 1775, the Continental Congress met in Philadelphia to establish an American "continental army" and appointed George Washington its commander. The delegates were also deeply concerned about keeping the neighboring Indian nations neutral in the escalating rebellion. After nearly a century of devastating wars against the French and their Indian allies, colonists knew firsthand that any chance of resisting the mighty British military depended on Indian neutrality. So members of the Continental Congress drafted an address to the powerful league of Iroquois nations. They explained their conflict with Britain as a family quarrel. Such imagery was familiar to the Six Nations of the Iroquois, who had developed their own familial language as metaphors for political relationships. As far back as perhaps the fifteenth century, the Mohawks, Seneca, Onondagas, Cayugas, and Oneidas stopped fighting one another and joined in the Iroquois confederation. By the eighteenth century, they had successfully maintained a peace with the often warring French and English, and their Indian allies, through their shrewd diplomatic skills. The Iroquois knew that New France's governors persisted in calling them children while demanding for themselves the honorific of "father"; but the Iroquois refused to assent to that relationship with any European authorities. Instead, the Iroquois expressed relationships of dependence and obligation with the terms "uncle" and "nephew" and used "brother" to denote equals—a title they demanded from English governors. Unfortunately, the Revolutionary War shattered the peace that the Iroquois confederation had so diligently nurtured. The Mohawks and Cayugas sided with the British; the Tuscaroras and Oneidas allied themselves with the Americans; and several of the nations were torn between rival factions on opposite sides. As one historian recently noted, "For the Iroquois, the Revolution was a war in which, in some cases literally, brother killed brother."

PROBLEMS TO CONSIDER

1. Why did the Continental Congress represent the colonists' dispute with Britain to the Iroquois in family terms? Compare this speech with the language in *Robinson Crusoe*.
2. How did the colonists apply the metaphor of family to relations between themselves and the Indians? Did that analogy differ from the one they used for their relationship with the British empire?

Brothers, *Sachems, and Warriors!* We, the Delegates from the twelve United Provinces . . . now sitting in General Congress at Philadelphia, send this talk to you our Brothers. We are sixty-five in number, chosen and appointed by the people throughout all these Provinces and Colonies, to meet and sit together in one great Council, to consult together for the common good of the land, and speak and act for them. . . .

Brothers and Friends, now attend! When our fathers crossed the great water and came over to this land, the King of England gave them a talk, assuring them that they and their children should be his children, and that if they would leave their native country and make settlements, and live here, and buy and sell, and trade with their brethren beyond the water, they should still keep hold of the same covenant chain and enjoy peace; and it was covenanted, that the fields, houses, goods and possessions which our fathers should acquire, should remain to them as their own, and be their children's forever, and at their sole disposal.

Trusting that this covenant should never be broken, our fathers came a great distance beyond the great water, laid out their money here, built houses, cleared fields, raised crops, and through their own labor and industry grew tall and strong. . . .

Brothers and Friends, open a kind ear! We will now tell you of the quarrel betwixt the Counselors of King George and the inhabitants and Colonies of America.

Many of his Counsellors are proud and wicked men. They persuade the King to break the covenant chain, and not to send us any more good Talks. . . .

If we submit, or comply with their demands, you can easily perceive to what state we will be reduced. If our people labor on the field, they will not know who shall enjoy the crop. If they hunt in the woods, it will be uncertain who shall taste of the meat, or have the skins. If they build houses, they will not know whether they may sit round the fire, with their wives and children. They cannot be sure whether they shall be permitted to eat, drink, and wear the fruits of their own labor and industry. . . .

Brothers, thus stands the matter betwixt old England and America. You Indians know how things are proportioned in a family—between the father and the son—the child carries a little pack. England we regard as the father; this island may be compared to the son.

The father has a numerous family—both at home and upon this island. He appoints a great number of servants to assist him in the government of his family. In process of time, some of his servants grow proud and ill-natured; they were displeased to see the boy so alert and walk so nimbly with his pack. They tell the father, and advise him to enlarge the child's pack; they prevail; the pack is increased; the child takes it up again—as he thought it might be the father's pleasure—speaks but few words—those very small—for he was loth to offend the father.

Those proud and wicked servants, finding they had prevailed, laughed to see the boy sweat and stagger under his increased load. By and by, they apply to the father to double the boy's pack, because they heard him complain; and without any reason, said they, he is a cross child; correct him if he complains any more. The boy entreats the father; addresses the great servants in a decent manner, that the pack might be lightened; . . . after all the tears and entreaties of the child, the pack is redoubled; the child stands a little while staggering under the weight, ready to fall every moment. . . . The child concludes the father could not hear; those proud servants had intercepted his supplications, or stopped the ears of the father. He therefore gives one struggle and throws off the pack, and says he cannot take it up again; such a weight would crush him down and kill him, and he can but die if he refuses.

Upon this, those servants are very wroth; and tell the father many false stories respecting the child; they bring a great cudgel to the father, asking him to take it in his hand and strike the child.

This may serve to illustrate the present condition of the King's American subjects or children. . . .

Brothers and Friends! We desire you will hear and receive what we have now told you, and that you will open a good ear and listen to what we are now going to say. This is a family quarrel between us and Old England. You Indians are not concerned in it. We don't wish you to take up the hatchet against the King's Troops. We desire you to remain at home, and not join on either side, but keep the hatchet buried deep. In the name and behalf of all our people, we ask and desire you . . . to love and sympathize with us in our troubles; that the path may be kept open with all our people and yours, to pass and repass, without molestation.

"A Speech to the Six Confederate Nations, Mohawks, Oneidas, Tuscaroras, Onondagas, Cayugas, Senecas, from the Twelve United Colonies, Convened in Council at Philadelphia (1775)," in *American Archives*, 4th ser., vol. 2, edited by Peter Force (Washington, D.C.: M. St. Clair Clarke and Peter Force, 1837–1853), 1880–82.

᧍

Common Sense (1776)

THOMAS PAINE

The tipping point in the movement for colonial independence was the publication of Thomas Paine's Common Sense *in January 1776. Although Paine had resided in America for little more than a year, still he captured the spirit of the colonists' growing discontent in his incendiary attack on monarchy and his impassioned call for independence from the British Crown.* Common Sense *was an overnight sensation. In its first three months of publication, 120,000 copies were sold (which would be more than 10 million in today's U.S. population). And those who purchased Paine's pamphlet represented only a fraction of the audience it reached, since colonists read it aloud in coffeehouses, taverns, and homes. The response throughout the American colonies was electric. George Washington reported that in Virginia* Common Sense *was "working a powerful change there in the minds of many men." And a writer in the* Connecticut Gazette *waxed rhapsodic over Paine's influence: "We were blind, but on reading these enlightening works the scales have fallen from our eyes. . . . The doctrine of Independence hath been in times past, greatly disgustful . . . it is now become our delightful theme."* Common Sense's *remarkable popular appeal can be attributed in part to Paine's decision to confront directly, in language accessible to nearly all classes, the family analogy that served as the foundation of Britain's authority over the colonies.*

PROBLEMS TO CONSIDER

1. What was Paine's most persuasive argument against the analogy of parent and child for Britain and the colonies? Did his argument endorse an ideal family relationship?
2. Why did Paine's pamphlet make so much "common sense" to American colonists on the eve of independence? How did his presentation enhance the message's appeal?

In the following pages I offer nothing more than simple facts, plain arguments, and common sense. . . .

Volumes have been written on the subject of the struggle between England and America. Men of all ranks have embarked in the controversy, from different motives, and with various designs; but all have been ineffectual, and the period of debate is closed. Arms as the last resource decide the contest; the appeal was the choice of the King, and the continent has accepted the challenge. . . .

The Sun never shined on a cause of greater worth. 'Tis not the affair of a City, a County, a Province, or a Kingdom; but of a Continent—of at least one eighth part of the habitable Globe. 'Tis not the concern of a day, a year, or an age; posterity are virtually involved in the contest, and will be more or less affected even to the end of time by the proceedings now. Now is the seed time of continental union, faith and honor. . . .

I have heard it asserted by some, that as America hath flourished under her former connection with Great Britain, that the same connection is necessary towards her future happiness and will always have the same effect—Nothing can be more fallacious than this kind of argument:—we may as well assert that because a child hath thrived upon milk, that it is never to have meat, or that the first twenty years of our lives is to become a precedent for the next twenty. But even this is admitting more than is true, for I answer, roundly, that America would have flourished as much, and probably much more, had no European power taken any notice of her. The commerce by which she hath enriched herself are the necessaries of life, and will always have a market while eating is the custom of Europe. . . .

But Britain is the parent country say some. Then the more shame upon her conduct. Even brutes do not devour their young, nor savages make war upon their families; wherefore the assertion, if true, turns to her reproach; but it happens not to be true, or only partly so, and the phrase, *parent* or *mother country*, hath been jesuitically adopted by the King and his parasites, with a low papistical design of gaining an unfair bias on the credulous weakness of our minds. Europe and not England is the parent country of America. This new world hath been the asylum for the persecuted lovers of civil and religious liberty from *every part* of Europe. Hither have they fled, not from the tender embraces of the mother, but from the cruelty of the monster; and it is so far true of England, that the same tyranny which drove the first emigrants from home, pursues their descendants still.

. . . And by a just parity of reasoning, all Europeans meeting in America, or any other corner of the Globe, are *countrymen*. . . . Not one third of the inhabitants, even of this province *[Pennsylvania]*, are of English descent. Wherefore, I reprobate the phrase of parent or mother country applied to England only, as being false, selfish, narrow and ungenerous. . . .

Men of passive tempers look somewhat lightly over the offences of Britain, and still hoping for the best, are apt to call out, *Come, come, we shall be friends again, for all this*. But examine the passions and feelings of mankind: Bring the doctrine of reconciliation to the touchstone of nature, and then tell me, whether you can here-after love, honour, and faithfully serve the power that hath carried fire and sword into your land? If you cannot do all these, then are you only de-ceiving yourselves, and by your delay bringing ruin upon posterity. Your future connection with Britain whom you can neither love nor honor, will be forced and unnatural, and being formed only on the plan of present convenience, will in a little time, fall into a relapse more wretched than the first. . . .

No man was a warmer wisher for reconcilia-tion than myself, before the fatal 19th of April 1775, but the moment the event of that day was made known I rejected the hardened, sullen tempered Pharaoh of England for ever; and dis-dain the wretch, that with the pretended title of FATHER OF HIS PEOPLE can unfeelingly hear of their slaughter, and composedly sleep with their blood upon his soul. . . .

But where, say some, is the King of America? I'll tell you Friend, he reigns above; and doth not make havoc of mankind like the Royal Brute of Great Britain. Yet that we may not appear to be defective even in earthly honours, let a day be solemnly set apart for proclaiming the Charter; let it be brought forth placed on the divine law, the word of God; let a crown be placed thereon, by which the world may know, that so far as we approve of monarchy, that in America THE LAW IS KING. For as in absolute governments the King is law, so in free countries the law *ought* to be King and there ought to be no other.

[Thomas Paine], *Common Sense: Addressed to the Inhabitants of America* . . . (Philadelphia: Edes & Gill, 1776), 17–22, 26–27, 32.

ꜱ

ꜱ PATRIOTISM: RITES (AND RIGHTS) OF RESISTANCE

The political event that more than any other first pushed some colonists to chal-lenge the analogy of parental authority was the passage of the Stamp Act in 1765. Great numbers of colonists interpreted this "taxation without representation" as a betrayal of the affectionate bonds that parents should naturally display toward their children. The Stamp Act also marked the beginning of the colonists' collective resistance against these hated measures. Many different social groups joined the dispute: laboring men and women rioted in the streets, destroying property and burning in effigy hated agents of the Crown; working men ordinarily excluded from political leadership joined the Sons of Liberty or committees of safety and corre-spondence; and men of letters engaged in a transatlantic debate over the meaning of representation, natural rights, and liberty. Crowds played a pivotal part in the colonists' successful undermining of British authority. In the process, colonists developed a set of rituals of collective behavior. Some of these actions, such as the notorious Boston "tea party," adapted traditions of festivals and crowds that had been prevalent throughout early modern Europe to the new American realities.

Contemporaries remembered the merriment exhibited as protesters engaged in a carnival-like mockery of making a big cup of tea in Boston Harbor. As with Euro-pean rituals of misrule, the participants donned disguises to protect themselves from detection and to displace responsibility for the destruction onto an unknown group of outsiders. But unlike riots in Europe, in which men usually avoided detection by disguising themselves as women, Boston's rioters donned the disguise and persona of Indians. These types of ritualized behavior, along with the symbolic language used in text and visual images (known as *iconography*), are what cultural historians seek to interpret as they explain the meanings that the American Revolution had for its contemporary participants.

Ideologies of gender and concepts of dependence again shaped the actions and symbolic language of the colonists' resistance, just as they had in their disputes over the family analogy of their relationship to the Crown. Because the colonists chose to represent themselves as Indians, slaves, or women in both passive and active ways, and because the actual acts of resisting the British empire depended on groups (such as women) usually excluded from political action, the gender, family, and racial language of colonial resistance touched on both the rites and the rights of patriotism in that society. Who was capable of the acts of a citizen at the very moment when subjects were being transformed into citizens?

Celebrating the Repeal of the Stamp Act (1766)

A View of the Obelisk Erected . . . for the Repeal of the —— Stamp Act (1766)
PAUL REVERE

The Able Doctor, or America Swallowing the Bitter Draught (1774)
PAUL REVERE

In May 1766, residents of Boston took to the city's streets and public spaces for a daylong celebration of the news that the Stamp Act had been repealed. The following account from the Boston Gazette *offers a glimpse at some of the public behavior of crowds during the Revolution. Of course, as a celebration rather than a protest, missing were the effigy burnings and violence that also characterized colonial mobs. A key part of Boston's repeal celebration was a giant obelisk erected by the Sons of Liberty, with four brightly lighted panels depicting the meaning of the event in both verse and illustrations. Within weeks, Paul Revere published an engraving that reproduced the images on this four-sided "pyramid." Revere's engraving displayed some of the symbolism that Americans commonly used to represent liberty and its enemies. An image of a Native American is meant to represent America, sitting under a liberty tree; Liberty is depicted as a woman, carrying a liberty pole and cap. The drawing also includes a devil (carrying the Stamp Act); two of the king's ministers, with iron chains and shackles slung over their shoulders; and a Catholic monk. Finally, another famous Revere engraving,* The Able Doctor, *was prompted by the Tea Act, which ultimately provoked further colonial resistance, including the famous Boston Tea Party.*

PROBLEMS TO CONSIDER

1. In what ways did Bostonians' celebration advance their political demands and contribute to their sense of common purpose?
2. Interpret the story depicted in the panel of the obelisk: What is the significance of representing Liberty as a woman, and America as an Indian? What similarities and differences do you see between Revere's *Able Doctor* engraving and the obelisk drawing?

CELEBRATING THE REPEAL OF THE STAMP ACT

Friday . . . [a week ago] to the inexpressible Joy of all, were received by Capt Coffin, the important News of the Repeal of the Stamp Act which was signed by His Majesty the 18th March last; upon which the Bells in the Town were set a ringing, the Ships in the Harbour display'd their Colours, Guns were discharged in different Parts of the Town, and in the evening were several Bonfires. According to a previous Vote of the Town the Selectmen met in the Afternoon at Faneuil Hall, and appointed Monday last for a Day of General Rejoicings on that happy Occasion. The Morning was ushered in with Musick, Ringing of Bells, and the Discharge of Cannon, the Ships in the Harbour and many of the Houses in Town being adorned with Colours—Joy smil'd in every Countenance, Benevolence, Gratitude and Content seemed the Companions of all. By the Generosity of some Gentlemen remarkable for their Humanity and Patriotism, our Goal *[jail]* was freed of Debtors.—At One o'clock, the Castle and Batteries, and Train of Artillery fired a Royal Salute; and the Afternoon was spent in Mirth and Jollity.—In the Evening the whole Town was beautifully illuminated:—On the Common the Sons of Liberty erected a magnificent Pyramid, illuminated with 280 Lamps: The four upper Stories of which were ornamented with the Figures of their Majesties, and fourteen of the worthy Patriots who have distinguished themselves by their Love of Liberty. The following Lines were on the four Sides of the next Apartment, which referred to the Emblematical Figures on the lower Story, the whole supported by a large Base of the Doric Order,

O thou whom next to Heav'n we most revere,
Fair LIBERTY! thou lovely Goddess hear!
Have we not woo'd thee, won thee, held thee long,
Lain in thy Lap and melted on thy Tongue:
Tho' Deaths and Dangers rugged Paths persu'd,
And led thee smiling to this SOLITUDE:
Hid thee within our Hearts most golden Cell,
And brav'd the Powers of Earth and Powers of Hell.
GODDESS! we cannot part, thou must not fly,
Be SLAVES; we dare to scorn it—dare to die. . . .
    Boast, foul Oppression, boast thy transient Reign,
While honest FREEDOM struggles with her Chain;
But know the Sons of Virtue, hardy, brave,
Disdain to lose thro' mean Despair to save:
Arrouz'd in Thunder, awful they appear,
With proud Deliverance stalking in their Rear:
While Tyrant Foes their pallid Fears betray,
Shrink from their Arms, and give their Vengeance way;
See in th' unequal War OPPRESSORS fall,
The Hate, Contempt, and endless Curse of all.
    Our FAITH approv'd, our LIBERTY restor'd,
Our Hearts bend grateful to our sov'r'gn Lord;
Hail darling Monarch! by this act endear'd,

Our firm Affections are thy best Reward;
Should Britains self, against herself divide,
And hostile Armies frown on either Side;
Should Hosts rebellions, shake our Brunswick's
    Throne,
And as they dar'd thy Parent, dare the Son;

To this Asylum stretch thine happy Wing,
And we'll contend, who best shall love our
    KING.

————

Boston Gazette, May 26, 1766.

Paul Revere, *A View of the Obelisk Erected . . . for the Repeal of the —— Stamp Act* (1766).
(Courtesy American Antiquarian Society.)

Boston cannonaded.

Boston Port Bill

BOSTON Petition

The able Doctor, or America Swallowing the Bitter Draught.

Paul Revere, *The Able Doctor, or America Swallowing the Bitter Draught* (1774).
(Hulton Archive/Getty Images.)

The Female Patriots (1768)

HANNAH GRIFFITTS

The Female Patriot, No. 1. Addressed to the Tea-Drinking Ladies of New-York (1770)

Women in the colonies had much greater involvement in acts of collective resistance than their symbolic representation as Liberty would imply. As was common in early modern crowds, women often joined men in bread riots or uprisings against impressment (kidnapping men to serve in the British navy), which threatened their families and neighborhoods. These types of riots continued as part of the American rebellion. In addition, as the colonists devised a strategy of economic pressure against the British empire by refusing to import or consume various luxury items subject to British taxes (British-made textiles, silverware, china, and especially tea), colonial women assumed even greater importance in the resistance movement. Unfortunately, increasing calls for women's patriotic activism ran square into gendered assumptions about the male-exclusive nature of public politics. After all, colonists were exhorting one another to exercise virtue—*the self-sacrifice for the public good that defined true patriotism. Yet virtue carried with it the presumption that this was an exclusively male ability; the word "virtue" even derives from the Latin word for "man." The following documents reveal two conflicting perspectives (in verse) on women's patriotism during the resistance movement; the first was written by a young Philadelphia woman, and the second was anonymously published on a broadside (poster) in New York City.*

PROBLEMS TO CONSIDER

1. When women became active patriots, how might their actions have reinforced or destabilized family analogies of political authority?
2. How would you explain the simultaneous existence of these two different perspectives on women's public service?

THE FEMALE PATRIOTS

Since the Men from a Party, or fear of a Frown,
Are kept by a Sugar-Plumb, quietly down.
Supinely asleep, & depriv'd of their Sight
Are strip'd of their Freedom, & rob'd of their
    Right.
If the Sons (so degenerate) the Blessing despise,
Let the Daughters of Liberty, nobly arise,
And tho' we've no Voice, but a negative here.
The use of the Taxables, let us forebear,
(Then Merchants import till your Stores are
    all full
May the Buyers be few & your Traffick be dull.)
Stand firmly resolved & bid Grenville to see
That rather than Freedom, we'll part with
    our Tea
And well as we love the dear Draught when
    a dry,
As American Patriots,—our Taste we deny,
Sylvania's, gay Meadows, can richly afford,
To pamper our Fancy, or furnish our Board,
And Paper sufficient (at home) still we have,
To assure the Wise-acre, we will not sign Slave.
When this Homespun shall fail, to remonstrate
    our Grief
We can speak with the Tongue or scratch on
    a Leaf.

Refuse all their Colours, tho richest of Dye,
The juice of a Berry—our Paint can supply,
To humour our Fancy—& as for our Houses,
They'll do without painting as well as our
    Spouses,
While to keep out the Cold of a keen winter
    Morn
We can screen the Northwest, with a well
    polish'd Horn,
And trust me a Woman by honest Invention
Might give this State Doctor a Dose of
    Prevention.
Join mutual in this, & but small as it seems
We may Jostle a Grenville & puzzle his
    Schemes
But a motive more worthy our patriot Pen,
Thus acting—we point out their Duty to Men,
And should the bound Pensioners, tell us to
    hush
We can throw back the Satire by biding them
    blush.

Hannah Griffitts, "The Female Patriots: Addressed to the Daughters of Liberty in America, by the Same, 1768," in *Milcah Martha Moore's Book: A Commonplace Book from Revolutionary America*, edited by Catherine La Courreye Blecki and Karin A. Wulf (University Park: Pennsylvania State University Press, 1997), 172–73.

THE FEMALE PATRIOT, NO. I.
ADDRESSED TO THE TEA-DRINKING
LADIES OF NEW-YORK

When ADAM first fell into SATAN's Snare,
And forfeited his Bliss to please the Fair;
God from his Garden drove the sinful Man,
And thus the Source of human Woes began.
'Twas weak in ADAM, for to please his Wife,
To lose his access to the Tree of Life:
His dear bought Knowledge all his Sons
    deplore,
DEATH their inheritance, and SIN their Store.
But why blame ADAM, since his Brainless Race
Will lose their ALL to obtain a beautious FACE;
And will their Honour, Pride, and Wealth lay
    down,
Rather than see a lovely Woman frown.
The Ladies are not quite so complisant,
If they want TEA, they'll storm and rave and rant,
And call their Lordly Husbands Ass and
    Clown,
The jest of Fools and Sport of all the Town.
A pleasant Story lately I heard told
Of MADAM HORNBLOOM, a noted Scold,
Last Day her Husband said, "My dearest Life,
My Kind, my Fair, my Angel of a Wife;
Just now, from LONDON, there's a Ship come in
Brings noble News will raise us Merchants
    Fame,

The Fruits of our non-importation Scheme.
The Parliament, dear Saint, may they be blest
Have great part of our Grievances redrest:"
"Have they indeed," replies the frowning
    Dame,
"Say, is there not some Tea and China come."
"Why no! We can't import that Indian Weed,
That Duty's still a Rod above our Head."
"Curse on your Heads, you nasty fumbling
    Crew,
Then round his Shoulders the hard Broom-
    Stick flew,
Go, dirty CLOD-POLE! get me some Shushong
    [tea],
This Evening I've invited MADAM STRONG.
—Silence—you BLOCKHEAD—hear, the Lady
    knocks!
Get to your Cock-Loft or expect some
    Strokes."
—"Your Servant Madam, Tea is on the Board
I really tho't you once had broke your Word."
"I ask your Pardon, dear MISS HORNBLOOM,
My sprailing Brats kept me so long at Home;
My stupid Husband too has gone astray
To wait upon the SONS of LIBERTY."

"The Female Patriot, No. 1. Addressed to the Tea-Drinking
Ladies of New-York" [Broadside] (New York, 1770).
☙

❧ Liberty's Key: Competing Visions of Freedom and Equality ❧

The movement for colonial independence ushered in an even more significant revolution. Americans went from defending an idea of British liberty ("the rights of
free-born Englishmen") to championing a language that asserted the universal
rights of humanity. Just months after colonists were reading aloud Paine's *Common
Sense* in coffeehouses, they were proclaiming the Declaration of Independence from
the steps of their statehouses, declaring it to be self-evident that "all men are created
equal; that they are endowed by their Creator with certain unalienable rights; that
among these are life, liberty, and the pursuit of happiness." Both freedom and
equality were embedded in this statement, and herein lies the revolution. The old

political culture that expressed authority through a patriarchal family metaphor required hierarchy and inequality—children could not be considered equals with parents any more than could subjects with kings. So when Americans challenged that analogy and fought a war on behalf of liberty, they opened the door for joining those two revolutionary ideas of freedom and equality. Together they became the standard for measuring the nation's fidelity to its ideals. As one leading historian has observed, "Freedom helps bind our culture together and exposes the contradictions between what America claims to be and what it actually is."

Nothing better illustrates the contradictory nature of freedom during the era of the American Revolution than the existence of slavery. The two words most frequently uttered during the Revolution were "liberty" and "slavery." Today we might see it as blatant hypocrisy for the loudest advocates of freedom to be slaveholders. Even some Revolutionary-era Americans (black and white) agreed with the words of one clergyman that this was "gross, barefaced, practiced inconsistence!" Nevertheless, slavery gave shape to the way white Americans understood freedom in a republic, because slavery offered the mirrored opposite that defined freedom. We need to keep in mind that liberty was commonly invoked from two different perspectives—either as the power to participate in public affairs or as the set of rights that needed to be protected from governmental interference. Thus, while slavery constrained the freedom and basic human rights of black Africans, it also was a property right that white slaveholders wished to be free to exercise without interference or constraint.

It is still a common myth that the Revolutionary generation was simply not familiar with the notions of economic, gender, or racial equality that are available to us today, and hence they should not be held accountable for falling short of the ideals they enshrined in the Declaration of Independence. The documents in this section demonstrate that many voices in this era, especially among those excluded from the privileges and rights of the new republic, did equate freedom and equality. Slaves, white women, and laborers on many occasions asked for or even demanded inclusion in the far-reaching promises of freedom and equality by which the Revolution was defined. And in listening to their voices, we are reminded that race, gender, and class have been the most common boundaries limiting the fulfillment of freedom and equality in the American republic.

Freedom Petitions by African Americans in Massachusetts (1773 and 1777)

Essay on Slavery (1774)
CAESAR SARTER

African American slaves did not sit by passively while the white population around them clamored for liberty. The American Revolution was the first significant self-emancipation movement in American history, not to be matched again until slaves began to run off and free themselves by joining the Union Army during the Civil War. Ironically, during the Revolutionary War most slaves saw their best hope for freedom on the side of the British. It all began in 1775, when the royal governor of Virginia, Lord Dunmore, issued a proclamation promising freedom to any slave who escaped from his master and joined the British troops. Tens of thousands of slaves in the South braved the danger of vengeful masters and fled to the British during the war. News of these events made their way to northern cities, too, where sizable slave communities emerged from the colonists' involvement in the Atlantic slave trade. Slaves in the North made their appeals by petitioning legislatures for their emancipation or by publishing antislavery essays in newspapers. The following two petitions to the Massachusetts General Court — one submitted before independence was declared, and the other after the war had begun — reveal the difficult balance that slaves achieved in pleading for their rights, while hoping not to offend white lawmakers. Also reproduced here is an antislavery appeal penned by a former slave for a New England newspaper in August 1774, just months before the crisis with Britain led to war. The arguments of antislavery advocates had some success during the Revolutionary era, as every northern state passed acts of gradual abolition, although it took nearly a generation for all northern slaves to be freed.

PROBLEMS TO CONSIDER

1. On what grounds did African Americans challenge their enslavement during the American Revolution?
2. What strategies did African Americans use in phrasing their demands for freedom to avoid alienating white Americans?

FREEDOM PETITIONS

Boston, April 20, 1773

Sir, The efforts made by the legislative of this province in their last sessions to free themselves from slavery, gave us, who are in that deplorable state, a high degree of satisfaction. We expect great things from men who have made such a noble stand against the designs of their *fellowmen* to enslave them. . . . The divine spirit of *freedom*, seems to fire every human breast on this continent, except such as are bribed to assist in executing the execrable plan.

We are very sensible that it would be highly detrimental to our present masters, if we were allowed to demand all that of *right* belongs to us for past services; this we disclaim. . . . We do not pretend to dictate to you Sir, or to the Honourable Assembly, of which you are a member.

We acknowledge our obligations to you for what you have already done, but as the people of this province seem to be actuated by the principles of equity and justice, we cannot but expect your house will again take our deplorable case into serious consideration, and give us that ample relief which, *as men*, we have a natural right to.

But since the wise and righteous governor of the universe, has permitted our fellow men to make us slaves, we bow in submission to him, and determine to behave in such a manner as that we may have reason to expect the divine approbation of, and assistance in, our peaceable and lawful attempts to gain our freedom.

A Documentary History of the Negro People in the United States, vol. 1, edited by Herbert Aptheker (New York: Citadel Press, 1951), 7–8.

1777

To the Honorable Counsel & House of [Representa]tives for the State of Massachusitte Bay in General Court assembled, January 13, 1777

The petition of A Great Number of Blackes detained in a State of slavery in the Bowels of a free and Christian Country Humbly sheweth that your Petitioners apprehend that they have in Common with all other men a Natural and Unali[en]able Right to that freedom which the Great Parent of the Unavers *[universe]* hath Bestowed equalley on all mankind and which they have Never forfeited by any Compact or agreement whatever—but they were Unjustly Dragged by the hand of cruel Power from their Dearest friends and some of them Even torn from the Embraces of their tender Parents—from A populous Pleasant and plentiful country and in violation of Laws of Nature and of Nations and in defiance of all the tender feelings of humanity Brought here Either to Be sold Like Beast of Burthen & Like them Condemnd to Slavery for Life—Among A People Profesing the mild Religion of Jesus A people Not Insensible of the Secrets of Rational Being Nor without spirit to Resent the unjust endeavours of others to Reduce them to a state of Bondage and Subjection your honour Need not to be informed that A Life of Slavery Like that of your petitioners Deprived of Every social privilege of Every thing Requisite to Render Life Tol[er]able is far worse than Nonexistance.

[In imit]ation of the Lawdable Example of the Good People of these States your petitioners have Long and Patiently waited the Event of petition after petition. . . . They Cannot but express their Astonishment that It has Never Been Considered that Every Principle from which Amarica has Acted in the Course of their unhappy Dificultes with Great Briton Pleads Stronger than A thousand arguments in favors of your petitioners they therfor humble Beseech your honours to give this petition its due weight & consideration and cause an act of the Legislatur to be past Wherby they may Be Restored to the Enjoyments of that which is the Naturel Right of all men. . . . May the Inhabitance of these States No longer chargeable with the inconsistancey of acting themselves the part which they condem and oppose in others Be prospered in their present Glorious struggle for Liberty and have those Blessing to them, &c.

"Negro Petitions for Freedom," *Collections of the Massachusetts Historical Society*, 5th ser., 3 (1877): 436–37.

ESSAY ON SLAVERY

As this is a time of great anxiety and distress among you, on account of the infringement not only of your Charter rights; but of the natural rights and privileges of freeborn men; permit a poor, though freeborn, African, who in his youth, was trepanned *[ensnared]* into Slavery, and who has born the galling yoke of bondage for more than twenty years; though at last, by the blessing of God, has shaken it off, to tell you, and that from experience, that as Slavery is the greatest, and consequently most to be dreaded, of all temporal calamities; so its opposite, Liberty, is the greatest temporal good, with which you can be blest. The importance of which, you clearly evince to the world you are sensible of, by your manly and resolute struggles to preserve it. . . . Now, if you are sensible, that slavery is in itself, and in its consequences, a great evil; why will you not pity and relieve the poor, distressed, enslaved Africans?—Who, though they are entitled to the same natural rights of mankind that you are, are, nevertheless groaning in bondage! . . . I shall not pretend a refutation of the arguments, generally brought in support of it; but request you, to let that excellent rule given by our Saviour, to do to others, as you would, that they should do to you, have its due weight with you. . . . . Suppose that you were trepanned away.—The husband from the dear wife of his bosom—the wife from her affectionate husband—children from their fond parents. . . . Suppose, I say, that you were thus ravished from such a blissful situation, and plunged into miserable slavery, in a distant quarter of the globe. . . . Now, are you willing all this should befall you? . . .

. . . Would you desire the preservation of your own liberty? As the first step let the oppressed Africans be liberated; then, and not till then, may you with confidence and consistency of conduct, look to Heaven for a blessing on your endeavours to knock the shackles with which your task masters are hampering you, from your own feet. On the other hand, if you are still determined to harden your hearts, and turn a deaf ear to our complaints, and the calls of God, in your present Calamities; Only be pleased to recollect the miserable end of Pharaoh, in Consequence of his refusal to set those at Liberty, whom he had unjustly reduced to cruel servitude. . . . I need not point out the absurdity of your exertions for liberty, while you have slaves in your houses. . . .

_____

The Essex Journal and Merrimack Packet, August 17, 1774.

∾

Salutatory Oration at the Young Ladies' Academy of Philadelphia (1794)

PRISCILLA MASON

To ensure that their revolution succeeded, many Americans were convinced that they needed not only to replace a monarchy with a republic but also to educate citizens in the principles of civic virtue—self-sacrifice of one's personal interests for the public good. Leading republican thinkers of the era, including Thomas Jefferson and Benjamin Franklin, devoted considerable energy to devising plans for the universal education of the American people. For many, this goal was too important to be left to the government alone. It required instead the help of the nation's mothers, who would teach the next generation of citizens. Education reformers endorsed a number of plans to improve the education of young white women. These plans, however, ran in the face of centuries of assumptions about the different capacities of the sexes. As Abigail Adams reminded her husband in 1778: "You need not be told how much female Education is neglected, nor how fashionable it has been to ridicule Female learning."

Reformers set out to revise a tradition of female education focused on preparing women with the skills and graces—fashion, music, and needlework—appropriate for marriage. In 1787, Dr. Benjamin Rush, a physician and a signer of the Declaration of Independence, proposed a model curriculum for a female academy, in which girls would be taught subjects that had been previously reserved for men, such as rhetoric, geography, advanced mathematics, and natural philosophy. The Young Ladies' Academy of Philadelphia was founded to perpetuate Rush's ideas. Rush did not advocate women's education in order to advance the independence or equality of women. His concern was for the young male citizens these women would be instructing "in the principles of liberty and government." Still, during the era of the American Revolution, several prophetic women raised their voices for women's equality, including Priscilla Mason, who in 1794 delivered the salutatory oration at the Young Ladies Academy, which Rush had helped found seven years earlier.

PROBLEMS TO CONSIDER

1. What did independence mean to this young woman orator in the wake of the American Revolution?
2. On what grounds did she assert women's equality with men? What are the limitations of her conception of women's freedom in this era?

Venerable Trustees of this Seminary, Patrons of the improvement of the female mind; suffer us to present the first fruits of your labors as an offering to you, and cordially to salute you on this auspicious day. . . .

A female, young and inexperienced, addressing a promiscuous [*i.e., both men and women present*] assembly, is a novelty which requires an apology, as some may suppose. I therefore, with submission, beg leave to offer a few thoughts in vindication of female eloquence.

. . . I claim for [women] the further right of being heard on more public occasions—of addressing the reason as well as the fears of the other sex.

Our right to instruct and persuade cannot be disputed, if it shall appear, that we possess the talents of the orator—and have opportunities for the exercise of those talents. Is a power of speech, and volubility of expression, one of the talents of the orator? Our sex possess it in an eminent degree.

Do personal attractions give charms to eloquence, and force to the orator's arguments? There is some truth mixed with the flattery we receive on this head. Do tender passions enable the orator to speak in a moving and forcible manner? This talent of the orator is confessedly ours. In all these respects the female orator stands on equal,—nay, on *superior* ground.

If therefore she should fail in the capacity for mathematical studies, or metaphysical profundities, she has, on the whole, equal pretensions to the palm of eloquence. . . . But seldom does it happen, that the abstruse sciences, become the subject of eloquence. And, as to that knowledge which is popular and practical,— that knowledge which alone is useful to the

orator; who will say that the female mind is incapable?

Our high and mighty Lords (thanks to their arbitrary constitutions) have denied us the means of knowledge, and then reproached us for the want of it. Being the stronger party, they early seized the sceptre and the sword; with these they gave laws to society; they denied women the advantage of a liberal education; forbid them to exercise their talents on those great occasions, which would serve to improve them. They doom'd the sex to servile or frivolous employments, on purpose to degrade their minds, that they themselves might hold unrivall'd, the power and pre-eminence they had usurped. Happily, a more liberal way of thinking begins to prevail. The sources of knowledge are gradually opening to our sex. . . .

But supposing now that we possess'd all the talents of the orator, in the highest perfection; where shall we find a theatre for the display of them? The Church, the Bar, and the Senate are shut against us. Who shut them? *Man*; despotic man, first made us incapable of the duty, and then forbid us the exercise. Let us by suitable education, qualify ourselves for those high departments—they will open before us. . . .

With respect to the bar, citizens of either sex, have an undoubted right to plead their own cause there. Instances could be given of females being admitted to plead the cause of a friend, a husband, a son; and they have done it with energy and effect. . . . In regard to the senate, prescription is clearly in our favour. We have one or two cases exactly in point.

Heliogabalus [*Marcus Aurelius Antoninus*], the Roman Emperor; of blessed memory, made his grand-mother a Senator of Rome. He also established a senate of women; appointed his mother President; and committed to them the important business of regulating dress and fashions. And truly methinks the dress of our own country, at this day, would admit of some regulation, for it is subject to no rules at all—It would be worthy the wisdom of Congress, to consider whether a similar institution, established at the seat of our Federal Government, would not be a public benefit. We cannot be independent, while we receive our fashions from other countries; nor act properly, while we imitate the manners of governments not congenial to our own. Such a Senate, composed of women most noted for wisdom, learning and taste, delegated from every part of the Union, would give dignity, and independence to our manners; uniformity, and even authority to our fashions.

It would fire the female breast with the most generous ambition, prompting to illustrious actions. It would furnish the most noble Theatre for the display, the exercise and improvement of every faculty. It would call forth all that is human—all that is *divine* in the soul of woman; and having proved them equally capable with the other sex, would lead to their equal participation of honor and office.

The Rise and Progress of the Young-Ladies' Academy of Philadelphia... (Philadelphia: Stewart and Cochran, 1794), 90–95.

The Key of Liberty (1797)
WILLIAM MANNING

Ordinary laboring men played a central role in the American Revolution. For all their importance in crowds, committees, and militias, farmers and laborers left us few written records that document their understanding of the meaning of the Revolution's ideas of freedom and equality. One of those rare documents is a lengthy essay by a self-educated Massachusetts farmer named William Manning, who signed himself "a Laborer" and entitled his work "The Key of Liberty." Manning's essay was a rational and yet impassioned example of egalitarian and democratic thought in the age of the American Revolution. Manning wrote the essay in response to the threat he perceived from the Federalists in power in the 1790s, but he was influenced by his participation in the rural uprisings of debtor farmers (Shays's Rebellion) a decade before. At the heart of Manning's philosophy was the belief that politics in the young American republic was the product of "the unreasonable desires of the Few to tyrannize over and enslave the Many." Manning's voice leads us to question those who view the Revolution as the unquestioned triumph of liberal capitalist values. He did not see this new democracy as a sanction for individual economic self-interest but chose rather to emphasize a set of collective values. Manning attached to "The Key of Liberty" a constitution for a political association of laboring men. These thoughts from an ordinary farmer offer a powerful vision of egalitarian democracy, although Manning apparently never thought to include women or slaves in his call for greater equality.

PROBLEMS TO CONSIDER

1. According to Manning, what are the principal differences that separate the interests of "the Few" from "the Many"? How would this perspective lead to a different understanding of the real purpose of the American Revolution?

2. What might have been the reasons for why Manning did not include women and slaves among "the Many" (his term for the people who embodied Revolution)?

[We have transcribed the beginning of this document exactly as it was written by Manning, to offer readers a feel for Manning's rudimentary skills in spelling, grammar, and punctuation. For the remainder of the document, the spelling and punctuation have been modernized for clarity of reading.]

To all the Republicans, Farmers, Mecanicks, and Labourers In America your Canded attention is Requested to the Sentiments of a Labourer

Introduction
Learning & Knowledg is essential to the preservation of Libberty & unless we have more of it amongue us we Cannot Seporte our Libertyes Long.

I am not a Man of Larning my selfe for I neaver had the advantage of six months schooling in my life. I am no travelor for I neaver was 50 Miles from whare I was born in no direction, & I am no grate reader of antiant history for I always followed hard labour for a living. But I always thought it My duty to search into & see for my selfe in all maters that consansed me as a member of society, & when the war began betwen Brittan & Amarica I was in the prime of Life & highly taken up with Liberty & a free Government. I See almost the first blood that was shed in Condord fite & scores of men dead, dying & wounded in the Cause of Libberty, which caused serious sencations in my mind.

[The text has been modernized from this point on.] But I believed then and still believe it is a good cause which we ought to defend to the very last, and I have been a constant reader of public newspapers and closely attended to men and measures ever since, through the war, through the operation of paper money, framing constitutions, making and constructing laws, and seeing what selfish and contracted ideas of interest would influence the best picked men and bodies of men. . . .

A General Description of the Causes
That Ruin Republics
The causes that I shall endeavor to make appear are a conceived difference of interests between those that labor for a living and those that get a living without bodily labor.

This is no new doctrine if I may judge from the many scraps of history I have seen of ancient republics. The best information I ever had on this subject and the greatest collection of historical accounts was by a writer who wrote ten long numbers in the Chronicle in December [17]85 and January [17]86, styling himself a Free Republican. . . .

I have looked over those ten numbers and searched other histories to satisfy myself as to the truth of his assertions, but [I] am very far from thinking as he does—that the destruction of free governments arises from the licentiousness of the many or their representatives, but on the contrary, [I] shall endeavor to prove that their destruction always arises from the ungoverned dispositions and combinations of the few, and the ignorance of the many. . . .

1. A Description of Mankind
and [the] Necessity of Government
. . . Men are born and grow up in this world with a vast variety of capacities, strength, and abilities both of body and mind, and have strongly implanted within them numerous passions and lusts continually urging them to fraud, violence, and

acts of injustice towards one another. . . . Yet as he is sentenced by the just decrees of heaven to hard labor for a living in this world, and has so strongly implanted in him a desire for self support, self defense, self conceit, self importance, and self aggrandizement, that it engrosses all his care and attention so that he can see nothing beyond self—for self (as once described by a divine) is like an object placed before the eye that hinders the sight of everything beyond.

This selfishness may be discerned in all persons, let their conditions in life be what they will, and it operates so powerfully as to disqualify them from judging impartially in their own cause, and a person raised to stations of high honor and trust does not clear him from selfishness. But on the contrary it is a solemn truth that the higher a Man is raised in stations of honor, power, and trust, the greater are his temptations to do wrong and gratify those selfish principles. Give a man honor and he wants more. Give him power and he wants more. Give him money and he wants more. In short, he is never easy, but the more he has the more he wants. . . .

From this disposition of man, or the depravity of the human heart, arises not only the advantage, but the absolute necessity, of civil government—without it mankind would be continually at war on their own species, stealing, roving, fighting with, and killing one another. . . .

2. A Description of a Free Government and Its Administration
. . . The sole end of government is the protection of life, liberty, and property. The poor man's shilling ought to be as much the care of government as the rich man's pound. Every person in the nation ought to be compelled to do justice and have it done to him promptly and without delay. All taxes for the support of government ought to be laid equally according to the property each person possesses and the advantages he receives from it. . . .

In short, a free government is one in which all the laws are made, judged, and executed according to the will and interest of a majority of the whole people, and not by the craft, cunning, and arts of the few. To support such a government, it is absolutely necessary to have a larger degree or better means of knowledge among the people than we now have, which I shall endeavor to make appear before I close.

3. Shows How the Few and Many Differ in Their Interests in Its Operation
. . . To be sentenced to hard labor during life is very unpleasant to human nature. There is a great aversion to it perceivable in all men—yet it is absolutely necessary that a large majority of the world should labor, or we could not subsist. For labor is the sole parent of all property. . . . Therefore no person can possess property without laboring, unless he gets it by force or craft, fraud or fortune, out of the earnings of others.

But, from the great variety of capacities, strength, and abilities of men, there always was, and always will be, a very unequal distribution of property in the world. Many are so rich that they can live without labor. Also, the merchant, physician, lawyer, and divine, the philosopher and school master, the Judicial and Executive officers, and many others who could honestly get a living without bodily labors. . . .

On the other hand, the laborer being conscious that it is labor that supports the whole, and that the more there is that live without labor and the higher they live or the greater their salaries and fees are, so much the harder he must work, or the shorter he must live, this makes the laborer watch the other with a jealous eye and often has reason to complain of real impositions. . . .

Here lays the great scuffle between the few and many. As the interests and incomes of the few lay chiefly in money and interest, rents, salaries, and fees that are fixed on the nominal value of money, they are interested in having money scarce and the price of labor and produce as low as possible. For instance, if the prices of labor and produce should fall one half, it would be just the same to the few as if their rents, fees, and salaries were doubled, all [of] which they would get out of the many. Besides, the fall of labor and produce and scarcity of money always brings the many into distress, and compels them into a state of dependence on the few for favors and assistance in a thousand ways.

On the other hand, if the many could raise the price of labor, etc. one half, and have the money circulate freely, they could pay their debts, eat and drink, and enjoy the good of their labor without being dependent on the few for assistance. . . .

The reasons why a free government has always failed is from the unreasonable demands and desires of the few. They can't bear to be on a level with their fellow creatures, or submit to the determinations of a Legislature where (as they call it) the Swinish Multitude *[Edmund Burke used this phrase to criticize the populace of France during the French Revolution]* are fairly represented, but sicken at the idea, and are ever hankering and striving after Monarchy or Aristocracy, where the people have nothing to do in matters of government but to support the few in luxury and idleness.

Samuel Eliot Morison, ed., "William Manning's *The Key of Libberty*," *William and Mary Quarterly*, 3rd ser., 13 (1956): 211–20.

ᴣ The Signs and Languages of a New Nationalism ᴣ

One of the most powerful ideas in American culture is the notion that the United States has a history unlike any other. Historians refer to this as the myth of American exceptionalism. Yet the United States was born in an age of democratic revolutions, the first of several in the Atlantic world, including the French, Haitian, and Latin American revolutions. The United States also gave rise to a new nationalism at the inauguration of an age of nationalism that continued through the twentieth century. The development of an American nationalism was indeed one of the most significant developments of the American Revolution.

How was it that a populace from thirteen different states across a huge geographic expanse, with different histories, regional identities, and ancestry, came to invent the belief that they were part of one nation? A person is not born with a national identity but instead acquires it through an ideological process created by very specific cultural practices. As a leading scholar has defined it, nationalism involves the idea of an "imagined community." Defining oneself as a nation requires imagining a group of individuals who constitute the members of that nation ("the people") and, conversely, those who are excluded from membership. Nationalism is an inventive process. Creating a sense of nationhood involves constructing a set of shared values, practices, and modes of communication—often through language, literature, civic culture, and political rituals—just as it often involves contests over the boundaries of who and what should be included in that nation. This process of exclusion reminds us that nationalism and racism are modern inventions that date from nearly the same era, and they have often worked in tandem with each other. Nationalism also relies on a set of myths that enable "newly emerging nations" to "imagine themselves antique." Nationalists believe that authority and identity are derived from ancient truths and values that their nation uniquely embodies. How could the newest nation on earth—the United States—make such a claim to antiquity?

This section examines the inventive process that fostered the belief that the United States was the star of westward empire, that it possessed its own language, its people their own unique character, and its political institutions originality, even in an era of republican revolutions. J. Hector St. John de Crevecoeur was not the only person asking this question at the end of the eighteenth century: "What then is the American, this new man?"

A Poem on the Rising Glory of America (1772)
PHILIP FRENEAU AND HUGH HENRY BRACKENRIDGE

*Some Americans had begun creating the idea of an American nation even before independence was declared. During the imperial crisis, two young graduates of the College of New Jersey (Princeton) strode to the stage and read a poem they had written for the College's commencement exercises in 1771. A dialogue in three voices (Leander, Eugenio, and Acasto), the poem narrated the history of the world and then prophesied that an American culture and empire would eclipse all others that had preceded it. Philip Freneau and Hugh Henry Brackenridge were tapping into a theory popular since the Middle Ages (*translatio studii et imperii*) that maintained that culture and political dominance had moved westward from Greece and Rome to western Europe, and now to America. Decades later, John Adams would recall that "there is nothing . . . more ancient in my memory than the observation that arts, sciences, and empire had traveled westward; and in conversation it was always added since I was a child, that their next leap would be over the Atlantic into America." Here then we catch the first glimpse of the idea that America as a nation was not a new invention, but something ancient. Is it any wonder that when Americans moved westward into upstate New York, they named the tiny hamlets they founded there Rome, Athens, Troy, Ithaca, and Syracuse? Both Freneau and Brackenridge became influential figures in the emergence of a new American literature and political culture in the early years of the republic — Freneau as a poet and newspaper editor, Brackenridge as a novelist and politician. James Madison, their classmate at Princeton and perhaps the single most important architect of American nationalism, was ill that day and missed the commencement ceremonies, but he certainly read and praised their sentiments.*

PROBLEMS TO CONSIDER

1. Why did the poets expect America's glory to surpass that of the ancients? Did America's genius require its independence from the Old World?
2. Why did Freneau and Brackenridge compare European Americans with the continent's Native American population?

Leander
No more of Memphis and her mighty kings,
Or Alexandria, where the Ptolemies
Taught golden commerce to unfurl her sails,

And bid fair science smile: No more of Greece
Where learning next her early visit paid,
And spread her glories to illume the world;
No more of Athens, where she flourished,

And saw her sons of mighty genius rise. . . .
No more of Rome, enlighten'd by her beams,
Fresh kindling there the fire of eloquence,
And poesy divine; imperial Rome! . . .
No more of Britain and her kings renown'd,
Edward's and Henry's thunderbolts of war;
Her chiefs victorious o'er the Gallic foe;
Illustrious senators, immortal bards,
And wise philosophers, of these no more,
A Theme more new, tho' not less noble, claims
Our ev'ry thought on this auspicious day;
The rising glory of this western world,
Where now the dawning light of science spreads
Her orient ray, and wakes the muse's song;
Where freedom holds her sacred standard high,
And commerce rolls her golden tides profuse
Of elegance and ev'ry joy of life. . . .

Eugenio
. . . For in her woods America contain'd,
From times remote, a savage race of men.
How shall we know their origin, how tell,
From whence or where the Indian tribes
    arose? . . .

Leander
How fallen, Oh!
How much obscur'd is human nature here!
Shut from the light of science and of truth
They wander'd blindfold down the steep of time;
Dim superstition with her ghastly train
Of dæmons, spectres and foreboding signs
Still urging them to horrid rites and forms
Of human sacrifice, to sooth the pow'rs
Malignant, and the dark infernal king. . . .

Leander
. . . Yet all these mighty feats to science owe
Their rise and glory. — Hail fair science! thou,
Transplanted from the eastern climes, dost
    bloom
In these fair regions, Greece and Rome no
    more. . . .
Hither they've wing'd their way, the last, the
    best

Of countries where the arts shall rise and grow
Luxuriant, graceful; and ev'n now we boast
A Franklin skill'd in deep philosophy,
A genius piercing as th' electric fire,
Bright as the light'ning's flash, explain'd so well
By him, the rival of Britannia's sage.
This is a land of ev'ry joyous sound
Of liberty and life; sweet liberty!
Without whose aid the noblest genius fails,
And science irretrievably must die. . . .

Eugenio
. . . A newer world now opens to her view,
She hastens onward to th' Americ shores
And bids a scene of recent wonders rise.
New states, new empires and a line of kings,
High rais'd in glory, cities, palaces,
Fair domes on each long bay, sea, shore or
    stream. . . .

Eugenio
And when a train of rolling years are past, . . .
A new Jerusalem sent down from heav'n
Shall grace our happy earth, perhaps this land,
Whose virgin bosom shall then receive, tho'
    late,
Myriads of saints with their almighty king,
To live and reign on earth a thousand years
Thence call'd Millennium. Paradise anew
Shall flourish, by no second Adam lost. . . .

Acasto
This is thy praise, America, thy pow'r,
Thou best of climes, by science visited,
By freedom blest and richly stor'd with all
The luxuries of life. Hail, happy land,
The seat of empire, the abode of kings,
The final stage where time shall introduce
Renowned characters, and glorious works
Of high invention and of wond'rous art. . . .

Philip Freneau and Hugh Henry Brackenridge, *A Poem on the Rising Glory of America* (Philadelphia, 1772). Reprinted in *The Poems of Philip Freneau*, 3 vols., edited by Fred Lewis Pattee (Princeton, N.J.: University Library, 1902), 1:50–51, 54, 58–59, 70–71, 75–76, 80–81, 82.

♌

The Contrast (1787)

ROYALL TYLER

After independence, not only did Americans need to invent the political structures of a new nation, but they also had to fill a void in the area of the arts. Before the American Revolution, no one born in the colonies would have been considered by either Europeans or colonists to be a legitimate painter, sculptor, composer, poet, playwright, actor, or novelist. But by the time the forms of a national government were in place, American painters such as Benjamin West were renowned in Europe, the first plays were written and performed by Americans, and the first American novel would soon be in print. In 1787, in the wake of Shays's Rebellion and the convention that drafted the new federal Constitution, Royall Tyler's play The Contrast *was performed for theatergoers in New York, Philadelphia, and Baltimore.* The Contrast *was the first play written by an American and performed before American audiences. The play lampooned those sentimental novels avidly consumed in Britain and America in the late eighteenth century. Still, Tyler also subtly exposed the cultural values — patriotism, equality, and gender conventions — of a new nationalism. Without subtlety, Tyler names the ideal man for the republic Colonel Manly. The simple-witted comical character of Manly's servant Jonathan voices the supposed perspectives and prejudices of common laboring people at this time. Jonathan became so popular that his type of character returned repeatedly as a stock figure in plays in the United States for the next several decades. Tyler begins the first scene reproduced here by having the character of Maria singing about an Indian warrior.*

PROBLEMS TO CONSIDER

1. What are "the contrasts" portrayed in this play, and how would they fuel sentiments of nationalism?
2. Why did Tyler focus on gender relations, courtship, and marriage at the founding moment of the new national government? What virtues make Colonel Manly so manly?

ACT I, SCENE II
A Room in Van Rough's House.
Maria sitting disconsolate at a Table,
    with Books, &c.

MARIA: There is something in this song which ever calls forth my affections. The manly virtue of courage, that fortitude which steels the heart against the keenest misfortunes, which interweaves the laurel of glory amidst the instruments of torture and death, displays something so noble, so exalted, that in despite of the prejudices of education, I cannot but admire it, even in a savage. The prepossession which our sex is supposed to entertain for the character of a soldier, is, I know, a standing piece of raillery among the wits. A cockade, a lapell'd coat, and a feather, they will tell you, are irresistible by a female heart. Let it be so. — Who is it that considers the helpless situation of our sex, that does not see we each moment stand in need of a protector, and that a brave one too. Formed of the more delicate materials of nature, endowed only with the softer passions, incapable, from our ignorance of the world, to guard against the wiles of mankind, our security for happiness often depends upon their generosity and courage. . . . Reputation is the life of woman; yet courage to protect it is masculine and disgusting; and the only safe asylum a woman of delicacy can find, is in the arms of a man of honour. How naturally then, should we love the brave, and the generous; how gratefully should we bless the arm raised for our protection, when nerv'd by virtue, and directed by honour! Heaven grant that the man with whom I may be connected—may be connected! . . . For, can the most frivolous manners, actuated by the most depraved heart, meet, or merit, any thing but contempt from every woman of delicacy and sentiment?

Van Rough *without*. Mary!

Ha! my father's voice—Sir!—

Enter Van Rough.

VAN ROUGH: What, Mary, always singing doleful ditties, and moping over these plaguy books. . . .

MARIA: Marriage, Sir, is, indeed, a very serious affair.

VAN ROUGH: You are right, child; you are right. I am sure I found it so to my cost.

MARIA: I mean, Sir, that as marriage is a portion for life, and so intimately involves our happiness, we cannot be too considerate in the choice of our companion.

VAN ROUGH: Right, child; very right. . . .

MARIA: My honoured mother, Sir, had no motive to melancholy; she married the man of her choice.

VAN ROUGH: The man of her choice! And pray, Mary, an't you going to marry the man of your choice—what trumpery notion is this?—It is these vile books [*throwing them away*]. I'd have you to know, Mary, if you won't make young Van Dumpling the man

of *your* choice, you shall marry him as the man of *my* choice.

MARIA: You terrify me, Sir. Indeed, Sir, I am all submission. My will is yours. . . .

VAN ROUGH: Well, well, Mary; do you be a good girl, mind the main chance, and never mind inclination. . . . [*Exit.*]

MARIA [*alone*]: How deplorable is my situation! How distressing for a daughter to find her heart militating with her filial duty! I know my father loves me tenderly, why then do I reluctantly obey him? . . . But to marry a depraved wretch, whose only virtue is a polished exterior; who is actuated by the unmanly ambition of conquering the defenceless . . . can he, who has no regard for the peace and happiness of other families, ever have a due regard for the peace and happiness of his own? . . . [*Exit.*]

ACT II, SCENE I
Enter Charlotte and Letitia.

. . .

LETITIA: What sort of a being is this brother of yours? If he is as chatty, as pretty, as sprightly as you, half the belles in the city will be pulling caps for him.

CHARLOTTE: My brother is the very counterpart and reverse of me: I am gay, he is grave; I am airy, he is solid; I am ever selecting the most pleasing objects for my laughter, he has a tear for every pitiful one. And thus, whilst he is plucking the briars and thorns from the path of the unfortunate, I am strewing my own path with roses. . . .

LETITIA: By what I can pick out of your flowery description, your brother is no beau.

CHARLOTTE: No, indeed; he makes no pretension to the character. He'd ride, or rather fly, an hundred miles to relieve a distressed object, or to do a gallant act in the service of his country: but should you drop your fan or bouquet in his presence, it is ten to one, that some beau at the farther end of the room would have the honour of presenting it to you before he had observed that it fell. I'll tell you one of his antiquated, anti-gallant notions.—He said once in my presence, in a room full of company—would you believe it—in a large circle of ladies, that the best evidence a gentleman could give a young lady of his respect and affection, was to endeavor in a friendly manner to rectify her foibles. I protest I was crimson to the eyes, upon reflecting that I was known as his sister.

LETITIA: Insupportable creature! tell a lady of her faults! If he is so grave, I fear I have no chance of captivating him.

CHARLOTTE: His conversation is like a rich, old fashioned brocade, it will stand alone; every sentence is a sentiment. Now you may judge what a time I had with him, in my twelve months visit to my father. He read me such lectures, out of pure brotherly affection, against the extremes of fashion, dress, flirting, and coquetry, and all the other dear things which he knows I dote upon, that, I protest, his conversation made me as melancholy as if I had been at church. . . .

Enter Colonel Manly.

. . .

CHARLOTTE: . . . And so, brother, you have come to the city to exchange some of your commutation notes for a little pleasure[?]

MANLY: Indeed you are mistaken; my errand is not of amusement, but business; and as I neither drink nor game, my expenses will be so trivial, I shall have no occasion to sell my notes.

CHARLOTTE: Then you won't have occasion to do a very good thing. Why, here was the Vermont General—he came down some time since, sold all his musty notes at one stroke, and then laid the cash out in trinkets for his dear Fanny. I want a dozen pretty

things myself; have you got the notes with you?

MANLY: I shall be ever willing to contribute as far as it is in my power, to adorn, or in any way to please my sister; yet, I hope, I shall never be obliged for this, to sell my notes. I may be romantic, but I preserve them as a sacred deposit. Their full amount is justly due to me, but as embarrassments, the natural consequences of a long war, disable my country from supporting its credit, I shall wait with patience until it is rich enough to discharge them. If that is not in my day, they shall be transmitted as an honourable certificate to posterity, that I have humbly imitated our illustrious WASHINGTON, in having exposed my health and life in the service of my country, without reaping any other reward than the glory of conquering in so arduous a contest. . . .

ACT II, SCENE II
The Mall
Enter Jessamy.

JESSAMY: . . .—Ah! who comes here? This, by his awkwardness, must be the Yankee colonel's servant. I'll accost him.

Enter Jonathan.

JESSAMY: Votre très-humble serviteur, Monsieur. I understand Colonel Manly, the Yankee officer, has the honour of your services.

JONATHAN: Sir!—

JESSAMY: I say, Sir, I understand that Colonel Manly has the honour of having you for a servant.

JONATHAN: Servant! Sir, do you take me for a neger,—I am Colonel Manly's waiter.

JESSAMY: A true Yankee distinction, egad, without a difference. Why, Sir, do you not perform all the offices of a servant? do you not even blacken his boots?

JONATHAN: Yes; I do grease them a bit some-times; but I am a true blue son of liberty, for all that. Father said I should come as Colonel Manly's waiter, to see the world, and all that; but no man shall master me: my father has as good a farm as the colonel. . . .

ACT III, SCENE II
The Mall
Enter Manly.

MANLY: It must be so, Montague! and it is not all the tribe of Mandevilles shall convince me, that a nation, to become great, must first become dissipated. Luxury is surely the bane of a nation: Luxury! which enervates both soul and body, by opening a thousand new sources of enjoyment, opens, also, a thou-sand new sources of contention and want: Luxury! which renders a people weak at home, and accessible to bribery, corruption, and force from abroad. When the Grecian states knew no other tools than the axe and the saw, the Grecians were a great, a free, and a happy people. . . . But when foreign gold, and still more pernicious, foreign lux-ury, had crept among them, they sapped the vitals of their virtue. . . . The common good was lost in the pursuit of private interest; and that people, who, by uniting, might have stood against the world in arms, by dividing, crumbled into ruin;—their name is now only known in the page of the historian, and what they once were, is all we have left to admire. Oh! that America! Oh! that my country, would in this her day, learn the things which belong to her peace!

———

[Royall Tyler], *The Contrast: A Comedy in Five Acts* (Phila-delphia: Prichard & Hall, 1790), 8–14, 16–20, 26–27, 48–49.

ᴣ

Dissertations on the English Language, with an Essay on the Necessity, Advantages and Practicability of Reforming the Mode of Spelling . . . (1789)

NOAH WEBSTER

Nationalists today are divided over the question of whether a nation can tolerate a citi-zenry that does not speak the same language. This problem is not new in American his-tory. Although the so-called "founding fathers" spoke the same language as the king they rebelled against, the 1790 census indicated that as few as one in four persons living in the United States regarded English as their first language. Could a nation of such lin-guistic diversity become a united nation? Noah Webster did not think so. He devoted his considerable energies to a plan for creating a distinctly American language. He was an ardent Federalist and an untiring supporter of the nationalist movement that produced a federal Constitution in 1787. But for Webster, this change of polity was not enough to make a nation. "Language as well as government should be national," he argued. He developed a system for teaching all Americans, regardless of region or ancestry, to speak and spell English in the same American way. Webster's plan for an American form of spelling, reproduced here, never fully caught on, but his ideas did reflect a set of national-istic sentiments prevalent in the new nation.

PROBLEMS TO CONSIDER

1. How did ideas about progress, anticolonialism, and capitalism fit into Webster's scheme for an American spelling of English?
2. Could Webster reconcile his new invention with the idea that the American nation had ancient roots?

It has been observed by all writers on the English language, that the orthography or spelling of words is very irregular; the same letters often representing different sounds, and the same sounds often expressed by different letters. . . .

In this progress, the English have lost the sounds of most of the guttural letters. The *k* before *n* in *know*, the *g* in *reign*, and in many other words, are become mute in practice; and the *gh* is softened into the sound of *f*, as in *laugh*, or is silent, as in *brought*. . . .

It is here necessary only to remark, that when words have been introduced from a foreign language into the English, they have generally retained the orthography of the original, however ill adapted to express the English pronunciation. Thus *fatigue, marine, chaise*, retain their French dress, while, to represent the true pronunciation in English, they should be spelt *fateeg, mareen, shaze*. Thus thro an ambition to exhibit the etymology of words, the English, in *Philip, physic, character, chorus*, and other Greek derivatives, preserve the representatives of the original φ and χ; yet these words are pronounced, and ought ever to have been spelt, *Filip, fyzzic* or *fizzic, karacter, korus*. . . .

The question now occurs; ought the Americans to retain these faults which produce innumerable inconveniencies in the acquisition and use of the language, or ought they at once to reform these abuses, and introduce order and regularity into the orthography of the AMERICAN TONGUE? . . .

A correct orthography would render the pronunciation of the language, as uniform as the spelling in books. A general uniformity thro the United States, would be the event of such a reformation as I am here recommending. All persons, of every rank, would speak with some degree of precision and uniformity. Such a uniformity in these states is very desireable; it would remove prejudice, and conciliate mutual affection and respect. . . .

The alteration, however small, would encourage the publication of books in our own country. It would render it, in some measure, necessary that all books should be printed in America. The English would never copy our orthography for their own use; and consequently the same impressions of books would not answer for both countries. . . .

Besides this, a *national language* is a band of *national union*. Every engine should be employed to render the people of this country *national*; to call their attachments home to their own country; and to inspire them with the pride of national character. However they may boast of Independence, and the freedom of their government, yet their *opinions* are not sufficiently independent; an astonishing respect for the arts and literature of their parent country, and a blind imitation of its manners, are still prevalent among the Americans. Thus an habitual respect for another country, deserved indeed and once laudable, turns their attention from their own interests, and prevents their respecting themselves. . . .

Now is the time, and *this* the country, in which we may expect success, in attempting changes favorable to language, science and government. Delay, in the plan here proposed, may be fatal; under a tranquil general government, the minds of men may again sink into indolence; a national acquiescence in error will follow; and posterity be doomed to struggle with difficulties, which time and accident will perpetually multiply.

Let us then seize the present moment, and establish a *national language*, as well as a national government.

Noah Webster Jr., *Dissertations on the English Language, with . . . an Essay on a Reformed Mode of Spelling . . .* (Boston: Isaiah Thomas, 1789), 391–94, 396–98, 406.

◌

Federalist and Democratic-Republican Toasts (1790s)

The new United States needed to create all the trappings of a national political culture overnight. Casting aside the calendar of British life, Americans created new holidays, new symbols to represent the nation and its values, a new civic religion that venerated sacred scriptures (the Declaration of Independence and the Constitution), and new sets of political rituals to accomplish the work of a democracy. One other new political invention had been neither anticipated nor desired: the formation of a system of opposing political parties. In Anglo-American politics in the eighteenth century, few men accepted the idea of a legitimate opposition to the party in power. Political parties, or "factions," were thought to be diseases in the body politic, threatening the health of the nation. Nevertheless, two competing political parties, the Federalists and the Democratic-Republicans, crystallized in opposition to each other in the 1790s. The parties differed most sharply in their attitudes about the French Revolution, with Federalists fearing that it was a dangerous disruption of the social order that might infect the new American republic. Federalist fears culminated in 1798 with the passage of the Alien and Sedition Acts, designed to punish any person who criticized the Adams administration's governance. The following documents are toasts that Federalists and Democratic-Republicans recited and sang at various political festivities. It was never enough, however, simply to speak these toasts. The new nationalism developed through an expanding print culture, so toasts were frequently printed in their entirety in newspapers, the engines of the new party politics.

PROBLEMS TO CONSIDER

1. What do these toasts reveal about the cultural practices of nationalism in the new republic?
2. Explain the toasts' symbolic language in light of other Revolutionary-era documents you have read.

FEDERALIST TOASTS AND SENTIMENTS

Lieutenant General WASHINGTON—the pride, the boast, the father, the protector of his country. In peace a Senate and in arms a Host.

The President of the United States—whose Spirit animates his Country—whose Wisdom foils the intrigues of Corruption, and whose Fortitude leads Anarchy in triumph.

The American Flag—may every nation respect its bearers—may the radiance of its stars shed a lustre over its friends, but its stripes lacerate the backs of its enemies. . . .

Old times—old principles, and none of the gipsey jargon of France. . . .

The Congress of the United States—while genius, eloquence and judgment preside, as they have done over our national councils, we may with justice sneer at the bombastic threats of our enemies.

The patriots of America, whose blood was shed at the altar of Liberty. May the sons never lose the fire of their fathers to preserve those blessings transmitted to them. . . .

The gallant Youth of America—may they justly appreciate the fair inheritance transmitted to them by their ancestors.

The Fair Sex—may their arms prove our sweetest refuge in adversity, and their smiles the truest antidote to care.

The sentiments of the day—"Millions for defence, but not a cent for tribute." . . .

Community of goods, unity of hearts, nobility of sentiments, and truth of feeling, to the real lovers of the fair sex.

The Echo; or, Federal Songster (Brookfield, Mass.: E. Merriam & Co., [1798]), 245–47.

DEMOCRATIC-REPUBLICAN TOASTS

TOASTS drank by the TAMMANY SOCIETY or COLUMBIAN ORDER, on the Fourth of July, 1799.

1. *America!* our Country! The mother of the doctrine of *equal rights*—May she refuse to nurse any other children but the sons of freedom, and may they ever be victorious.

2. The *President* of the United States—May he be as wise as a serpent, and as harmless as a dove.—3 cheers.

3. *Jefferson, the friend of the people*—May the Declaration of Independence which he framed, secure him the confidence of his country; and may his honest and patriotic exertions in the cause of universal Liberty meet with success. 6 cheers.

4. A *free* and *uncorrupted* representation of the *People*—May no *sycophant* or *time server* ever obtain the suffrages of freemen.

5. Perpetuity to the *principles of* our late revolution—May the death wound to tyranny be dated from that period.

6. A *tarry vest* and a *coat of feathers* to the slaves of monarchy, and all who oppose the freedom and happiness of the human race.—3 cheers.

7. Wisdom, virtue, and integrity to the councils of our nation.—May they keep a watchful eye on the fawning *Lyon*, and all his *whelps*.— 3 cheers. . . .

9. The Martyrs to American Independence —May their patriotism be handed down to posterity, and their memories honoured at every celebration of freemen.

10. May the *terrorists of our late election* who have threatened to deprive the *labouring poor of bread*, not only have their names registered; but (unless they repent) meet a like fate with *Robespierre [leader of the French Revolution, who was executed by guillotine]* their *progeniture*.— 9 cheers. . . .

16. *American Mothers*—May they teach their sons to love liberty, and their daughters to hate tyranny and adore virtue.

Greenleaf's New York Journal and Patriotic Register, July 6, 1799.

᧠

∿ CHAPTER 5 ∿

An Entrepreneurial and Industrial North: 1790–1840

CONSIDER THE STORY of the Patch family of Massachusetts: their experiences illustrate the life-changing developments common throughout the North after the American Revolution. Mayo Greenleaf Patch, born in 1766, was the youngest of his father's ten surviving children. Needless to say, little remained of his father's 114 acres of poor farm land for Greenleaf to inherit when he reached adulthood. He joined thousands of others who became landless in a rural society in which farmland was the only real guarantee of a comfortable life. He married Abigail McIntire when he was twenty-two and she was seventeen and pregnant (like one out of every three New England brides of her generation). Greenleaf attempted to gain control of some of his wife's family's property during the 1790s and tried his hand as a shoemaker until his combined failures and debts forced him to abandon the prospect of an independent household in a rural family economy. The Patches relocated to Pawtucket, Rhode Island, where Abigail and the children could sell their labor for wages in the newly built textile mills. Within a few years, Greenleaf turned to drinking and abandoned his family, and Abigail became the head of household for a family of wage-laboring women and children. During the 1820s, the Patches' oldest son, Sam Patch, became a renowned daredevil and one of the nation's first celebrities, known for leaping over waterfalls, including Niagara Falls.

The Patches were certainly a colorful family. Still, their experiences reveal the transformation of northern society in the half century following the American Revolution. Recently historians have adopted the term "market revolution" to portray the various upheavals that changed the lives of northerners such as the Patches. In truth, the market revolution was really a series of different but related transformations all coalescing at the same time. Between 1790 and 1840 in the North, an industrial revolution, a transportation revolution (the invention and proliferation of canals and railroads), a consumer revolution, and a print revolution took place. And these so-called revolutions still do not encompass other important developments, such as the emergence of a working class and a middle class, and a new ideology of sexual difference, that resulted from these social transformations.

The Patch family were participants in these transformations. Their lives exposed the declining power of traditional rural patriarchs, the indispensable role of women's labor at the beginnings of industrialization, and new expressions of masculinity that conformed to the aggressive ambitions of men in the marketplace. The Patches were also marginal people, but it was those on the margins of a rural society who were forced to seek wage labor when landowner-ship was no longer possible. Once larger segments of the working population fit that profile, northerners began to embrace a political ideology that glorified that status — now calling it "free labor" and contrasting it with the dangerous spread of "slave labor" to their south.

Abigail Patch and her daughters also illustrate the conflict between the real lives of working women and the cultural discourses of gender that were spreading in the early republic. Through a variety of different texts, the northern middle class began to promote an ideal of womanhood that was all about repro-duction rather than production, while demonizing independent women by associating them with prostitution. In the new market economy, the emergent middle class effectively married an ambitious, entrepreneurial manhood with a domesticated and religious womanhood. The ideal man was defined as assertive and self-interested, and the ideal woman as spiritual, nurturing, and home-bound. This chapter probes the developments that ushered in a new social order for the young republic and began to set apart the culture of the North from that of the South.

☙ A Market Revolution ❧

The transformation that historians call the market revolution was based on the mass production of cheap manufactured goods and their penetration into local communities on a scale never witnessed before. And as the rural North became more dependent on consuming and producing for internal markets, more imper-sonal relationships of credit and money replaced the local networks of exchange among neighbors. The population in the North also became increasingly mobile, as men and women moved both westward and into cities in search of the wages necessary to purchase those goods. Industrialization meant that the nature, scale, and location of work began to change, and with it the type of community structures that had characterized rural colonial America. A new set of values associated with a successful man emerged as well, justifying ambition and entrepreneurial striving as the manly alternative to the dependent labor to which women, children, and slaves were confined.

∿ CREATING CONSUMER DESIRE

Advertisements and Trade Cards from a Philadelphia Newspaper (1798)

It was the unprecedented expansion of consumer goods—items that ordinary farmers' and tradesmen's families suddenly decided were necessities of life, such as manufactured textiles, ceramic, glass and silver tableware, and furniture—that fueled the market's influence over northern cities and rural villages. This "consumer revolution" began a few decades before the American Revolution, and it became a defining feature of the middle-class capitalist society that developed in the North after the Revolution. Merchants and shopkeepers used newspaper advertisements to get consumers to think, "I've just got to have that!" From the start, consumerism and newspapers went hand in hand; eighteenth-century newspapers commonly included the word "advertiser" in their title. But retailers also began to transform their advertisements in the early republic. Previously, merchants' ads simply contained a long list of the new items available at their stores. Even these rudimentary ads excited the desires of new consumers, with strategically placed words that emphasized "the latest fashions" or "reasonable prices." What changed in the decades after the Revolution was the way in which stories were now used to elicit consumer desires. It was no longer enough to let potential buyers know that the goods existed; now consumers needed to be enticed to choose one set of goods over others. At the same time, newspapers spread rapidly throughout the northern countryside, subsidized by the government and serving as an engine of both popular democracy and a money-based market economy.

PROBLEMS TO CONSIDER

1. What type of stories did each of these advertisements tell, and how might these tales increase the consumer appeal of their products? What role do the various characters (merchant, satisfied customers, and so on) play in the crafting of these ads?
2. What similarities or differences can you perceive between these ads and popular advertisements today?

Barbers all in an Uproar!

A PETITION is expected to be presented to Mr. H——, to withdraw his DOUBLE CUTTING RAZOR STROP, shaving twosides, consequently works with double force at first, it has so peculiar an effect on an old Razor, usually thrown away as good for nothing; now you may fancy the beard shaved off one day's growth within the skin — Secondly, the honest Barber deplores to see each private family become a Barber's shop, whilst the Cutter is lost in surprize, to see notches removed from Razors, penknives, Surgeon's instruments, &c. by the powers of

HOPKINS' CELEBRATED RAZOR
STROPS AND COMPOSITION.

Sold in three sizes, at 5∫7½ — 9∫4½ — and 15∫ each — and a box of Composition to repair the strop, that will last for years, at 3∫9 — the money returned within one week, if not found to answer the description given.

Sold by J. Hopkins, No. 119, South Third-street. . . . .

THE NAKED TRUTH.

Sans doute Mr. Hopkins your elegant STROPS,
   Are the best that e'er MORTAL invented;
We have nothing to do but to lather our chops —
   The RAZOR soon makes us contented;
Surely magic herself has been lending her aid,
   To assist in the brilliant invention,
And the fam'd composition you also have made
   Will assuredly gain you attention.

TO THE AFFLICTED

With *Rheumatism, Gout, Lumbago, Palsy, Numbness, Bruises, Sprains, &c.* is recommended
WHITEHEAD's
Essence of Mustard,

As the most safe and effectual remedy for the above complaints, "Even to the Aged in cases most desperate," this extraordinary Medicine gives immediate relief and generally effects an absolute and speedy CURE.

The Pills have also, removed Cold or Windy complaints and Pains in the Stomach of many years duration, — In addition to the many instances of its efficacy already published in this Paper, we insert the following recent ones.

Mrs. ANN MOORE, of No. 76, Almond street, had been THIRTY-FIVE YEARS afflicted with the RHEUMATISM, and in December last, when she heard of the ESSENCE OF MUSTARD, her arms were so violently affected, that she could neither dress or undress: By the second application of the Fluid Essence, the use of her arms were restored to her, and she was perfectly cured with less than ONE BOTTLE.
March, 1798

Mr. N. COLEMAN, No. 117, North Third-street, had the RHEUMATISM so severely in both Ankles, that he could not move up or down stairs except on his hands and knees: — He was cured by ONE BOTTLE of WHITEHEAD's ESSENCE OF MUSTARD.
February 1, 1798.

March 14th, 1798.
GENTLEMEN,

Some time since, I was seized with a PARALYTIC AFFECTION in my left arm, which entirely deprived me of the use of it — I had been some time in this situation, expecting to remain a cripple for life, as I had applied to several of the Faculty and had tried every remedy I could hear of, without effect, when I was informed by Mrs. Irving of Dock Street, of the great benefit she had received by the use of WHITEHEAD's ESSENCE OF MUSTARD, in a severe attack of RHEUMATISM. — I applied to you for a bottle, and in the course of a few days I had the satisfaction of finding my arm restored to its natural state, and I can now use it as well as ever. — For the Benefit of the afflicted, I request you to make this public.

PETER ADAMS,
No. 108, South Second-street.
Messrs. Shaw, & Co.

Aurora General Advertiser (Philadelphia), June 9, 1798; May 3, 1798.

∽

The Clockmaker; or, The Sayings and Doings of Sam Slick, of Slickville (1839)

THOMAS HALIBURTON

In addition to newspapers, an army of traveling peddlers brought a consumer market-place into all reaches of the northern countryside. Peddlers were the agents of a market transformation. They facilitated a new distribution network that brought scores of man-ufactured products into the hands of consumers, thereby breaking down the old patterns of local exchange that had previously characterized rural economies and making distant villages connected to (and dependent on) distant markets. Book publishers were among the first entrepreneurs to hire bands of traveling salesmen. The New England clock industry also used traveling peddlers in the 1820s and 1830s to sell tens of thousands of cheaply made shelf clocks. Peddlers marketed something else besides the goods they were hawking; they sold northern residents on a consumer culture, popularizing a gospel of self-fulfillment through the acquisition of goods. We have few firsthand accounts of shop-ping practices in the rural North, but we can glimpse the cultural reaction to traveling salesmen in the humorous tale of Sam Slick the clockmaker (actually clock peddler). Thomas Haliburton's story — itself an example of the new mass commodity of cheap, entertaining fiction — is a trickster tale (see chapter 6), but it also tapped into northern middle-class anxieties about the prevalence of deceitful men in this new market-driven society.

PROBLEMS TO CONSIDER

1. How do you think readers in the North responded to this story? Would they have identified more with Slick or the Flints? Would they have considered the book itself a luxury or a necessity?
2. What are all the various factors in this tale that helped Slick create sufficient desire for a consumer item? What does Haliburton's tale reveal about the gen-der behavior involved in the new consumerism?

Here's a book they've namesaked arter me, Sam Slick, the Clockmaker, but it tante mine, and I can't altogether jist say rightly whose it is. . . . It's a wise child that knows its own father. It wipes up the blue-noses consider-able hard, and don't let off the Yankees so very easy neither, but it's generally allowed to be about the prettiest book ever writ in this coun-try; and although it aint altogether jist gospel what's in it, there's some pretty home truths in it, that's a fact. Whoever wrote it must be a funny feller, too, that's sartin; for there are some queer stories in it that no soul could help larfin at, that's a fact. It's about the wittiest book I ever see'd. It's nearly all sold off, but jist a few copies I've kept for my old customers. The price is just 5*s*. 6*d*., but I'll let you have it for 5*s*., because you'll not get another chance to have one. Al-ways ask a sixpence more than the price, and then bait it, and when blue-nose hears that, he thinks he got a bargain, and bites directly. I never see'd one on 'em yet that didn't fall right into the trap. . . .

SAMUEL SLICK

CHAPTER 2: THE CLOCKMAKER

I had heard of Yankee clock pedlars, tin pedlars, and bible pedlars, especially of him who sold

Polyglot Bibles (*all in English*) to the amount of sixteen thousand pounds. The house of every substantial farmer had three substantial ornaments, a wooden clock, a tin reflector, and a Polyglot Bible. How is it that an American can sell his wares, at whatever price he pleases, where a blue-nose would fail to make a sale at all? I will enquire of the Clockmaker the secret of his success. . . .

But how is it, said I, that you manage to sell such an immense number of clocks, (which certainly cannot be called necessary articles) among a people with whom there seems to be so great a scarcity of money?

Mr. Slick paused, as if considering the propriety of answering the question, and looking me in the face, said, in a confidential tone, Why, I don't care if I do tell you, for the market is glutted, and I shall quit this circuit. It is done by a knowledge of *soft sawder* and *human natur*. But here is Deacon Flint's, said he, I have but one clock left, and I guess I will sell it to him.

At the gate of a most comfortable looking farm house stood Deacon Flint, a respectable old man, who had understood the value of time better than most of his neighbors, if one might judge from the appearance of every thing about him. After the usual salutation, an invitation to "alight" was accepted by Mr. Slick, who said, he wished to take leave of Mrs. Flint before he left Colchester. . . .

As the old gentleman closed the door after him, Mr. Slick drew near to me, and said in an under tone, Now that is what I call "*soft sawder*.". . . Here his lecture on "*soft sawder*" was cut short by the entrance of Mrs. Flint. Jist come to say good bye, Mrs. Flint.—What, have you sold all your clocks? Yes, and very low, too, for money is scarce, and I wished to close the concarn; no, I am wrong in saying all, for I have jist one left. Neighbor Steel's wife asked to have the refusal of it, but I guess I won't sell it; I had but two of them, this one and the feller of it that I sold Governor Lincoln. General Green, the Secretary of State for Maine, said he'd give me

50 dollars for this here one—it has composition wheels and patent axles, it is a beautiful article—a real first chop—no mistake, genuine superfine, but I guess I'll take it back; and beside, Squire Hawk might think kinder harder that I didn't give him the offer. Dear me, said Mrs. Flint, I should like to see it; where is it? It is in a chest of mine over the way, at Tom Tape's store. I guess he can ship it on to Eastport. That's a good man, said Mrs. Flint, jist let's look at it.

Mr. Slick, willing to oblige, yielded to these entreaties, and soon produced the clock—a gawdy, highly varnished, trumpery looking affair. He placed it on the chimney-piece where its beauties were pointed out and duly appreciated by Mrs. Flint, whose admiration was about ending in a proposal, when Mr. Flint returned from giving his directions about the care of the horses. The Deacon praised the clock, he too thought it a handsome one; but the Deacon was a prudent man, he had a watch—he was sorry, but he had no occasion for a clock. I guess you're in the wrong furrow this time, Deacon, it an't for sale, said Mr. Slick; and if it was, I reckon neighbor Steel's wife would have it, for she gives me no peace about it. Mrs. Flint said, that Mr. Steel had enough to do, poor man, to pay his interest, without buying clocks for his wife. It's no concarn of mine, said Mr. Slick, so long as he pays me, what he has to do, but I guess I don't want to sell it, and besides it comes too high; that clock can't be made at Rhode Island under 40 dollars. Why it an't possible, said the Clockmaker, in apparent surprise, looking at his watch, why as I'm alive it is 4 o'clock, and I hav'nt been two blessed hours here—how on earth shall I reach River Philip to-night? I'll tell you what, Mrs. Flint, I'll leave the clock in your care till I return on my way to the States—I'll set it a goin and put it to the right time.

As soon as this operation was performed, he delivered the key to the Deacon with a sort of serio-comic injunction to wind up the clock every Saturday night, which Mrs. Flint said she would take care should be done, and promised to remind her husband of it, in case he should chance to forget it.

That, said the Clockmaker, as soon as we were mounted, that I call "*human natur!*" Now that clock is sold for 40 dollars—it cost me just 6 dollars and 50 cents. Mrs. Flint will never let Mrs. Steel have the refusal—nor will the Deacon learn, until I call for the clock, that having once indulged in the use of a superfluity, how difficult it is to give it up. We can do without any article of luxury we have never had, but when once obtained, it isnt "*in human natur*" to surrender it voluntarily. Of fifteen thousand sold by myself and partners in this Province, twelve thousand were left in this manner, and only ten clocks were ever returned—when we called for them they invariably bought them. We trust to "*soft sawder*" to get them into the house, and to "*human natur*" that they never come out of it.

[Thomas Haliburton], *The Clockmaker; or, The Sayings and Doings of Sam Slick, of Slickville*, 5th ed. (London: Richard Bentley, 1839), ix–x, 9–15.

ॐ

ॐ DEBATES OVER MANUFACTURING

Although Americans had become eager consumers as early as the 1740s, the colonies had remained dependent on goods manufactured in Britain. On the eve of independence, the colonies imported more than one-quarter of all that Britain manufactured, while not a single factory could be found anywhere in North America. The British empire prohibited colonial industries that competed with British manufacturing, but that hardly explains their absence, given that colonists had no qualms about ignoring imperial regulations in other cases. Quite simply, there was little interest in manufacturing in America.

With independence, however, came the first serious commitment to manufacturing schemes. Even then, Americans exhibited a profound ambivalence toward the idea of introducing large-scale manufacturing in their midst. As early as 1760, Benjamin Franklin exposed the social context of manufacturing: "Manufactures are founded in poverty. It is the multitude of poor without land in a country, and who must work for others at low wages or starve, that enables undertakers to carry on a manufacture." In Franklin's mind, as long as sufficient land was available for the American population, manufactures would never take hold on the continent. But even as he was writing, population pressures were already threatening the future of independent landownership for New England farm families. By the 1780s, more and more farm families were being forced to supplement their meager farm incomes by resorting to wage labor, like the experience of the Patch family. It was this ever-growing population in search of wages who supplied the necessary cheap labor force that made the earliest manufacturing enterprises profitable in the North.

Proponents of manufacturing ran headlong into strong ideological opposition to introducing the social order of British manufacturing towns. They would have to convince skeptical Americans that manufacturing in the United States would somehow be exempt from the evils that most Americans associated with Britain's manufacturing cities: urban blight and a dependent laboring population that was characterized by vice rather than virtue.

Notes on the State of Virginia (1781)
THOMAS JEFFERSON

Report on Manufactures (1791)
ALEXANDER HAMILTON

The debate over manufacturing raised certain questions: what type of economic culture should the new nation embrace, and what characteristics should its working citizens possess? These questions were so pivotal to the founding of the republic that the principal architects of the nation's first political parties—Thomas Jefferson and Alexander Hamilton—devoted their best intellectual energies to them. Jefferson announced his opinions on manufacturing in his only published book, Notes on the State of Virginia *(1781), written while he was the governor of Virginia. Hamilton's opposing viewpoint was articulated in his report to Congress on manufacturing, delivered while he was the first secretary of the treasury during George Washington's presidency. For centuries, their economic philosophies have influenced competing visions of the ideal American life.*

PROBLEMS TO CONSIDER

1. Independence and dependence were key concepts for both Jefferson and Hamilton. How did these ideas influence their thinking about manufacturing?
2. What are the differences in the way that Jefferson and Hamilton thought about human nature and the natural characteristics of working men and women?

NOTES ON THE STATE OF VIRGINIA

Query 19
The present state of manufactures, commerce, interior and exterior trade?

We never had an interior trade of any importance. Our exterior commerce has suffered very much from the beginning of the present contest. During this time we have manufactured within our families the most necessary articles of cloathing. Those of cotton will bear some comparison with the same kinds of manufacture in Europe; but those of wool, flax and hemp are very coarse, unsightly, and unpleasant: and such is our attachment to agriculture, and such our preference for foreign manufactures, that be it wise or unwise, our people will certainly return as soon as they can, to the raising raw materials, and ex-

changing them for finer manufactures than they are able to execute themselves.

The political economists of Europe have established it as a principle that every state should endeavour to manufacture for itself: and this principle, like many others, we transfer to America, without calculating the difference of circumstance which should often produce a difference of result. In Europe the lands are either cultivated, or locked up against the cultivator. Manufacture must therefore be resorted to of necessity not of choice, to support the surplus of their people. But we have an immensity of land courting the industry of the husbandman. Is it best then that all our citizens should be employed in its improvement, or that one half should be called off from that to exercise manufactures and handicraft arts for the other? Those who labour in the earth are the chosen people of God, if ever he had a chosen people, whose breasts he has made his peculiar deposit for substantial and genuine virtue. It is the focus in which he keeps alive that sacred fire, which otherwise might escape from the face of the earth. Corruption of morals in the mass of cultivators is a phenomenon of which no age nor nation has furnished an example. It is the mark set on those, who not looking up to heaven, to their own soil and industry, as does the husbandman, for their subsistance, depend for it on the casualties and caprice of customers. Dependance begets subservience and venality, suffocates the germ of virtue, and prepares fit tools for the designs of ambition. This, the natural progress and consequence of the arts, has sometimes perhaps been retarded by accidental circumstances: but, generally speaking, the proportion which the aggregate of the other classes of citizens bears in any state to that of its husbandmen, is the proportion of its unsound to its healthy parts, and is a good-enough barometer whereby to measure its degree of corruption. While we have land to labour then, let us never wish to see our citizens occupied at a work-bench, or twirling a distaff. Carpenters, masons, smiths, are wanting in husbandry: but, for the general operations of manufacture, let our work-shops remain in Europe. It is better to carry provisions and materials to workmen there, than bring them to the provisions and materials, and with them their manners and principles. The loss by the transportation of commodities across the Atlantic will be made up in happiness and permanence of government. The mobs of great cities add just so much to the support of pure government, as sores do to the strength of the human body. It is the manners and spirit of a people which preserve a republic in vigour. A degeneracy in these is a canker which soon eats to the heart of its laws and constitution.

Thomas Jefferson, *Notes on the State of Virginia* (Philadelphia: Prichard and Hall, 1788), 174–75.

REPORT ON MANUFACTURES

[To the Speaker of the House of Representatives]

The Secretary of the Treasury, in obedience to the order of the House of Representatives . . . has applied his attention . . . to the subject of Manufactures, and particularly to the means of promoting such as will tend to render the United States independent on foreign nations for military and other essential supplies; and he thereupon respectfully submits the following report. . . .

. . . The substitution of foreign for domestic manufactures is a transfer to foreign nations of the advantages accruing from the employment of machinery, in the modes in which it is capable of being employed with most utility and to the greatest extent.

The cotton-mill, invented in England, within the last twenty years, is a signal illustration of the general proposition which has been just advanced. In consequence of it, all the different processes for spinning cotton are performed by means of machines, which are put in motion by water, and attended chiefly by women and children—and by a smaller number of persons, in the whole, than are requisite in the ordinary mode of spinning. And it is an advantage of great moment, that the operations of this mill continue with convenience during the night as well as through the day. The prodigious effect of such a machine is easily conceived. To this invention is to be attributed, essentially, the immense progress which has been so suddenly made in Great Britain, in the various fabrics of cotton.

3. *As to the additional employment of classes of the community not ordinarily engaged in the particular business*

This is not among the least valuable of the means by which manufacturing institutions contribute to augment the general stock of industry and production. In places where those institutions prevail, besides the persons regularly engaged in them, they afford occasional and extra employment to industrious individuals and families, who are willing to devote the leisure resulting from the intermissions of their ordinary pursuits to collateral labors, as a resource for multiplying their acquisitions or their enjoyments. The husbandman himself experiences a new source of profit and support from the increased industry of his wife and daughters, invited and stimulated by the demands of the neighboring manufactories.

Besides this advantage of occasional employment to classes having different occupations, there is another, of a nature allied to it, and of a similar tendency. This is the employment of persons who would otherwise be idle, and in many cases a burthen on the community, either from the bias of temper, habit, infirmity of body, or some other cause, indisposing or disqualifying them for the toils of the country. It is worthy of particular remark that, in general, women and children are rendered more useful, and the latter more early useful, by manufacturing establishments, than they would otherwise be. . . .

And thus it appears to be one of the attributes of manufactures, and one of no small consequence, to give occasion to the exertion of a greater quantity of industry, even by the same number of persons, where they happen to prevail, than would exist if there were no such establishments. . . .

6. *As to the affording a more ample and various field for enterprise*

. . . To cherish and stimulate the activity of the human mind, by multiplying the objects of enterprise, is not among the least considerable of the expedients by which the wealth of a nation may be promoted. Even things in themselves not positively advantageous sometimes become so, by their tendency to provoke exertion. Every new scene which is opened to the busy nature of man to rouse and exert itself, is the addition of a new energy to the general stock of effort. . . .

7. *As to the creating, in some instances, a new, and securing, in all a more certain and steady demand for the surplus produce of the soil*

This is among the most important of the circumstances which have been indicated. It is a principal means by which the establishment of manufactures contributes to an augmentation of the produce or revenue of a country, and has an immediate and direct relation to the prosperity of agriculture.

It is evident that the exertions of the husbandman will be steady or fluctuating, vigorous or feeble, in proportion to the steadiness or fluctuation, adequateness or inadequateness, of the markets on which he must depend for the vent of the surplus which may be produced by his labor; and that such surplus, in the ordinary course of things, will be greater or less in the same proportion.

For the purpose of this vent, a domestic market is greatly to be preferred to a foreign one; because it is, in the nature of things, far more to be relied upon. . . .

It merits particular observation, that the multiplication of manufactories not only furnishes a market for those articles which have been accustomed to be produced in abundance in a country; but it likewise creates a demand for such as were either unknown or produced in inconsiderable quantities. The bowels as well as the surface of the earth are ransacked for articles which were before neglected. Animals, plants and minerals acquire an utility and value which were before unexplored.

Alexander Hamilton, Report on Manufactures (1791), in *The Works of Alexander Hamilton*, 12 vols., edited by Henry Cabot Lodge (New York: G. P. Putnam's Sons, 1904), 4:70, 90–92, 94–95, 98.

ᴧ

Laboring Classes (1840)
ORESTES BROWNSON

Factory Girls (1840)
THE LOWELL OFFERING

Despite a growing discourse in the North that equated productive labor with masculinity, ironically it was women laborers who ushered in the industrial age in the United States. In scattered small mills radiating through Rhode Island's Blackstone River valley, where Samuel Slater established the nation's first textile mills, and then in larger-scale mill towns such as Lowell, Massachusetts, manufacturers relied on women's labor to create a market revolution. And farm families, such as the Patches, relied on young women's earnings to ease their transition to a dependence on wage labor. By the 1840s, tens of thousands of young New England women labored in the textile and shoe industries, and many more women on farms and in big cities depended on piecework in their homes or in sweatshops to make ends meet. From the outset, Americans often expressed their ambivalence toward manufacturing by raising concerns about how this work might corrupt the morals of workers, especially women. Samuel Slater had hoped to avoid disrupting the traditional household economy by paying the wages of his young women employees directly to their fathers. When the Waltham and Lowell mills opened in the 1820s and 1830s, however, the owners paid the women directly, thereby opening the door to women's independence. To alleviate fears of women's unregulated freedom, the Lowell mill owners tried to fill the role of supervisory parents, insisting that "factory girls" live in company boardinghouses, attend church services, abide by curfews, and keep their minds active. The association of women workers with suspect morals, however, never vanished. Orestes Brownson offered his critique of factory work in the Boston Quarterly Review *in 1840. A minister, activist, and essayist, Brownson was also a labor radical who had supported the Workingmen's Party in the 1830s. Brownson's criticism of female factory workers prompted women workers in Lowell to pen a defense of their fellow laborers in their own newspaper, the* Lowell Offering.

PROBLEMS TO CONSIDER

1. How do you account for Brownson's apparently demeaning comments about factory laborers, when his intent was to offer a defense of labor against the cruelties of a capitalist system?
2. How are Brownson and the Lowell women arguing more about ideas of manhood and womanhood than about industrial labor?

LABORING CLASSES

What we would ask is, throughout the Christian world, the actual condition of the laboring classes, viewed simply and exclusively in their capacity of laborers? . . .

All over the world this fact stares us in the face, the workingman is poor and depressed, while a large portion of the non-workingmen, in the sense we now use the term, are wealthy. . . . The whole class of simple laborers are poor, and in general unable to procure anything beyond the bare necessaries of life.

In regard to labor two systems obtain; one that of slave labor, the other that of free labor. Of the two, the first is, in our judgment, except so far as the feelings are concerned, decidedly the least oppressive. If the slave has never been a free man, we think, as a general rule, his sufferings are less than those of the free laborer at wages. As to the actual freedom one has just about as much as the other. The laborer at wages has all the disadvantages of freedom and none of its blessings, while the slave, if denied the blessing, is freed from the disadvantages. We are no advocates of slavery, we are as heartily opposed to it as any modern abolitionist can be; but we say frankly that, if there must always be a laboring population distinct from proprietors and employers, we regard the slave system as decidedly preferable to the system at wages. It is no pleasant thing to go days without food, to lie idle for weeks, seeking work and finding none, to rise in the morning with a wife and children you love, and know not where to procure them a breakfast, and to see constantly before you no brighter prospect than the almshouse. Yet these are no unfrequent incidents in the lives of our laboring population. . . .

We pass through our manufacturing villages, most of them appear neat and flourishing. The operatives are well dressed, and we are told, well paid. They are said to be healthy, contented, and happy. This is the fair side of the picture; the side exhibited to distinguished visitors. There is a dark side, moral as well as physical. Of the common operatives, few, if any, by their wages, acquire a competence. . . . But the great mass wear out their health, spirits, and morals, without becoming one whit better off than when they commenced labor. The bills of mortality in these factory villages are not striking, we admit, for the poor girls when they can toil no longer go home to die. The average life, working life we mean, of the girls that come to Lowell, for instance, from Maine, New Hampshire, and Vermont, we have been assured, is only about three years. What becomes of them then? Few of them ever marry; fewer still ever return to their native places with reputations unimpaired. "She has worked in a Factory," is almost enough to damn to infamy the most worthy and virtuous girl. We know no sadder sight on earth than one of our factory villages presents, when the bell at break of day, or at the hour of breakfast, or dinner, calls out its hundreds or thousands of operatives. We stand and look at these hard working men and women hurrying in all directions, and ask ourselves, where go the proceeds of their labors? The man who employs them, and for whom they are toiling as so many slaves, is one of our city nabobs [*i.e., persons of great wealth*], revelling in luxury; or he is a member of our legislature, enacting laws to put money in his own pocket; or he is a member of Congress, contending for a high Tariff to tax the poor for the benefit of the rich; or in these times he is shedding crocodile tears over the deplorable condition of the poor laborer, while he docks his wages twenty-five per cent.; building miniature log cabins, shouting Harrison and "hard cider." And this man too would fain pass for a Christian and a republican. He shouts for liberty, stickles for equality, and is horrified at a Southern planter who keeps slaves. . . .

The actual condition of the workingman today, viewed in all its bearings, is not so good as it was fifty years ago. If we have not been altogether misinformed, fifty years ago, health and industrious habits, constituted no mean stock in trade, and with them almost any man might aspire to competence and independence. But it is so no longer. . . .

Now the great work for this age and the coming, is to raise up the laborer, and to realize in our own social arrangements and in the actual condition of all men, that equality between man and man, which God has established between the rights of one and those of another. In other words, our business is to emancipate the proletaries, as the past has emancipated the slaves. . . .

Orestes Brownson, "Laboring Classes," *Boston Quarterly Review* 3 (July 1840): 367–73.

FACTORY GIRLS

"SHE HAS WORKED IN A FACTORY, *is sufficient to damn to infamy the most worthy and virtuous girl*."

So says Mr. Orestes A. Brownson; and either this horrible assertion is true, or Mr. Brownson is a slanderer. I assert that it is *not* true, and Mr. B. may consider himself called upon to prove his words, if he can.

This gentleman . . . may now see what will probably appear to him quite as marvellous; and that is, that a *factory girl* is not afraid to oppose herself to the *Editor of the Boston Quarterly Review*. True, he has upon his side fame, learning, and great talent; but I have what is better than either of these, or all combined, and that is *truth*. Mr. Brownson has not said that this thing should be so; or that he is glad it is so; or that he deeply regrets such a state of affairs; but he has said it *is* so; and *I* affirm that it is *not*.

And whom has Mr. Brownson slandered? A class of girls who in this city alone are numbered by thousands, and who collect in many of our smaller towns by hundreds; girls who generally come from quiet country homes, where their minds and manners have been formed under the eyes of the worthy sons of the Pilgrims, and their virtuous partners, and who return again to become the wives of the free intelligent yeomanry of New England, and the mothers of

quite a proportion of our future republicans. Think, for a moment, how many of the next generation are to spring from mothers doomed to infamy! "Ah," it may be replied, "Mr. Brownson acknowledges that you may still be worthy and virtuous." Then we must be a set of worthy and virtuous idiots, for no virtuous girl of common sense would choose for an occupation one that would consign her to infamy. . . .

That there has been prejudice against us, we know; but it is wearing away, and has never been so deep nor universal as Mr. B's statement will lead many to believe. Even now it may be that "the mushroom aristocracy," and "would-be-fashionables" of Boston, turn up their eyes in horror at the sound of those vulgar words, *factory girls*; but *they* form but a small part of the community, and theirs are not the opinions which Mr. Brownson intended to represent.

Whence has arisen the degree of prejudice which has existed against factory girls, I cannot tell; but we often hear the condition of the factory population of England, and the station which the operatives hold in society there, referred to as descriptive of *our* condition. . . . And again: it has been asserted that to put ourselves under the influence and restraints of corporate bodies, is contrary to the spirit of our institutions, and to that love of independence which we ought to cherish. . . . We are under restraints, but they are voluntarily assumed; and we are at liberty to withdraw from them, whenever they become galling or irksome. Neither have I ever discovered that any restraints were imposed upon us, but those which were necessary for the peace and comfort of the whole, and for the promotion of the design for which we are collected, namely, to get money, as much of it and as fast as we can, and it is because our toil is so unremitting, that the wages of factory girls are higher than those of females engaged in most other occupations. It is these wages which, in spite of toil, restraint, discomfort, and prejudice, have drawn so many worthy, virtuous, intelligent, and well-educated girls to Lowell, and other factories; and it is the wages which are in a great degree to decide the characters of the factory girls as a class. . . . Mr. Brownson may rail as much as he pleases against the real injustice of capitalists against operatives, and we will bid him *God speed*; if he will but keep truth and common sense upon his side. Still, the avails of factory labor are now greater than those of many domestics, seamstresses, and school-teachers; and strange would it be, if in money-loving New England, one of the most lucrative female employments should be rejected because it is toilsome, or because some people are prejudiced against it. Yankee girls have too much *independence* for *that*.

But it may be remarked, "You certainly cannot mean to intimate, that all factory girls are virtuous, intelligent," &c. No, I do not; and Lowell would be a stranger place than it has ever been represented, if among eight thousand girls there were none of the ignorant and depraved. Calumniators have asserted, that *all* were vile, because they knew *some* to be so; and the sins of *a few* have been visited upon *the many*. . . . The erroneous idea, wherever it exists, must be done away, that there is in factories but one sort of girls, and *that* the baser and degraded sort. There are among us *all sorts* of girls. I believe that there

are few occupations which can exhibit so many gradations of piety and intelligence; but the majority may at least lay claim to as much of the former as females in other stations of life. . . . The Improvement Circles, the Lyceum and Institute, the social religious meetings, the Circulating and other libraries, can bear testimony that the little time they have is spent in a better manner. Our well filled churches and lecture halls, and the high character of our clergymen and lecturers, will testify that the state of morals and intelligence is not low. . . .

And now, if Mr. Brownson is *a man*, he will endeavor to retrieve the injury he has done; he will resolve that "the dark shall be light, and the wrong made right," and the assertion he has publicly made will be as publicly retracted. If he still doubts upon the subject, let him come among us: let him make himself as well acquainted with us as our pastors and superintendents are; and though he will find error, ignorance, and folly among us, (and where would he find them not?) yet he would not see worthy and virtuous girls consigned to infamy, because they work in a factory.

A FACTORY GIRL

"Factory Girls," *Lowell Offering*, December 1840, 17–19.

↜

↜ MEN ON THE MAKE: ENTREPRENEURS AND THE MYTHICAL CULTURE OF SELF-MADE MEN

Journal (1818–1824)
JAMES GUILD

A key feature of the market transformation in the North was how pervasive a culture of ambition became for young men. Contemporaries were struck by the entrepreneurial spirit that reigned in the early republic. In the words of one observer, the society was literally "teeming with business." Another foreign traveler noted the "feverish ardor [with which] the Americans pursue prosperity and how they are ever tormented by the shadowy suspicion that they may not have chosen the shortest route to get it." Of course, as Greenleaf Patch's story reminds us, these commercial ambitions might have been a response to

declining opportunities for men in traditional farming and artisan work once industri-
alization had begun. Yet other men plunged wholeheartedly into the pursuit of wealth
and business success. These were the entrepreneurial strivings that established the middle
class in the North. And with these commercial ambitions emerged new ideals of mas-
culinity. Enterprise, energy, action, aggression — and, above all, self-interest — became
the defining characteristics of this self-achieving manhood. Behind these ideals also lay
the fears of the all-too-common flip side of this manly behavior, found in debt, business
failure, drinking, and violence. We can take a peek at the culture of this new aggressive
masculinity in the extraordinary journal kept by a Vermont farmboy named James
Guild, who set out on a personal quest to make something of himself. His account offers
a striking parallel to the fictional tale of Sam Slick.

PROBLEMS TO CONSIDER

1. Analyze the various performances that Guild enacts during his travels: how
   were Guild's performances part of his self-representation as a man?
2. How would you characterize Guild's system of values? What does he value
   most and least? Compare his values with those espoused by Colonel Manly in
   The Contrast (chapter 4).

Tunbridge, [Vermont], Oct. 5th 1818
At this time I became of age. . . . Then I sough[t]
for some happier situation. My disposition would
not allow me to work on a farm, and some other
employment I must pursue. At this time I was
worth a note of $70 Dollars, and I could not com-
mand the cash for it. So I had a disposition to sell
it for goods which I moved to my great disadvan-
tage. No one knows the feelings of my heart when
parting with my little all for a trunk of goods and
losing my character if I had any by being a pedler.
I not only had the disagreeable sensations of leaving my friends, but I wondered why I should
stoop so low as to follow so mean a calling. . . .

After biding all friends adieu I took my little
trunk and stears for the west. Now my sorrows
began to rise. . . . I began my peddleing. You
must know it was awkward for a farmer boy who
had been confined to the hoe or ax to put on a
pedlers face, but I believe I was as apt as any
one, I got my things in rotation pedler form, so
when I went into a house, ["]do you wish to buy
some haircombs, needles, buttons, buttonmolds,
sewing silk, beeds?["] If they wished to pur-

chase, they would want to banter untill they
could get it for nothing. . . .

The best you could say of me I was a poor
sorry boy. To indulge myself in thinking of home
I found was a burden to my sorrows. . . .

Soon it began to rain and . . . while I was traveling over the dreary forrest, my mind was not
without its thoughts. Some times I was thinking of pleasure I used to take with my young
companions. Some times I would think of my
Mother, Brothers or sister. Sometimes I would
think of my God but not as I ought. Sometimes
would sing, but if I sang any thing that was
mournful I would burst out in tears. . . . While
contemplateing on these things my foot slipt
and down went guile, I, trunk and all, and hurt
myself and bruised my trunk. I got up and cried
out, ["]O heaven what shall I do, was I born for
misfortune? O' I am poorer than a beger, and I
can never prosper, nor my friends will never
more embrace my society with that loveing affection. O misery, I wish my goods were never
seen by me, but since I was born for misfortune,
I will sit down and sing a song.["]

Thus while the rain was driping my face and all covered with mud, I sat down and sang the following verses:

In my youth I was blest by the smiles of a
  mother,
Whose kindness love no longer can express.
There's happy a lass though deprived of a
  Father
Who died ere I clung to a kind parents
  breast.

Now manhood advances my young breast
  with ambition,
For fame and for fortune with raptures do
  glow.
On pursuant of this notion I'm traveling
  abroad the ocean
While amid perils so manhood will grow.

After this I shouldered my trunk and went on. . . .

In the meantime I had a chance to buy four or five dozen scissors at 3 cents each and thought if I could sell them for 12 cents, I was making good profit, so I offerd them for sale, but the reply was they are good for nothing; if they were, you would ask more for them. I tried about a fortnight but sold none, then I took and made two packs of them and marked one 12 and the other 25 cents, new scissors for sale; and when I went into a house it was, ["]do you want any tin cups, tin pans, tin or pewter dishes of any kind mended and do you want to buy some scissors?["] ["]Yes, if you have got some good ones.["] ["]Well, ma'am, I have got some good ones and some poor ones; my best come at 25 cents and the other at 12 cents.["] So I would show them, to them, and they would look of them. ["]Now mother you must get me a pair of scissors for me, for you never got me a pair.["] ["]O well dear child I suppose you must have a pair or I shall be teased to death.["] Now the girl would say ["]mother which is it best to get 12 or 25 cents one?["] ["]O it is best to get a good pair if any.["]. . .

Now I had got slicked up a little and into Albany I went heads up, and in the most important way I could to make folks think I was something I was not. The first dash I made was into the museum. Here I observed they played on the hand organs, and I criticized them to see how they maneuvered it, and soon I asked the leave to play a tune as I was used to playing on them and pretended I had a favorite tune I wanted to play. Here I used deception, for I never had played on one before. Then I asked the owner of the Museum if he would not be glad to have me play on a tambourine that evening and the reply was yes, for we are going to have an uncommon collection this evening. So I went and borrowed tambourine and came on to the stage with a bold face, and after I had been introduced to the musicians I began to knock round the tambourine while the people were collecting. Now Guild exerted himself, I can asure you, for I drew the attention of two or three hundred people.

After the evening exercise was over the man asked me to call in and see him in the morning. Of course I did, and he gave me five dollars and said if I would stay one month longer, he would give me $15. I accepted of this offer and the course of that time learned to cut profile likenesses. . . . Now then I called myself a profile cutter. . . .

Now I went to Canadagua. Here I went into a painters shop, one who painted likenesses, and my profiles looked so mean when I saw them I asked him what he would show me one day for, how to distinguish the colors & he said $5, and I consented to it and began to paint. He showed me one day and then I went to Bloomfield and took a picture of Mr Goodwins painting for a sample on my way. I put up at a tavern and told a Young Lady if she would wash my shirt, I would draw her likeness. Now then I was to exert my skill in painting. I opperated once on her but it looked so like a wretch I throwed it away and tried again. The poor Girl sat nipped up so prim and look so smileing it makes me smile when I think of while I was daubing on paint on a piece of paper, it could not be called painting, for it looked more like a strangled cat than it did like her. However I told her it looked like her and she believed it, but I cut her profile and she had a profile if not a likeness. . . .

Now I begin [to] learn human nature. I find people are not always what they seem to be. . . . I find by experience if a man thinks he is something and puts him self forward he will be something. I dont mean he must put himself forward by crowding himself into company but despising those who haunt the grog shop or the gambleing table, and act with an independent manner and face the rich proud and haughty, with the same ease and politeness of manner as though . . . you belonged to the same class. . . .

For about three weeks I was in low spirits and sought solitude. I found my health impairing very fast and to grieve about spilt milk would only shorten my days and deprive me of that independant spirit and ambition which I had to shine in the world. I was and always was unhappy because I could not obtain a fortune. I thought that I should be one of the happiest fellows in the world if I could only be rich, and I thought as others had began with nothin and became men of fortune that I might I threw asside all my dull notions and went to painting and paid off all my debts and a little to clear out. . . .

Here I said to myself that I will make money. . . .

After I failed in Baltimore I would not write to my friends [i.e., his family] too proud to own that I had been taken in and lost all my money. I said to myself money I must and will have. I found I lacked very much for instruction, and I made up my mind to go to N.Y. and receive instruction from the first artists and then take a trip to the south, and when I can go home in Style then will I go but in any other way I will not show my face. . . .

Now my sole object was to make money. I cared not for this society, nor friendship any more than to have them treat me with politeness, and

I do the same to them. I commenced my profession and soon found incouragement. . . .

My object was money, and when I had settled up my concerns, I found I had made one Thousand dollars from, Oct, untill June. Now I have surmounted the great difficulty I so long sought. I loved my friends my dear Mother and Sister & but three years had passed, and I had not seen her.

My whole happiness was in anticipating the pleasure I should receive in visiting them. I engagued my passage for New York. . . . I landed safe in N.Y. I had 4 Hundred dollars in the bank and $1000, which made $1400. Now I felt as though I could go home and see my friends in the character of an independent Gentleman, and something to foot the bill. I always bare in mind, Shoemaker go not above your last. I was now worth about, $2000, and by good conduct my profession would always furnish me with the best society. . . .

[I] returned to Albany from thence I crossed the green mountains and returned once more to my beloved friends, in Vt.

I had been absent from them three years, and for two years I had never heard from them nor they from me. I would not write them, because I had failed in business, and unless I could go home in Style. I Surprised them all very much, for I could go home with my pockets well lined, and of what a happy time I spent with them. I could embrace my dear Mother and Sister with an affectionate kiss, and embrace in my arms, that Mother who watched over my youthful days. . . .

I soon paid my old Master a visit. . . . How changed the sun seven years before that I was Subject to my masters will, and tied to the hoe and harrow. Now I could ride in my cariage, and ask no man, any favors. I had never done any work since I left him, and had become so accustomed to dressing in style and keeping Stylish company, it seemed very odd to return to my friends who live as I used to with a tow Shirt and frock on with a beard a week old. The young Ladies that I used to think so very nice now look

. . . more like servants Girls. In the style I had been living and society that I associated with had accustomed me to treat such as was not able to dress in style at all times and have the title of Ladies and Gentlemen, with indifferance, and never thought them companions for me; but when I saw so much harmony existing in their little family circles, the strong attachments they held for each other, how happy they were in, spending time in industry, contented to please, no ambition to shine, I was ready to exclaim, give me domestic happiness. I could not help but admire them, and stronger attachments I have never seen, neither felt in those circles where they could dress in style every day. After having made my visits to all my friends finding them all well, I began to feel a desire to get back again to N.Y. where I could enjoy my usual ocupation and visiting those families who have daughters that play so beautiful on the pianoforte, and where there is constantly some new thing to attract the eye and attention.

———

"From Tunbridge, Vermont, to London, England: The Journal of James Guild, Peddler, Tinker, Schoolmaster, Portrait Painter, from 1818 to 1824," *Proceedings of the Vermont Historical Society* 5 (1937): 250–53, 259–61, 267–68, 279, 300–301, 305–8.

Dr. Stramonium (1830)
SAMUEL WOODWORTH

Not everyone was comfortable with the new self-interested manhood displayed in the early republic. One of its greatest dangers, in the minds of many, was the possibility that arts of deception might be practiced not only in competition with other men but also in the market for marriage and sex. Alongside the mythical self-made man emerged another character: the rake or seducer, the man who exploits women's "virtue" for his own pleasure. As the next section reveals, stories of seduction were the most popular fiction of the early republic, and they usually featured a man as aggressive in his sexual conquests as he might be in business. Samuel Woodworth exploited this real and imagined "man on the make" in his song "Dr. Stramonium." Woodworth's own life fit the patterns traced in this chapter: he was the son of poor farmers in Massachusetts, faced several business failures and was nearly imprisoned for debts, and eventually moved to New York City, where he struggled to support a family as the author of songs, popular verses, and musical comedies for the theater. Stramonium (also called the "devil's apple") was an herbal recipe popular with homeopathic doctors, so Woodworth was alluding both to Eve's seduction in the Garden of Eden and to another group of men on the make, alternative medical practitioners, upstarts who challenged university-trained doctors for the new status of professional physicians.

PROBLEMS TO CONSIDER

1. What similarities does "Mr. Rover," Woodworth's seducer of women, share with other men on the make, such as James Guild or Sam Slick?
2. In Woodworth's song, what are the parallels between the deceptions of men in commerce or personal ambition and the sexual relationships between men and women?

Air—Nothing at All

[1.]

A last and a lapstone, were once my delight,
And I sung while I hammered, from morning
    till night;
But all the day's earnings, at eve, I would spend,
Till the *thread* of my credit was brought to an
    end.

Spoken

For I was up to a thing or two, and loved fun;
passed the night in reciting Shakespeare at the
ale-house, and kept myself awake the next day,
by beating time with the hammer, while I sung—

Make a death, cut a stick, high time I tramp'd,
Rise again, tick again, credit new vamp'd.

2.

I next taught the gamut, the sharps, and the flats,
To a nasal-twang'd bass, and a treble of cats;
Till my *private* duet with a miss, got abroad,
Which chang'd the *key note*, and produced a
    discord.

Spoken

A little love affair, that ran *counter* to my wishes,
and induced some slanderous tongues to pronounce the whole *tenor* of my conduct to be
thorough *bass.* . . .

3.

A travelling merchant I quickly became,
With a new stock in trade, a new dress, and
    new name;
And I bartered my goods with such exquisite
    grace,
That I left a fair mourner in every place.

Spoken

"O Tabitha, what will become of me! The dear
sweet Mr. Rover, (for that was my travelling
name,) my dear sweet Mr. Rover, the pedler, is
gone, and perhaps I shall never see him again.
O dear!" "*Your* dear sweet Mr. Rover, indeed!
I'd have you to know, cousin Keziah, that he is
my dear sweet Mr. Rover, and he has left me
something to remember him by."—"O the base,

wicked deceiver! He has left me something too."

. . .

5.

I then became preacher without any call,
When a sweet village lass came to hear brother
    Paul;
And told her experience o'er with such grace,
That I gave the dear creature an ardent embrace.

Spoken

There was the devil to pay, and poor I once more
in the vocative. But, I made my escape to the
back-woods, singing my old Crispin ditty—

Make a death, cut a stick, high time I tramp'd,
Rise again, tick again, credit new vamp'd.

6.

And now a physician, with cock'd hat and wig,
I can feel ladies' pulses, look wise, and talk big;
With a fine ruffled shirt, and good coat to my
    back,
I pluck the poor *geese*, while the ducks exclaim
    quack!

Spoken

"O Doctor, I am so glad you are come. I have
such a concerned beating of the heart, that I can
hardly draw a breath. Oh!" "Let me see your
tongue, Miss."—"My tongue! Law souls, Doctor, what in the world has the tongue to do with
the heart?" "In general, Miss, not much; but
your case is an exception." "An exception! O
goody gracious! now, you don't say so; is an exception a dangerous disorder, Doctor?" "Not at
all dangerous, Miss. An application of stramonium externally, and copious draughts of catnip
tea internally, will soon restore you."—The lady's
heart becomes composed, I pocket my fee, and
make my exit, singing—

Feel the pulse, smell the cane, look at the
    tongue,
Touch the gold, praise the old, flatter the young.

Samuel Woodworth, *Melodies, Duets, Trios, Songs, and Ballads,* . . ., 3rd ed. (New York: Author, 1831), 171–73.

✆

↝ *Heart and Hearth:*
Seduction and Domesticity for Women ↝

The market revolution in the North produced for the first time a distinct and dominant middle class in America. From the perspective of economics, the middle class established its identity by having access to capital, engaging in nonmanual work, and becoming either the employers of labor or the retailers who sold the products made by wage laborers. The authority of members of the middle class, however, rested squarely on their ability to shape cultural ideals and to convince others that their ideologies were not peculiar to their class, but rather were expressions of human nature. Through the writings and actions of reformers, ministers, and businessmen, a middle-class ethos of "respectability" was forged around the values of self-denial and the expectations that men's and women's nature and responsibilities would be both different and separate.

Perhaps the biggest change associated with the market and industrial revolutions was the displacement of work from the home. For centuries in Europe and America, nearly everyone worked and resided in the same location. But in the early nineteenth century, it became clear that people of all classes were now working and living in different places. For the working class, this meant going off to work in factories and workshops rather than working on farms or in shops at home, as in a traditional economy. For the middle class, this change was manifested in moving away from their laboring employees into new class-segregated neighborhoods in towns and cities. A quick glance at city directories (the equivalent of phone books for that era) reveals that in the eighteenth century most merchants, shopkeepers, and master craftsmen were listed with one address; by the early nineteenth century, they had separate work and home addresses.

To make sense of these changes, middle-class Americans constructed a cultural ideology of gender, in which men and women were said to inhabit "separate spheres." Once home was no longer considered a place of production, the middle class began to glorify a woman's separate existence in the home. "To render *home* happy," wrote one essayist, "is woman's peculiar province; home is *her* world." Women were presented as naturally suited for the private and domestic sphere, creating an oasis of piety to which men could return after they had exerted themselves in the cutthroat public world of business and politics. Sexual difference was now defined as a set of categorical opposites: men were depicted as public, selfish, passionate, in the world, and peripheral to child rearing; women were seen as private, selfless, passionless, in the home, and central to child rearing. With each passing year, the architects of this gender ideology emphasized women's maternal and domestic roles until these roles assumed the character of an office or occupation and were accorded significance for the nation and the race.

This notion of women as sexually passionless and unsuited for independence outside of the home was, of course, a direct response to new market-oriented changes. The middle-class ideology of "true womanhood" sought to erase women's presence in the wage labor force and reestablish controls over marriage and women's sexuality, in the face of rising rates of premarital pregnancies. Even before middle-class reformers promulgated an ideology of domesticity for women, these changes were first addressed in a new form of popular culture for women: novel reading.

Charlotte Temple: A Tale of Truth (1791)

SUSANNA ROWSON

Americans became enthusiastic readers of novels and short fiction in the early republic, and the most common plot involved a tragic tale of seduction. The story of a young woman torn from her loving (sometimes tyrannical) parents by a deceitful and dishonorable seducer, and then left to die a lonely death, was the narrative that American readers returned to again and again in cheap books, magazines, and newspapers. This form of popular culture spurred on a print revolution in the North. Book publishers and traveling book peddlers made these novels readily available, and increasing literacy rates made young women both the intended audience and the central protagonists of this fiction. Northern readers were attracted to these stories because they dramatized the dilemmas of young women and men in a changing society, in which traditional controls over marriage and sexuality exerted by families and close-knit communities were fractured by the mobility and anonymity of industrial cities. Some seduction novels were based on real women's experiences, and novelists quickly learned that posing their fiction as a real story gave their tales legitimacy and popularity at a time when readers were told that novels were morally corrupt. Written for women and about women, seduction tales give us insights into attitudes about marriage and women's sexuality during the early years of the republic. Susanna Rowson's novel Charlotte Temple *(1791), the best-selling book during the nation's first fifty years, is the story of a young woman lured away from her parents in England, taken to America, and, after she gives up her virginity, abandoned by her seducer, who had no intention of marrying her.*

PROBLEMS TO CONSIDER

1. What does this story reveal about contemporary attitudes about young women, sexuality, marriage, and family during the early republic?
2. How could the character of Charlotte Temple be read as a metaphor for the upheavals in a dynamic and uncertain market society?

PREFACE

For the perusal of the young and thoughtless of the fair sex, this Tale of Truth is designed; and I could wish my fair readers to consider it as not merely the effusion of Fancy, but as a reality. The circumstances on which I have founded this novel were related to me some little time since by an old lady who had personally known Charlotte, though she concealed the real names of the characters, and . . . I have thrown over the whole a slight veil of fiction, and substituted names and places according to my own fancy. The principal characters in this little tale are now consigned to the silent tomb: it can therefore hurt the feelings of no one; and may, I flatter myself, be of service to some who are so unfortunate as to have neither friends to advise, or understanding to direct them, through the various and unexpected evils that attend a young and unprotected woman in her first entrance into life.

While the tear of compassion still trembled in my eye for the fate of the unhappy Charlotte, I may have children of my own, said I, to whom this recital may be of use, and if to your own children, said Benevolence, why not to the many daughters of Misfortune who, deprived of natural friends, or spoilt by a mistaken education, are thrown on an unfeeling world without the least power to defend themselves from the snares not only of the other sex, but from the more dangerous arts of the profligate of their own. . . .

CHAPTER I: A BOARDING SCHOOL

. . . Montraville was a Lieutenant in the army: Belcour was his brother officer: they had been to take leave of their friends previous to their departure for America, and were now returning to Portsmouth, where the troops waited orders for embarkation. They had stopped at Chichester to dine; and . . . to take a survey of the Chichester ladies as they returned from their devotions.

They had gratified their curiosity, and were preparing to return to the inn without honoring any of the belles with particular notice, when Madame Du Pont, at the head of her school, descended from the church. Such an assemblage of youth and innocence naturally attracted the young soldiers: they stopped; and, as the little cavalcade passed, almost involuntarily pulled off their hats. A tall, elegant girl looked at Montraville and blushed: he instantly recollected the features of Charlotte Temple, whom he had once seen and danced with at a ball at Portsmouth. . . .

But Charlotte had made too great an impression on his mind to be easily eradicated: having therefore spent three whole days in thinking on her and in endeavoring to form some plan for

seeing her, he determined to set off for Chichester, and trust to chance either to favor or frustrate his designs. . . .

He soon found means to ingratiate himself with her companion, who was a French teacher at the school, and, at parting, slipped a letter he had purposely written, into Charlotte's hand, and five guineas into that of Mademoiselle, who promised she would endeavor to bring her young charge into the field again the next evening. . . .

CHAPTER 6: AN INTRIGUING TEACHER

. . . Gracious heaven! when I think on the miseries that must rend the heart of a doting parent, when he sees the darling of his age at first seduced from his protection, and afterwards abandoned, by the very wretch whose promises of love decoyed her from the paternal roof—when he sees her poor and wretched, her bosom torn between remorse for her crime and love for her vile betrayer—when fancy paints to me the good old man stooping to raise the weeping penitent, while every tear from her eye is numbered by drops from his bleeding heart, my bosom glows with honest indignation, and I wish for power to extirpate those monsters of seduction from the earth.

Oh my dear girls—for to such only am I writing—listen not to the voice of love, unless sanctioned by paternal approbation: be assured, it is now past the days of romance: no woman can be run away with contrary to her own inclination: then kneel down each morning, and request kind heaven to keep you free from temptation, or, should it please to suffer you to be tried, pray for fortitude to resist the impulse of inclination when it runs counter to the precepts of religion and virtue. . . .

CHAPTER II: CONFLICT OF LOVE AND DUTY

Almost a week was now gone, and Charlotte continued every evening to meet Montraville, and in her heart every meeting was resolved to be the last; but alas! when Montraville at parting would earnestly entreat one more interview, that treacherous heart betrayed her; and, forgetful of its resolution, pleaded the cause of the enemy so powerfully, that Charlotte was unable to resist. Another and another meeting succeeded; and so well did Montraville improve each opportunity, that the heedless girl at length confessed no idea could be so painful to her as that of never seeing him again.

"Then we will never be parted," said he.

"Ah, Montraville," replied Charlotte, forcing a smile, "how can it be avoided? My parents would never consent to our union; and even could they be brought to approve it, how should I bear to be separated from my kind, my beloved mother?" ...

"All these distressing scenes, my dear Charlotte," cried Montraville, "are merely the chimeras of a disturbed fancy. Your parents might perhaps grieve at first; but when they heard from your own hand that you was with a man of honor, and that it was to insure your felicity by an union with him, to which you feared they would never have given their assent, that you left their protection, they will, be assured, forgive an error which love alone occasioned, and when we return from America, receive you with open arms and tears of joy." ...

CHAPTER 15: EMBARKATION

It was with the utmost difficulty that the united efforts of Mademoiselle and Montraville could support Charlotte's spirits during their short ride from Chichester to Portsmouth, where a boat waited to take them immediately on board the ship in which they were to embark for America.

As soon as she became tolerably composed, she entreated pen and ink to write to her parents. This she did in the most affecting, artless manner, entreating their pardon and blessing, and describing the dreadful situation of her mind, the conflict she suffered in endeavoring to conquer this unfortunate attachment, and concluded with saying, her only hope of future comfort consisted in the (perhaps delusive) idea she indulged, of being once more folded in their protecting arms, and hearing the words of peace and pardon from their lips.

The tears streamed incessantly while she was writing, and she was frequently obliged to lay down her pen: but when the task was completed, and she had committed the letter to the care of Montraville to be sent to the post office, she became more calm. ...

But Montraville knew too well the consequences that must unavoidably ensue, should this letter reach Mr. Temple: he therefore wisely resolved to walk on the deck, tear it in pieces, and commit the fragments to the care of Neptune, who might or might not, as it suited his convenience, convey them on shore. ...

In the mean time every enquiry that could be thought of was made by Mr. and Mrs. Temple; for many days did they indulge the fond hope that she was merely gone off to be married, and that when the indissoluble knot was once tied, she would return with the partner she had chosen, and entreat their blessing and forgiveness.

"And shall we not forgive her?" said Mr. Temple.

"Forgive her!" exclaimed the mother. "Oh yes, whatever be our errors, is she not our child? and though bowed to the earth even with shame and remorse, is it not our duty to raise the poor penitent, and whisper peace and comfort to her desponding soul? would she but return, with rapture would I fold her to my heart, and bury every remembrance of her faults in the dear embrace."

But still day after day passed on, and Charlotte did not appear, nor were any tidings to be heard of her. ...

CHAPTER 18: REFLECTIONS

... Montraville had placed her in a small house a few miles from New York: he gave her one female attendant, and supplied her with what money she wanted; but business and pleasure so entirely occupied his time, that he had little to devote to the woman, whom he had brought from all her connections, and robbed of innocence. Sometimes, indeed, he would steal out at the close of evening, and pass a few hours with her; and then so much was she attached to him, that all her sorrows were forgotten while blest with his society: she would enjoy a walk by moonlight, or sit by him in a little arbor at the bottom of the garden, and play on the harp, accompanying it with her plaintive, harmonious voice. But often, very often, did he promise to renew his visits, and, forgetful of his promise, leave her to mourn her disappointment. . . .

Who can form an adequate idea of the sorrow that preyed upon the mind of Charlotte? . . . But the poor girl by thoughtless passion led astray, who, in parting with her honor, has forfeited the esteem of the very man to whom she has sacrificed everything dear and valuable in life, feels his indifference in the fruit of her own folly, and laments her want of power to recall his lost affection; she knows there is no tie but honor, and that, in a man who has been guilty of seduction, is but very feeble: he may leave her in a moment to shame and want; he may marry and forsake her forever; and should he, she has no redress, no friendly, soothing companion to pour into her wounded mind the balm of consolation, no benevolent hand to lead her back to the path of rectitude; she has disgraced her friends, forfeited the good opinion of the world, and undone herself; she feels herself a poor solitary being in the midst of surrounding multitudes; shame bows her to the earth, remorse tears her distracted mind, and guilt, poverty, and disease close the dreadful scene: she sinks unnoticed to oblivion. . . .

[As often happens in seduction tales, the tragic heroine unfortunately becomes mortally ill just as she is to be reconciled with her forgiving parents.]

CHAPTER 33: WHICH PEOPLE VOID OF FEELING NEED NOT READ

. . . The ardent manner in which he uttered these words occasioned him to raise his voice. It caught the ear of Charlotte: she knew the beloved sound: and uttering a loud shriek, she sprang forward as Mr. Temple entered the room. "My adored father." "My long lost child." Nature could support no more, and they both sunk lifeless into the arms of the attendants.

Charlotte was again put into bed, and a few moments restored Mr. Temple: but to describe the agony of his sufferings is past the power of any one, who, though they may readily conceive, cannot delineate the dreadful scene. Every eye gave testimony of what each heart felt—but all were silent.

When Charlotte recovered, she found herself supported in her father's arms. She cast on him a most expressive look, but was unable to speak. A reviving cordial was administered. She then asked, in a low voice, for her child: it was brought to her: she put it in her father's arms. "Protect her," said she, "and bless your dying—"

Unable to finish the sentence, she sunk back on her pillow: her countenance was serenely composed; she regarded her father as he pressed the infant to his breast with a steadfast look; a sudden beam of joy passed across her languid features, she raised her eyes to heaven—and then closed them forever.

[Susanna Rowson], *Charlotte: A Tale of Truth*, 2 vols. (Philadelphia: Printed by D. Humphreys for Mathew Carey, 1794), 1:v–vii, 9–12, 38, 57–59, 75–77; 2:4–6, 77–78.

Novel Reading, A Cause of Female Depravity (1802)

The protagonist in Royall Tyler's novel The Algerine Captive *(1797) observes that before he spent seven years in captivity in North Africa, the most common books in a family's home in rural New England were sermons of clergymen and other works of piety. When he returned, "he found a surprising alteration in the public's taste." Country booksellers had fostered a passion for "books designed to amuse rather than to instruct," filling "the whole land with modern travels and novels almost as incredible." In the same year that Tyler's book was released, the editor of* New York Magazine *declared: "This is a novel-reading age." The popularity of novel reading was matched by the frequency and prevalence of its critics. Not only did leading statesmen, clergy, and reformers make the point of thrashing novels, but nearly every popular novel defended itself either by suggesting it was not really a novel ("a tale of truth," as Rowson phrased it) or by telling readers that this book was the exception, the novel worthy of reading for the moral lessons it contained. Because women were novels' targeted audience, criticisms of novel reading became statements about the ideals of womanhood in the new nation. It was not just that novels contained seduction tales thought to be bawdy and indecent; critics feared that novel reading itself was an act of seducing women. In the words of one critic: "Novels . . . are the powerful engines with which the seducer attacks the female heart." Hence, both reading and sexuality became sites where moralists feared women's independent action and thought. Originally printed in the* New England Quarterly *in 1802, the following essay, attacking the presumed depravity of novel reading, offers the most pointed example of these concerns.*

PROBLEMS TO CONSIDER

1. How exactly did novels threaten gender conventions in the new republic? How would you compare this critique of novel reading to Orestes Brownson's criticism of "factory girls"?
2. How might this critic of novel reading have engaged in the same vices that he or she accuses novelists of fomenting through their texts?

Mr. Editor,

I now begin to hope I shall see good old days come round again—that moderately stiff stays, covered elbows, and concealed bosoms, will soon be prevailing fashions; and, what is of far greater importance, that chastity—pure and spotless CHASTITY!—will once more be the darling attribute of women. Had fashionable depravity been confined to the higher circles of life, I think I should hardly have troubled you with

these my sentiments. . . . But, like every other fashion, a little day hands it down to *the million*, and woman is now but another name for infamy.

I have been at some trouble to trace to its source this great calamity, in the middling orders of society . . . and I find those who first made *novel-reading* an indispensable branch in forming the minds of young women, have a great deal to answer for. Without this poison instilled, as it were, into the blood, females in ordinary life would never have been so much the slaves of vice. The plain food, wholesome air, and exercise they enjoy, would have exempted them from the tyranny of lawless passions, and, like their virtuous grandmothers, they would have pointed the finger of shame at the impure and licentious. But those generous sentiments, those liberal opinions, those tender tales abounding with fine feeling, soft ideas, fascinating gentleness, and warm descriptions, have been the ruin of us. A girl with her intellectual powers enervated by such a course of reading, falls an easy prey to the first *boy* who assumes the languishing lover. He has only to stuff a piece of dirty paper into the crevice of her window, full of *thous* and *thees* and *thys* and mellifluous compounds, hieroglyphically spelled, perhaps, and Miss is not long in finding out that "many waters cannot quench love, neither can the floods drown it;" so as Master is yet in his apprenticeship, and friends would disapprove of an early marriage, they agree to dispense with the ceremony. Nay, even when brooding over a helpless base-born infant, and surrounded by a once respectable and happy family, now dejected and dishonored, too often does the infatuated fair one take pleasure in the misery she has created, and fancy floods of sorrow *sweetly graceful*, because, forsooth, she is just in the same point of view as the hapless, the distressed, the love-lorn Sappho of some novel or other.

And yet this, bad as it is, is not the worst result of such pernicious reading. It is no uncommon thing for a young lady who has attended her dearest friend to the altar, a few months after a marriage which, perhaps, but for *her*, had been a happy one, to fix her affections on her friend's husband, and by artful blandishments allure him to herself. Be not staggered, moral reader, at the recital! such serpents are really in existence; such dæmons in the form of women

are now too often to be found! Three instances, in as many years, have occurred in the little circle I move in. I have seen two poor disconsolate parents drop into premature graves, miserable victims to their daughter's dishonor, and the peace of several relative families wounded, never to be healed again in this world.

"And was novel-reading the cause of this?" inquires some gentle fair one, who, deprived of such an amusement, could hardly exist; "was novel-reading the foundation of such frail conduct?" I answer yes! It is in that school the poor deluded female imbibes erroneous principles, and from thence pursues a flagrantly vicious line of conduct; it is there she is told that love is involuntary, and that attachments of the heart are decreed by fate. Impious reasoning! . . . The first idle prepossession, therefore, such a person feels, if it happens to be for the husband of her most intimate friend, instead of calling herself to a severe account for the illegal preference, she sets to work to reconcile it to nature—"There is a fatality in it," argues she; "it is the will of Heaven our souls should be united in the silken bonds of reciprocal love, and there is no striving against fate." This once settled, criminality soon follows; the gentle, the sympathizing, the faithful friend, undauntedly plants a dagger in the bosom of the mother, and ruthlessly tears from the innocent children the parent stem on which their support and comfort depends. And yet this very female has cried, oh how she has cried! over relations of fictitious distress—has railed at hardhearted fathers, cruel mothers, barbarous uncles, and treacherous friends, till her tongue denied its office, and she sunk beneath the weight of sympathy, for misery far short of *that* she herself is creating.

"Novel Reading, A Cause of Female Depravity," *New England Quarterly Magazine* (1802): 172–74.

❧

Godey's Lady's Book (1836–1837)

The ideals of "true womanhood," which maintained that women were more naturally suited to a life of domesticity, were not invented and disseminated by men to keep women in their place; they were produced and popularized by women as well as men. Ironically, those white, middle-class women who created this canon of domesticity had themselves stepped outside of the home and into a more public sphere as writers, educators, and reformers. One of the leading voices promoting the ideals of domesticity was Sarah Josepha Hale, an entrepreneurial woman editor and publisher. Hale published a number of different "ladies' magazines" in northern cities during the first half of the nineteenth century. None was more popular than Godey's Lady's Book, *which she produced in Philadelphia between 1832 and 1845.* Godey's *was the Bible of respectable womanhood, the primer on bourgeois class and gender conventions. The following selections offer a glimpse at the prescribed values of "true womanhood" espoused in Hale's magazine for "ladies."*

PROBLEMS TO CONSIDER

1. Analyze the marriage of ideals of both womanhood and manhood presented here. What was expected of women, and what was expected of men?
2. How did ideas about domesticity define white American attitudes toward other cultures and races in this era? What were the implications of the "empire" and "mission" of woman for American actions in the 1830s and 1840s?

WOMAN

The good government of families leads to the comfort of communities, and the welfare of States. Of every domestic circle, woman is the centre. Home, that scene of purest and dearest joy, home is the empire of woman. There she plans, directs, performs; the acknowledged source of dignity and felicity. Where female virtue is most pure, female sense most improved, female deportment most correct, there is most propriety of social manners. . . . She, therefore, may be presumed to lay the foundation of all the virtue and all the wisdom that enrich the world.

THE LADIES MENTOR

A great anxiety is now manifested, in certain quarters, to determine precisely the "sphere of woman." It will not be found a more easy question to settle, than was Pilate's query, what is truth? Indeed the settling of the latter will determine, in a good measure, the former. Where men understand the truth in regard to their own nature and destiny, improvement and happiness, and are prepared to obey its dictates, then will they be able to comprehend the true sphere of woman. At present, there is scarcely a correct notion on the subject advanced by any of the writers who discuss it. Men, even those who desire the high appellation of Christian teachers, and profess to believe that women have souls as immortal as their own, and a moral responsibility, as rational and accountable beings, as irrevocable and personal, yet these men deny to woman the right to equal privileges of knowledge and independence of judgment, and would fain restrict her to man's opinion for her rule of morals, and manners, and conduct. It is strange the good men do not perceive how liable their opinions are to error, and how utterly evil in its consequences, both for himself and society, has been the exercise of the prerogative of which man boasts, his mortal superiority to his female companion.

We only need to advert to those countries where the "sphere of woman" is marked out and restricted wholly by the power and devices of man, to be convinced of the sins and miseries which must ever attend the mental degradation of one half of the human race.

In India, and throughout the East, it is the received opinion, that woman was made solely to gratify man's physical propensities. She has no companionship in mind with her lord. "I should as soon think of offering a Bible to a donkey as to a woman in India," is the remark of one of the missionaries to that country—"the females are never taught to read."—It is not their sphere. . . .

But why, it may be asked, do we advert to customs and opinions which no person, in a Christian country, approves or would uphold?

Because we wish to impress on the minds of our readers the fallibility of human opinion, and the iniquity of perpetuating customs, which are manifestly contrary to the intention of the Creator and injurious to the human race. Man's fiat cannot fix woman's sphere; she must go to the word of God, to the precepts of the Saviour to learn her moral duties, and she must judge for herself how she can best perform them. And further, we would impress on every Christian heart this truth, that the sphere of woman is as certainly extending as the moral light of the Gospel is diffusing clearer and wider views of the truths it indicates. . . .

And these denunciations were made because she established schools for the poor, and female friendly societies to improve the habits and character of those who had none to help them. They were made by men, by clergymen, who feared that a woman, by outvying them in doing good, would rob them of their exclusive glory.

How contemptible now does the conduct of those men appear. . . . As men come more and more to comprehend the spirit and truth of Christianity, so will their estimation of woman's sphere increase. They will see that the religion of Jesus is, throughout, in harmony with female character, that he poured contempt on all those pursuits from which men claim to derive their exclusive power and glory. Riches, and dignities, and honors, and even the pride of human learning were counted as nought in his scale of greatness—but to be meek, and lowly, and forgiving, pure in heart, peaceful and charitable; these were the virtues that elevated his followers. These were the examples he exhibited. And are not these virtues more in unison with the nature of woman than of man? It would be strange, indeed, were it not so, for the human nature of the Son of God was derived from woman, the Saviour was her seed, and if her intellectual and moral faculties are inferior to that of man, so must the Saviour's also be.

Instead, therefore, of there being any danger that the intellectual and moral progress of woman will make her, what is termed, masculine, we hold that her enlightened influence, by diffusing more clearly the simple truths of the Gospel, and establishing right habits in the young, will, by making men better Christians, make them more like women. . . .

Yet, it is woman's mission to educate, and she will yet be qualified to discharge her high calling. As surely as moral power gains the ascendancy over physical might, so surely will her sphere be enlarged, till it embraces every sort of knowledge, which increases real wisdom, and influences every movement of society that promotes truth and goodness.

"Woman" and "The Ladies Mentor," *Godey's Lady's Book*, January 1836, 26; November 1837, 229. Accessible Archives: http://www.accessible.com.

Rights and Wrongs of Women (1829)
FRANCES WRIGHT

Despite the dominance of middle-class conventions of domesticity, we must remember that these were class-based prescriptions for women's behavior rather than actual descriptions of women's lives. Working women could be excluded from this ideal of domestic respectability (see the debate over "factory girls" earlier in the chapter). As such, a few women voiced their criticisms of this gender ideology. Frances Wright was easily the most controversial woman in America before the Civil War, and she was vilified by moralists and conservatives alike. Wright inspired this controversy because she stood at a convergence of three radical ideas in the late 1820s, each of which was a direct attack on the cherished values of the white middle class. Wright was known as a freethinker, because she voiced a critique of religion as irrational; she was accused of advocating "free love," because she maintained that women and men could freely end their marriages when mutual affection or kindness had ceased; and she was an outspoken opponent of private property.

In 1829, Wright's contemporary, Thomas Skidmore, had called for a radical redistribution of property, claiming that every man possessed a right to property and that no one had the right to monopolize its passage from one generation to the next. This idea became one of the pillars of the Workingmen's Party, which Wright and her fellow editor, Robert Dale Owen, supported in the late 1820s and early 1830s. Nothing was more threatening to the middle class than a simultaneous assault on religion, marriage, and property. In one essay in her newspaper, the Free Enquirer, *Wright discussed the justice of marriage laws that gave a husband absolute control over any property his wife brought into their marriage.*

PROBLEMS TO CONSIDER

1. How was this defense of women's rights a threat to the ideals of domesticity?
2. How was Wright's essay a challenge to the kind of nationalistic arguments about sexual difference espoused in *Godey's Lady's Book*?

A law has recently passed the legislature of Massachusetts, providing that when a woman shall be divorced, the court passing such decree shall have power to assign her, for her own use, all the personal estate which her husband received by reason of the marriage; and such part of the personal estate of the husband, as may be necessary for her comfort, and the support of such children as may be assigned to her care. The wife also to hold all promissory notes and other things in action, belonging to her before marriage; and all legacies to her, and

personal property, in every way appertaining to her in her own right. . . .

It is truly inconceivable and truly monstrous, that that mass of absurdity, injustice, and cruelty, styled the common law of England, should be still the law of revolutionized America. An anomaly so extraordinary could not have obtained one hour after the established independence of these states, but for the ascendancy invariably held by lawyers in the states' assemblies. That they should protect their own craft, is but in the common order of things, as things now are; but that a whole nation should consent to uphold their craft at expense of all justice, all common sense, and all national interests, would be astounding but for the simple fact which renders simple the mystery—viz. that the nation is in absolute ignorance of *what the law is* which it upholds. . . .

But without adverting at present to all its parts, or even commenting on its general complexion, I would ask every father not absolutely dead to all human feeling, how he can permit his daughters blindly to immolate all their rights, liberties, and property by the simple utterance of a word, and thus place themselves, in their tender, ignorant, and unsuspecting youth, as completely at the disposal and mercy of an individual, as is the negro slave when bought for gold in the market of Kingston or New Orleans?

The insensibility of American parents with respect to their daughters would appear incredible to an ordinary French parent, and not a little singular to an English parent of any intelligence or solicitude. The French law affords much protection to women, the English *none*. (I have reference at present to married women only.) . . .

The American law is that of England; and Americans, in their double character of a self governing people, and of parents, equally neglect the duty incumbent on both.

But what say I of *protection*? The law of this land inflicts absolute spoliation, and allows of absolute robbery, and all *but* murder, against the unhappy female who swears away, at one and the same moment, her person and her property, and, as it but too often is, her peace, her honor, and her life.

Imagine the case—and we need but to look round and we may *see* the case, or, if we will, a thousand cases—*see* a young creature, untaught to reason, and knowing only to feel, placing in the hands of a man who has won her affections . . . I say, pledging her troth to one who, some moons, or, it may be, years after, turns gambler, or drunkard, or speculator, staking at one throw, or wasting over nightly potations, not *his* property only, but hers also—see this, and then see her obliged, constrained by unrighteous law and profligate public opinion, to stand silent by and watch the ruin—that ruin, which is to overwhelm alike herself and her children! See her, moreover, compelled to endure the company of her destroyer, experience its vitiating example, and entail its evils on a yearly multiplying progeny! Look at this, ye that praise existing institutions, and *dare* to call them moral, rational, or just!

Time was it that Massachusetts, who rung the first alarm of political revolution, should commence the civil one. Time was it that she, who drew valiantly the pen and the sword for the rights of man, should remember *woman*, and commence the good work of adjusting her wrongs and establishing her rights! Small is the justice the Massachusetts assembly has now accorded, but every generous heart that hath ever bled over the wrongs and sufferings of the better, the neglected half of humankind will hail this first and feeble effort, and say to its projectors and executors "good speed!"

———
Frances Wright, "Rights and Wrongs of Women," *Free Enquirer*, April 29, 1829.

ᨠ

CHAPTER 6

The Southern Culture of Slavery and a Slave Culture: 1790–1860

AT ROUGHLY the same time that a group of New England merchants was financing Samuel Slater's introduction of factory-based textile manufacturing, another New Englander invented the technology that ensured a divergence between the economic cultures of the South and the North. Eli Whitney's cotton gin made possible an economic and geographic reconfiguration of the South, pushing the region's free and slave population perpetually westward in search for arable land. By 1860, the South was supplying three-quarters of all the cotton used in English textile manufacturing and two-thirds of all the cotton grown in the entire world. Cotton accounted for more than half of all American exports in the decades before the Civil War. But most significant, cotton production encouraged the South's extensive reliance on a labor system based on the legal enslavement of African Americans.

Even historians intent on shattering the myths that have persisted about the "Old South" are still forced to make generalizations about a southern culture in these years. There never was *one* South, but rather a multiplicity of different subregions and ways of life: eastern seaboard states or cotton-rich Gulf states or frontier western settlements; mountain or river or tidewater landscapes; wheat, sugar, rice, or cotton economies. But despite all those differences, the legal institution of slavery shaped the economic and social development of all southern states. Although the percentage of white families owning slaves declined from 36 percent to 24 percent between 1830 and 1860, slavery affected every social arrangement in southern society. It established the legal and philosophical meanings for the property rights, freedoms, and nominal equality of all white southerners. It defined race relations and encoded notions of white racial superiority into law. Slavery constrained the slave's autonomy, defined the limits of his or her personhood, and controlled his or her relationship with any white person. As a result, in southern society the richest and most powerful individuals lived in an intricate interdependence with the powerless and exploited. All the determinants of the status, wealth, and autonomy of one group were shaped by the presence of the other, and the dynamic interaction between the two was an elaborate dance of dominance and resistance.

This chapter examines the culture of southern slavery from two points of view—that of slaves and that of slave owners. The first section investigates the cultural forms and texts created by slaves in their efforts to develop communities of resistance against their enslavers. Slaves' texts of resistance might usually be hidden, but on some occasions they were openly public. The second section exposes the proslavery ideology that defenders of slavery developed in the South after 1830, contrasting myths of caring parental slaveholders with a harsh racist and anticapitalist position that justified slavery under a cloak of "science."

᧞ Double Consciousness as a Slave: An African American Culture Amidst Slavery ᧞

At the beginning of the twentieth century, black scholar and activist W. E. B. Du Bois reflected on what he termed the "double consciousness" of African Americans. "One ever feels this twoness," Du Bois wrote in *The Souls of Black Folks* (1903), "an American, a Negro; two souls, two thoughts, two unreconciled strivings." Du Bois's notion of double consciousness aptly captured the cultural experience of African Americans during slavery's reign in the South. Even amid the violence and degradation of slavery, slaves developed and nurtured a rich and complex culture that maintained tenuous connections to their African past, while supporting both the survival of individuals and the sense of community among millions of the enslaved.

Slaves confirmed their double consciousness as African and American—slave but human—most strongly in their folk culture and religious life. Folktales and music were two of the most vibrant expressions of this rich culture. Both of these cultural forms functioned in a multitude of ways within the slave community. They provided a moral compass, a mode of communication, and a performer's art. They also involved a dynamic process of give and take—"call and response"—between performer and audience that exemplified the slave community.

Historians have examined many societies with great disparities of power, in which race, class, or caste kept large populations of peasants, serfs, laborers, prisoners, or slaves under the dominance of powerful ruling classes. These rulers maintained their power through violent means of coercion sanctioned by law, and by gaining the tacit consent of subordinated groups. When subordinated peoples appear to embrace their rulers' ideas and values, scholars call this *hegemony*. Using the dynamic of hegemony, some historians have assumed that slaves accepted slavery under the terms that masters presented it. Recently, one scholar developed a framework for challenging this perspective. He suggests that the powerless can often express both "public transcripts" and "hidden transcripts" when voicing their ideas about a power relationship. Slaves communicated one thing in the presence of their masters, a pretended form of obedience, thus assuring masters that both parties accepted the system. They also spoke in a secret or "hidden transcript," most commonly found among all subordinated groups in such forms as "rumors, gossip, folktales, songs, gestures, jokes, and theater of the powerless." These cultural forms cemented the bonds of a slave community. Hidden messages might be spoken in the presence of masters and not threaten the masters' veneer of dominance. But whenever a slave's "public transcript" challenged the very foundations of slavery, then the slave had stepped over the line into open rebellion, if not revolution.

∾ TRICKSTERS: SLAVE FOLKTALES

In a slave society with extreme disparities of autonomy, wealth, and power, it is not surprising that a popular expression of the slave community's folk culture was trickster tales — stories in which the small, weak, and less powerful often outwit their larger, stronger, and more dominant neighbors. Slaves were not the only Americans who told such tales. Tricksters were a staple of Native American folklore, and white Americans in the early republic devoured stories of backwoods characters who got the best of their adversaries with comic chicanery. Slaves with memories of Africa were already conversant with trickster fables, and those born in the Americas had plenty of reasons for wanting to tell stories in which the powerful (namely, the master), like "brother wolf" in the animal tales, gets what's coming to him. Telling and listening to these tales served a variety of functions in the cultural experiences of slaves. These stories provided entertainment for a slave community; they offered a festive manner of imagining the world turned upside down; they gave expression to deeply held religious and moral beliefs; and they were educational, teaching young and old alike lessons about human nature and life's cruelties while asserting that existing inequalities were not necessarily natural.

It was the hidden or multiple meanings behind folktales that made them so vital to the popular culture of an exploited people; and in this, folklore shared many of the same features and significance as the music and dance of slaves. Whether in spirituals or work songs, slaves developed a popular art form that possessed multiple hidden layers of meaning. The singer of songs, like the storyteller, invoked both the cunning and moral sense of the trickster. This should not surprise us. After all, deception was an inherent feature of slave societies, for both masters and slaves. Masters frequently complained about the lying and stealing of slaves; but slaves understood the larger deceit and thievery behind the "peculiar institution." As one Texas slave stated, "Dey allus done tell us it am wrong to lie and steal, but why did de white folks steal my mammy and her mammy? . . . Dat de sinfulles' stealin' dey is." Slaves thus nourished an independent folk culture through tales and songs.

De Rabbit, de Wolf, an' de Tar Baby

Mr. Deer's My Riding Horse

Slaves frequently performed tales among family and friends that featured animals as the central characters, with small animals, especially the rabbit, as the most common trickster heroes (remember that Bugs Bunny is a later version of a trickster). Storytellers made the animals seem as human as possible; they live in cabins, tend gardens, cook with pots over stoves, court lovers, have wives and children, and, most important, exhibit all the desires and passions of humans—greed, pride, envy, vanity, lust, and power. Listeners were expected to recognize patterns of human behavior and to learn about the workings of the world around them. Usually every tale involved a struggle over the symbols of power and mastery in the South's slave society, especially food or sex. And although animals frequently address each other as "brother [buh, brer] rabbit" or "brother fox," their relationships resemble those of rivals or adversaries rather than of friends. This exposes the complexity of these folktales. They were not just hidden protest tales in which the strong (that is, masters) get what's coming to them or the good but powerless get their just reward. Slave folktales contained much greater ambiguity. All too often the strong outwit the weak, or the trickster is a cruel and morally suspect character. The following two tales, collected by white folklorists after the Civil War, offer us examples of the hundreds of animal tales that slaves performed for one another.

PROBLEMS TO CONSIDER

1. With whom would slaves identify in these folktales?
2. What effect did it have on slaves to tell these tales on the plantation, often within earshot of their masters?

DE RABBIT, DE WOLF, AN' DE TAR BABY

Now de Wolf, 'e bery wise man; but not so wise as de Rabbit. De Rabbit 'e mos' cunnin' man dat go on four leg. 'E lib in de brier-bush. Now, de Wolf 'e done plant corn one 'ear *[year]*, but Rabbit 'e aint plant nuttin tall. E' lib on Wolf corn all winter. Nex' 'ear Wolf aint plant corn, 'e tink corn crop too poo'; so 'e plant groun'-nut *[peanuts]*. Rabbit, 'e do jes' de same as befo'.

Well, Wolf 'e biggin for tink something wrong. 'E gone out in de mawnin' look at 'e groun'-nut patch, look bery hard at Rabbit track, say: "I 'spicion somebordy ben a tief my groun'-nut."

Nex' mawnin' 'e go 'gen, meet mo' groun-nut gone, say same ting. Den 'e say, "I gwine mek one skeer-crow for set up in dis yere groun'-nut patch,

for skeer de tief." So 'e mek one ol' skeer-crow an' set um in de middle ob de groun'-nut patch.

Dat night when Rabbit come wid 'e bag for git groun'-nut, 'e see de skeer-crow stan' bery white in de moonshine, an' 'e say, "Wha' dat?" Nobordy aint say anyting. "Wha' dat?" 'e say 'gen. Den nobordy aint say nuttin', an' he aint see nuttin moobe *[move]*, so 'e gone up leetle closer, an' leetle closer, tel 'e git *close* up ter um, den 'e put out e' paw an' touch de skeer-crow. Den 'e say, "You aint nuttin but one ol' bundle o' rag! Wolf tink I gwine fraid *you*? mus' be fool!" So 'e kick ober the skeer-crow an' fill 'e bag wid groun'-nut, an' gone back home to de brier-bush.

Nex' mawnin' Wolf gone out for look at 'e groun'-nut patch, an' when 'e meet mo groun'-nut gone an' de skeer-crow knock down, 'e bery mad. 'E say, "Neber you min', I fix ol' Rabbit dat done tief all my groun'-nut. Jes' le' me show you!" So 'e mek one baby out o' tar, an' set up in 'e groun'-nut patch, an' say, "Jes' le' ol' Rabbit try for knock ober dis yere Tar Baby an' 'e 'll see! I jes' wan' um for try!"

Dat night, when Rabbit come 'gen wid 'e bag in 'e han' an' see de Tar Baby stan' bery black in de moonshine, 'e say, "Wha' dat?—ol' Wolf done gone set up nodder skeer-crow? mus' be." So 'e moobe leetle nearer, an' say, "Dis yere enty no skeer-crow, dis yere mus' be one gal; I mus' study 'pon dis."

So 'e tu'n roun' an' spread out 'e bag an' sit down on um in de middle ob de groun'-nut patch an' look hard at de Tar Baby. Bimeby *[By and by]* 'e say, "Gal, wha' you name?" Gal aint say anyting. "Gal, why don' you speak? Wha you da do dere?" . . .

So 'e gone close ter um an' say, "Gal, you speak ter me, you min'! Gal, ef you aint speak to me I knock you! I knock you wid my right paw, den you tink it tunder!" Tar Baby aint say nuttin, so 'e knock um wid 'e right paw, and 'e paw stick!

Den 'e biggin for holler. "Gal, le' go me! I tell you, le' go me! Wha' for you da hol' me? Ef you aint le' go me I knock you wid my lef' paw; den you tink 'e tunder an' lighten too!" So 'e knock um 'gen wid 'e lef' paw, an' 'e lef' paw stick!

Den 'e say, "Gal, lef me loose! lef me loose, I tell you! Ef you don't I kick you wid my right foot; den you tink colt kick you!" So 'e kick um wid 'e right foot, an 'e right foot stick.

Den 'e say, "Now, gal, ef you aint tu'n me loose mighty quick I gwine kick you wid my lef' foot; den you tink hoss kick you!" So 'e kick um wid 'e lef' foot, an' 'e lef' foot stick.

Den 'e say, "Min' now, gal, I aint done nuttin to you, wha' for you hol' me? tu'n me loose an I aint gwine meddle you 'gen sho'. Mebbe you tink I can't do nuttin to you? aint you know I kin bite you do? Ef you aint tu'n me loose I gwine bite you sho'. Aint you know my bite wuss dan snake bite?" So 'e bite um, an' 'e nose stick!

Nex' mawnin', fo' sun-up, Wolf gone up to de groun'-nut patch for see wha' he kin fin', an' dere 'e meet poo' Rabbit wid 'e paw an' 'e foot an' 'e nose all farsten on Tar Baby, an' 'e say, "Enty I done tol' you so? look a yawnder! I reckon Tar Baby done cotch ol' Rabbit dis time." So 'e tuk Rabbit off an say, "You done tief half my groun'-nut; now what I gwine do wid you?"

Den Rabbit biggin for beg: "Oh, Maussa Wolf, do le' me go, an' I nebber tief groun'-nut no mo'." Wolf say, "No, Brudder Rabbit, you ben a tief my corn las' 'ear an' you ben a tief groun'-nut dis 'ear, an' now I gwine eat you up." Den Rabbit say, "Oh, Maussa Wolf, do don't do me so, but le' me beg you. You ma' [may] roas' me, you ma' toas' me, you ma' cut me up, you ma' eat me, but do, Maussa Wolf, whatebber you do, don't t'row me in de brier-bush! Ef you t'row me in de brier-bush I gwine dead!"

So Wolf say, "You aint wan' me for t'row you in de brier-bush, enty? dat de bery ting I gwine to do wid you, den." So 'e fling um in de brier-bush, an' *den* Rabbit laugh and say, "Hi! Maussa Wolf, aint you know I *lib* in de brier-bush? Aint you know all my farmbly *[family]* bawn *[born]* an bred in de brier-bush? *Dat* what mek I tol' you for t'row me yere. How you is gwine get me 'gen?"

Den Wolf bery mad, 'cause 'e see Rabbit too wise man for him. 'E gone home, tell 'e wife, "No Rabbit soup for dinner to-day." . . .

Abigail M. H. Christensen, *Afro-American Folk Lore* (Boston: Author, 1898; repr., Freeport, N.Y.: Books for Libraries Press, 1971), 62–70.

MR. DEER'S MY RIDING HORSE

Now, children, I'm tired tellin' you every even' 'bout Mr. Rabbit and Tar-Baby over and over agin; I'll see ef I can't 'member a story Mammy used ter tell 'bout "Mr. Deer's my riding horse."

Well, once upon a time, when Mr. Rabbit was young and frisky, he went a courting Miss Fox, who lived way far back in the thick woods. . . . Mr. Deer he had his eyes set on Miss Fox, too. But he din' suspicion [suspect] Mr. Rabbit was a lookin' that way, but kep' on being jus' as frenly with Mr. Rabbit as he ever been. One day Mr. Rabbit call on Miss Fox, and wile they was tawkin, Miss Fox she tells him what a fine gentleman she thinks Mr. Deer is. Mr. Rabbit jes threw back his head and he laf and he laf. "What you laffin 'bout?" Miss Fox says; and . . . at las' Mr. Rabbit stop laffin an' say, "Miss Fox, you bear me witness I did n' want to tell you, but you jes made me. Miss Fox, you call Mr. Deer a fine gentleman; Miss Fox, Mr. Deer is my riding horse!" Miss Fox she nearly fell over in a faintin' fit, and she say she done *[don't]* bleve it, and she will not till Mr. Rabbit give her the proof. An' Mr. Rabbit he says, "Will you bleve it ef you sees me riding pass yo' do'?" and Miss Fox says she will, and she wone *[won't]* have nothin' to do with Mr. Deer if the story is true. Now, Mr. Rabbit is ben fixing up a plan for some time to git Mr. Deer outer his way; so he says good even' to Miss Fox, and clips it off to Mr. Deer's house, and Mr. Rabbit he so frenly with Mr. Deer he done suspec' nothin'. Presently Mr. Rabbit jes fall over double in his cheer *[chair]* and groan and moan, and Mr. Deer he says, "What's the matter, Mr. Rabbit, is you sick?" But Mr. Rabbit he jes groan; then Mr. Rabbit fall off the cheer and roll on the floor, and Mr. Deer says, "What ails you, Mr. Rabbit, is you sick?" And Mr. Rabbit he jes groans out, "Oh, Mr. Deer, I'm dying; take me home, take me home." An' Mr. Deer he's mighty kinehearted, and he says, "Get up on

my back, and I'll tote you home;" but Mr. Rabbit says, "Oh, Mr. Deer, I'm so sick, I can't set on your back 'less you put a saddle on." So Mr. Deer put on a saddle. Mr. Rabbit says, "I can't steady myself 'less you put my feets in the stirrups." So he puts his feets in the stirrups. "Oh, Mr. Deer, I can't hold on 'less you put on a bridle." So he put on a bridle. "Oh, Mr. Deer, I done feel all right 'less I had a whip in my hand." So Mr. Deer puts the whip in his hand. "Now I'm ready, Mr. Deer," says Mr. Rabbit, "but go mighty easy, for I'm likely to die any minute. Please take the short cut through the wood, Mr. Deer, so I kin get home soon." So Mr. Deer took the short cut, an' forgot that it took him pass Miss Fox's house. Jes as he 'membered it, an' was 'bout to turn back, Mr. Rabbit, who had slipped a pair of spurs on unbeknownst to him, stuck 'em into his sides, and at the same time laid the whip on so that po' Mr. Deer was crazy with the pain, and ran as fas' as his legs could carry him right by where Miss Fox was standin' on the gallery, and Mr. Rabbit a standin' up in his stirrups and hollerin', "Did n't I tell you Mr. Deer was my riding horse!" But after a while Miss Fox she found out 'bout Mr. Rabbit's trick on Mr. Deer, and she would n't have nothin' more to do with him.

Mrs. William Preston Johnston, "Two Negro Tales," *Journal of American Folk-Lore* 9 (1896): 195–96.

᠀

Malitis

How the Boss-Man Found Out John Was Taking His Chickens

Slaves also told trickster tales involving slaves and masters. Here they had to be more guarded because stories about besting their masters, if overheard by whites, could prove dangerous for the safety of the slave storyteller. A common series of tales involved contests between a slave named John and his master. And as before, even though John often outwitted his master, there were many variations in which the master successfully donned the role of trickster. Tales that involved slave characters remind us how slaves needed to play the trickster in their actual relationships with white authorities. Trickery and deception were regular features of slaves' lives in the South. Because outright rebellion involved such severe risks, slaves resorted instead to various acts of deceiving their own-ers and other white people. Folktales allowed slaves to recount acts of cunning and hidden resistance or to rehearse strategies for survival and stealth in their battles with their mas-ters. The two tales reproduced here illustrate the slave as trickster; the first derives from the recollections of an elderly ex-slave from Tennessee interviewed during the 1930s, and the second is a tale that continued to be told in Texas well into the twentieth century.

PROBLEMS TO CONSIDER

1. Analyze the "hidden transcripts" of these stories: what are all the possible meanings these tales held for slaves listening in the Old South?
2. The brief tale "Malitis" offers a glimpse at the storyteller's performance in slave folktales. What particular features of this slave woman's performance enhanced the meaning of the tale, and how was this accomplished?

MALITIS

. . . I remember mammy told me about one master who almost starved his slaves. Mighty stingy, I reckon he was.

Some of them slaves was so poorly thin they ribs would kinda rustle against each other like corn stalks a-drying in the hot winds. But they gets even one hog-killing time, and it was funny, too, mammy said.

They was seven hogs, fat and ready for fall hog-killing time. Just the day before old master told off they was to be killed, something hap-pened to all them porkers. One of the field boys found them and come a-telling the master: "The hogs is all died, now they won't be any meats for the winter."

When the master gets to where at the hogs is laying, they's a lot of Negroes standing round looking sorrow-eyed at the wasted meat. The master asks: "What's the illness with 'em?"

"Malitis," they tells him, and they acts like they don't want to touch the hogs. Master says to dress them anyway for they ain't no more meat on the place.

He says to keep all the meat for the slave families, but that's because he's afraid to eat it hisself account of the hogs' got malitis.

"Don't you all know what is malitis?" Mam-my would ask the children when she was telling of the seven fat hogs and seventy lean slaves. And she would laugh, remembering how they fooled the old master so's to get all them good meats.

"One of the strongest Negroes got up early in the morning," Mammy would explain, "long 'fore the rising horn called the slaves from their cabins. He skitted to the hog pen with a heavy mallet in his hand. When he tapped Mister Hog 'tween the eyes with that mallet, 'malitis' set in mighty quick, but it was a uncommon 'disease,' even with hungry Negroes around all the time."

"Mrs. Josie Jordan," in *The American Slave: A Composite Autobiography*, 19 vols., edited by George P. Rawick (West-port, Conn.: Greenwood Publishing, 1972), 7: 162–63.

HOW THE BOSS-MAN FOUND OUT JOHN WAS TAKING HIS CHICKENS

Colonel Clemons thought that chicken was too good for plantation hands to eat, so he would never let his hands eat one. The only kind of meat he would let them have was dry salt bacon from his commissary, and the only kind of wild game he allowed them to eat was possum. If he caught a hand with a chicken, he would punish him. For this reason the poor field hands very seldom had chicken for dinner. Now and then they would take a nice fat hen off the Colonel's chicken roost, but they had to slip out and cook it, because Colonel Clemons was always coming down to their cabins at meal times and looking at the food on their tables. If he saw any kind of meat except salt bacon or possum, he would take it and throw it out of the cabin door on the ground.

Most of the hands on the plantation had got to the place where they were afraid to take any more chickens, but John wasn't. Every Saturday night he went to Colonel Clemons' chicken roost and took two fat hens for his Sunday dinner.

The Colonel would always miss his chickens but he never could catch the thief. He felt somehow that it must be John; so one Sunday about twelve o'clock he walked down to John's cabin. When he went in, the first thing that attracted his attention was the odor of some kind of meat cooking.

"What's that cooking, John?" said the Colonel.

"Possum, boss, possum," replied John.

"I've been hearing about what a good possum cook Mariah is," said the Colonel, "so I think I'll stay here and sample some of her cooking."

"Sho, boss, sho," replied John. "Takes long time to cook possum good."

So the Colonel stayed another half an hour. Still Mariah didn't serve dinner. The Colonel got up from the stool, walked over to John and said, "John, looks like to me that possum ought to be done by now; I'm going over there and see about him myself."

And with these words the Colonel walked over to the fireplace where the meat was cooking and pulled the lid off the pot. Instead of possum he saw two of his fattest hens.

"John, you thievin' rascal," he said, "these aren't possums, they're chickens."

"Says dey is, Boss, says dey is," replied John. "Well, dey wuz possums when Ah put 'em in dere, if dey's chickens now Ah'm gonna th'ow 'em away."

J. Mason Brewer, "John Tales," in *Publications of the Texas Folk-lore Society* 21 (1946): 81–83.

ᔑ

ᔑ REBELS: SLAVE NARRATIVES AND RESISTANCE

Slaves did not limit their resistance or their cultural production to "hidden transcripts." They also resisted their enslavement in deliberate acts of rebellion against their masters and the slave system. Large-scale rebellions, such as those in Caribbean and South American slave societies, were quite rare in the antebellum South. Slaves in the southern states most frequently expressed their rebellion in acts of "stealing themselves"—running away. Fugitive slaves, in turn, contributed in significant ways to the ultimate downfall of slavery. Although the majority of slaves ran off for limited purposes and distances, a number of those who ran away as far as the nonslave states to the North published accounts of their enslavement, known as slave narratives.

For historians, using slave narratives as evidence for reconstructing the history of southern slavery is filled with both problems and rewards. Several texts claiming to be slave narratives were merely the fictional imaginings of antislavery reformers. Moreover, slave narratives were written as abolitionist polemics and hence were designed more to advance the antislavery cause than to present accurate historical memories. And finding the voice of the actual fugitive slave is sometimes difficult, because nearly all of these narratives had been altered, ghost-written, or edited by white northern editors. Nonetheless, these narratives do contain the rare voices of former slaves from a close proximity to their actual time in slavery, giving us first-hand accounts of how slaves themselves experienced and understood their enslavement. Despite the tampering of white abolitionists, many of the most powerful slave narratives have been corroborated by scholars and by the other writings of the slave narrator. The texts that ex-slaves produced were acts of rebellion against slavery (a rebel's "public transcript") in several different ways. After all, they were the products of slaves who stole themselves in order to be free; they narrate numerous acts of outright resistance by the narrator and his or her fellow slaves; and ultimately they constitute a powerful testimony of antislavery activism on the part of the former slave author.

The two slave narratives in this section—one by a man and the other by a woman—were published near the end of the slave era. Both were undoubtedly influenced by the conventions of other antislavery texts, especially the hugely popular novel *Uncle Tom's Cabin* (1852) (see chapter 9). They were certainly written to expose a slave's perspective on slavery, yet they were also written to capture the attention of, and move to action, a clearly defined audience in the North.

Twelve Years a Slave (1853)
SOLOMON NORTHUP

Nearly all of the slaves who published a narrative had never known freedom until they emancipated themselves by escaping to the North, but not so for Solomon Northup. He was born a freeman in New York state, but at thirty-three years of age, he was kidnapped, spirited away to a slave market in Washington, D.C., and then sold into slavery in Louisiana for twelve years, until he was rescued and returned to his wife and children in New York. Despite his obvious debt to Harriet Beecher Stowe's Uncle Tom's Cabin *and the climate of abolitionism in the 1850s, Northup's narrative provides a very reliable portrait of slave life in the Gulf South. Not only did Northup enter slavery as an educated northern freeman with a keener basis for critical observation, but in those instances where the facts of his account could be checked, they have been verified by scholars as accurate. In the excerpt below, Northup contrasts his two masters and narrates his resistance to one master's attempt to whip him unjustly.*

PROBLEMS TO CONSIDER

1. One historian has recently argued that slaveholders told stories about themselves to their neighbors through how they owned and treated slaves. How were Ford and Tibeats trying to represent themselves to other white southerners?
2. What made it difficult for slaves to adopt Northup's strategy of resistance on a regular basis? What ultimately saved Northup's life?

Our master's name was William Ford. He resided then in the "Great Pine Woods," in the parish of Avoyelles . . . in the heart of Louisiana. He is now a Baptist preacher. Throughout the whole parish of Avoyelles . . . he is accounted by his fellow-citizens as a worthy minister of God. In many northern minds, perhaps, the idea of a man holding his brother man in servitude, and the traffic in human flesh, may seem altogether incompatible with their conceptions of a moral or religious life. . . . But I was some time his slave, and had an opportunity of learning well his character and disposition, and it is but simple justice to him when I say, in my opinion, there never was a more kind, noble, candid, Christian man than William Ford. The influences and associations that had always surrounded him, blinded him to the inherent wrong at the bottom of the system of Slavery. He never doubted the moral right of one man holding another in subjection. Looking through the same medium with his fathers before him, he saw things in the same light. Brought up under other circumstances and other influences, his notions would undoubtedly have been different. Nevertheless, he was a model master, walking uprightly, according to the light of his understanding, and fortunate was the slave who came to his possession. Were all men such as he, Slavery would be deprived of more than half its bitterness. . . .

John M. Tibeats was the opposite of Ford in all respects. He was a small, crabbed, quick-tempered, spiteful man. He had no fixed residence that I ever heard of, but passed from one plantation to another, wherever he could find employment. He was without standing in the community, not esteemed by white men, nor even respected by slaves. He was ignorant, withal, and of a revengeful disposition. . . . Certain it is, it was a most unlucky day, for me that brought us together. . . .

William Ford unfortunately became embarrassed in his pecuniary affairs. A heavy judgment was rendered against him in consequence of his having become security for his brother,

Franklin Ford, . . . who had failed to meet his liabilities. He was also indebted to John M. Tibeats to a considerable amount in consideration of his services in building the mills on Indian Creek, and also a weaving-house, corn-mill and other erections on the plantation at Bayou Boeuf, not yet completed. It was therefore necessary, in order to meet these demands, to dispose of eighteen slaves, myself among the number. . . .

I was sold to Tibeats, in consequence, undoubtedly, of my slight skill as a carpenter. This was in the winter of 1842. . . . At the time of my sale to Tibeats, the price agreed to be given for me being more than the debt, Ford took a chattel mortgage of four hundred dollars. I am indebted for my life, as will hereafter be seen, to that mortgage. . . .

Ford's overseer on this plantation, and who had the exclusive charge of it, was a Mr. Chapin, a kindly disposed man, and a native of Pennsylvania. In common with others, he held Tibeats in light estimation, which fact, in connection with the four hundred dollar mortgage, was fortunate for me.

I was now compelled to labor very hard. From earliest dawn until late at night, I was not allowed to be a moment idle. Notwithstanding which, Tibeats was never satisfied. He was continually cursing and complaining. He never spoke to me a kind word. I was his faithful slave, and earned him large wages every day, and yet I went to my cabin nightly, loaded with abuse and stinging epithets.

We had completed the corn mill, the kitchen, and so forth, and were at work upon the weaving-house, when I was guilty of an act, in that State punishable with death. It was my first fight with Tibeats. The weaving-house we were erecting stood in the orchard a few rods from the residence of Chapin, or the "great house," as it was called. One night, having worked until it was too dark to see, I was ordered by Tibeats to rise very early in the morning, procure a keg of nails from Chapin, and commence putting on the clapboards. . . .

As the day began to open, Tibeats came out of the house to where I was, hard at work. He seemed to be that morning even more morose and disagreeable than usual. He was my master, entitled by law to my flesh and blood, and to exercise over me such tyrannical control as his mean nature prompted; but there was no law that could prevent my looking upon him with intense contempt. I despised both his disposition and his intellect. I had just come round to the keg for a further supply of nails, as he reached the weaving-house.

"I thought I told you to commence putting on weather-boards this morning," he remarked.

"Yes, master, and I am about it," I replied.

"Where?" he demanded.

"On the other side," was my answer.

He walked round to the other side, examined my work for a while, muttering to himself in a fault-finding tone.

"Didn't I tell you last night to get a keg of nails of Chapin?" he broke forth again.

"Yes, master, and so I did; and overseer said he would get another size for you, if you wanted them, when he came back from the field."

Tibeats walked to the keg, looked a moment at the contents, then kicked it violently. Coming towards me in a great passion, he exclaimed,

"G—d d—n you! I thought you *knowed* something."

I made answer: "I tried to do as you told me, master. I didn't mean anything wrong. Overseer said—" But he interrupted me with such a flood of curses that I was unable to finish the sentence. At length he ran towards the house, and going to the piazza, took down one of the overseer's whips. The whip had a short wooden stock, braided over with leather, and was loaded at the butt. The lash was three feet long, or thereabouts, and made of raw-hide strands.

. . . I knew he intended to whip me, and it was the first time any one had attempted it since my arrival at Avoyelles. I felt, moreover, that I had been faithful—that I was guilty of no wrong whatever, and deserved commendation rather than punishment. My fear changed to anger, and before he reached me I had made up my mind fully not to be whipped, let the result be life or death.

Winding the lash around his hand, and taking hold of the small end of the stock, he walked up to me, and with a malignant look, ordered me to strip.

"Master Tibeats," said I, looking him boldly in the face, "I will *not*." I was about to say something further in justification, but with concentrated vengeance, he sprang upon me, seizing me by the throat with one hand, raising the whip with the other, in the act of striking. Before the blow descended, however, I had caught him by the collar of the coat, and drawn him closely to me. Reaching down, I seized him by the ankle, and pushing him back with the other hand, he fell over on the ground. Putting one arm around his leg, and holding it to my breast, so that his head and shoulders only touched the ground, I placed my foot upon his neck. He was completely in my power. My blood was up. It seemed to course through my veins like fire. In the frenzy of my madness I snatched the whip from his hand. He struggled with all his power; swore that I should not live to see another day; and that he would tear out my heart. But his struggles and his threats were alike in vain. I cannot tell how many times I struck him. Blow after blow fell fast and heavy upon his wriggling form. At length he screamed—cried murder—and at last the blasphemous tyrant called on God for mercy. . . .

His screams had been heard in the field. Chapin was coming as fast as he could ride. I struck him a blow or two more, then pushed him from me with such a well-directed kick that he went rolling over on the ground.

Rising to his feet, and brushing the dirt from his hair, he stood looking at me, pale with rage. We gazed at each other in silence. Not a word was uttered until Chapin galloped up to us.

"What is the matter?" he cried out.

"Master Tibeats wants to whip me for using the nails you gave me," I replied.

"What is the matter with the nails?" he inquired, turning to Tibeats.

Tibeats answered to the effect that they were too large, paying little heed, however, to Chapin's question, but still keeping his snakish eyes fastened maliciously on me.

"I am overseer here," Chapin began. "I told Platt *[the name given to Northup after he had been kidnapped into slavery]* to take them and use them, and if they were not of the proper size I would get others on returning from the field. It is not his fault. Besides, I shall furnish such nails as I please. I hope you will understand *that*, Mr. Tibeats."

Tibeats made no reply, but, grinding his teeth and shaking his fist, swore he would have satisfaction, and that it was not half over yet. Thereupon he walked away, followed by the overseer, and entered the house, the latter talking to him all the while, in a suppressed tone, and with earnest gestures.

I remained where I was, doubting whether it was better to fly or abide the result, whatever it might be. Presently Tibeats came out of the house, and, saddling his horse, the only property he possessed besides myself, departed on the road to Cheneyville. . . .

As I stood there, feelings of unutterable agony overwhelmed me. I was conscious that I had subjected myself to unimaginable punishment. The reaction that followed my extreme ebullition of anger produced the most painful sensations of regret. An unfriended, helpless slave—what could I *do*, what could I *say*, to justify, in the remotest manner, the heinous act I had committed, of resenting a *white* man's contumely and abuse. . . . For at least an hour I remained in this situation, finding relief only in tears, when, looking up, I beheld Tibeats, accompanied by two horsemen, coming down the bayou. They rode into the yard, jumped from their horses, and approached me with large whips, one of them also carrying a coil of rope.

"Cross your hand," commanded Tibeats, with the addition of such a shuddering expression of blasphemy as is not decorous to repeat.

"You need not bind me, Master Tibeats, I am ready to go with you anywhere," said I.

One of his companions then stepped forward, swearing if I made the least resistance he would break my head—he would tear me limb from limb—he would cut my black throat—and giving wide scope to other similar expressions. . . . With a remaining piece of rope Tibeats made an awkward noose, and placed it about my neck.

"Now, then," inquired one of Tibeats' companions, "where shall we hang the nigger?" . . .

At length, as they were dragging me towards the tree, Chapin, who had momentarily disappeared from the piazza, came out of the house and walked towards us. He had a pistol in each hand, and as near as I can now recall to mind, spoke in a firm, determined manner, as follows:

"Gentlemen, I have a few words to say. You had better listen to them. Whoever moves that slave another foot from where he stands is a dead man. In the first place, he does not deserve this treatment. It is a shame to murder him in this manner. I never knew a more faithful boy than Platt. You, Tibeats, are in the fault yourself. You are pretty much of a scoundrel, and I know it, and you richly deserved the flogging you have received. In the next place, I have been overseer of this plantation seven years, and, in the absence of William Ford, am master here. My duty is to protect his interests, and that duty I shall perform. You are not responsible—you are a worthless fellow. Ford holds a mortgage on Platt for four hundred dollars. If you hang him, he loses his debt. Until that is canceled you have no right to take his life. You have no right to take it any way. There is a law for the slave as well as for the white man. You are no better than a murderer." . . .

Tibeats, in a few minutes, evidently in fear, and overawed by the decided tone of Chapin, sneaked off like a coward, as he was, and mounting his horse, followed his companions.

Solomon Northup, *Twelve Years a Slave* (Auburn, N.Y.: Derby and Miller, 1853), 89–90, 103, 105–16.

Incidents in the Life of a Slave Girl (1861)
HARRIET JACOBS

Female slaves were doubly oppressed in the antebellum South—both as slaves and as women. For centuries, women of African ancestry were compelled to perform arduous field labor alongside slave men, even as separation from physical labor became an emblem of womanhood for white Americans. At the same time, slave women had numerous additional responsibilities, such as child rearing and domestic labor for both white and black families on a plantation. Female slaves also suffered from a unique exploitation as women. Once the importation of slaves ended in 1808, slaveholders increasingly valued female slaves for their reproductive capacity as much as for their labor. Hence, female slaves were frequently the target of sexual exploitation by numerous white men (masters, their sons, or overseers), while they faced greater constraints in the types of resistance available to them. Few female slaves could fight back against their oppressors (although some did), and slave women ran away less frequently because they often had to choose between taking along young children or leaving them behind. Harriet Jacobs, writing under the pseudonym Linda Brent, penned a powerful portrait of the dilemmas facing a sexually exploited female slave.

PROBLEMS TO CONSIDER

1. Analyze the dynamic between Jacobs, her master, and his wife: What kinds of exploitation occurred here? Why did Jacobs's mistress refuse to forge a bond of solidarity with Jacobs?
2. Jacobs eventually escaped, but what types of resistance did she employ before her escape?

CHAPTER 5: THE TRIALS OF GIRLHOOD

. . . I now entered on my fifteenth year—a sad epoch in the life of a slave girl. My master began to whisper foul words in my ear. Young as I was, I could not remain ignorant of their import. I tried to treat them with indifference or contempt. The master's age, my extreme youth, and the fear that his conduct would be reported to my grandmother, made him bear this treatment for many months. . . . He peopled my young mind with unclean images, such as only a vile monster could think of. I turned from him with disgust and hatred. But he was my master. I was compelled to live under the same roof with him—where I saw a man forty years my senior daily violating the most sacred commandments of nature. He told me I was his property; that I

must be subject to his will in all things. My soul revolted against the mean tyranny. But where could I turn for protection? No matter whether the slave girl be as black as ebony or as fair as her mistress. In either case, there is no shadow of law to protect her from insult, from violence, or even from death; all these are inflicted by fiends who bear the shape of men. The mistress, who ought to protect the helpless victim, has no other feelings towards her but those of jealousy and rage. The degradation, the wrongs, the vices, that grow out of slavery, are more than I can describe. They are greater than you would willingly believe. . . .

If God has bestowed beauty upon her, it will prove her greatest curse. That which commands admiration in the white woman only hastens the degradation of the female slave. I know that some are too much brutalized by slavery to feel the humiliation of their position; but many slaves feel it most acutely, and shrink from the memory of it. I cannot tell how much I suffered in the presence of these wrongs, nor how I am still pained by the retrospect. My master met me at every turn, reminding me that I belonged to him, and swearing by heaven and earth that he would compel me to submit to him. . . . The other slaves in my master's house noticed the change. Many of them pitied me; but none dared to ask the cause. They had no need to inquire. They knew too well the guilty practices under that roof; and they were aware that to speak of them was an offence that never went unpunished. . . .

O, what days and nights of fear and sorrow that man caused me! Reader, it is not to awaken sympathy for myself that I am telling you truthfully what I suffered in slavery. I do it to kindle a flame of compassion in your hearts for my sisters who are still in bondage, suffering as I once suffered. . . .

In view of these things, why are ye silent, ye free men and women of the north? Why do your tongues falter in maintenance of the right? Would that I had more ability! But my heart is so full, and my pen is so weak! There are noble men and women who plead for us, striving to help those who cannot help themselves. God bless them! God give them strength and courage to go on! God bless those, every where, who are laboring to advance the cause of humanity!

CHAPTER 6: THE JEALOUS MISTRESS

. . . Mrs. Flint possessed the key to her husband's character before I was born. She might have used this knowledge to counsel and to screen the young and the innocent among her slaves; but for them she had no sympathy. They were the objects of her constant suspicion and malevolence. She watched her husband with unceasing vigilance; but he was well practiced in means to evade it. . . .

I had entered my sixteenth year, and every day it became more apparent that my presence was intolerable to Mrs. Flint. Angry words frequently passed between her and her husband. He had never punished me himself, and he would not allow any body else to punish me. In that respect, she was never satisfied; but, in her angry moods, no terms were too vile for her to bestow upon me. Yet I, whom she detested so bitterly, had far more pity for her than he had, whose duty it was to make her life happy. I never wronged her, or wished to wrong her; and one word of kindness from her would have brought me to her feet. . . .

After a while my mistress sent for me to come to her room. . . .

She handed me a Bible, and said, "Lay your hand on your heart, kiss this holy book, and swear before God that you tell me the truth." . . .

". . . Now take this stool, sit down, look me directly in the face, and tell me all that has passed between your master and you."

I did as she ordered. As I went on with my account her color changed frequently, she wept, and sometimes groaned. She spoke in tones so sad, that I was touched by her grief. The tears came to my eyes; but I was soon convinced that her emotions arose from anger and wounded pride. She felt that her marriage vows were desecrated, her dignity insulted; but she had no compassion for the poor victim of her husband's perfidy. She pitied herself as a martyr; but she was incapable of feeling for the condition of shame and misery in which her unfortunate, helpless slave was placed.

. . . She was not a very refined woman, and had not much control over her passions. I was an object of her jealousy, and, consequently, of her hatred; and I knew I could not expect kindness or confidence from her under the circumstances in which I was placed. I could not blame her. Slaveholders' wives feel as other women would under similar circumstances. The fire of her temper kindled from small sparks, and now the flame became so intense that the doctor was obliged to give up his intended arrangement. . . .

The secrets of slavery are concealed like those of the Inquisition. My master was, to my knowledge, the father of eleven slaves. But did the mothers dare to tell who was the father of their children? Did the other slaves dare to allude to it, except in whispers among themselves? No, indeed! They knew too well the terrible consequences.

[Harriet Jacobs], *Incidents in the Life of a Slave Girl* (Boston: Author, 1861), 44–55.

ᴈ

⌁ *Saddles and Spurs: Creating a Proslavery Ideology* ⌁

Slaveholders, like all groups who maintain their dominance through hierarchy, possessed a deep desire for social stability. Yet two events in 1831 profoundly reshaped their cultural assumptions: Nat Turner's bloody rebellion in Virginia and the inaugural issue of William Lloyd Garrison's newspaper *The Liberator*, the first step of a new abolitionist movement in the North. Following these developments, white southerners felt compelled to defend slavery more strongly than ever before. Some wished to put an acceptable face on the institution either for their own sake or to justify themselves before the nonslaveholding regions of the country. Others chose to extend to the fullest the logic of a slave society—not merely to defend the practice of slavery but to promote it as the best of all social systems or the best for maintaining racial dominance. Apologists for the "southern way of life" forged the apparatus of a proslavery ideology in domestic novels, in advice essays in agriculture journals, and in treatises on religion, political economy, and a newly developed "science" of racial thinking. In the process of creating this proslavery ideology, slave owners gave us not so much a realistic picture of master-slave relations on plantations, but rather a set of ideals and justifications for their slaveholding activities. Over time, a more benign defense of slavery as a duty, a responsibility, and an opportunity for benevolence was dramatically joined by strident arguments for slavery as the desirable social condition for the dominance of a superior race over an allegedly inferior race. On the eve of the Civil War, some proslavery advocates in the South were defending slavery as the ideal societal arrangement for the whole nation—a positive good rather than a necessary evil.

⌁ MYTHS OF PATERNALIST CARE

Swallow Barn (1832)

JOHN PENDLETON KENNEDY

Since the American Revolution, it was common for slave owners to defend the continuation of slavery by maintaining that it was a "necessary evil." Like poverty or disease, the existence of slavery predated its current practitioners; and because no one was personally responsible for its origin, slaveholders spoke of slavery as a legacy or debt passed on by their parents' generation. Out of this notion of inherited responsibility grew the mythology that slaveholders were essentially the parental protectors and benevolent caretakers of slaves—a set of ideas known as paternalism. *Paternalism depicts an organic society, one in which duty and mutual obligations rather than individual self-interest govern human relationships and in which the family offers an analogy for all social organization. Whether slave owners really believed these notions has been a matter of considerable debate among historians. Certainly, slaveholders' diaries and letters are filled with phrases such as "my family, white and black." As one master wrote: "All living on the plantation, whether colored or not, are members of the same family and are to be treated as such." Nonetheless, slave owners willfully sold away black members of their "families" but never their white children.*

A pioneering work in the mythology of the paternalistic master was John Pendleton Kennedy's novel Swallow Barn, *published soon after Nat Turner's rebellion. Kennedy's novel tells the story of Frank and Lucretia Meriwether of Virginia, who represent the ideal planter family. For Kennedy, the plot of this novel was inconsequential; his objective was to depict a southern slave plantation in all its benevolent glory and to represent slavery as a benign institution that served the mutual needs, and provided for the mutual happiness, of both master and slave.*

PROBLEMS TO CONSIDER

1. According to Kennedy, what characteristics make slaveholders into benevolent caretakers, and what characteristics of slaves make them in need of paternalistic caretaking?
2. On what basis does Kennedy assert that slavery was a necessary evil?

Every thing at Swallow Barn, that falls within the superintendence of my cousin Lucretia is a pattern of industry. In fact, I consider her the very priestess of the American system, for, with her, the protection of manufactures is even more of a passion than a principle. . . .

It is refreshing to behold how affectionately vain our good hostess is of Frank, and what deference she shows to his judgment in all matters, except that belong to the home department;—for there she is confessedly and without appeal, the paramount power. It seems to be a dogma with her, that he is the very "first man of Virginia." . . . Frank, in return, is a devout admirer of her accomplishments. . . .

CHAPTER 46: THE QUARTER

Having despatched these important matters at the stable, we left our horses in charge of the servants, and walked towards the cabins, which were not more than a few hundred paces distant. These hovels, with their appurtenances, formed an exceedingly picturesque landscape. They were scattered, without order, over the slope of a gentle hill; and many of them were embowered under old and majestic trees. The rudeness of their construction rather enhanced the attractiveness of the scene. . . . But the more lowly of these structures, and the most numerous, were nothing more than plain log-cabins, compacted pretty much on the model by which boys build partridge-traps. . . .

From this description, which may serve to illustrate a whole species of habitations very common in Virginia, it will be seen, that on the score of accommodation, the inmates of these dwellings were furnished according to a very primitive notion of comfort. Still, however, there were little garden-patches attached to each, where cymblings, cucumbers, sweet potatoes, watermelons and cabbages flourished in unrestrained luxuriance. Add to this, that there were abundance of poultry domesticated about the premises, and it may be perceived that, whatever might be the inconveniences of shelter, there was no want of what, in all countries, would be considered a reasonable supply of luxuries.

Nothing more attracted my observation than the swarms of little negroes that basked on the sunny sides of these cabins, and congregated to gaze at us as we surveyed their haunts. They were nearly all in that costume of the golden age which I have heretofore described; and showed their slim shanks and long heels in all varieties of their grotesque natures. Their predominant love of sunshine and their lazy, listless postures, and apparent content to be silently looking abroad, might well afford a comparison to a set of terrapins luxuriating in the genial warmth of summer, on the logs of a mill-pond.

And there, too, were the prolific mothers of this redundant brood,—a number of stout negro-women who thronged the doors of the huts, full of idle curiosity to see us. And, when to these are added a few reverend, wrinkled, decrepit old men, with faces shortened as if with drawing-strings, noses that seemed to have run all to nostril, and with feet of the configuration of a mattock, my reader will have a tolerably correct idea of this negro-quarter, its population, buildings, external appearance, situation and extent.

Meriwether, I have said before, is a kind and considerate master. It is his custom frequently to visit his slaves, in order to inspect their condition, and, where it may be necessary, to add to their comforts or relieve their wants. His coming amongst them, therefore, is always hailed with pleasure. He has constituted himself into a high court of appeal, and makes it a rule to give all their petitions a patient hearing, and to do justice in the premises. . . . On the present occasion, in almost every house where Frank entered, there was some boon to be asked; and I observed, that in every case, the petitioner was either gratified or refused in such a tone as left

no occasion or disposition to murmur. Most of the women had some bargains to offer, of fowls or eggs or other commodities of household use, and Meriwether generally referred them to his wife, who, I found, relied almost entirely on this resource, for the supply of such commodities; the negroes being regularly paid for whatever was offered in this way. . . .

The air of contentment and good humor and kind family attachment, which was apparent throughout this little community, and the familiar relations existing between them and the proprietor struck me very pleasantly. I came here a stranger, in great degree, to the negro character, knowing but little of the domestic history of these people, their duties, habits or temper, and somewhat disposed, indeed, from prepossessions, to look upon them as severely dealt with, and expecting to have my sympathies excited towards them as objects of commiseration. I have had, therefore, rather a special interest in observing them. The contrast between my preconceptions of their condition and the reality which I have witnessed, has brought me a most agreeable surprise. . . . I am quite sure they never could become a happier people than I find them here. Perhaps they are destined, ultimately, to that national existence, in the clime from which they derive their origin—that this is a transition state in which we see them in Virginia. If it be so, no tribe of people have ever passed from barbarism to civilization whose middle stage of progress has been more secure from harm, more genial to their character, or better supplied with mild and beneficent guardianship, adapted to the actual state of their intellectual feebleness, than the negroes of Swallow Barn. And, from what I can gather, it is pretty much the same on the other estates in this region. . . .

What the negro is finally capable of, in the way of civilization, I am not philosopher enough to determine. In the present stage of his existence, he presents himself to my mind as essentially parasitical in his nature. I mean that he is, in his moral constitution, a dependant upon the white race; dependant for guidance and direction even to the procurement of his most indispensable necessaries. Apart from this protection he has the helplessness of a child,—without foresight, without faculty of contrivance, without thrift of any kind. . . . Taking instruction from history, all organized slavery is inevitably but a temporary phase of human condition. Interest, necessity and instinct, all work to give progression to the relations of mankind, and finally to elevate each tribe or race to its maximum of refinement and power. We have no reason to suppose that the negro will be an exception to this law.

. . . In short, I think them the most good-natured, careless, light-hearted, and happily-constructed human beings I have ever seen. Having but few and simple wants, they seem to me to be provided with every comfort which falls within the ordinary compass of their wishes; and, I might say, that they find even more enjoyment,—as that word may be applied to express positive pleasures scattered through the course of daily occupation—than any other laboring people I am acquainted with.

I took occasion to express these opinions to Meriwether. . . .

This, as I expected, brought him into a discourse.

. . . For slavery, as an original question, is wholly without justification or defence. It is theoretically and morally wrong—and fanatical and one-sided thinkers will call its continuance, even for a day, a wrong, under any modification of it. But, surely, if these people are consigned to our care by the accident, or, what is worse, the premeditated policy which has put them upon our commonwealth, the great duty that is left to us is, to shape our conduct, in reference to them, by a wise and beneficent consideration of the case as it exists, and to administer wholesome laws for their government, making their servitude as tolerable to them as we can consistently with our own safety and their ultimate good. We should not be justified in taking the hazard of internal convulsions to get rid of them; nor have we a right, in the desire to free ourselves, to whelm them in greater evils than their present bondage. A violent removal of them, or a general emancipation, would assuredly produce one or the other of these calamities. . . . In the mean time, we owe it to justice and humanity to treat these people with the most considerate kindness. As to what are ordinarily imagined to be the evils or sufferings of their condition, I do not believe in them. The evil is generally felt on the side of the master. . . . The slaveholders in this region are, in the main, men of kind and humane tempers—as pliant to the touch of compassion, and as sensible of its duties, as the best men in any community, and as little disposed to inflict injury upon their dependents. . . ."

John Pendleton Kennedy, *Swallow Barn, or, A Sojourn in the Old Dominion* (New York: Putnam, 1851), 39–40, 445–57.

⅋

Management of Negroes Upon Southern Estates (1851)

Another picture of the paternalist attitudes of white southern slaveholders emerged from essays on plantation management published during the antebellum years. After 1819, nearly two dozen journals, with names like American Cotton Planter *or* Southern Cultivator, *emanated from southern presses dedicated to the agricultural concerns of southern planters. Frequently, planters submitted their advice for the proper operation of a slave plantation. By the 1850s, as sectional hostilities heightened, these publications encouraged effective plantation management and strategies for the kindhearted control of slaves. Written by white southerners for white southerners, without any concern for reaching a national audience, these essays leave us with one of the best instances of the ideology of a slave master's benevolence.*

PROBLEMS TO CONSIDER

1. How did this "Mississippi Planter" balance "humanity" and "self-interest" in his strategies for managing slaves on a plantation?
2. Would his slaves have interpreted his management strategies differently than this planter did?

[We regard this as a practical and valuable paper for the planters, and hope that those of them who have been experimenting in the matter, will give us the results. — EDITOR.]

Some very sensible and practical writer in the March No. of "The Review," under the "*Agricultural Department*" has given us an article upon the *management of negroes*, which entitles him to the gratitude of the planting community . . . because it has opened up this subject, to be thought of, written about, and improved upon, until the comforts of our black population shall be greatly increased, and their services become more profitable to their owners. Surely there is no subject which demands of the planter more careful consideration than the proper treatment of his slaves, by whose labor he lives, and for whose conduct and happiness he is responsible in the eyes of God. We very often find planters comparing notes and making suggestions as to the most profitable modes of tilling the soil, erecting gates, fences, farm-houses, machinery, and, indeed, everything else conducive to their comfort and prosperity; but how seldom do we find men comparing notes as to their mode of feeding, clothing, nursing, working, and taking care of those human beings intrusted to our charge, whose best condition is slavery, when they are treated with humanity, and their labor properly directed! . . . For it is a fact established

beyond all controversy, that when the negro is treated with humanity, and subjected to constant employment without the labor of thought, and the cares incident to the necessity of providing for his own support, he is by far happier than he would be if emancipated, and left to think, and act, and provide for himself. And from the vast amount of experience in the management of slaves, can we not deduce some general, practicable rules for their government, that would add to the happiness of both master and servant? I know of no other mode of arriving at this great desideratum, than for planters to give to the public their rules for feeding, clothing, housing and working their slaves, and of taking care of them when sick, together with their plantation discipline. In this way, we shall be continually learning something new upon this vitally interesting question, filled, as it is, with great responsibilities; and while our slaves will be made happier, our profits from their labor will be greater, and our consciences be made easier. . . .

To begin, then, I send you my plantation rules. . . . My first care has been to select a proper place for my "Quarter," well protected by the shade of forest trees, sufficiently thinned out to admit a free circulation of air, so situated as to be free from the impurities of stagnant water, and to erect comfortable houses for my negroes. Planters do not always reflect that there is more sickness, and consequently greater loss of life, from the decaying logs of negro houses, open floors, leaky roofs, and crowded rooms, than all other causes combined; and if humanity will not point out the proper remedy, let self-interest for once act as a virtue, and prompt him to save the health and lives of his negroes, by at once providing comfortable quarters for them. . . . The negroes are never permitted to sleep before the fire, either lying down or sitting up, if it can be avoided, as they are always prone to sleep with their hands to the fire, are liable to be burnt, and to contract disease: but beds with ample clothing are provided for them, and in them they are *made to sleep.* As to their habits of amalgamation and intercourse, I know of no means whereby to regulate them, or to restrain them; I attempted it for many years by preaching virtue and decency, encouraging marriages, and by punishing, with some severity, departures from marital obligations; but it was all in vain. I allow for each hand that works out, four pounds of clear meat and one peck of meal per week. Their dinners are cooked for them, and carried to the field, always with vegetables, according to the season. There are two houses set apart at mid-day for resting, eating, and sleeping, if they desire it, and they retire to one of the weather-sheds or the grove to pass this time, not being permitted to remain in the hot sun while at rest. They cook their own suppers and breakfasts; each family being provided with an oven, skillet, and sifter, and each one having a coffee-pot, (and generally some coffee to put in it,) with knives and forks, plates, spoons, cups, &c., of their own providing. The wood is regularly furnished them; for, I hold it to be absolutely mean, for a man to require a negro to work until daylight closes in, and then force him to get wood, sometimes half a mile off, before he can get a fire, either to

warm himself or cook his supper. Every negro has his hen-house, where he raises poultry, which he is not permitted to sell, and he cooks and eats his chickens and eggs for his evening and morning meals to suit himself; besides, every family has a garden, paled in, where they raise such vegetables and fruits as they take a fancy to. A large house is provided as a nursery for the children, where all are taken at daylight, and placed under the charge of a careful and experienced woman, whose solo occupation is to attend to them. . . .

I also employ a good preacher, who regularly preaches to them on the Sabbath day, and it is made the duty of every one to come up clean and decent to the place of worship. As Father Garritt regularly calls on Brother Adam (the foreman of the prayer meetings) to close the exercises, he gives out and sings his hymn with much unction, and always cocks his eye at Charley, the fiddler, as much as to say, "Old fellow, you had your time last night; now it is mine."

I would gladly learn every negro on the place to read the bible, but for a fanaticism which, while it professes friendship to the negro, is keeping a cloud over his mental vision, and almost crushing out his hopes of salvation.

These are some of the leading outlines of my management, so far as my negroes are concerned. That they are imperfect, and could be greatly improved, I readily admit; and it is only with the hope that I shall be able to improve them by the experience of others, that I have given them to the public. . . .

A MISSISSIPPI PLANTER.

"Management of Negroes Upon Southern Estates," *DeBow's Review* 10 (June 1851): 621–25.

༄

The Black Gauntlet: A Tale of Plantation Life in South Carolina (1860)
MARY HOWARD SCHOOLCRAFT

Throughout the southern states, white women were expected to remain silent in public regarding the issue of slavery. No plantation mistress published an essay like the "Mississippi Planter," outlining her advice for managing her household or handling her slaves. But elite white southern women did value their participation in a literate culture. They read popular sentimental and moralizing literature as attentively as did northern women. And they nourished a mythology that suggested that white women served as the spiritual conscience of a southern slave society—nurturing and caring for their households (black and white), as well as tempering the excessive cruelty of white men toward slaves. Historians have extensively debated how true to reality that mythology might have been. Yet when Harriet Beecher Stowe's antislavery novel Uncle Tom's Cabin *(1852) became an international sensation (see chapter 9), white southern women writers added their public voice to this national issue by combining representations of the paternalistic plantation mistress with new arguments that justified slavery as a positive good rather than a necessary evil. Mary Schoolcraft's* The Black Gauntlet *bridges the ideas expressed in the earlier plantation literature, such as Kennedy's* Swallow Barn, *and the more aggressive proslavery ideas that flourished in the South in the 1850s (see the next section). Schoolcraft was the second wife of Henry Rowe Schoolcraft, one of the leading interpreters of Native American culture, who had previously married a Chippewa woman and maintained that Indians could never be "civilized" unless they abandoned hunting and settled on reservations.*

PROBLEMS TO CONSIDER

1. How did Schoolcraft blend religion, gender, and family ideas into a single proslavery argument? On what basis did she contend that the Bible sanctions slavery?
2. As you read selections by Josiah Nott and George Fitzhugh in the next section, consider how Schoolcraft's narrative might have been influenced by their proslavery ideas.

DEDICATION

Ne na baim *[Indian word, meaning "my husband"]*, you have so repeatedly urged me to write sketches of . . . plantation life, in my own native State of South Carolina, where my ancestors have lived from its earliest settlement, that I have, for two months past, snatched every moment I could dutifully spare from my innumerable domestic cares, to comply with your wishes, by describing every-day life on the plantations. South Carolinians, you know, are "old fogies," and consequently *they* do not believe with the Abolitionists, that *God* is a progressive being; but that throughout eternity *He* has been the same; perfect in wisdom, perfect in justice, and perfect in love to all his creatures; we cannot comprehend, therefore, the new-light doctrine,

"That slavery is a sin;" for it seems quite incredible that God, through his servant Moses, should have ordered his own peculiar people (to whom he delivered his commandments under the thunderings of Sinai), to take their bondsmen from among the heathen nations around them, and keep them as an inheritance forever to their children's children, if slavery was a *crime* against the moral law. I have for twenty years studied the Bible with more intense interest than any other book; yet from Genesis to Revelation, I cannot find a sentence that holds out the idea, that slavery will ever cease while there are any heathen nations in this world. . . .

Surely every Bible Christian is willing to let God Almighty be the expositor of *his own* laws; and even when He was made flesh, and dwelt among us thirty-three years, He never uttered one single word against slavery, though Jesus Christ rebuked all kinds of sin with the unsparing energy of Omnipotence itself. . . .

Neither the Old Testament nor the New; neither Moses, Jesus Christ, the Apostles, or our own historical experiences for six thousand years, agrees with the Honorable Thomas Jefferson, that "All men are born free and equal." . . . [We] might as well strive to prevent the return of day and night, as divorce what God hath joined together; and if Thomas Jefferson is right, we must search at once for an anti-slavery Bible, and an Abolition God, to make "all men equal;" and we must blot out the history of the whole human race, whose glaring inequality of mind, body, and condition, has been manifest to every observer, from the time that God created it between our first parents, and ordered Adam, in consequence of his superiority, to rule over Eve.

This primitive, radical inauguration of strength over weakness, has continued from that day to this, and will continue as long as this world lasts, for God has willed it so. . . . Our whole duty then is to bow to His revelation.

I do not, Ne na baim, own a slave, and I never again expect to be a slave-holder, though it is a high moral vocation to civilize and christianize the heathen, brought to our very doors in the South by the providence of God; — still, in the deepest recesses of my conscience, from the study of the Bible, and my own experience among Africans all my life, I am so satisfied that slavery is the school God has established for the conversion of barbarous nations, that were I an absolute Queen of these United States, my first missionary enterprise would be to send to Africa, to bring its heathen as *slaves* to this Christian land, and keep them in bondage until *compulsory* labor has tamed their beastliness, and civilization and Christianity had prepared them to return as missionaries of progress to their benighted black brethren.

God has placed a mark on the negro, as distinctive as that on Cain; and I do not believe there is a *white* man, woman, or child, on the face of the earth, who does not, in his deepest heart, regard the African an inferior race to his own. The fiat of the great God Almighty, the researches of ethnology, history, and experience, and our very instincts, teach us this fact; and I believe a refined Anglo-Saxon lady would sooner be burnt at the stake, than married to one of these black descendants of Ham. . . .

CHAPTER 5

Although it is reported that the Northern ladies arrogate to themselves all the enterprise and industry as housekeepers in these United States, they never saw a day in all their lives that could comprise all the responsibilities of a Southern planter's wife—as she has not only every principle of self-interest to urge her to be up and doing at sunrise; but from her very nursery she is taught that the meanest creature on God's earth is a master or mistress who neglects those that Providence has made utterly dependent on them. Her conscience, educated to this self-denying nobility of action, would feel as wounded by the neglect of her helpless children as by disregard for her hard working slaves. And this world cannot furnish more healthy unpharisaical sensibility than what God sees . . . the planter's wife expend in the humble cabin of the sick or afflicted negro, on her plantation, night or day; for no storm prevents personal attention from house to house of a very ill servant, though they invariably have a nurse of their own color.

The author has repeatedly spent the whole night walking around the cabin of a dying, or dangerously ill negro, so as to be able to administer every dose of medicine herself, and report every change in the developments of the disease to the Doctor the next morning. This loss of rest was endured, not because the said negro was her own property, but because she lived in the same house with the owner of the slave, and had, from earliest youth, regarded it the most morally dignified of employments to wait on the poor and afflicted around her, whether they were red, white, or black. . . .

Let a Yankee lady fancy herself surrounded by a family of two hundred persons (as is often the case with a Southern planter's wife), all dependent, more or less, on herself. . . .

I would candidly ask my Northern sister, who has so harshly condemned the ladies of the South, is this yearly enterprise of a planter's wife, with all the other daily etceteras, living a life of idleness? 'Tis true, before she is a wife, or head of a plantation, the miss in her teens does no work in South Carolina. . . . But the moment she becomes a planter's wife, her domestic talents grow by the square-yard every year; for by a quick transformation, she is changed from a laughing, thoughtless flirt, seeking only to make herself beautiful and admired, into a responsible, conscientious "sister of charity" to her husband's numerous dependants.

Mrs. Henry R. Schoolcraft, *The Black Gauntlet: A Tale of Plantation Life in South Carolina* (Philadelphia: J. B. Lippincott, 1860), iii–vii, 113–15.

ᐟ

ᐛ SCIENCE FOR RACIAL DOMINANCE

During the same year in which the U.S. Supreme Court reached its decision in *Dred Scott v. Sandford* (1857), declaring that black persons were "beings of an inferior order," "and so far inferior, that they had no rights which the white man was bound to respect," two controversial southern apologists published books that revealed that the defense of slavery had moved a great distance from the romantic paternalism found in *Swallow Barn*. In their writings from the late 1840s to secession, Josiah C. Nott and George Fitzhugh pushed the assumptions of a slaveholder's ideology to their logical extremes. Neither man was typical or representative of white southern thinkers; both were bombastic and had a penchant for statements that shocked their readers. Yet both men sought to ground their proslavery ideas in the appearance of scientific inquiry. Nott's principal concern was to provide scientific proof for the separate creation, and hence the superiority and inferiority, of the races; Fitzhugh's attention was directed toward a theory of economics and labor. Their notions that "science" proved the necessity and advantage of slavery might strike twenty-first-century readers as absurd or disingenuous, but in an era in which scientific inquiry and racial hatred could be easily joined, Nott and Fitzhugh would be neither the first nor the last to cloak crude racism in the garments of "science." (In the twentieth century, eugenics and Nazism would continue that trend.)

Types of Mankind (1854)

JOSIAH C. NOTT

A physician from Mobile, Alabama, Josiah C. Nott might have been remembered in history for his contributions to new understandings of the origins of yellow fever or the germ theory, but his greater fame is as one of the leading voices of a new pseudo-scientific racism that his contemporaries called "ethnology." Nott was one of a handful of post-Enlightenment scientists who wished to challenge the orthodoxy that physical differences in the appearances of human groups could be caused by environmental influences, such as climate. Nott was not the first to challenge this environmentalist theory, but he was the first to take it to the point of arguing that Caucasians, Negroes, and Indians were, in fact, different species of mankind. Nott himself stated in one of his earliest publications that his objective was to prove "that there is a Genus, Man, comprising two or more species—that physical causes cannot change a White man into a Negro, and that to say this change has been effected by a direct act of providence, is an assumption which cannot be proven, and is contrary to the great chain of Nature's laws."

Nott reveled in his rebellious rejection of Scripture's narrative of a single creation, a stance that did not sit well with clergymen in either New England or the Deep South. But his writings got widespread circulation and praise in southern journals such as DeBow's Review. *Southern slaveholders neither created the ideas of polygenesis and "scientific racialism" nor retained them as their exclusive property. Nott's closest colleagues were men of science and medicine in northern cities such as Philadelphia. But for Nott, his inquiries into human anatomical distinctions, and his conclusion that humanity was divided into different species (races), were not matters of science for science's sake. Rather, Nott intended his "scientific racialism" to justify the continued enslavement of Negroes, as well as the conquest and subjugation of other inferior races, such as Native Americans. In the introduction to his book* Types of Mankind, *Nott outlines what he considered to be the irrefutable scientific proof that the races of "Negroes," "Caucasians," and "Indians" were actually different species with distinct origins.*

PROBLEMS TO CONSIDER

1. How did Nott establish the scientific authority of his arguments? By our standards today, would we regard Nott's methods and arguments as scientific?
2. Were Nott's ideas compatible with other defenses of slavery presented in this chapter? Would paternalist defenders of slavery have agreed with his conclusions?

Ethnology demands to know what was the primitive organic structure of each race?—what such race's moral and psychical character?—how far a race may have been, or may become, modified by the combined action of time and moral and physical causes?—and what position in the social scale Providence has assigned to each type of man? . . .

The grand problem, more particularly interesting to all readers, is that which involved the *common origin* of races; for upon the latter deduction hang not only certain religious dogmas, but the more practical question of the equality and perfectibility of races—we say "more practical question," because, while Almighty Power, on the one hand, is not responsible to Man for the distinct origin of human races, these, on the other, are accountable to Him for the manner in which their delegated power is used towards each other.

Whether an original diversity of races be admitted or not, the *permanence* of existing physical types will not be questioned by any Archæologist or Naturalist of the present day. Nor, by such competent arbitrators, can the consequent permanence of moral and intellectual peculiarities of types be denied. The intellectual man is inseparable from the physical man; and the nature of the one cannot be altered without a corresponding change in the other.

The truth of these propositions had long been familiar to the master-mind of JOHN C. CALHOUN; who regarded them to be of such paramount importance as to demand the fullest consideration from those who, like our lamented statesman in his day, wield the destinies of nations and of races. . . . A correspondence ensued between Mr. Calhoun and Dr. [Samuel] Morton on the subject, and the Doctor presented to him copies of the *Crania Americana* and *Ægyptiaca*, together with minor works, all of which Mr. Calhoun studied with no less pleasure than profit. He soon perceived that the conclusions which he had long before drawn from history, and from his personal observations in America, on the Anglo-Saxon, Celtic, Teutonic, French, Spanish, Negro, and Indian races, were entirely corroborated by the plain teachings of modern science. He beheld demonstrated in Morton's works the important fact, that the Egyptian, Negro, several White, and sundry Yellow races, had existed, in their present forms, for at least 4000 years; and that it behoved the statesman to lay aside all current speculations about the origin and perfectibility of races, and to deal, in political argument, with the simple facts as they stand. . . .

Looking back over the world's history, it will be seen that human progress has arisen mainly from the war of races. All the great impulses which have been given to it from time to time have been the results of conquests and colonizations. Certain races would be stationary and

barbarous for ever, were it not for the introduction of new blood and novel influences; and some of the lowest types are hopelessly beyond the reach even of these salutary stimulants to melioration. . . .

One of the main objects of this volume is to show . . . that the diversity of races must be accepted by Science as a *fact*, independently of theology, and of all analogies or reasonings drawn from the animal kingdom. . . .

The views, moreover, that we expressed in 1849, touching Physical Causes, Congenital Varieties, &c., need no modification at the present day; but, on the contrary, will be found amply sustained by the progress of science, as set forth in the succeeding chapters. We make bold to add an extract from our opinions published at that time:

. . . A few generations in animals are sufficient to produce all the changes they usually undergo from climate, and yet the races of men retain their leading characteristics for ages, without approximating to aboriginal types. . . .

We beg leave to fix your attention on this vital point. It is a commonly received error that the influence of a hot climate is gradually exerted on successive generations, until one species of mankind is completely changed into another; a dark shade is impressed on the first, and transmitted to the second; another shade is added to the third, which is handed down to the fourth; and so on, through successive generations, until the fair German is transformed, by climate, into the black African!

This idea is *proven to be false*, and is abandoned by the well-informed writers of all parties. A sunburnt cheek is never handed down to succeeding generations. The exposed parts of the body alone are tanned by the sun, and the children of the white-skinned Europeans in New Orleans, Mobile, and the West Indies, are *born* as fair as their ancestors, and would remain so, if carried back to a colder climate. The same may be said of other *acquired* characters, (except those from want and disease.) They die with the individual, and are no more capable of transmission than a flattened head, mutilated limb, or tattooed skin. We repeat, that this fact is settled, and challenge a denial.

The only argument left, then, for the advocates of the *unity* of the human species to fall back upon, is that of "*congenital*" varieties or peculiarities, which are said to spring up, and be transmitted from parent to child, so as to form new races.

Let us pause for a moment to illustrate this fanciful idea. The Negroes of Africa, for example, are admitted not to be offsets from some other race, which have been gradually blackened and changed in moral and physical type by the action of climate; but it is asserted that, "once in the flight of ages past," some genuine little Negro, or rather many such, were born of Caucasian, Mongol, or other light-skinned parents, and then have turned about and changed the type of the inhabitants of a whole continent. So in America: the countless aborigines found on this continent . . . are the offspring of a race changed by accidental or congenital varieties. Thus, too, old China, India, Australia, Oceania, etc., all owe their types, physical and mental, to *congenital* or *accidental varieties*, and all are descended from Adam and Eve! Can human credulity go farther, or human ingenuity invent any argument more absurd? Yet the whole groundwork of a common origin for some nine or ten hundred millions of human beings, embracing numerous distinct types, which are lost in an antiquity far beyond all records or chronology, sacred or profane, is narrowed down to this "baseless fabric."

. . . Did any one ever hear of a club-foot, cross-eyed, or six-fingered *race*, although such individuals are exceedingly common? Are they not, on the contrary, always swallowed up and lost? Is it not strange, if there be any truth in this argument, that no race has ever

been formed from those congenital varieties which we *know* to occur frequently, and yet races should originate from congenital varieties which cannot be proved, and are not believed, by our best writers, ever to have existed? No one ever saw a Negro, Mongol, or Indian, born from any but his own species. Has any one heard of an Indian child born from white or black parents in America, during more than two centuries that these races have been living here? Is not this brief and simple statement of the case sufficient to satisfy any one, that the diversity of species now seen on the earth, cannot be accounted for on the assumption of congenital or accidental origin? . . .

The unity of the human species has also been stoutly maintained on psychological grounds. Numerous attempts have been made to establish the intellectual quality of the dark races with the white; and the history of the past has been ransacked for examples, but they are nowhere to be found. Can any one call the name of a full-blooded Negro who has ever written a page worthy of being remembered?

. . . On former occasions, and in the most respectful manner, we had attempted to conciliate sectarians, and to reconcile the plain teachings of science with theological prejudices; but to no useful purpose. In return, our opinions and motives have been misrepresented and vilified by self-constituted teachers of the Christian religion! We have, in consequence, now done with all this; and no longer have any apologies to offer, nor favors of lenient criticism to ask. The broad banner of science is herein nailed to the mast. Even in our own brief day, we have beheld one flimsy religious dogma after another consigned to oblivion, while science, on the other hand, has been gaining strength and majesty with time.

J. C. Nott and George R. Gliddon, *Types of Mankind: Or, Ethnological Researches, Based on Ancient Monuments, Paintings, Sculptures, and Crania of Races*, 7th ed. (Philadelphia: Lippincott, Grambo & Co., 1855), 49–61.

∾

Cannibals All! (1857)

GEORGE FITZHUGH

Slavery gained its most controversial apologist in the person of George Fitzhugh of Virginia. He declared that Thomas Jefferson's Declaration of Independence had no practical relevance to the social order of either the slave South or the "free labor" North. As he wrote in 1854: "Men are not 'born entitled to equal rights!' It would be far nearer the truth to say, 'that some were born with saddles on their backs, and others booted and spurred to ride them,'—and the riding does them good. They need the reins, the bit and the spur." If this statement is not shocking, it is because we have come to expect racist language from persons who hold other men and women as slaves. Yet ironies abound in Fitzhugh's case: first, he was never a very successful slaveholder or planter, although he descended from one of Virginia's "first families"; second, Fitzhugh was speaking here of all workers (white and black, slave and free, north and south), all of whom were born with "saddles on their backs" and were meant to be exploited by their propertied masters.

In his boldest defense of slavery, his book Cannibals All!, *Fitzhugh devotes himself to a systematic critique of capitalism that resembles Marx's discussion of class struggle and the labor theory of value. On the eve of the Civil War, Fitzhugh's book inflamed a northern body politic that placed ever greater emphasis on "free labor" as the defining feature of its social order. Abolitionist William Lloyd Garrison called Fitzhugh a "cool audacious defender of the soul-crushing, blood-reeking system of slavery" and a spokesman for "the cradle-plunderers and slave-drivers" of the South. But in a final irony, although his writings became associated with fire-eating southern politicians who trumpeted a severing of the Union, Fitzhugh actually opposed secession until the very last moment.*

PROBLEMS TO CONSIDER

1. Compare and contrast Fitzhugh's *Cannibals All!* with John Pendleton Kennedy's *Swallow Barn*. What features of paternalism were still present in this harsh defense of slavery, and how did it differ from Kennedy's paternalism?
2. In what ways did Fitzhugh distort the realities of slavery in his case against a "free labor" society?

CHAPTER I: THE UNIVERSAL TRADE

We are, all, North and South, engaged in the White Slave Trade, and he who succeeds best, is esteemed most respectable. It is far more cruel than the Black Slave Trade, because it exacts more of its slaves, and neither protects nor governs them. We boast, that it exacts more, when we say, "that the *profits* made from employing free labor are greater than those from slave labor." . . . But we not only boast that the White Slave Trade is more exacting and fraudulent (in fact, though not in intention,) than Black Slavery; but we also boast, that it is more cruel, in leaving the laborer to take care of himself and family out of the pittance which skill or capital have allowed him to retain. When the day's labor is ended, he is free, but is overburdened with the cares of family and household, which make his freedom an empty and delusive mockery. But his employer is really free, and may enjoy the profits made by others' labor, without a care, or a trouble, as to their well-being. The negro slave is free, too, when the labors of the day are over, and free in mind as well as body; for the master provides food, raiment, house, fuel, and everything else necessary to the physical well-being of himself and family. The master's labors commence just when the slave's end. No wonder men should prefer white slavery to capital, to negro slavery, since it is more profitable, and is free from all the cares and labors of black slave-holding.

Now, reader, . . . we will dispel illusions which have promoted your happiness, and shew you that what you have considered and practiced as virtue, is little better than moral Cannibalism. But you will find yourself in numerous and respectable company; for all good and respectable people are "Cannibals all," who do not labor, or who are successfully trying to live without labor, on the unrequited labor of other people. . . .

The respectable way of living is, to make other people work for you, and to pay them nothing for so doing—and to have no concern about them after their work is done. Hence, white slave-holding is much more respectable than negro slavery—for the master works nearly as hard for the negro, as he for the master. But you, my virtuous, respectable reader, exact three thousand dollars per annum for white labor, (for your income is the product of white labor,) and make not one cent of return in any form. You retain your capital, and never labor, and yet live in luxury on the labor of others. . . . You, with the command over labor which your capital gives you, are a slave owner—a master, without the obligations of a master. They who work for you, who create your income, are slaves, without the rights of slaves. Slaves without a master! Whilst you were engaged in amassing your capital, in seeking to become independent, you were in the White Slave Trade. To become independent, is to be able to make other people support you, without being obliged to labor for *them*. . . . The capitalists, in free society, live in ten times the luxury and show that Southern masters do, be-

cause the slaves to capital work harder and cost less, than negro slaves.

The negro slaves of the South are the happiest, and, in some sense, the freest people in the world. The children and the aged and infirm work not at all, and yet have all the comforts and necessaries of life provided for them. They enjoy liberty, because they are oppressed neither by care nor labor. The women do little hard work, and are protected from the despotism of their husbands by their masters. The negro men and stout boys work, on the average, in good weather, not more than nine hours a day. The balance of their time is spent in perfect abandon. . . . We do not know whether free laborers ever sleep. They are fools to do so; for, whilst they sleep, the wily and watchful capitalist is devising means to ensnare and exploitate them. The free laborer must work or starve. He is more of a slave than the negro, because he works longer and harder for less allowance than the slave, and has no holiday, because the cares of life with him begin when its labors end. He has no liberty, and not a single right. . . .

Free laborers have not a thousandth part of the rights and liberties of negro slaves. Indeed, they have not a single right or a single liberty, unless it be the right or liberty to die. . . .

CHAPTER 21: NEGRO SLAVERY

. . . To insist that a status of society, which has been almost universal, and which is expressly and continually justified by Holy Writ, is its natural, normal, and necessary status, under the ordinary circumstances, is on its face a plausible and probable proposition. To insist on less, is to yield our cause, and to give up our religion; for if white slavery be morally wrong, be a violation of natural rights, the Bible cannot be true. Human and divine authority do seem in the general to concur, in establishing the expediency of having masters and slaves of different races. . . . In some respects, the wider the difference the better, as the slave will feel less mortified by his position. In other respects, it may be that too wide a difference hardens the hearts and brutalizes the feelings of both master and slave. The civilized man hates the savage, and the savage returns the hatred with interest. Hence, West India slavery, of newly caught negroes, is not a very humane, affectionate or civilizing institution. Virginia negroes have become moral and intelligent. They love their master and his family, and the attachment is reciprocated. Still, we like the idle, but intelligent houseservants, better than the hard-used, but stupid out-hands; and we like the mulatto better than the negro; yet the negro is generally more affectionate, contented and faithful. . . .

CHAPTER 26: CHRISTIAN MORALITY IMPRATICABLE IN FREE SOCIETY— BUT THE NATURAL MORALITY OF SLAVE SOCIETY

. . . Good treatment and proper discipline renders the slave happier, healthier, more valuable, grateful, and contented. Obedience, industry and loyalty on the part of the slave, increases the master's ability and disposition to protect and take care of him. The interests of all the members of a natural family, slaves included, are identical. Selfishness finds no place, because nature, common feelings and self-interest dictate to all that it is their true interest "to love thy neighbor as themselves," and "to do as they would be done by,"—at least, within the precincts of the family. To throw off into the world wife, children, and slaves, would injure, not benefit them. To neglect to punish children or slaves when they deserved it, would not be to do as we would be done by. Such punishment is generally the highest reach of self-abnegation and self-control. . . . Christian morality is neither difficult nor unnatural where dependent, family, and slave relations exist, and Christian morality was preached and only intended for such.

The whole morale of free society is, "Every man, woman and child for himself and herself." Slavery in every form must be abolished. Wives must have distinct, separate, and therefore antagonistic and conflicting interests from their husbands, and children must as soon as possible be remitted to the rights of manhood. . . . Their world of universal liberty was a world of universal selfishness, discord, competition, rivalry, and war of the wits. . . . But the family, including slaves, which the Abolitionists would destroy, has been almost universal, and is therefore natural. Christian morality is the natural morality in slave society, and slave society is the only natural society. . . . In such society it is natural for men to love one another. The ordinary relations of men are not competitive and antagonistic as in free society; and selfishness is not general, but exceptionable. Duty to self is the first of duties: free society makes it the only duty. Man is not naturally selfish or bad, for he is naturally social. Free society dissociates him, and makes him bad and selfish from necessity.

George Fitzhugh, *Cannibals All! Or, Slaves Without Masters* (Richmond, Va.: A. Morris, 1857), 25–31, 295–96, 317–19.

ᴔ

CHAPTER 7

Reforming America: 1820–1860

EARLY IN THE NINETEENTH CENTURY, biographies of pious women philanthropists, such as Hannah More and Isabella Graham, offered guides for women wishing to dedicate their lives to humanitarian deeds. Half a century later, on the eve of the Civil War, Mary Louise Hankins published a parody of that life, which she entitled "Mrs. Biffles, the Philanthropist" (1861). By that time, Americans were quite familiar with the persona of the reformer, as tens of thousands of Americans pursued hundreds of different causes to improve the lives of the less fortunate or to purge sin from their society. In Hankins's tale, Mrs. Biffles had been a young girl who "was early taught to sit up straight . . . and go to church three times every Sunday." By the time she reached adulthood, she had devoured books about the deaths of perfectly devout children and missionaries saving foreign heathens, until her mother noticed the similarity to novel reading and took all the books away. Mrs. Biffles then determined to assist the poor by making "them all go to church," to improve the lives of prisoners, and to set straight the errant ways of drunken neighbors. By the time she discovered abolitionism, she "was for freeing the whole mass of southern negroes in one day, and allowing them to run pell-mell over the United States." "She attended abolition meetings, made speeches, called the southerners hard names, . . . and advised freemen 'to arm in aid of their enslaved brethren.'" All the while, her own household was neglected, her children ran wild, poor Mr. Biffles "seldom had buttons on his linen," and deserving poor white men and women received "no favors at her hands."

Hankins's parody makes sense only in the context of the reform impulse of the antebellum years. During the pre–Civil War decades, social movements to transform the wayward and redress troubling social problems dominated the nation's social and cultural landscape. Historians have often characterized this period as the nation's first great age of reform. Spurred by a belief that they lived at a pivotal moment in human history, and by a faith in both an intimate God and the power of individual self-transformation, thousands of Americans joined together in collective endeavors to remake people's minds and behavior. To accomplish their goals, they relied on three new cultural phenomena: revivals, voluntary associations, and cheap print resources. This chapter examines the interrelationship of all three of these features of the culture of reform. By looking at controversies surrounding revival meetings and then analyzing how reformers employed the devices of popular culture, we can see how the reform impulse almost always involved deeper concerns than any single change of behavior. For example, temperance reformers might have wanted to encourage people to abstain from drinking, but beneath this action was a larger anxiety about the unrestrained behavior of men in leisure and in the marketplace.

Reform was a set of interdependent ideas, fears, and actions. It unleashed an unprecedented creative energy for joining. Alexis de Tocqueville noted in the 1830s that Americans had a habit of "forever forming associations." The smorgasbord of different voluntary societies and reform movements generated at this time makes any quick summary impossible. What unites Sunday schools and Bible societies with utopian communes or mental health asylums? Were there common threads that linked abolition, anti-Catholicism (nativism), the penitentiary movement, peace activism, and women's rights? As we will see, the commonality of such disparate movements rested in the methods and strategies of the lecturers, preachers, and writers who produced the cultural apparatus around which a shared community of reform-minded Americans rallied.

∾ *Meeting the Spirit: Cultural Disputes Over Revivalist Religion* ∾

The early years of the republic witnessed an explosive and contentious development in the arena of religious life — revivalism — that heralded a cultural reorientation as profound as the spread of democracy or the market revolution. Within a matter of a few decades, the foundation was laid for the tremendous influence of evangelical Protestantism on American culture in the nineteenth century.

It is a mistake to think of evangelical Protestants in this era as backward, nostalgic folks trying to return to some "old-time religion." Instead, they were innovators and experimenters, working at the cutting edge of new technologies and exploiting new forms of popular culture. Evangelical Protestants pushed ahead with new advances in print culture (newspapers and cheaply produced and distributed literature) and devised innovations in the social organization of people's lives. It might be more accurate to refer to the organizers of revivals as religious entrepreneurs. What, after all, is an entrepreneur? He or she is someone who takes an existing technology or organizational strategy and finds new applications for it, in order to generate a release of productive energy and new growth. That is what evangelicals got from revivals. Revivalism promoted a competitive religious marketplace in the United States that paralleled and matched the individual consumer choices that Americans were making in their economic and political lives.

Revivalist religion also generated its share of contention and conflict. New religious ideas emphasizing free moral agency and individual self-determination, and openly mocking the usefulness of traditional ministers, church worship, and theology, were bound to rankle the defenders of orthodoxy. The most contested phenomenon of all was the camp meeting.

Camp meetings were a uniquely American invention. They began partly by accident in the western frontier. Churches and clergymen could not keep up with the flood of people surging westward after the Revolution. Leaders of Baptist, Methodist, Presbyterian, and other churches decided that since their members needed to travel great distances to be baptized, take communion, or listen to a sermon, there was no point in making people travel hundreds of miles for a one-day church service. So they decided to extend the services to last a whole week, and travelers pitched tents and camped in the woods while they listened to spirited preaching. Camp meetings were an immediate popular sensation, drawing immense crowds. A camp meeting held at Cain Ridge, Kentucky, in 1801 attracted more than 20,000 people. Here, the extraordinary emotional outpouring that became a defining feature of camp meetings was on display. Men and women, deeply moved by conviction of their sins and the joy of rebirth, became overcome with emotion and exhibited behavior that came to be called "exercises," with bodies falling, fainting, shaking, or jerking and noises of shouting, shrieking, and even barking. To some, these were the undisputed signs of God's spirit at work. For a growing body of critics, however, camp meetings represented unimaginable excesses of uncontrolled passions ("fanaticism"), evils that threatened both religion and the social order.

Just as Europeans traveled across the Atlantic in order to witness camp meetings for themselves, let's travel back in time to critically examine this uniquely American phenomenon. What all three documents in this section have in common is that they are based on personal experiences. All three authors, who came from very different backgrounds, turn to their own encounters with revivalist religion or with camp meetings and devote their narratives to the question, is this the work of God?

The Life and Religious Experience of Jarena Lee (1836)
JARENA LEE

It might seem strange to our ears to use the words "counterculture" and "evangelical" together in the same sentence. But at the end of the eighteenth century, evangelical religion was a countercultural force that threatened the dominance of the gentry class's leisure culture during the Great Awakening (see chapter 3). Still, the aspect of early evangelical Protestantism that most cut against the grain of social mores was its idea of the spiritual equality of all persons, including slaves and free blacks. Baptist and Methodist revivalists in the late eighteenth century not only preached to African Americans and admitted them as equal members in their fellowships but also encouraged gifted black preachers to take up their calling and preach to congregations, white or black. Black preachers and white congregants — it is hard to imagine anything more countercultural at that time. Jarena Lee was one of a handful of black women whose powerful visionary encounter with the divine led them to assume a status reserved for white men — preacher. The racial equality in evangelical churches did not last long, however. As revivals became popular, and more and more white slaveholders embraced evangelical religion, Baptists and Methodists watered down their positions on antislavery and racial equality. By 1815, black evangelicals had left white churches in the North and had even created their own denomination, the African Methodist Episcopal (AME) Church, led by the Reverend Richard Allen.

PROBLEMS TO CONSIDER

1. How would you characterize Lee's conversion? What was empowering about evangelical conversions?
2. What gave Lee, a black woman, the authority and the courage to challenge the tradition of male-only preachers?

I was born February 11th, 1783, at Cape May, state of New Jersey. At the age of seven years I was parted from my parents and went to live as a servant maid, with a Mr. Sharp, at the distance of about sixty miles from the place of my birth.

My parents being wholly ignorant of the knowledge of God, had not therefore instructed me in any degree in this great matter. Not long after the commencement of my attendance on this lady, she had bid me do something respecting my work, which in a little while after, she asked me if I had done, when I replied, Yes — but this was not true.

At this awful point, in my early history, the spirit of God moved in power through my conscience, and told me I was a wretched sinner. On this account so great was the impression, and so strong were the feelings of guilt, that I promised in my heart that I would not tell an other lie.

But notwithstanding this promise my heart grew harder, after a while, yet the spirit of the Lord never entirely forsook me, but continued mercifully striving with me, until his gracious power converted my soul. . . .

Soon after this I again went to the city of Philadelphia; and commenced going to the English Church, the pastor of which was an Englishman, by the name of [Joseph] Pilmore, one of the number, who at first preached Methodism in America, in the city of New York.

But while sitting under the ministration of this man, which was about three months, and at the last time, it appeared that there was a wall between me and a communion with that people, which was higher than I could possibly see over, and seemed to make this impression upon my mind, *this is not the people for you.*

But on returning home at noon I inquired of the head cook of the house respecting the rules of the Methodists, as I knew she belonged to that society, who told me what they were; on which account I replied, that I should not be able to abide by such strict rules not even one year; — however, I told her that I would go with her and hear what they had to say.

The man who was to speak in the afternoon of that day, was the Rev. Richard Allen, since bishop of the African Episcopal Methodists in

America. During the labors of this man that afternoon, I had come to the conclusion, that this is the people to which my heart unites, and it so happened, that as soon as the service closed he invited such as felt a desire to flee the wrath to come, to unite on trial with them—I embraced the opportunity. Three weeks from that day, my soul was gloriously converted to God, under preaching, at the very outset of the sermon. The text was barely pronounced, which was: "I perceive thy heart is not right in the sight of God," when there appeared to *my* view, in the centre of the heart *one* sin; and this was *malice*, against one particular individual, who had strove deeply to injure me, which I resented. At this discovery I said, *Lord* I forgive *every* creature. That instant, it appeared to me, as if a garment, which had entirely enveloped my whole person, even to my fingers ends, split at the crown of my head, and was stripped away from me, passing like a shadow, from my sight—when the glory of God seemed to cover me in its stead.

That moment, though hundreds were present, I did leap to my feet, and declare that God, for Christ's sake, had pardoned the sins of my soul. Great was the ecstacy of my mind, for I felt that not only the sin of *malice* was pardoned, but all other sins were swept away together. That day was the first when my heart had believed, and my tongue had made confession unto salvation—the first words uttered, a part of that song, which shall fill eternity with its sound, was *glory to God*. For a few moments I had power to exhort sinners, and to tell of the wonders and of the goodness of him who had clothed me with *his* salvation. During this, the minister was silent, until my soul felt its duty had been performed, when he declared another witness of the power of Christ to forgive sins on earth, was manifest in my conversion. . . .

MY CALL TO PREACH THE GOSPEL

Between four and five years after my sanctification, on a certain time, an impressive silence fell upon me, and I stood as if some one was about to speak to me, yet I had no such thought in my heart. But to my utter surprise there seemed to sound a voice which I thought I distinctly heard, and most certainly understood, which said to me, "Go preach the Gospel!" I immediately replied aloud, "No one will believe me." Again I listened, and again the same voice seemed to say—"Preach the Gospel; I will put words in your mouth, and will turn your enemies to become your friends."

At first I supposed that Satan had spoken to me, for I had read that he could transform himself into an angel of light, for the purpose of deception. Immediately I went into a secret place, and called upon the Lord to know if he had called me to preach, and whether I was deceived or not; when there appeared to my view the form and figure of a pulpit, with a Bible lying thereon; the back of which was presented to me as plainly as if it had been a literal fact.

In consequence of this, my mind became so exercised, that during the night following, I took a text, and preached in my sleep. I thought there stood before me a great multitude, while I expounded to them the things of religion. . . . Two days after, I went to see the preacher in charge of the African Society, who was the Rev. Richard Allen, the same before named in these pages, to tell him that I felt it my duty to preach the gospel. But as I drew near the street in which his house was, which was in the city of Philadelphia, my courage began to fail me. . . . Several times on my way there, I turned back again; but as often I felt my strength again renewed, and I soon found that the nearer I approached to the house of the minister, the less was my fear. Accordingly, as soon as I came to the door, my fears subsided, the cross was removed, all things appeared pleasant—I was tranquil.

I now told him, that the Lord had revealed it to me, that I must preach the gospel. He replied, by asking, in what sphere I wished to move in? I said, among the Methodists. He then replied, that a Mrs. Cook, a Methodist lady, had also some time before requested the same privilege;

who it was believed, had done much good in the way of exhortation, and holding prayer meetings; and who had been permitted to do so by the verbal license of the preacher in charge at the time. But as to women preaching, he said that our Discipline knew nothing at all about it—that it did not call for women preachers. This I was glad to hear, because it removed the fear of the cross—but not no sooner did this feeling cross my mind, than I found that a love of souls had in a measure departed from me; that holy energy which burned within me, as a fire, began to be smothered. This I soon perceived.

O how careful ought we to be, lest through our by-laws of church government and discipline, we bring into disrepute even the word of life. For as unseemly as it may appear now-a-days for a woman to preach, it should be remembered that nothing is impossible with God. And why should it be thought impossible, heterodox, or improper, for a woman to preach? seeing the Saviour died for the woman as well as the man.

If the man may preach, because the Saviour died for him, why not the woman? seeing he died for her also. Is he not a whole Saviour, instead of a half one? as those who hold it wrong for a woman to preach, would seem to make it appear. . . .

In my wanderings up and down among men, preaching according to my ability, I have frequently found families who told me that they had not for several years been to a meeting, and yet, while listening to hear what God would say by his poor coloured female instrument, have believed with trembling—tears rolling down their cheeks, the signs of contrition and repentance towards God. I firmly believe that I have sown seed, in the name of the Lord, which shall appear with its increase at the great day of accounts, when Christ shall come to make up his jewels.

———

Jarena Lee, *The Life and Religious Experience of Jarena Lee, A Coloured Lady, Giving an Account of Her Call to Preach the Gospel* (Philadelphia: Author, 1836), 3–6, 12–15.

ॐ

A History of the Methodist Episcopal Church (1839)
NATHAN BANGS

The phenomenon of camp meetings became synonymous with Methodists in America. While other Protestant denominations shied away from the excesses associated with camp meetings, Methodists embraced them as their own. Why? They simply could not resist the extraordinary number of people these meetings brought into their fold. Bishop Francis Asbury once compared camp meetings to "fishing with a large net." The Methodists' growth was nothing less than phenomenal: from about 20,000 members in 1790 to more than 1 million in 1845, they quickly became the nation's largest Protestant denomination, with nearly twice as many followers as their nearest competitor.

As camp meetings came to define Methodism, they also became the vehicle for spreading new democratic religious ideas. Methodists moved evangelicals increasingly away from Calvinist notions that salvation was limited to a select few. They taught that Christianity should be preached in common folk's language, encouraged preachers who possessed limited education, and attracted converts among poor farmers, factory workers, slaves, free blacks, and other marginal groups. By the 1830s, urban revivalists (such as Charles Finney) were copying the techniques of Methodist camp meetings for weeklong meetings in cities, and camp meetings spread throughout the Northeast and Northwest, not just in the rural and frontier South. At that time, Nathan Bangs emerged as the best

voice to defend camp meetings against critics' vociferous attacks. Bangs began with a lim-
ited education and labored as a circuit-riding preacher before his talents led him to New
York City to oversee Methodist newspapers, magazines, and book publishing. By the
1830s, some Methodists in the Northeast, including Bangs, wanted to make the church
more respectable in order to increase its appeal among the growing middle class. This
movement toward respectability led Methodists to found Wesleyan College, in Connecti-
cut, and in 1841 Bangs was appointed president of the college. Respectability meant
playing down the excesses of camp meetings, while still supporting their usefulness for
making new converts.

PROBLEMS TO CONSIDER

1. How did Bangs defend the practice of camp meetings, and how did he choose
   to address the kind of excesses that critics noticed?
2. Bangs ended his defense of camp meetings as authentic works of God by
   asserting, "What I experience I know." Why was this axiom important to an
   evangelical's identity?

The camp-meetings continued to be held . . . more generally than ever, and were owned of God to the awakening and conversion of sinners, and tended much to quicken the people of God in their own souls, and to stimulate them to more vigorous exertions for the salvation of others. And as this history may be read by some who have never attended these meetings, it may not be out of place to give a description of the manner in which they are attended. . . .

The rules and orders of the meeting are generally as follows, varying so as to suit different circumstances:—

1. The times of preaching are 10 o'clock, A.M., and 3 and 7 o'clock, P.M., notice of which is given by the sound of a trumpet or horn at the preachers' stand.

2. The intermediate time between preaching is occupied in prayer meetings, singing, and exhortation.

3. In time of worship persons are prohibited from walking to and fro, talking, smoking, or otherwise disturbing the solemnities of the meeting.

4. All are required, except on the last night of the meeting, to be in their tents at 10 o'clock, P.M., and to rise at 5, A.M.

5. At 6 o'clock, A.M., they are required to take their breakfast, before which family prayer is attended in each tent occupied by a family.

6. In time of preaching all are required to attend, except one to take care of the tent. . . .

This is a general description of a camp-meeting. . . . That good has resulted from these meetings must be evident to every impartial person who has either attended them or witnessed their effects—although it must be admitted that some accidental evils have flowed from them. But these have originated chiefly from the attendance of persons who have gone for other purposes than to worship God. . . . There are those in the community who, actuated by mercenary motives, will go and set up hucksters' shops, sell strong liquors and other things, and then invite the thoughtless rabble to convene for convivial purposes, to the annoyance of the peaceable worshipers of God. . . . But they who provide those things and partake of them, are alone responsible for the evils which they create. Neither camp-meetings nor those who attend them for religious purposes are accountable for the disorderly conduct of those who, in defiance of law, of religion, and decency, violate the order of the meeting, and bring on themselves the disgrace of being disturbers of the peace. . . .

It has been objected that professors of religion themselves often violate the rules of religious order by unseemly gesticulations and boisterous exclamations. It may, indeed, be so — and we no more justify these things than we do the same exceptionable conduct in other places — but there is nothing in the time, the place, or the object of coming together, which need excite these censurable manifestations, more than in any other place of worship. "Let all things be done decently and in order" at camp-meetings, and they shall still be rendered a blessing, as they have heretofore been, to the souls of the people. There is greater danger at present arising from their degenerating into seasons of idle recreation, than of their being abused by ranting fanaticism. . . .

I know not that I can furnish the reader with a juster idea of a well conducted camp-meeting, than by inserting the following account of one held at Cowharbor, Long Island, in the state of New-York, August 11, 1818. It was written indeed under the impulse of those vivid sensations which were produced by a participation in the solemn exercises of the occasion, and by a glow of fervent feeling which may have betrayed the writer into a warmth of expression which none but those similarly situated know how to interpret and appreciate. . . . The following is the account alluded to: — . . .

"According to the order of the meeting, the people this night retired to rest at ten o'clock. The next morning opened a delightful prospect to a contemplative mind. The rising sun in the east, darting his lucid beams through the grove, which was now rendered vocal by the voice of morning prayer in the several tents, announced the superintending care, and proclaimed the majesty of Him who maketh the sun to rise on the evil and on the good. . . . Not a turbulent passion was permitted to interrupt the sacred peace and divine harmony which the heavenly

Dove had imparted to God's beloved people. The exercises of this day were solemn, impressive, and divinely animating. The falling tear from many eyes witnessed the inward anguish which was produced in the hearts of sinners by the word of eternal truth. Those trembling sinners, groaning under the weight of their sins, were encircled by God's people, and lifted to his throne in the arms of faith and prayer. Some were disburthened of their load; and their shouts of praise testified that Jesus had become their Friend,

"The departure of the sun under the western horizon indicated the time to have arrived for the intelligent creation to lose themselves once more in . . . [sleep]. But, while some obeyed the impulse of nature, . . . others, animated by the love of God, and attracted by the sympathetic groans of wounded sinners, whose piercing cries ascended to heaven, committing themselves to the protection of God, assembled in groups, and united their petitions and intercessions to almighty God in behalf of themselves and their mourning fellow-creatures. . . . About midnight I was attracted by the shouts of an intimate friend, who had been sometime overwhelmed upon the stand with the power of God. In company with some of the young disciples of Christ, I drew near, while he proclaimed the wonders of redeeming love. I at first looked on with the criticising eye of cool philosophy, determined not to be carried away with passionate exclamations. Bracing myself as much as possible, I was resolved my passions should not get the ascendancy over my judgment. But, in spite of all my philosophy, my prejudice, and my resistance, my heart suddenly melted like wax before the fire, and my nerves seemed in a moment relaxed. . . .

"Friday was the day appointed to close our meeting. It had been unusually solemn, and profitable to many, very many souls; and the hour of separation was anticipated with reluctance. The exercises of this day were attended with an uncommon manifestation of the power and presence of God. The mournful cries of penitent sinners were many and strong; and the professors of religion were ardently engaged in praying for them; and not a few were groaning for full redemption in the blood of the Lamb. While engaged in this exercise, some of the preachers were baptized afresh *with the Holy Ghost and fire*; and their cup ran over with love to God and to the souls of men.

". . . Many fell to the ground under the mighty power of God, while the shouts of the redeemed seemed to rend the heavens, and to be carried on the waves of the undulating air to the distant hills, and in their rolling melody proclaimed the praises of Him who sits upon the throne and of the Lamb.

"This was one of the most awfully solemn scenes my eyes ever beheld. Such a sense of the ineffable Majesty rested upon my soul, that I was lost in astonishment, wonder, and profound adoration. Human language cannot express the solemn, the delightful, the deep and joyful sensation which pervaded my soul. . . . Singing, prayer, and exhortation were continued more or less until 3 o'clock next morning, the hour appointed to prepare to leave the consecrated ground. Many were the subjects of converting grace; and great was the joy of the happy Christians.

". . . May they never violate their solemn vow, nor suffer their serious impressions to be effaced. Let no vain amusement, no trifling company, nor any worldly concern divert your attention, ye young professors of religion, or ever efface from your minds those solemn impressions of God, and of his goodness, which you have received. . . .

"Sometimes when I have indulged in the cool speculations which worldly prudence would suggest, so many objections have been raised in my mind against camp-meetings, that I have been ready to proclaim war against them; but these objections have uniformly been obviated by witnessing the beneficial effects of the meetings while attending them. My theories have all been torn in pieces while testing them by actual experiment—but never more effectually than by this last. This is more convincing than all the arguments in the world. What I experience I know; and hundreds of others, equally competent to decide, would, were they called upon, bear a similar testimony. O! ye happy souls that were bathed in the love of God at this meeting! May you ever evince to the world by the uniformity of your Christian conduct, that such meetings are highly useful."

Nathan Bangs, *A History of the Methodist Episcopal Church*, 2 vols. (New York: T. Mason & G. Lane, 1839), 2:265–75.

ꝵ

Fall River: An Authentic Narrative (1833)

CATHARINE WILLIAMS

Camp meetings ignited the hot fires of controversy in 1833, when a Methodist minister named Ephraim K. Avery was tried in Rhode Island for the murder of an unmarried (and pregnant) "factory girl," Sarah Maria Cornell. Cornell was a Methodist convert and an avid attender at camp meetings, and she maintained that at one meeting Avery coerced her into having sex and impregnated her. At the time, Methodists had reached the height of their success in gaining new converts through revivalist preaching and camp meetings. The scandal continued even beyond the long trial. (Avery was acquitted by a jury, based in part on arguments that a promiscuous factory girl must have committed suicide.) Using the burgeoning print resources of the 1830s, a public outcry was directed at Avery and the Methodists. Catharine Williams, a divorced mother who supported herself and her child as an author, jumped into the fray. Williams published a local best-seller that argued for Avery's guilt and for the Methodists' complicity in conspiring to assure his acquittal. In an appendix to that book, Williams offers her reflections on, and personal experiences at, a camp meeting.

PROBLEMS TO CONSIDER

1. How do you explain the differences between Nathan Bangs and Catharine Williams? Are they describing the same phenomena?
2. Examine the way gender and sexuality influence Williams's depiction of this camp meeting: what is her point with regard to women, sexuality, and religion?

So much has been said of late of Camp Meetings, and such intense curiosity excited on the subject, that the author of these sheets feels called upon to give a history of one of which she was an eye and ear witness, i.e. for the time she passed there. The meeting was held in R.I. and was I should say some ten or twelve years ago. It is said that the regulations of those places have been much more strict of late years, and that the disorders in the immediate vicinity of a Camp have lessened since. That their moral tendency is better than it was before is however doubtful. Witness the affair of the unfortunate girl *[i.e., Sarah Maria Cornell]* who perished at the stack-yard.—That her latest misfortune was occasioned by her attendance there, cannot be doubted. . . . Men's eyes are now partially open to the great evils of fanaticism generally, and of Camp-Meetings in particular; and every thing known on that subject ought to come out. The following diary or memorandum, or whatever it may be called, was taken at the time, except a very little added from memory. . . . This is brought before the world; but with the hope that it may have a tendency to assist in putting down a great evil, a sore affliction in the land, a pestilence walking in darkness, an enormity that calls loudly for the strong arm of the law, in the opinion of many good judges. . . .

Extracted from a Journal of a Camp Meeting, held in Smithfield, R.I.
The long expected time at length arrived, the meeting was to be held in an extensive wood

about nine miles from the town of——several very respectable young ladies had agreed to stay at a house within two miles of the meeting, where they could ride backwards and forwards as often as they chose through its continuance. . . . For my own part I felt determined to endure all hardships rather than be disappointed in this opportunity of seeing and hearing. So many stories had been told me of Camp Meetings, and such various and contradictory ones, that I felt determined to see and hear for myself. The meetings had not commenced upon our arrival, but the Camp was said to be in order. . . .

I was never more amazed than by the scene before me. It was a beautiful spot in a pine wood. The trees were felled here and there with a sufficiency left for shade, and had the appearance of a fine grove within an impenetrable wood. . . . The setting sun lent its last bright beams to the scene, while the snowy tents stretched far and wide, discovered many happy faces peeping from beneath their white curtains. . . .

The plain dress of the people was very pleasant to me, and about the place there was an air of quiet, inviting to heavenly contemplation. And is this, I asked, a Camp Meeting? I do not believe a word about the confusion. . . .

I made the remark, "it is very quiet here." She [i.e., a companion] answered, "the meetings have not began."

Upon re-entering the avenue our wagon had to turn out often for companies of rude young men, who, though the pass was so extremely dangerous, drove Jehu-like *[i.e., furiously]*, unmindful of stumps or stones, and appeared in a high frolic. I inquired the meaning of this. The landlord's son who was driving us, answered, "They were professional gamblers and horse jockies, who followed a Camp Meeting as regularly as crows and vultures followed an army." I was amazed, but I soon forgot the circumstance and relapsed into my former pleasing reverie. . . .

The excessive heat and fatigue drove us back to our lodgings at noon; but towards night we rode again to the Camp. We observed, as we came near the wood, the recent erection of stalls to sell liquors and refreshments; and around many were congregated people notorious for dissolute morals and disgraceful conduct. The wood appeared to be swarming with people of all descriptions, and it looked as though it might be extremely hazardous for any one to venture there alone and on foot.

The first object that met our eyes upon coming within the barrier was a young woman of extreme beauty, who was staggering through the Camp, with her clothes torn and her locks dishevelled, wringing her hands and mourning that the people were not more engaged. She was a girl of about middling height, rather fat, with large, languishing black eyes, and a profusion of raven hair which floated on her shoulders and reached below her waist, with the fairest complexion that could be imagined. She appeared to excite great attention wherever she moved through the crowd. We observed, as she passed along, that the young men exchanged winks and jogged each others elbows. We subsequently saw the same young woman lying in a tent, apparently insensible, i.e. in a perfect state of happiness, as they assured us. There was a great deal of joggling, pinching and looking under bonnets, which was extremely annoying. We met a young lady from our town, who showed us her arms pinched black and blue by she could not tell who, while she was listening to the preaching of a woman at the stand. She was quite enraged about it, and protested she would get

home as soon as she could get her party to go, and that no persuasion should induce her to come again. . . .

Thursday afternoon, rode again to the Camp, saw the most drunken people in the road I ever saw on any other occasion. Many of them, I was told, had families at home destitute, even in this land of plenty, of the common necessaries of life. I could not help groaning in spirit all the way, which was literally perfumed by the odour of the spirit which they had drank. . . .

When we entered the Camp, there was what they called a powerful preacher, on the stand. He was exhorting the people to repentance with great vehemence and gesticulation. The bad English he used provoked many a smile from his hearers, while another class of his hearers seemed to listen with profound attention, and expressed their approbation by many an exclamation of delight, accompanied with groans and amens. One man fell down near us in strong convulsions; the crowd pressed around him, but the brethren, pushing them back, drew him into a tent, saying he was "full of the spirit," &c. We now got crowded between a woman of most infamous character and some young men, who were holding a whispering dialogue over our shoulders:—astonishing impudence! . . . The brutal intoxication and profanity visible on the road home was truly shocking; and as we went past the stalls, the thought struck me, that these buyers and sellers were after all perhaps the smallest sinners on the ground; that they, who were the means of bringing this tumultuous assemblage together, unless there was some redeeming merit about it that I had not yet discovered, had much to answer for. . . .

Friday was the last day of the meeting, and I who had now firmly resolved to see it out, and be a judge myself how far it was a work of the Spirit, went prepared to spend the day and night in the Camp. . . .

As no interesting preacher now occupied the stand, we resolved to stroll round and look up some of our friends from the neighboring towns, many of whom we doubted not were there. In passing one of the tents we could not forbear stopping to look at a young woman reclining on the straw in a very languishing attitude, and apparently quite helpless: two or three young men had seated themselves near her and were enquiring how she felt? Upon closely observing her I discovered she was the same young woman whose disordered appearance and extraordinary beauty had struck me so forcibly, and invited so much observation a few day[s] before. It was she, but oh how changed! even in the brief space of time that had intervened since we saw her before. Her bloom was entirely gone, and her haggard look and tangled hair gave her the appearance of something that had recently escaped from a mad house. I shuddered with horror, and thought oh! if you were a sister or daughter of mine how should I feel. Humanity towards the poor victim induced me to draw near and ask her if she had no mother to take care of her? She turned a look of scorn and anger upon me, and then exchanged a look with each of the young men, and they all three laughed, and I walked off convinced I had been mistaken. . . .

Before it was quite dark we returned, and by the time we arrived, the camp was lighted. . . . We avowed our determination to pass the night in the Camp. . . . Prayer meetings had commenced in the different tents, yet there was a continual travelling from place to place—nobody except the immediate actors in the scene seemed stationary for a moment at a time; crowds of people passing and repassing all the time. One woman flew past, throwing her arms abroad, and shouting "there are grapes here and they are good, heavenly times! heavenly times!" A few moments after our ears were assailed with the most piercing shrieks of a female voice, which proceeded from behind one of the neighboring tents. Two of us sprang up and almost involuntarily ran to the place—the other two rather hung back as they afterwards told us from fear, thinking it might be some one murdered,

or some terrible assault, a few moments brought us to the spot, and beheld two young women stretched upon the ground, no human creature touching them, screaming with all their strength. Some females from the neighboring tents rushed out to them, and sinking down by their side, began to talk to them all at once. "Sink right into Jesus" said one, "and you will be happy in a minute." I enquired of an old lady standing by what the matter was? she said they were slain, and there was a great many slain there every night. Several persons now raised them to carry them into the tent, and we in a whisper agreed to follow close in the rear, which by keeping hold of each other's clothes and following close upon the heels of those who had borne in the slain, we succeeded in getting into the centre of the tent, where, within a circle formed by the meeting they were laid upon the straw. They, the meeting people, were singing a hymn, which rose to deafening uproar upon our approach. After the hymn, the women commenced praying over them, using many strange expressions and the most violent gesticulation, the power of which was acknowledged by many a groan, shout, and interjection, intermingled with the agonizing shrieks of the slain, which still continued.

The loud Amen, the cries for mercy, the groans of distress, (either real or imaginary) resounded from every quarter, while the triumphant exclamations of those who shouted "I'm full—I'm running over—I'm eating heavenly manna—glory! hallelujah!" &c. &c. were as distinctly heard: and this, this scene of discordant noise and unseemly riot (as it appeared to me) was what they called "the power of God." Forgive, thou insulted Being, the use I am here obliged to make of thy great and dreadful name! Occasionally some of the young men who were within the circle would draw near the young women, whose shrieks gradually changed to groans, and ask, in a low voice, "do you feel any better?" I could not hear that they made any answer. One young man, while the prayer was going on, began to shake violently, and then falling flat upon the straw, exclaimed "God, I'm willing—I will own my Saviour—I will, I will:" at the same time, his feet kicking at such a rate, that the dust from the straw nearly suffocated us all. His feet chancing to lodge, in his fall, just between me and another young lady, we endured no small share of inconvenience. . . .

The din and confusion increased every moment. Stamping, slapping hands, and knocking fists together, formed altogether a scene of confusion that beggars description, and really terrified us. We looked at each other in despair, and then at the door, which was completely wedged up with faces, one above another; no way to get out, and no one to help us; when fortunately the uncle of two of the young ladies . . . descried us, and in a moment comprehending our distress, opened a passage to the circle. . . .

We felt rejoiced that this was the last night of the meeting, for the camp began to smell very offensive. Many were remarking that the danger to health would be very great should the meetings continue twenty-four hours longer. . . . The inhabitants of the neighbourhood long had cause to remember that meeting. The effects of it were distinctly visible. Fences torn to pieces, and fields of grain wantonly trod down and destroyed, with other excesses, absurd and unnecessary, bear witness to the little reformation in morals the meeting had occasioned. . . .

It must be obvious to every person, of common sense, that if camp meetings exhibit such scenes to moral persons, to those who penetrate the recesses in their neighbourhood the view must be still more revolting. Stories have been told and still are, that almost stagger credulity itself, and they carry with them this proof of their authenticity, that the most depraved and abandoned of the human species, are always fond of resorting to them. If the writer of this true sketch can be a means of opening the eyes of any well disposed persons, who have hitherto been disposed to uphold them, it will be a source of lasting satisfaction, and a full reward for all the resentment which ignorance and fanaticism may award.

C. R. Williams, *Fall River: An Authentic Narrative* (Boston: Lilly, Wait & Co., 1833), 165–94.

ᔧ

ᔧ *Sensational Tales of Ruin: The Cultural Production of Reformers* ᔧ

Moral reformers were certainly aware of the tremendous popular successes (as well as the controversies) surrounding revivalism. Many of the leaders of the temperance, abolitionist, and antiprostitution reforms (to name a few) had themselves been converts of this new evangelical message of individual free moral agency. And they patterned their reform movements after many of the methods of revivalists.

In time, reformers also resorted to popular culture to achieve their goals. Reformers made clear that the battles they waged to remake American society in their own image were not just a struggle to control individual behavior but also a contest to shape the emerging democratic culture of the United States. In turning to the forms of popular culture—songs, plays, novels, and personal narratives—reformers tried to expand the audience for their ideas as well as offer alternative options for evangelicals to partake of these moral amusements. But, as one American literature scholar has noted, the cultural productions of moral reformers often became as salacious and immoral as the behavior they wished to reform. Good examples of these were the nativist tales depicting lurid fantasies of lascivious priests and imprisoned nuns in Catholic convents. The most popular of these convent tales was the *Awful Disclosures of Maria Monk*. It made no difference to Protestant readers that the real Maria Monk had never been a nun, only a mentally disturbed prostitute, or that the *Awful Disclosures* had been ghost-written by Catholic-phobic Protestant ministers. It was one of the best-selling books of the pre–Civil War era, outsold only by Harriet Beecher Stowe's *Uncle Tom's Cabin*. The irony behind this anti-Catholic literature was that in an effort to expose the supposed sexual iniquities of Catholics, these Protestant reformers produced a form of popular pornography for a broad antebellum reading public. The documents in this section offer two examples of reform literature that straddled the fence between sentimental instruction and immoral reform.

Ten Nights in a Bar-Room (1854)

T. S. ARTHUR

Temperance reform transformed the drinking habits of numerous Americans in the antebellum years. The premise behind the movement was that each individual drinker (almost always figured as a man, not a woman) would pledge to abstain from the consumption of alcoholic beverages, especially hard liquor. American consumption of hard liquor (whiskey and other distilled spirits) had skyrocketed in the decades following the American Revolution, but with a new market and industrial economy in the early nineteenth century, opponents of drinking began by the 1820s to organize societies that advocated abstinence as a new ethic that provided its followers with a badge of respectability, economic credit, and class standing.

As the movement gained more and more followers across class and racial lines in the 1830s and 1840s, temperance advocates exploited available forms of popular culture to get out their message. Temperance reformers wrote songs, hymns, and poems; performed theatrical melodramas; and penned popular sentimental fiction. Tales of families, livelihoods, and characters destroyed by the bottle soon abounded in these sentimental novels. As one temperance tale concluded: "How many broken hearted mothers are sorrowing over their fallen offspring, brought to disgrace and ruin by a father's folly!" The best-selling temperance novel, and one of the best-selling books, of the nineteenth century was T. S. Arthur's Ten Nights in a Bar-Room. *Arthur's narrator returns to a tavern on ten different evenings over several years and charts the steady ruin that a male culture of drinking brings to many men's lives. The following selection exposes the sentimental conventions and melodramatic plot that Arthur employs in the story of the death of young Mary Morgan.*

PROBLEMS TO CONSIDER

1. How is Mary Morgan's death an act of reform? What was Arthur's purpose in employing a female child to accomplish this work of reformation?
2. How might Arthur's melodrama be interpreted as a critique of the market revolution? What did drinking and taverns represent in this culture, and why did they need reforming?

The First Night

Ten years ago, business required me to pass a day in Cedarville. It was late in the afternoon when the stage set me down at the "Sickle and Sheaf," a new tavern, just opened by a new landlord, in a new house, built with the special end of providing "accommodations for man and beast." As I stepped from the dusty old vehicle . . . the good-natured face of Simon Slade, the landlord, beaming as it did with a hearty welcome, was really a pleasant sight to see, and the grasp of his hand was like that of a true friend. . . .

"If our excellent friend, Mr. Slade," said Harvey Green, "is not the richest man in Cedarville at the end of ten years, he will at least enjoy the satisfaction of having made his town richer." . . .

"And the graveyard too"—muttered the individual who had before disturbed the self-satisfied harmony of the company, remarking upon the closing sentence of Harvey Green. "Come, landlord," he added, as he strode across to the bar, speaking in a changed, reckless sort of way, "fix me up a good hot whisky-punch, and do it right; and there's another sixpence toward the fortune you are bound to make." . . .

I looked at Simon Slade, his eyes rested on mine for a moment or two, and then sunk beneath my earnest gaze. I saw that his countenance flushed, and that his motions were slightly confused. The incident, it was plain, did not awaken agreeable thoughts. Once I saw his hand move toward the sixpence, that lay upon the counter; but, whether to push it back, or draw it toward the till, I could not determine. The whisky-punch was in due time ready, and with it the man retired to a table across the room, and sat down to enjoy the tempting beverage. As he did so, the landlord quietly swept the poor unfortunate's last sixpence into his drawer. The influence of this strong potation was to render the man a little more talkative. To the free conversation passing around him he lent an attentive ear, dropping in a word, now and then, that always told upon the company like a well-directed blow. At last, Slade lost all patience with him, and said, a little fretfully,—

"Look here, Joe Morgan, if you will be ill-natured, pray go somewhere else, and not interrupt good feeling among gentlemen." . . .

Just at this moment the outer door was pushed open with a slow, hesitating motion; then a little pale face peered in, and a pair of soft blue eyes went searching about the room. Conversation was instantly hushed, and every face, excited with interest, turned toward the child, who had now stepped through the door. She was not over ten years of age; but it moved the heart to look upon the saddened expression of her young countenance, and the forced bravery therein, that scarcely overcame the native timidity so touchingly visible.

"Father!" I have never heard this word spoken in a voice that sent such a thrill along every nerve. It was full of sorrowful love—full of a tender concern that had its origin too deep for the heart of a child. As she spoke, the little one sprang across the room, and laying her hands upon the arm of Joe Morgan, lifted her eyes, that were ready to gush over with tears, to his face.

"Come, father! won't you come home?" I hear that low, pleading voice even now, and my heart gives a quicker throb. Poor child! Darkly shadowed was the sky that bent gloomily over thy young life.

Morgan arose, and suffered the child to lead him from the room. He seemed passive in her hands. I noticed that he thrust his fingers nervously into his pocket, and that a troubled look went over his face as they were withdrawn. His last sixpence was in the till of Simon Slade! . . .

[The narrator listens while another customer tells him the history of Slade and Morgan.]

". . . Poor Joe Morgan! He is an old and early friend of Simon Slade. They were boys together, and worked as millers under the same roof for many years. In fact, Joe's father owned the mill, and the two learned their trade with him. When old Morgan died, the mill came into Joe's hands. It was in rather a worn-out condition, and Joe went in debt for some pretty thorough repairs and additions of machinery. By and by, Simon

Slade, who was hired by Joe to run the mill, received a couple of thousand dollars at the death of an aunt. This sum enabled him to buy a share in the mill, which Morgan was very glad to sell in order to get clear of his debt. Time passed on, and Joe left his milling interest almost entirely in the care of Slade, who, it must be said in his favour, did not neglect the business. But it somehow happened—I will not say unfairly—that, at the end of ten years, Joe Morgan no longer owned a share in the mill. The whole property was in the hands of Slade. . . .

"A year or two before his ownership in the mill ceased, Morgan married one of the sweetest girls in our town—Fanny Ellis. . . . Joe was an attractive young man, take him as you would, and just the one to win the heart of a girl like Fanny. What if he had been seen, now and then, a little the worse for drink! What if he showed more fondness for pleasure than for business! Fanny did not look into the future with doubt or fear. She believed that her love was strong enough to win him from all evil allurements. . . .

"Well. Dark days came for her, poor soul! And yet, in all the darkness of her earthly lot, she has never, it is said, been any thing but a loving, forbearing, self-denying wife to Morgan. And he—fallen as he is, and powerless in the grasp of the monster intemperance—has never, I am sure, hurt her with a cruel word. Had he added these, her heart would, long ere this, have broken. Poor Joe Morgan! Poor Fanny! Oh, what a curse is this drink!" . . .

"It was unfortunate for Joe, at least, that Slade sold his mill, and became a tavern-keeper. . . .

"But, after Slade sold the mill, a sad change took place. The new owner was little disposed to pay wages to a hand who would not give him all his time during working hours; and in less than two weeks from the day he took possession, Morgan was discharged." . . .

The Second Night

"Look here, Joe Morgan!"—the half angry voice of Simon Slade now run through the bar-room,—"just take yourself off home!"

I had not observed the entrance of this person. He was standing at the bar, with an emptied glass in his hand. A year had made no improvement in his appearance. On the contrary, his clothes were more worn and tattered; his countenance more sadly marred. What he had said to irritate the landlord, I know not; but Slade's face was fiery with passion, and his eyes glared threateningly at the poor besotted one, who showed not the least inclination to obey.

"Off with you, I say! And never show your face here again. I won't have such low vagabonds as you are about my house. If you can't keep decent and stay decent, don't intrude yourself here."

"A rum-seller talk of decency!" retorted Morgan. "Pah! You were a decent man once, and a good miller into the bargain. But that time's past and gone. Decency died out when you exchanged the pick and facing-hammer for the glass and muddler. Decency! Pah! How you talk! As if it were any more decent to sell rum than to drink it."

There was so much of biting contempt in the tones, as well as the words of the half intoxicated man, that Slade, who had himself been drinking rather more freely than usual, was angered beyond self-control. Catching up an empty glass from the counter, he hurled it with all his strength at the head of Joe Morgan. The missive just grazed one of his temples, and flew by on its dangerous course. The quick sharp cry of a child startled the air, followed by exclamations of alarm and horror from many voices.

"It's Joe Morgan's child!" "He's killed her!" "Good heavens!" Such were the exclamations that rang through the room. . . .

The Third Night

[The scene shifts to Morgan's apartment, where his young daughter is in bed, nearing death.]

"Father!" . . .

"Yes, poor child."

"Now, won't you promise me one thing?"

"What is it, dear?"

"Not to go out in the evening until I get well."

Joe Morgan hesitated.

"Just promise me that, father. It won't be long. I shall be up again in a little while."

How well the father knows what is in the heart of his child. Her fears are all for him. Who is to go after her poor father, and lead him home when the darkness of inebriety is on his spirit, and external perception so dulled that not skill enough remains to shun the harm that lies in his path.

"Do promise just that, father, dear."

He cannot resist the pleading voice and look.

"I promise it, Mary; so shut your eyes now and go to sleep. I'm afraid this fever will increase."

"Oh! I'm so glad—so glad!" . . .

Later

"Father!"

"What, love?"

"Stoop down closer; I don't want mother to hear; it will make her feel so bad."

The father bends his ear close to the lips of Mary. How he starts and shudders! What has she said?—only these brief words—

"I shall not get well, father; I'm going to die."

The groans, impossible to repress, that issued through the lips of Joe Morgan, startled the ears of his wife, and she came quickly to the bed-side.

"What is it? What is the matter, Joe?" she inquired with a look of anxiety.

"Hush, father. Don't tell her. I only said it to you." And Mary put a finger on her lips, and looked mysterious. "There, mother—you go away; you've got trouble enough, any how. Don't tell her, father." . . .

"Joe,"—Mrs. Morgan aroused herself as quickly as possible, for she had that to say which she feared she might not have the heart to utter—"Joe, if Mary dies, you cannot forget the cause of her death."

"Oh, Fanny! Fanny!"

"Nor the hand that struck the cruel blow." . . .

"Nor the place where the blow was dealt," said Mrs. Morgan, interrupting him.

"Poor—poor child!" moaned the conscience-stricken man.

"Nor your promise, Joe—nor your promise given to our dying child." . . .

[Later, when experiencing withdrawal from alcohol addiction (the "DTs"), Morgan crawls into bed next to his daughter.]

"You're an angel—my good angel, Mary," he murmured, in a voice yet trembling with fear. "Pray for me, my child. Oh, ask your Father in heaven to save me from these dreadful creatures. There now!" he cried, rising up suddenly, and looking toward the door. "Keep out! Go away! You can't come in here. This is Mary's room; and she's an angel. Ah, ha! I know you wouldn't dare come in here. . . ."

"Poor father!" sighed the child, as she gathered both arms about his neck. "I will be your good angel. Nothing shall hurt you here."

"I knew I would be safe where you were," he whispered back—"I knew it, and so I came. Kiss me, love."

How pure and fervent was the kiss laid instantly upon his lips! There was a power in it to remand the evil influences that were surrounding and pressing in upon him like a flood. All was quiet now, and Mrs. Morgan neither by word nor movement disturbed the solemn stillness that reigned in the apartment. In a few minutes the deepened breathing of her husband gave a blessed intimation that he was sinking into sleep. . . .

The Fourth Night

"Father, I dreamed something about you, while I slept to-day." Mary again turned to her father.

"What was it, dear?"

"I thought it was night, and that I was still sick. You promised not to go out again until I was well. But you did go out; and I thought you went over to Mr. Slade's tavern. When I knew this, I felt as strong as when I was well, and I got up and dressed myself, and started out after you . . . until I came to the tavern, and there you stood in the door. And you were dressed so nice. You had on a new hat and a new coat; and your boots were new, and polished just like Judge

Hammond's. I said—'O father! is this you?' And then you took me up in your arms and kissed me, and said—'Yes, Mary, I am your real father. Not old Joe Morgan—but Mr. Morgan now.' It seemed all so strange, that I looked into the bar-room to see who was there. But it wasn't a bar-room any longer; but a store full of goods. The sign of the Sickle and Sheaf was taken down; and over the door I now read your name, father. Oh! I was so glad, that I awoke—and then I cried all to myself, for it was only a dream."

The last words were said very mournfully, and with a drooping of Mary's lids, until the tear-gemmed lashes lay close upon her cheeks. . . .

Morgan answered, and bent down his ear.

"You will only have mother left," she said—"only mother. And she cries so much when you are away."

"I won't leave her, Mary, only when I go to work," said Morgan, whispering back to the child. "And I'll never go out at night any more."

"Yes; you promised me that."

"And I'll promise more."

"What, father?"

"Never to go into a tavern again."

"Never!"

"No, never. And I'll promise still more."

"Father?"

"Never to drink a drop of liquor as long as I live."

"Oh, father! dear, dear father!" And with a cry of joy Mary started up and flung herself upon his breast. Morgan drew his arms tightly around her, and sat for a long time, with his lips pressed to her cheek—while she lay against his bosom as still as death. As death? Yes; for, when the father unclasped his arms, the spirit of his child was with the angels of the resurrection!

[The rest of this melodrama focuses on the Slade family, and how Simon Slade's decision to open a tavern results in the ultimate ruin of his family. Slade's tavern slips into financial ruin. Slade is prosecuted for Mary's death (but acquitted by influential friends). His son Frank becomes an insolent, intemperate young man, who eventually kills his father by hurling a brandy bottle at his head (inverting the death of young Mary Morgan from earlier in the novel). Arthur could not have chosen a stronger temperance metaphor—the bottle kills Slade and results in the final ruin of his son. Slade's wife ends up in an insane asylum.]

T. S. Arthur, *Ten Nights in a Bar-Room, and What I Saw There* (Philadelphia: J. W. Bradley, 1854), 7, 20–24, 28–30, 50–51, 63–64, 70–74, 78–79, 92–94.

๛

A Lecture to Young Men, on Chastity (1837)
SYLVESTER GRAHAM

Besides advocating temperance, moral reformers set their sights on many other "sins" that they hoped to purge from society, including Sabbath breaking, Masonic lodges, war, slavery, and prostitution. Temperance was just one among many reforms directed at the bodies and health of Americans during the antebellum era. The man who best tied together these various health, body, and sex reforms was Sylvester Graham, a popular lecturer who became associated with a health and diet craze. Graham began his career as a revivalist preacher, but he was soon hired by the Pennsylvania Temperance Society to convince laboring men in working-class neighborhoods of the dangers of drink. Realizing that he could garner substantially better compensation as a health reform lecturer than as a temperance agent, Graham developed a system of health reforms based on the consumption of coarse grains and vegetables and abstinence from stimulants of any kind (such as spices, coffee, and alcohol).

Today, we are familiar with Graham more for his whole-wheat graham flour (an important ingredient of graham crackers) than for his ideas about health, sex, and the body. But for many of Graham's contemporaries, diet and sex reforms were inseparably linked. Both required an ethic of self-denial, by which an emergent middle class displayed its respectability and differentiated itself from the allegedly immoral, pleasure-seeking working class and nonwhite population. One of Graham's most popular lectures was an advice manual to young men against the dangers of sexual excess in any form, whether it be masturbation ("self-pollution"), premarital sex, or even too-frequent sexual intercourse for married men. At the height of his popularity, Graham earned more than $200 per night for his lectures (the equivalent of the annual income for a working man), and his Lecture to Young Men *ran through fifteen editions over the next ten years. The following excerpts reveal how Graham unified his ideas about health, the body's systems, and the dangers associated with lack of sexual self-restraint. Ironically, reformers such as Graham exploited their titillating subject matter to attract readers, despite their stated objective to curtail the evils of "lascivious thoughts."*

PROBLEMS TO CONSIDER

1. How did Graham link the body's digestive system to its sexual functions, and what reforms did he advocate for both?
2. Graham repeatedly used several key words—"excitement," "stimulation," "irritability," "debility," "nerves." Explain how these might be metaphors for social changes in antebellum America.

I am fully aware of the delicacy and difficulty attending the discussion of the subject of the following Lecture; and have seriously and solemnly considered all the objections which can be made against its publication. But I am also aware of the immense importance, that young men should be correctly and properly instructed on this subject. He who in any manner endeavors to excite the sensual appetites, and arouse the unchaste passions of youth, is one of the most heinous offenders against the welfare of mankind; and, so far as effects are considered, it is not enough that he who meddles with this matter, *means well.* Irreparable mischief may be done, with the best *intentions.* . . .

In the first place, self-pollution is actually a very great and rapidly increasing evil in our country. It is, indeed, all that I have described in the following lecture—yes, far more than I dare describe, lest I should do harm; for there are some things that may not even be named.

In the second place, illicit commerce between the sexes is a very great and rapidly increasing evil in society.

In the third place, sexual excess within the pale of wedlock is really a very considerable and an increasing evil.

In the fourth place, efforts to encourage illicit and promiscuous commerce between the sexes are already very extensive, and are daily becoming more extensive, bold and efficient. . . .

I did not write this lecture to oppose infidelity, nor to vindicate the Bible, but simply to set forth, in a clear and concise manner, the true physiological and pathological principles which relate to the sexual organization, functions, propensities and passions of man, and to illustrate their practical bearing; and I am confident that I have done this with an accuracy of scientific truth which defies refutation; and in so doing, without going out of my way for the purpose, I have proved beyond all controversy, that the Bible doctrine of marriage and sexual continence and purity, is founded on the physiological principles established in the constitutional nature of man. . . .

Constituted as man is, two grand FUNCTIONS of his system are necessary for his existence as an individual and as a species. The first is NUTRITION; the second is REPRODUCTION. . . .

The functions of nutrition and reproduction depend on the vital properties of the tissues which form the organs of the system — particularly the muscular and nervous tissues, and more especially the nervous. . . .

The genital organs are, as it were, woven into the same grand web of organic life with the stomach, heart, lungs, &c., by being largely supplied with the same class of nerves on which the organs of nutrition depend for their functional power: but the genital organs are also supplied with nerves of animal life, or those which are connected with the brain and spinal marrow. Hence the influences of the brain may act directly on the genital organs; and of these latter on the brain. Lascivious thoughts and imaginations will excite and stimulate the genital organs, cause an increased quantity of blood to flow into them, and augment their secretions and peculiar sensibilities; and, on the other hand, an excited state of the genital organs, either from the stimulations of semen, or from diseased action in the system, will throw its influence upon the brain, and force lascivious thoughts and imaginations upon the mind.

The same reciprocity of influence, also, exists between the organs of reproduction and nutrition. The stomach, heart, lungs, skin, &c., are immediately and strongly affected by the condition of the genital organs; and these latter participate, to a greater or less extent, in the affections of the former; — and always share fully in those conditions of the former, which result from the general state of the nerves of organic life. . . .

All kinds of stimulating and heating substances, high-seasoned food, rich dishes, the free use of flesh, and even the excess of aliment, all, more or less — increase the concupiscent excitability and sensibility of the genital organs,

and augment their influence on the functions of organic life, and on the intellectual and moral faculties.

SEXUAL DESIRE, again, in turn, throws its influence over the whole domain of the nerves of organic life, . . . and when it kindles into a passion, its influence is so extensive and powerful, that it disturbs and disorders all the functions of the system. Digestion is retarded, or wholly interrupted; — circulation is accelerated, and an increased quantity of blood is injected into the brain, stomach, lungs, and other important organs; respiration is obstructed and oppressed, and imperfectly performed, — and insensible perspiration is considerably diminished. These irritations and disturbances cannot long be continued, nor frequently repeated, without serious injury to the whole system. . . .

The convulsive paroxysms attending venereal indulgence, are connected with the most intense excitement, and cause the most powerful agitation to the whole system, that it is ever subject to. The brain, stomach, heart, lungs, liver, skin, and the other organs, feel it sweeping over them, with the tremendous violence of a tornado. The powerfully excited and convulsed heart drives the blood, in fearful congestion, to the principal viscera, — producing oppression, irritation, debility, rupture, inflammation, and sometimes disorganization; — and this violent paroxysm is generally succeeded by great exhaustion, relaxation, lassitude and even prostration.

These excesses, too frequently repeated, cannot fail to produce the most terrible effects. The nervous system, even to its most minute filamentary extremities, is tortured into a shocking state of debility, and excessive irritability, and uncontrollable mobility, and aching sensibility. . . .

But we are perfectly certain, that the peculiar *excitement* of venereal indulgence, is more diffusive, universal and powerful, than any other to which the system is ever subject; and that it more rapidly exhausts the vital properties of the tissues, and impairs the functional powers of the organs: and consequently . . . deteriorates all the vital processes of nutrition . . . and hence the terrible fact, that venereal excesses occasion the most loath-some, and horrible, and calamitous diseases that human nature is capable of suffering. . . .

Hence, therefore, SEXUAL DESIRE, cherished by the mind and dwelt on by the imagination, not only increases the excitability and peculiar sensibility of the genital organs themselves, but always throws an influence, equal to the intensity of the affection, over the whole nervous domain;—disturbing all the functions depending on the nerves for vital energy, . . . and if this excitement is frequently repeated, or long continued, it inevitably induces an increased degree of irritability and debility, and relaxation generally throughout the nervous and muscular tissues, and especially the nerves of organic life. And hence, those LASCIVIOUS DAY-DREAMS, and *amorous reveries*, in which young people too generally,—and especially the idle, and the voluptuous, and the sedentary, and the nervous,—are exceedingly apt to indulge, are often the sources of general debility, effeminacy, disordered functions, and permanent disease, and even premature death, without the actual exercise of the genital organs! Indeed, this unchastity of thought—this *adultery of the mind*—is the beginning of immeasurable evil to the human family. . . .

If we will train our offspring into the early and free use of flesh-meat, and accustom them to high-seasoned food, and richly prepared dishes, and learn them to drink tea, and coffee, and wine, and to indulge in various other stimulants, with which civic life is universally cursed, and effeminate their bodies with feather beds and enervating dress,—in short, if we will sedulously educate them to all the degenerating habits of luxury, indolence, voluptuousness and sensuality, we shall be more indebted to their want of *opportunity to sin*, than to any other cause, for the preservation of their bodily chastity. . . . For these lascivious, and exceedingly pernicious day-dreams of the young, are but the first buddings of a depraved instinct, which will

not be satisfied with the passive reveries of the mind and affections of the body. . . .

To what avail, then, are moral laws, and civil legislation, and philanthropic efforts, in the cause of chastity, while all the elements combine to give invincible efficiency to the work of ruin? As well might we attempt to prevent the eruption of volcanic mountains, when the internal fires were kindled, and the molten entrails were boiling and heaving like the exasperated ocean! As well might we think to stand before the gushing mouth of a crater, and roll back the burning tide, and save the world below from desolation! . . .

The mere fact that a man is married to one woman, and is perfectly faithful to her, will by no means prevent the evils which flow from venereal excess, if his commerce with her transgresses the bounds of that connubial chastity which is founded on the real wants of the system. Beyond all question, an immeasurable amount of evil results to the human family from sexual excess within the precincts of wedlock. Languor, lassitude, muscular relaxation, general debility and heaviness, depression of spirits, loss of appetite, indigestion, faintness and sinking at the pit of the stomach, increased susceptibilities of the skin and lungs to all the atmospheric changes, feebleness of circulation, chilliness, head-ache, melancholy, hypochondria, hysterics, feebleness of all the senses, impaired vision, loss of sight, weakness of the lungs, nervous cough, pulmonary consumption, disorders of the liver and kidneys, urinary difficulties, disorders of the genital organs, spinal diseases, weakness of the brain, loss of memory, epilepsy, insanity, apoplexy—abortions, premature births, and extreme feebleness, morbid predispositions, and early death of offspring,—are among the too common evils which are caused by sexual excesses between husband and wife.

Sylvester Graham, *A Lecture to Young Men, on Chastity* (Boston: Light & Stearns, 1837), 7, 15–16, 19, 29, 34, 36–37, 40–43, 48–52, 55, 68–69.

❧

The Bible Argument for Complex Marriage ("Free Love") (1849)

JOHN HUMPHREY NOYES

During the time that Graham's health and sex reforms were gaining popularity, other reformers, influenced by revivalist religion, adopted very different outlooks on religion and sexuality. A new American religious group, the Mormons, led by their prophet Joseph Smith, adopted the practice of plural marriage. Equally controversial was the religious commune founded by John Humphrey Noyes in Oneida, New York, where members of the community shared not only all their worldly possessions but their sexual partners as well. Noyes called this "complex marriage," but his critics denounced it as "free love." It became all too clear that experiments in religious community and sexuality might become the objects of the very same sensational tales of ruin that they were designed to eradicate. To some respectable middle-class Americans, even reformers needed reforming. (To avoid the practical dilemmas of pregnancy and parentage that might result from multiple partners, Noyes also encouraged birth control based on men's self-control — "male continence.") The following document is Noyes's detailed defense of the biblical support for his ideas on sexual love between believers.

PROBLEMS TO CONSIDER

1. How could two religious reformers such as Sylvester Graham and John Humphrey Noyes come to such divergent opinions on the nature of sexuality and the best method to achieve moral reform? Where do they agree, and where do their perspectives diverge?
2. Which do you think Noyes's critics found more threatening, Noyes's rejection of marriage or his insistence that the Bible encouraged "free love"?

P ROPOSITION I.—The Bible predicts the coming of the kingdom of heaven on earth. Dan. 2:44. Isa. 25:6–9. . . .

PROPOSITION II.—The administration of the will of God in his kingdom on earth, will be the same as the administration of his will in heaven. Matt. 6:10. Eph. 1:10. . . .

PROPOSITION III.—In heaven God reigns over the body, soul, and estate, without interference from human governments; and consequently, the advent of his kingdom on earth will supplant all human governments. Dan. 2:44.1 Cor. 15:24, 25. Isa. 26:13, 14, and 33:22. . . .

PROPOSITION V.—In the kingdom of heaven, the institution of marriage which as-signs the exclusive possession of one woman to one man, does not exist. Matt. 22:23–30. "In the resurrection they neither marry nor are given in marriage." . . .

PROPOSITION VI.—In the kingdom of heaven, the intimate union of life and interests, which in the world is limited to pairs, extends through the whole body of believers; i.e. *complex* marriage takes the place of simple. John 17:21. Christ prayed that *all* believers might be one, even as he and the Father are one. His unity with the Father is defined in the words, *"All mine are thine, and all thine are mine."* Ver. 10. This perfect community of interests, then, will be the condition of *all*, when his prayer is answered.

The universal unity of the members of Christ, is described in the same terms that are used to describe marriage-unity. . . .

PROPOSITION VIII. — The abolishment of appropriation is involved in the very nature of a true relation to Christ in the gospel. This we prove thus: — The *possessive* feeling which expresses itself by the possessive pronoun *mine*, is the same in essence, when it relates to woman, as when it relates to money, or any other property. Amativeness [*i.e., sexual love*] and acquisitiveness are only different channels in one stream. . . .

PROPOSITION IX. — The abolishment of sexual exclusiveness is involved in the love-relation required between all believers by the express injunction of Christ and the apostles, and by the whole tenor of the New Testament. "The new commandment is, that we love one another," and that, not by pairs, as in the world, but *en masse*. We are required to love one another *fervently* (1 Peter 1:22) or, as the original might be rendered, *burningly*. The fashion of the world forbids a man and woman who are otherwise appropriated, to love one another burningly — to flow into each other's hearts. But if they obey Christ they must do this; and whoever would allow them to do this, and yet would forbid them . . . to express their unity of hearts by bodily unity, would "strain at a gnat and swallow a camel;" for unity of hearts is as much more important than the bodily expression of it. . . .

Note. — The tendency of religious unity to flow into the channel of amativeness, manifests itself in revivals and in all the higher forms of spiritualism. Marriages or illegitimate amours usually follow religious excitements. Almost every spiritual sect has been troubled by amative tendencies. These facts are not to be treated as unaccountable irregularities, but as expressions of a law of human nature. Amativeness is in fact . . . the first and most natural channel of religious love. . . .

PROPOSITION XIII. — The law of marriage "worketh wrath." 1. It provokes to secret adultery, actual or of the heart. — 2. It ties together unmatched natures. 3. It sunders matched natures. 4. It gives to sexual appetite only a scanty and monotonous allowance, and so produces the natural vices of poverty, contraction of taste, and stinginess or jealousy. 5. It makes no provision for the sexual appetite at the very time when that appetite is the strongest. . . .

Note. — The only hopeful scheme of Moral Reform, is one which will bring the sexes together according to the demands of nature. The desire of the sexes is a stream ever running. If it is dammed up, it will break out irregularly and destructively. The only way to make it safe and useful, is to give it a free natural channel. . . . Reform, in order to be effectual, must base itself on the principle of restoring and preserving equilibrium by free intercourse. . . . A system of complex-marriage, which shall match the demands of nature, both as to time and variety, will open the prison doors to the victims both of marriage and celibacy: to those in married life who are starved, and those who are oppressed by lust; . . . to those in the unmarried state who are withered by neglect, diseased by unnatural abstinence, or plunged into prostitution and self-pollution, by desires which find no lawful channel.

First Annual Report of the Oneida Association (Oneida, N.Y.: Leonard & Co., 1849). Reprinted in John Humphrey Noyes, *Bible Communism: A Compilation from the Annual Reports and Other Publications of the Oneida Association and Its Branches* (Brooklyn, N.Y.: Office of the Circular, 1853), 24, 26–27, 30–31, 37–38.

↢ *New Freedoms: Abolitionism, Colonization, and Woman's Rights* ↣

For most white Americans in the northern states during the antebellum years, slavery was something they knew only in their imaginations. Few had traveled to the South to witness how the institution actually worked. So when reformers sought to resolve the problems of slavery, the slaves they discussed were more of an abstraction than a reality. In creating mental images of slaves, northern reformers drew upon what they considered to be familiar and natural in human relationships. Thus, they relied heavily on contemporary ideas about men and women, conventions of gender and family, to make sense of what they thought to be true about slaves.

Imagining slaves in gendered terms involved more than just familiarity. Gender was the language by which disparities of power, and freedom and equality, were best communicated, because it could connect those power relationships to nature. Gender imagery gave some women abolitionists an idea of slaves with which they could personally identify as they became keenly aware of their own oppression. Radical women abolitionists came to see themselves as slaves, enchained by a social system similar to the southern slavery they denounced. The movement to abolish slavery thus assumed an additional dimension: it became a cause to advance the emancipation of women from their bondage as well.

Yet women abolitionists were not the first to turn to gender imagery to make sense of slavery and to enact its reform. An alternative reform movement in the North, deeply competitive with abolitionists, was the colonization movement. Colonizationists imagined their reform as an adventurous, manly endeavor to colonize another continent while also solving the country's domestic problems. This perspective first required a set of gendered ideas about slaves and free African Americans in both America and Africa.

A Man of Sense (1839)

Even before a new abolitionist movement began in the 1830s, some white Americans in both the North and the South devised a reform that promised a solution to the problems of slavery and the country's growing numbers of free blacks. Their solution was to return African Americans to a colony in West Africa. The American Colonization Society, founded in 1817, promised to be a catchall reform that appealed to individuals who were concerned with several different objectives: the gradual end of slavery; a society in which freedom and whiteness were synonymous; and a missionary and commercial engagement with Africa. The underlying premise of this movement was that white Americans had such an unalterable prejudice against black people that the only charitable solution was removal. As one colonizationist stated: "There appears to exist in the breasts of white men in this country a prejudice against the colour of the African, which nothing short of divine power can remove." Ironically, colonizationists attributed great promise and capacity to African Americans once they agreed to go to the colony of Liberia. To remove a slave "to the land of his fathers," one colonizationist maintained, "would present the man [as] an entirely new being." A story (most likely fictional) printed in a northern colonizationist newspaper illustrates the distinctions that these white reformers made between the "nuisances" (as they liked to call northern free blacks) and the worthy men who chose to brave the oceans for the colonization scheme.

PROBLEMS TO CONSIDER

1. What does this story reveal about the mindset of colonization reformers?
2. What is the significance of putting the words "the making of a man of me" into the mouth of an imagined free black man?

On the morning of the day fixed for the embarkation of the emigrants for Cape Palmas, in the brig Oberon, a stout, athletic coloured man of about thirty years of age, to judge from his appearance, came to the Colonization office, and said he wanted to join the expedition, then on the eve of departure. He was referred to the President of the Society, and as near as the writer can recollect, the following dialogue took place:

"Well, my friend, what may your business be with me?"

"I wish to go to Africa, sir."

"When?"

"I wish to go to-day, sir. They tell me a vessel is to sail to-day, and I wish to sail in her."

"I am afraid you are too late, the emigrants are now on their way, and it will take some time to get you ready. Why did you not apply sooner? Why did you apply at all?"

"I hope I'm not too late, sir. I was employed last week to do some work at a house where the people who are to go to-day boarded, and I heard them talk, and say what led them to go, and I thought I should like to go myself—but I did not know where to apply for leave. This morning early, I met one of them, and he brought me here."

"Well, my friend, it is short notice for you to get ready, or for us to receive you as an emigrant. What do you think you'll get by going to Africa?

We should be sorry if you went from a mere freak, and without having weighed the matter well."

"Why, sir, I think that if you will let me go, it will be the MAKING OF A MAN OF ME, that's all."

"In what respect?—people have to work at Cape Palmas as well as in Baltimore—somewhat harder too, in the first instance, for it is a new country, and hardships are to be expected."

"I know I'll have to work, sir, and to work hard; but I'm used to that. I've been for seven years working with Mr. Crey, the street paver, and at the end of seven years I'm no better off than when I begun. Mr. Crey treats me well too, and pays me regular; but it all comes to nothing after all—I was a labourer seven years ago, and I am a labourer now. The white men I labour with don't respect people of my colour. I'm shoved here and there, and don't feel encouraged, and I don't see any change. Things if any thing, are getting worse. Germans come, Irish come, and if any thing, it's harder for me to get on every year. I think from all I hear, that if I work as hard at Cape Palmas as I've been working in Baltimore, I could raise out of the ground enough to live on, and after a-while, lay something by—and if I behave well, I might get to be respectable. They tell me I'd have a lot of land given to me, and that's more than I'll ever get here, the way things are going. I've thought the matter over as well as I could, and I've made up my mind—I may have a hard time at first, but some how or other, I have a notion that IF I GO TO THE COLONY IT WILL BE THE MAKING OF A MAN OF ME."

"Well, my friend, your views are certainly very satisfactory to me, and if you will bring evidence of your being a free man, and a certificate of good character, from some respectable white person, who has known you, Mr. Easter, the agent, will see whether you can get ready to go out this fall."

The man left the office, and in a short time returned with the necessary proof of his freedom and good character, and he is now on his way, with the other emigrants of the Oberon, to Cape Palmas.

How many other coloured persons are there in the state of Maryland to whom this man's description of his situation is applicable? Are there not ninety-nine out of the hundred of them all? The difference between this individual and those whom he has left behind him is, that he has a liberal and proper view of his interest—they are blinded by ignorance, prejudice, or evil purposes. He is worthy to be a freeman in fact, as well as name, they are not. He, the poor street paver, has set them all an example. He has enterprise, judgment and courage. In them these qualities have yet to be developed.

"A Man of Sense," *The Colonization Herald*, n.s. 1 (January 1839): 15–16.

⚮

Antislavery Song: "A Man's a Man for a' That" (1843)

Soon after the American Colonization Society was founded, 3,000 free African Americans rallied in Philadelphia, declaring that they would "renounce and disdain every connection with" the colonization idea and "respectfully and firmly declare our determination not to participate in any part of it." By the 1830s, African Americans in the North had convinced their white abolitionist allies that an anticolonization stance was critical to the identity of the abolitionist movement. The colonization movement remained the abolitionists' greatest rival for support among reformers. Many abolitionists, including William Lloyd Garrison, had begun their reform careers in the colonization society. Garrison eventually denounced colonization as "anti-republican and anti-christian," declaring that "its pretences are false, its doctrines odious, its means contemptible." And like temperance activists, abolitionists also resorted to forms of popular culture, such as songs and fiction, to get their reform message to as large an audience as possible. The following song underscores the anticolonization rhetoric that united white and black abolitionists.

PROBLEMS TO CONSIDER

1. How does this song challenge the notions of manhood articulated in "A Man of Sense"?
2. What are the possible meanings of the phrase "the slave's a man for a[ll] that" in this song?

Though stripped of all the dearest rights
 Which nature claims, and a' that,
There's that which in the slave unites
 To make the man for a' that:
For a' that and a' that,
 Though dark his skin, and a' that,
We cannot rob him of his kind,
 The slave's a man for a' that.

Though by his brother bought and sold,
 And beat, and scourged, and a' that,
His wrongs can ne'er be felt or told,
 Yet he's a man for a' that:
For a' that and a' that,
 His body chained, and a' that,
The image of his God remains,
 The slave's a man for a' that. . . .

If those who now in bondage groan
 Were white, and fair, and a' that,
O should we not their fate bemoan,
 And plead their cause, and a' that?
For a' that and a' that,
 Would any say, in a' that

We've nought to do, they are not here,
 We'll mind our own, and a' that?

O tell us not they're clothed and fed,
 'Tis insult, stuff, and a' that;
With freedom gone, all joy is fled,
 For Heaven's best gift is a' that:
For a' that and a' that,
 Free agency, and a' that,
We get from Him who rules on high,
 The slave we rob of a' that.

Then think not to escape his wrath,
 Who's equal, just, and a' that;
His warning voice is sounded forth,
 We heed it not, for a' that:
For a' that and a' that,
 'Tis not less sure, for a' that;
His vengeance, though 'tis long delayed,
 Will come at last, for a' that.

———————

The Liberator, January 13, 1843.

❧

Letters on the Equality of the Sexes (1838)
SARAH GRIMKÉ

Declaration of Sentiments (1848)
SENECA FALLS CONVENTION

Two sisters from South Carolina, Angelina and Sarah Grimké, created quite a stir within the community of northern reformers when they began lecturing to audiences of both men and women on behalf of the American Antislavery Society in the 1830s. Traditionalists maintained that it was dangerously inappropriate (out of a "woman's sphere") for women to be public speakers on a topic of such economic and political importance. Angelina Grimké refused to back down, asking on one occasion: "Are we bereft of citizenship because we are the mothers, wives, and *daughters of a mighty people? Have* women *no country—no interest staked in public weal—. . . no partnership in the nation's guilt and shame?" Grimké's radical conclusion was that "whatever it is* morally right for a man to do, it is *morally* right for a woman to do.*" Once radical women abolitionists encountered opposition as their antislavery activism crossed the boundaries of gender norms, they became increasingly aware not only of the slaves' oppression but also of their own. As Abby Kelley, another prominent abolitionist lecturer, stated, "In striving to strike his chains off, we found, most surely, that we were manacled ourselves." This growing self-consciousness spurred Sarah Grimké to pen one of the earliest declarations of feminist principles in her* Letters on the Equality of the Sexes *(1838). A decade later, a group of women, all of whom were abolitionists, met in Seneca Falls, New York, for the first ever Woman's Rights Convention, at which they issued a* Declaration of Sentiments, *the most definitive call for women's emancipation to be issued before the Civil War.*

PROBLEMS TO CONSIDER

1. Analyze the parallels made in these documents between slaves and women: what aspects of slavery did these women most clearly identify with, and what experiences of the slave did they erase with this comparison?
2. What is the relationship of property to these imagined parallels between slaves and women, masters and men?

LETTERS ON THE EQUALITY OF THE SEXES

LETTER 12

Concord, 9th Mo., 6th, 1837

MY DEAR SISTER, — There are few things which present greater obstacles to the improvement and elevation of woman and her appropriate sphere of usefulness and duty, than the laws which have been enacted to destroy her independence, and crush her individuality; laws which, although they are framed for her government, she has had no voice in establishing, and which rob her of some of her *essential rights*. Woman has no political existence. With the single exception of presenting a petition to the legislative body, she is a cipher in the nation; or, if not actually so in representative governments, she is only counted, like the slaves of the South, to swell the number of law-makers who form decrees for her government, with little reference to her benefit, except so far as her good may promote their own. . . .

Here now, the very being of a woman, like that of a slave, is absorbed in her master. All contracts made with her, like those made with slaves by their owners, are a mere nullity. Our kind defenders have legislated away almost all our legal rights, and in the true spirit of such injustice and oppression, have kept us in ignorance of those very laws by which we are governed. . . .

Yet a man may spend the property he has acquired by marriage at the ale-house, the gambling table, or in any other way that he pleases. Many instances of this kind have come to my knowledge; and women, who have brought their husbands handsome fortunes, have been left, in consequence of the wasteful and dissolute habits of their husbands, in straitened circumstances, and compelled to toil for the support of their families. . . .

If the wife be injured in her person or property, she can bring no action for redress without her husband's concurrence, and his name as well as her own: neither can she be sued, without making her husband a defendant.

This law that "a wife can bring no action," &c., is similar to the law respecting slaves. "A slave cannot bring a suit against his master, or any other person, for an injury — his master, must bring it." So if any damages are recovered for an injury committed on a wife, the husband pockets it; in the case of the slave, the master does the same.

> In criminal prosecutions, the wife may be indicted and punished separately, unless there be evidence of coercion from the fact that the offence was committed in the presence, or by the command of her husband. A wife is excused from punishment for theft committed in the presence, or by the command of her husband.

It would be difficult to frame a law better calculated to destroy the responsibility of woman as a moral being, or a free agent. Her husband is supposed to possess unlimited control over her; and if she can offer the flimsy excuse that he bade her steal, she may break the eighth commandment with impunity, as far as human laws are concerned. . . .

> The husband, by the old law, might give his wife moderate correction, as he is to answer for her misbehavior. The law thought it reasonable to entrust him with this power of restraining her by domestic chastisement. The courts of law will still permit a husband to restrain a wife of her liberty, in case of any gross misbehavior.

What a mortifying proof this law affords, of the estimation in which woman is held! She is placed completely in the hands of a being subject like herself to the outbursts of passion, and therefore unworthy to be trusted with power. Perhaps I may be told respecting this law, that it is a dead letter, as I am sometimes told about the slave laws; but this is not true in either case. The slaveholder does kill his slave by moderate correction, as the law allows; and many a husband, among the poor, exercises the right given him by the law, of degrading woman by personal chastisement. And among the higher ranks, if actual imprisonment is not resorted to, women are not unfrequently restrained of the liberty of going to

places of worship by irreligious husbands, and of doing many other things about which, as moral and responsible beings, *they* should be the *sole* judges. Such laws remind me of the reply of some little girls at a children's meeting held recently at Ipswich. The lecturer told them that God had created four orders of beings with which he had made us acquainted through the Bible. The first was angels, the second was man, the third beasts; and now, children, what is the fourth? After a pause, several girls replied, "WOMEN."

> A woman's personal property by marriage becomes absolutely her husband's, which, at his death, he may leave entirely away from her.

And farther, all the avails of her labor are absolutely in the power of her husband. All that she acquires by her industry is his; so that she cannot, with her own honest earnings, become the legal purchaser of any property. . . .

The laws above cited are not very unlike the slave laws of Louisiana.

> All that a slave possesses belongs to his master; he possesses nothing of his own, except what his master chooses he should possess. . . . With regard to the property of women, there is taxation without representation; for they pay taxes without having the liberty of voting for representatives.

And this taxation, without representation, be it remembered, was the cause of our Revolutionary war, a grievance so heavy, that it was thought necessary to purchase exemption from it at an immense expense of blood and treasure, yet the daughters of New England, as well as of all the other States of this free Republic, are suffering a similar injustice—but for one, I had rather we should suffer any injustice or oppression, than that my sex should have any voice in the political affairs of the nation. . . .

As these abuses do exist, and women suffer intensely from them, our brethren are called upon in this enlightened age, by every sentiment of honor, religion and justice, to repeal these unjust and unequal laws, and restore to woman those rights which they have wrested from her. Such laws approximate too nearly to the laws enacted by slaveholders for the government of their slaves, and must tend to debase and depress the mind of that being, whom God created as a help meet for man, or "helper like unto himself," and designed to be his equal and his companion. Until such laws are annulled, woman never can occupy that exalted station for which she was intended by her Maker. And just in proportion as they are practically disregarded, which is the case to some extent, just so far is woman assuming that independence and nobility of character which she ought to exhibit. . . .

Hoping that in the various reformations of the day, women may be relieved from some of their legal disabilities, I remain,

Thine in the bonds of womanhood,

SARAH M. GRIMKE

Sarah M. Grimké, *Letters on the Equality of the Sexes and the Condition of Woman* (Boston: Isaac Knapp, 1838), 74–83.

DECLARATION OF SENTIMENTS

When, in the course of human events, it becomes necessary for one portion of the family of man to assume among the people of the earth a position different from that which they have hitherto occupied, but one to which the laws of nature and of nature's God entitle them, a decent respect to the opinions of mankind requires that they should declare the causes that impel them to such a course.

We hold these truths to be self-evident: that all men and women are created equal; that they are endowed by their Creator with certain inalienable rights; that among these are life, liberty, and the pursuit of happiness; that to secure these rights governments are instituted, deriving their just powers from the consent of the governed. Whenever any form of government be-

comes destructive of these ends, it is the right of those who suffer from it to refuse allegiance to it, and to insist upon the institution of a new government, laying its foundation on such principles, and organizing its powers in such form, as to them shall seem most likely to effect their safety and happiness. . . . But when a long train of abuses and usurpations, pursuing invariably the same object evinces a design to reduce them under absolute despotism, it is their duty to throw off such government, and to provide new guards for their future security. Such has been the patient sufferance of the women under this government, and such is now the necessity which constrains them to demand the equal station to which they are entitled.

The history of mankind is a history of repeated injuries and usurpations on the part of man toward woman, having in direct object the establishment of an absolute tyranny over her. To prove this, let facts be submitted to a candid world.

He has never permitted her to exercise her inalienable right to the elective franchise.

He has compelled her to submit to laws, in the formation of which she had no voice.

He has withheld from her rights which are given to the most ignorant and degraded men — both natives and foreigners.

Having deprived her of this first right of a citizen, the elective franchise, thereby leaving her without representation in the halls of legislation, he has oppressed her on all sides.

He has made her, if married, in the eye of the law, civilly dead.

He has taken from her all right in property, even to the wages she earns.

He has made her, morally, an irresponsible being, as she can commit many crimes with impunity, provided they be done in the presence of her husband. In the covenant of marriage, she is compelled to promise obedience to her husband, he becoming, to all intents and purposes, her master — the law giving him power to deprive her of her liberty, and to administer chastisement.

He has so framed the laws of divorce, as to what shall be the proper causes, and in case of separation, to whom the guardianship of the children shall be given, as to be wholly regardless of the happiness of women—the law, in all cases, going upon a false supposition of the supremacy of man, and giving all power into his hands.

After depriving her of all rights as a married woman, if single, and the owner of property, he has taxed her to support a government which recognizes her only when her property can be made profitable to it.

He has monopolized nearly all the profitable employments, and from those she is permitted to follow, she receives but a scanty remuneration. He closes against her all the avenues to wealth and distinction which he considers most honorable to himself. As a teacher of theology, medicine, or law, she is not known.

He has denied her the facilities for obtaining a thorough education, all colleges being closed against her.

He allows her in Church, as well as State, but a subordinate position, claiming Apostolic authority for her exclusion from the ministry, and, with some exceptions, from any public participation in the affairs of the Church.

He has created a false public sentiment by giving to the world a different code of morals for men and women, by which moral delinquencies which exclude women from society, are not only tolerated, but deemed of little account in man.

He has usurped the prerogative of Jehovah himself, claiming it as his right to assign for her a sphere of action, when that belongs to her conscience and to her God.

He has endeavored, in every way that he could, to destroy her confidence in her own powers, to lessen her self-respect, and to make her willing to lead a dependent and abject life.

Now, in view of this entire disfranchisement of one-half the people of this country, their social and religious degradation—in view of the unjust laws above mentioned, and because women do feel themselves aggrieved, oppressed, and fraudulently deprived of their most sacred rights, we insist that they have immediate admission to all the rights and privileges which belong to them as citizens of the United States.

In entering upon the great work before us, we anticipate no small amount of misconception, misrepresentation, and ridicule; but we shall use every instrumentality within our power to effect our object. We shall employ agents, circulate tracts, petition the State and National legislatures, and endeavor to enlist the pulpit and the press in our behalf. We hope this Convention will be followed by a series of Conventions embracing every part of the country.

The following resolutions were discussed by Lucretia Mott, Thomas and Mary Ann McClintock, Amy Post, Catharine A. F. Stebbins, and others, and were adopted:

WHEREAS, The great precept of nature is conceded to be, that "man shall pursue his own true and substantial happiness." . . . Therefore,

Resolved, That such laws as conflict, in any way, with the true and substantial happiness of woman, are contrary to the great precept of nature and of no validity, for this is "superior in obligation to any other."

Resolved, That all laws which prevent woman from occupying such a station in society as her conscience shall dictate, or which place her in a position inferior to that of man, are contrary to the great precept of nature, and therefore of no force or authority.

Resolved, That woman is man's equal—was intended to be so by the Creator, and the highest good of the race demands that she should be recognized as such. . . .

Resolved, That inasmuch as man, while claiming for himself intellectual superiority, does accord to woman moral superiority, it is preeminently his duty to encourage her to speak and teach, as she has an opportunity, in all religious assemblies.

Resolved, That the same amount of virtue, delicacy, and refinement of behavior that is required of woman in the social state, should also be required of man, and the same transgressions should be visited with equal severity on both man and woman.

Resolved, That the objection of indelicacy and impropriety, which is so often brought against woman when she addresses a public audience, comes with a very ill-grace from those who encourage, by their attendance, her appearance on the stage, in the concert, or in feats of the circus.

Resolved, That woman has too long rested satisfied in the circumscribed limits which cor-

rupt customs and a perverted application of the Scriptures have marked out for her, and that it is time she should move in the enlarged sphere which her great Creator has assigned her.

Resolved, That is the duty of the women of this country to secure to themselves their sacred right to the elective franchise.

Resolved, That the equality of human rights results necessarily from the fact of the identity of the race in capabilities and responsibilities. . . .

Seneca Falls Convention, *Declaration of Sentiments* (1848), in *The History of Woman Suffrage*, 6 vols., edited by Elizabeth Cady Stanton et al. (Rochester, N.Y.: Susan B. Anthony, 1881–1922), 1:70–73.

ᴖ

∽ CHAPTER 8 ∼

The Culture of Democracy:
1820–1870

JOHN L. O'SULLIVAN, a newspaper editor and a Jacksonian Democrat, set out to define the principles of American democracy in 1837: "We have an abiding confidence in the virtue, intelligence, and full capacity for self-government, of the great mass of our people—our industrious, honest, manly, intelligent millions of freemen." O'Sullivan is famous for publishing the newspaper that coined the phrase "manifest destiny." He issued the preceding declaration of democracy in the same confident spirit, as a self-evident description of the natural and historically necessary expansion of freedom in the fertile, uncorrupted soil of the New World.

O'Sullivan was conscious that he lived in a new era, even for the United States. That era was an inventive age. Technological advances in transportation and communication (railroads, telegraphs, and new printing presses) were matched by new types of cultural production in the realm of religion, politics, literature, and the arts. The democracy that Americans experienced at this time was never limited only to political campaigns and voting, in which universal white manhood suffrage and the ascendancy of a system of competitive party politics created a new political universe. Americans also lived their vision of a new equality in the fully developed market economy, in new promises of religious salvation to all, and in new civic and reform associations to make a godly society.

Yet democracy, as it was developed and practiced in the United States during the antebellum period, was neither natural, necessary, nor—by our standards today or by those of early-nineteenth-century Americans—truly democratic. It is important to examine critically and historically the many claims of American democracy in order to understand how declaring democracy was in itself a cultural act of mythmaking with enormous political consequences. American political culture, in other words, did not grow as most "freemen" claimed it did, like a rising oceanic tide of freedom that equally lifted all boats, large and small. Rather, this version of democracy involved inclusion *and* exclusion, the deliberate assertion of power in the interests of some and against the interests of others. To understand its history, we must also examine the notions of nationalism, the racial and cultural privileging of whiteness, and the exalting of a natural landscape with the purposeful annihilation of both nature and natural man to advance an ideal of progress and destiny.

To any observer at the time, the most obvious features of a democratic culture were westward expansion, popular entertainments, and party politics. The readings and images in this chapter focus on these topics in an attempt to unravel the workings of the culture of democracy. They expose the myriad ways that ordinary Americans lived out their lives—their work and their leisure—and gave meaning to this new culture.

✌ *Nature's Vistas and Visages: Cultural Meanings of Expansionism and the Western Frontier* ✌

✌ AMERICAN SCENERY

It is hard to resist being charmed by Thomas Cole's 1839 painting of Crawford Notch in the White Mountains of New Hampshire, showing a farmhouse nestled at the base of a mountain covered in the rich tones of a New England autumn. Yet during its era, much of the power of this painting arose from the ways in which the artist addressed, negotiated, and assigned meanings to the rapid and often destructive *changes* that Americans were making in the land. The ax and the log cabin in the woods were among the symbols favored by artists of Cole's generation who sought to represent the relationship of the era's gospel of progress to a rapidly disappearing "wilderness." It sometimes seemed that, in America, "the sounds of the ax were ceaseless, while the falling of the trees was like a distant cannonading," as James Fenimore Cooper wrote in his novel *The Pioneers* (1823). American progress achieved its greatest social and cultural importance with the invention and spread of the telegraph and steam-powered railroad during the 1830s and 1840s.

What united Cole with ordinary midcentury Americans was the certainty that the nation's unique identity and its God-appointed destiny were wrapped up in the fate of the American wilderness. By the time the portraitist George Catlin launched his monumental quest to compose a painted record of the "looks and customs" of every existing Indian tribe, Andrew Jackson's policy of the forced removal of Native Americans to territories west of the Mississippi was a foregone conclusion. The nation's founders had assumed that environment and culture accounted for the major differences between whites and Indians; they imagined a day when Indians would disappear by fading into white civilization. But after 1800, more white Americans embraced the popular belief that "savagery" and "civilization" were unchanging, incompatible racial traits, and thus no amount of education or indoctrination in Protestant Christianity could alter the fundamental savagery of an Indian. The majority of white Americans came to believe that the extinction of aboriginal Americans was a natural and necessary outcome of progress. The painting of Crawford Notch and the other images in this section suggest the high moral significance that antebellum Americans assigned to nature and the powerful emotional, commercial, and political interests that they invested in American scenery.

The Notch of the White Mountains (1839)
THOMAS COLE

Lecture on American Scenery (1841)
THOMAS COLE

Thomas Cole's painting of the New Hampshire mountains and his brief "Lecture on American Scenery" express widely held nationalist sentiments about the particular advantages of rural America as the subject of art. But they also show his reformist concern for the moral influence of art to temper the reckless commercial spirit of his age. Cole immigrated to America from England in 1818, eventually settling with his family in Philadelphia. His landscapes, which were "discovered" in the 1820s, reflected both his prodigious talents and his keen appreciation of the artistic tastes of New York City's rising class of wealthy bankers and merchants, such as the grocery magnate Luman Reed, who commissioned Cole's famous series The Course of Empire. *As Cole expressed in a letter to Reed, he hoped his canvases would be "maledictions on all dollar-godded utilitarians."*

PROBLEMS TO CONSIDER

1. Examine the two prominent *man*-made stumps and the stubbled field behind them in Cole's painting. Is the landscape scarred or improved? Do the remains represent a decline from nature's original perfection or the mark of human progress?
2. How would you describe the tone in which Cole used terms such as "improvements" and "civilization" in his essay? Did he think that taste and imagination (art) will ultimately win out against modern improvements, or did he think the days of wilderness are numbered?

Thomas Cole, *A View of the Mountain Pass Called the Notch of the White Mountains (Crawford Notch)*, 1839.
(Andrew W. Mellon Fund. Image courtesy of the Board of Trustees, National Gallery of Art, Washington, D.C.)

The essay that with your indulgence I shall now offer is a mere sketch of an almost exhaustless subject—American Scenery; and in selecting the theme the author has placed more confidence in its overflowing richness than in his own capacity for treating it in a manner worthy of its vastness and importance.

It is a subject that to every American ought to be of surpassing interest; for whether he beholds the Hudson mingling its waters with the Atlantic, explores the central wilds of this vast continent, or stands on the margin of the distant Pacific, he is still in the midst of American scenery—it is his own land; its beauty, its magnificence, its sublimity, all are his; and how undeserving of such a birthright if he can turn towards it an unobserving eye, an unaffected heart!

Before entering into the proposed subject, . . . I shall be excused for saying a few words on the advantages of cultivating a taste for scenery and for exclaiming against the apathy with which the beauties of external nature are regarded by a great mass, even of our refined community. It is generally admitted that the liberal arts tend to soften our manners; but they do more—they carry within them the power to mend our hearts. Poetry and painting sublime and purify thought, and *rural nature* is full of the same quickening spirit; it is in fact the exhaustless mine from which the poet and painter have brought such wondrous treasures—an unfailing fountain of intellectual enjoyment where all may drink and be awakened to a deeper feeling of the works of genius, a keener perception of the beauty of our existence, and a more profound reverence for the Creator of all things.

For those whose days are consumed in the low pursuit of avarice, or the gaudy frivolities of fashion, unobservant of nature's loveliness are unconscious of the harmony of creation. . . .

In this age, when a meagre utilitarianism seems ready to absorb every feeling and sentiment, and what is called improvement, in its march, makes us fear that the bright and tender flowers of the imagination will be crushed beneath its iron tramp, it would be well to cultivate the oasis that yet remains to us, and to cherish the impressions that nature is ever ready to give, as an antidote to the sordid tendencies of modern civilization. The spirit of our society is to contrive and not to enjoy—toiling in order to produce more toil—accumulating in order to aggrandize. . . .

And to this cultivated state our western *[American]* world is fast approaching; but nature is still predominant, and there are those who regret that with the improvements of cultivation the sublimity of the wilderness must pass away; for those scenes of solitude from which the hand of nature has never been lifted, affect the mind with more deep-toned emotion than aught which the hand of man has touched. Amid them the consequent associations are of God, the Creator; they are his undefiled works, and the mind is cast into the contemplation of eternal things. . . .

. . . Yet I cannot but express my sorrow that much of the beauty of our landscapes is quickly passing away; the ravages of the axe are daily increasing, and the most noble scenes are often laid desolate with a wantonness and barbarism scarcely credible in a people who call themselves civilized. The wayside is becoming shadeless, and another generation will behold spots now rife with beauty, bleak and bare. This is a *regret* rather than a complaint. I know, full well, that the forests must be felled for fuel and tillage, and that roads and canals must be constructed, but I contend that beauty should be of *some* value among us; that where it is not NECESSARY to destroy a tree or a grove, the hand of the woodman should be checked, and even the consideration, which alas, weighs too heavily with us, of a few paltry dollars, should be held as nought in comparison with the pure and lasting pleasure that we enjoy, or ought to enjoy, in the objects which are among the most beautiful creations of the Almighty. . . . But I will now conclude, and in the hope that, though feebly urged, the importance of cultivating a taste for scenery will not be forgotten. Nature has spread for us a rich and delightful banquet—shall we turn away from it? We are still in Eden; the wall that shuts us out of the garden is our own ignorance and folly.

Thomas Cole, *The Collected Essays and Prose Sketches*, edited by Marshall Tymn (St. Paul, Minn.: John Colet Press, 1980), 197–202, 210–11.

∽

Wi-jun-jon, The Pigeon's Egg Head Going to and Returning from Washington (1832)

GEORGE CATLIN

Letters and Notes on the Manners, Customs, and Condition of the North American Indians (1842)

GEORGE CATLIN

George Catlin was one of many nineteenth-century writers and artists, including James Fenimore Cooper, who devoted themselves to committing the "last" of the Indians to immortal images or words. Catlin had in mind the "noble savage," an image of the Indian as the highest expression of human liberty in a state of nature. Catlin painted often stunning, true-to-life portraits of all ranks and sexes. Yet even the scrupulous Catlin could not avoid "modernizing" his subjects, by rendering them in poses of conventional European portraiture and by underscoring the autonomous individuality of each subject. In this way, Catlin attached a modern way of understanding the "self" that was alien to premodern Native American cultures but was a perfect fit for the romantic, democratic individualism of the era. Catlin's Indians were painted to communicate in a visual language that urban Americans could understand; they were "white man's Indians." Yet Catlin also operated in a complicated cultural zone that was characteristic of the era's market revolution. He was simultaneously a philanthropist, missionary, entrepreneur, showman, and schoolteacher. In 1837, with more than four hundred paintings and thousands of sketches completed, he opened his first "Indian Gallery" in New York City. This massive exhibit of portraits, artifacts, costumes, and lectures also attracted paying crowds in other American cities and later in European capitals. Still, Catlin was never able to turn his venture in philanthropy, enlightenment, and entertainment into the paying proposition he wished for.

The image reproduced here—the "before-and-after" portrait of Wi-jun-jon, the Assiniboine chief's son who had been sent as an emissary to Washington, D.C.—is described in detail in the selections from Catlin's Letters and Notes, *which were published in London nearly a decade after Catlin's expedition to the Indian lands west of the Mississippi. Together the visual and written texts expose the attitudes of mid-nineteenth-century white Americans toward Indians and "primitivism" in the period after removal. They also suggest how representations of Indians also were used as critical tools for unmasking the moral flaws and corrupting artificialities of "civilization," an entertaining exposé that Americans would pay to see.*

PROBLEMS TO CONSIDER

1. How were Indians the tools as well as the models for Catlin's artistic quest? What was Catlin's purpose in portraying these "last" Indians?
2. What was Catlin hoping to accomplish in this visual and written portrait of Wi-jun-jon? How might white and Indian viewers have attributed different meanings to this portrayal?

George Catlin, *Wi-jun-jon, The Pigeon's Egg Head Going to and Returning from Washington*, 1832.

(The Granger Collection, New York.)

LETTER—NO. 2

Mouth of Yellow Stone, Upper Missouri, *1832*

I arrived at this place yesterday in the steamer "Yellow Stone," after a voyage of nearly three months from St. Louis, a distance of two thousand miles, the greater part of which has never before been navigated by steam. . . .

A voyage so full of incident, and furnishing so many novel scenes of the picturesque and romantic, as we have passed the numerous villages of the "astonished natives," saluting them with the puffing of steam and the thunder of artillery, would afford subject for many epistles; and I cannot deny myself the pleasure of occasionally giving you some little sketches of scenes that I have witnessed, and *am witnessing.* . . . I am here in the full enthusiasm and practice of my art. That enthusiasm alone has brought me into this remote region, 3500 miles from my native soil; the last 2000 of which have furnished me with almost unlimited models, both in landscape and the human figure, exactly suited to my feelings. . . . I [am] surrounded by living models of such elegance and beauty, that I feel an unceasing excitement of a much higher order—the certainty that I am drawing knowledge from the true source. My enthusiastic admiration of man in the honest and elegant simplicity of nature, has always fed the warmest feelings of my bosom, and shut half the avenues to my heart against the specious refinements of the accomplished world. This feeling, together with the desire to study my art, independently of the embarrassments which the ridiculous fashions of civilized society have thrown in its way, has led me to the wilderness for a while, as the true school of the arts. . . .

In addition to the knowledge of human nature and of my art, which I hope to acquire by this toilsome and expensive undertaking, I have another in view, which, if it should not be of equal service to me, will be of no less interest and value to posterity. I have, for many years past, contemplated the noble races of red men who are now spread over these trackless forests and boundless prairies, melting away at the approach of civilization. Their rights invaded, their morals corrupted, their lands wrested from them, their customs changed, and therefore lost to the world; and they at last sunk into the earth, and the ploughshare turning the sod over their graves, and I have flown to their rescue—not of their lives or of their race (for they are "*doomed*" and must perish), but to the rescue of their looks and their modes, at which the acquisitive world may hurl their poison and every besom [*broom*] of destruction, and trample them down and crush them to death; yet, phoenix-like, they may rise from the "stain on a painter's palette," and live again upon canvass, and stand forth for centuries yet to come, the living monuments of a noble race. For this purpose, I have designed to visit every tribe of Indians on the Continent, if my life should be spared; for the purpose of procuring portraits of distinguished Indians, of both sexes in each tribe, painted in their native costume. . . .

LETTER—NO. 8

Mouth of Yellow Stone, Upper Missouri

. . . The Blackfeet are, perhaps, the most powerful tribe of Indians on the Continent; and being sensible of their strength, have stubbornly resisted the Traders in their country. . . . Their country abounds in beaver and buffalo, and most of the fur-bearing animals of North America; and the American Fur Company, with an unconquerable spirit of trade and enterprize, has pushed its establishments into their country; and the numerous parties of trappers are tracing up their streams and rivers, rapidly destroying the beavers which dwell in them. . . . Trinkets and whiskey, however, will soon spread their charms amongst these, as they have amongst other tribes; and white man's voracity will sweep the prairies and the streams of their wealth, to the Rocky Mountains and the Pacific Ocean; leaving the Indians to inhabit, and at last to starve upon, a dreary and solitary waste. . . .

I have painted the portrait of a very distinguished young man, and son of the chief; his dress is a very handsome one, and in every respect answers well to the descriptions I have given above. The name of this man is Wi-jun-jon (the pigeon's egg head). . . .

I have just had the satisfaction of seeing this travelled-gentleman (Wi-jun-jon) meet his tribe, his wife and his little children; after an absence of a year or more, on his journey of 6000 miles to Washington City, and back again (in company with Major Sanford, the Indian agent); where he has been spending the winter amongst the fashionables in the polished circles of civilized society. And I can assure you, readers, that his entrée amongst his own people, in the dress and with the airs of a civilized beau, was one of no ordinary occurrence. . . .

On his way home from St. Louis to this place, a distance of 2000 miles, I travelled with this gentleman, on the steamer Yellow-Stone; and saw him step ashore (on a beautiful prairie, where several thousands of his people were encamped), with a complete suit *en militaire*, a colonel's uniform of blue, presented to him by the President of the United States, with a beaver hat and feather, with epaulettes of gold—with sash and belt, and broad sword; with high-heeled boots—with a keg of whiskey under his arm, and a blue umbrella in his hand. In this plight and metamorphose, he took his position

on the bank, amongst his friends—his wife and other relations; not one of whom exhibited, for an half-hour or more, the least symptoms of recognition, although they knew well who was before them. He also gazed upon them—upon his wife and parents, and little children, who were about, as if they were foreign to him, and he had not a feeling or thought to interchange with them. . . .

This man, at this time, is creating a wonderful sensation amongst his tribe, who are daily and nightly gathered in gaping and listless crowds around him, whilst he is descanting upon what he has seen in the fashionable world; and which to them is unintelligible and beyond their comprehension; for which I find they are already setting him down as a liar and impostor.

What may be the final results of his travels and initiation into the fashionable world, and to what disasters his incredible narrations may yet subject the poor fellow in this strange land, time only will develop.

He is now in disgrace, and spurned by the leading men of the tribe, and rather to be pitied than envied, for the advantages which one might have supposed would have flown from his fashionable tour.

George Catlin, *Letters and Notes on the Manners, Customs, and Condition of the North American Indians*, 2nd ed., 2 vols. (London: Author, 1842), 1:14–16, 49, 51–52, 55–57.

ﹶ

American Progress (1872)

JOHN GAST

John Gast's American Progress *(1872) was one of countless nineteenth-century representations of western settlement that showed Native Americans and wildlife retreating before the symbols of "manifest destiny." Little is known about Gast except that* American Progress *did not spring freely from his imagination. An entrepreneur needing an image to promote a travel guide told him what to paint: a floating figure who bears the "Star of Empire" and a book symbolizing the "common school—the emblem of education and the testimonial of our national enlightenment, while with the left hand she unfolds . . . the slender wires of the telegraph, that are to flash intelligence throughout the land."*

PROBLEMS TO CONSIDER

1. Who are the principal characters in Gast's painting, and what various narratives are being conveyed?
2. How are the artist's techniques (light and shadows, foreground and background) used to communicate to his audience?

(© Christie's Images/Corbis.)

∽ EXPANSIONISM AND CONQUEST

Although some Americans remained loyal to the eighteenth-century pessimism about the fortunes of large and expansive republics, by the 1830s and 1840s many more were convinced that God had a particular destiny in mind for them and their nation—to extend the nation's boundaries to the Pacific and to impose its democratic political, religious, and economic practices on the "unfree" peoples of the Americas. The popular doctrine of "manifest destiny" seemed to harmonize aspirations for greater national power and greater individual liberty—"empire" and "freedom," two ideas that earlier generations of Americans had regarded as incompatible.

In 1835, when the writer Edgar Allan Poe hailed the "romance" and "charm" of fictional and historical accounts of the "Spanish conquests of America," he identified a literary taste that contained its own version of "manifest destiny." Hernán Cortés's conquest of Mexico in 1519–1521 provided the page-turning drama of daring, chivalrous exploits amid an exotic, otherworldly setting that was native to the Western Hemisphere. In the 1830s and 1840s, the United States was so awash with popular (and unpopular) novels, stage productions, paintings, travelogues, and historical studies centering on the violent, early-sixteenth-century Spanish venture that the events seemed as much American as they were Mexican and European. But more was at play in these accounts than the nationalist literary or artistic agenda of a young culture that seemed insubstantial in comparison to Europe. An assumption running through many of these visual and written texts was that Mexico had changed little in the intervening three centuries; to know the Mexico of 1519 was to know the Mexico of 1846. The desire for and use of such "knowledge" had important implications during this period because contemporary Mexico and Mexicans both troubled and excited Americans with visions of national expansion and destiny, incorporating Texas, California, and, perhaps, beyond.

History of the Conquest of Mexico (1843)
WILLIAM H. PRESCOTT

The "conquest of Mexico" told a story in which white men triumphed in a savage war against dark-skinned Indians, a tale in which technological superiority, Christianity, and civilization prevailed against a race of human-sacrificing pagans, and a manly hero (Cortés) vanquished his effeminate and corrupt antagonist (Montezuma). The most celebrated and influential version of this story was William Hickling Prescott's History of the Conquest of Mexico, *a "masterpiece" of midcentury literature first published in 1843, two and a half years before the Mexican War. Prescott was a wealthy Boston Whig deeply suspicious of popular enthusiasms such as the war, which he regarded as a "mad ambition for conquest." Yet his history became part of America's military and political arsenal.* History of the Conquest *inspired readers to enlist, served as a guidebook to the invaders, and seemed to provide a sense of larger historical purpose to the war. The following selections include Prescott's description of the Aztec practice of human sacrifice and his conclusions about the nature of the conflict between Spaniard and Mexican.*

PROBLEMS TO CONSIDER

1. What additional meanings could Americans in 1843 read into the aspersions Prescott casts at "superstition," "the influence of the priesthood," and the "tyranny . . . of a blind fanaticism"?
2. How might Prescott's use of the ideas of "civilization" and "race" have been understood in the era of "manifest destiny"?

BOOK I: VIEW OF THE AZTEC CIVILIZATION

Chapter 3: Human Sacrifices

The civil polity of the Aztecs is so closely blended with their religion that without understanding the latter it is impossible to form correct ideas of their government or their social institutions. . . .

From the construction of their temples *[teocallis]*, all religious services were public. The long processions of priests, winding round their massive sides, as they rose higher and higher towards the summit, and the dismal rites of sacrifice performed there, were all visible from the remotest corners of the capital, impressing on the spectator's mind a superstitious veneration for the mysteries of his religion, and for the dread ministers by whom they were interpreted. . . .

Human sacrifices were adopted by the Aztecs early in the fourteenth century, about two hundred years before the Conquest. Rare at first, they became more frequent with the wider extent of their empire; till, at length, almost every festival was closed with this cruel abomination. These religious ceremonials were generally arranged in such a manner as to afford a type of the most prominent circumstances in the character or history of the deity who was the object of them. . . .

Such was the form of human sacrifice usually practised by the Aztecs. . . . Women, as well as the other sex, were sometimes reserved for sacrifice. On some occasions, particularly in seasons of drought, at the festival of the insatiable Tlaloc, the god of rain, children, for the most part infants, were offered up. . . . These innocent victims were generally bought by the priests of parents who were poor, but who stifled the voice of nature, probably less at the suggestions of poverty than of a wretched superstition. . . .

The influence of these practices on the Aztec character was as disastrous as might have been expected. Familiarity with the bloody rites of sacrifice steeled the heart against human sympathy, and begat a thirst for carnage, like that excited in the Romans by the exhibitions of the circus. The perpetual recurrence of ceremonies, in which the people took part, associated religion with their most intimate concerns, and spread the gloom of superstition over the domestic hearth, until the character of the nation wore a grave and even melancholy aspect, which belongs to their descendants at the present day. The influence of the priesthood, of course, became unbounded. . . . The whole nation, from the peasant to the prince, bowed their necks to the worst kind of tyranny, that of a blind fanaticism. . . .

In this state of things, it was beneficently ordered by Providence that the land should be delivered over to another race, who would rescue it from the brutish superstitions that daily extended wider and wider with extent of empire. The debasing institutions of the Aztecs furnish the best apology for their conquest. It is true, the conquerors brought along with them the Inquisition. But they also brought Christianity, whose benign radiance would still survive when the fierce flames of fanaticism should be extinguished. . . .

BOOK VI: SIEGE AND SURRENDER OF MEXICO

Chapter 8: Reflections

Yet we cannot regret the fall of an empire which did so little to promote the happiness of its subjects or the real interests of humanity. Notwithstanding the lustre thrown over its latter days by the glorious defence of its capital, by the mild munificence of Montezuma, . . . the Aztecs were emphatically a fierce and brutal race, little calculated, in their best aspects, to excite our sympathy and regard. Their civilization, such as it was, was not their own, but reflected, perhaps imperfectly, from a race whom they had succeed in the land. It was, in respect to the Aztecs, a generous graft on a vicious stock, and could have brought no fruit to perfection. They ruled over their wide domains with a sword, instead of a sceptre. . . .

The right of conquest necessarily implies that of using whatever force may be necessary for overcoming resistance to the assertion of that right. For the Spaniards to have done otherwise than they did would have been to abandon the siege, and, with it, the conquest of the country. To have suffered the inhabitants, with their high-spirited monarch, to escape, would but have prolonged the miseries of war by transferring it to another and more inaccessible quarter. They literally, so far as the success of the expedition was concerned, had no choice. If our imagination is struck with the amount of suffering in this and in similar scenes of the Conquest, it should be borne in mind that it was a natural result of the great masses of men engaged in the conflict. The amount of suffering does not of itself show the amount of cruelty which caused it; and it is but justice to the Conquerors of Mexico to say that the very brilliancy and importance of their exploits have given a melancholy celebrity to their misdeeds, and thrown them into somewhat bolder relief than strictly belongs to them. . . .

Its fate may serve as a striking proof that a government which does not rest on the sympathies of its subjects cannot long abide; that human institutions, when not connected with human prosperity and progress, must fall,—if not before the increasing light of civilization, by the hand of violence; by violence from within, if not from without. And who shall lament their fall?

William H. Prescott, *History of the Conquest of Mexico*, 3 vols., edited by John Foster Kirk (Philadelphia, 1843; repr., Philadelphia: J. B. Lippincott, 1873), 1:55, 76–81, 85–86, 89; 3:201, 204–5, 207.

❧

Relations Between Texas, the United States of America, and the Mexican Republic (1837)

JOSÉ MARÍA TORNEL Y MENDÍVIL

Mexico won its independence from Spain in 1821, at a moment when the United States had just emerged from the Missouri Compromise crisis, which shockingly exposed the bitter divisions within the nation over the continued westward expansion of slavery. Because the northern reaches of Mexico's state of Texas were sparsely populated and vulnerable to assault by the Spanish, French, and Comanche, Mexico was initially willing to grant land to a select group of American settlers who promised to become Mexican citizens and convert to Catholicism. By 1828, more than 20,000 Americans were squatters ("illegal aliens") in Texas. When Mexico shifted to a stronger central government, legislated against American immigration, outlawed slavery, and increased taxes, these Anglos determined to declare their independence, much like their fathers had in 1776. The newly elected governor of the Republic of Texas, Stephen Austin, described the conflict as one pitting barbarism on the part of "a mongrel Spanish-Indian and negro race, against civilization and the Anglo-American race." No Mexican official was better acquainted with the arrogance of American expansionism than José María Tornel y Mendívil, the Mexican minister to Washington in the 1830s and the secretary of war during the Texas rebellion. Tornel's book on the relations between Mexico, Texas, and the United States provides one of the best accounts of Mexican attitudes toward the United States during the era of western expansionism, "manifest destiny," and war.

PROBLEMS TO CONSIDER

1. What was Tornel's explanation for the United States' insatiable desire to acquire the lands of other nations to its west? What role did race play in his criticism of the United States?
2. Tornel also described how Mexico contributed to this crisis. What were his criticisms of Mexico?

For more than fifty years, that is, from the very period of their political infancy, the prevailing thought in the United States of America has been the acquisition of the greater part of the territory that formerly belonged to Spain, particularly that part which to-day belongs to the Mexican nation. Democrats and Federalists, all their political parties, whatever their old or new designations, have been in perfect accord upon one point, their desire to extend the limits of the republic to the north, to the south, and to the west, using for the purpose all the means at their command, guided by cunning, deceit, and bad faith. It has been neither an Alexander nor a Napoleon, desirous of conquest in order to extend his dominions or add to his glory, who has inspired the proud Anglo-Saxon race in its desire, its frenzy to usurp and gain control of that which rightfully belongs to its neighbors; rather it has been the nation itself which, possessed of that roving spirit that moved the barbarous hordes of a former age in a far remote north, has swept away whatever has stood in the way of its aggrandizement. . . .

Our continuous revolts made that country conceive the hope that we would neglect or abandon our national and sacred charge, while the ill-advised colonization laws and our still more imprudent and scandalous mismanagement of the public lands, so coveted and yet so freely and generously distributed and given away, clearly showed that we knew neither how to appreciate nor how to keep the precious heritage of the Spaniards. Unfortunately they were not mistaken in their assumption, for at every step we have displayed that candor, weakness, and inexperience so characteristic of infant nations. Too late have we come to know the restless and enterprising neighbor who set himself up as our mentor, holding up his institutions for us to copy them, institutions which transplanted to our soil could not but produce constant anarchy, and which, by draining our resources, perverting our character, and weakening our vigor, have left us powerless against the attacks and the invasions of this modern Rome. . . .

In spite of the advantageous position of the United States, of their growing maritime power, of the war-like disposition of their inhabitants, of the determination displayed in their struggles, of the abundant resources of their soil and the bright prospects of their industry, they could not aspire to a superior rank among the nations of the world, as long as they had to compete with the old and powerful countries of Europe. The setting changed, however, with the appearance of other independent nations in the New World. It was, therefore, to the essential interest of the United States to encourage by their example, their counsel, and their material help the insurrection of Spanish America. . . .

What the cunning of the United States lacked was made up by our unexplainable candor. Though the plan of operations was conceived in Washington, Mexico contributed directly to its execution. The colonization of Texas, thrown open to adventurers from the United States, afforded them the best means for gaining that territory *without the disregard, the violation, or the infringement of existing treaties.* Who does not sense the devious spirit of a policy which, in this ruthless manner rendered the most solemn and sacred efforts to maintain the rights of our nation useless? . . .

If it is written in the uncertain and obscure book of destiny that we are some day to lose the department of Texas, let the fact remain buried in the inscrutable designs of fate as evidence of the unexampled perfidy displayed by the colonists and settlers and as testimony of ill-requited Mexican generosity. . . . They have even encouraged the very scum of the United States, those who because of debt or crimes found themselves obliged to flee from the rigor of the law in search of a more secure refuge in an unsettled country which was nominally governed by a well-regulated and organized body politic. . . .

Nowhere else on the face of the globe is the feeling of the white race stronger against those which, in its pride, it designates as colored. This was sufficient for the expulsion of the men of bronze, the redmen, and for the despoliation of their property. This policy was all the more advisable because in the lands occupied by some of these tribes deposits of the fatal and coveted metal *[gold]* had been discovered. Furthermore, the Indians had cleared the woods, and the lands were now ready for cultivation. What was there to restrain Anglo-American greed? Nothing! Might was on their side, the miserable Indians had nothing but their weakness. . . . In 1830 it was definitely decided to expel the Indian tribes from Georgia and Alabama. . . . It is not my purpose in relating this recent catastrophe that has just befallen the primitive dwellers of this continent to place upon the United States the curse of having exterminated an innocent people and of having driven the survivors to unknown deserts. The world has passed judgment upon this classic example of injustice and it is not for me to excite the sensibility of those who sorrow for the misfortunes of humanity. What I aim to point out clearly is that at the same time that the Indians were despoiled of their territory, it was planned to deprive the Mexican Republic of its own. . . .

The loss of Texas will inevitably result in the loss of New Mexico and the Californias. Little by little our territory will be absorbed, until only an insignificant part is left to us. Our destiny will be similar to the sad lot of Poland. Our national existence, acquired at the cost of so much blood, recognized after so many difficulties, would end like those weak meteors which, from time to time, shine fitfully in the firmament and disappear.

José María Tornel y Mendívil, *Tejas y Los Estados-Unidos de America, en Sus Relaciones con las Republica Mexicana (Relations Between Texas, the United States of America, and the Mexican Republic)* (Mexico, 1837), in *The Mexican Side of the Texan Revolution*, translated by Carlos Castañeda (Dallas: P. L. Turner, 1928; repr., Austin: Graphic Ideas, 1970), 295–96, 303–4, 315–16, 330–31, 335–36, 380.

ᕐ

The Emigrants' Guide to Oregon and California (1845)
LANSFORD W. HASTINGS

Even before Texas was annexed to the United States and the war with Mexico began, residents of the United States had set their sights on California, the culmination of the myth of "manifest destiny" that promised the United States a nation across the entire continent. Lansford W. Hastings's The Emigrants' Guide to Oregon and California *was one of a number of widely read guidebooks of the West published in the 1830s and 1840s for curious — and enterprising — Americans, who were especially interested in the "character" of the lands and peoples of the former Spanish empire.*

PROBLEMS TO CONSIDER

1. Using this traveler's guide, reconstruct the racial foundations for the doctrine of "manifest destiny." How were these ideas similar to or different from the types of racial thinking expressed at other times in early American history, such as European colonization, the defense of slavery, or the removal of Indians?
2. How does Hastings's description of Mexicans compare with Prescott's depiction of the Aztecs prior to Spanish conquest?

The entire population of Upper California, including foreigners, Mexicans and Indians, may be estimated at about thirty-one thousand human souls, of whom, about one thousand are foreigners, ten thousand are Mexicans, and the residue are Indians. By the term foreigners, I include all those who are not native citizens of Mexico, whether they have become citizens by naturalization, or whether they remain in a state of alienage. They consist, chiefly, of Americans, Englishmen, Frenchmen, Germans and Spaniards, but there is a very large majority of the former. . . . The foreigners of this country are, generally, very intelligent; many of them have received all the advantages of an education; and they all possess an unusual degree of industry and enterprise. Those who are emigrating to that remote and almost unknown region, like those who are emigrating to Oregon, are, in all respects, a different class of persons, from those who usually emigrate to our frontier. They generally, possess more than an ordinary degree of intelligence, and that they possess an eminent degree of industry, enterprise and bravery, is most clearly evinced, from the very fact, of their entering upon this most arduous and perilous undertaking. Very few cowards ever venture voluntarily, to meet all those imaginary and real dangers, . . . but extraordinary kindness, courtesy and hospitality, are additional traits, which they possess to an unusual degree. A more kind and hospitable people are nowhere found; they seem to vie with each other, in their kindness and hospitality to strangers; and at the same time, they treat each other as brothers. Here, you see the citizens and subjects, of almost every nation in the civilized world, united by the silken chains of friendship, exerting every energy, and doing every thing in their power, to promote the individual and general welfare. . . .

The Mexicans differ, in every particular, from the foreigners; ignorance and its concomitant, superstition, together with suspicion and superciliousness, constitute the chief ingredients, of the Mexican character. More indomitable ignorance does not prevail, among any people who make the least pretentions to civilization; in truth, they are scarcely a visible grade, in the scale of intelligence, above the barbarous tribes by whom they are surrounded; but this is not surprising, especially when we consider the relation, which these people occupy to their barbarous neighbors, in other particulars. Many of the lower order of them, have intermarried with the various tribes, and have resided with them so long, and lived in a manner so entirely similar, that it has become almost impossible, to trace the least distinctions between them, either in reference to intelligence, or complexion. There is another class, which is, if possible, of a lower order still, than those just alluded to, and which consists of the aborigines themselves, who have been slightly civilized, or rather *domesticated*. These two classes constitute almost the entire Mexican population, of California, and among them almost every variety and shade of complexion may be found, from the African black, to the tawny brown of our southern Indians. Although there is a great variety, and dissimilarity among them, in reference to their complexions, yet in their beastly habits and an entire want of all moral principle, as well as a perfect destitution of all intelligence, there appears to be a perfect similarity. . . . The priests are not only the sole proprietors, of the learning and intelligence, but also, of the liberty and happiness of the people, all of which they parcel out to their blind votaries, with a very sparing hand; and thus it is, that all the Mexican people are kept, in this state of degrading ignorance, and humiliating vassalage. The priests here, not only have the possession of the keys of the understanding, and the door of liberty, but they also, have both the present and ultimate happiness, of these ignorant people, entirely at their disposal. Such at least, is the belief of the people, and such are the doctrines there taught by the priests. At times, I sympathize with these unfortunate beings, but again, I frequently think, that, perhaps, it is fortunate for the residue of mankind, that these semi-barbarians, are thus *ridden* and restrained, and if they are to be thus priest ridden, it is, no doubt, preferable, that they should retain their present *riders*.

———

Lansford W. Hastings, *The Emigrants' Guide to Oregon and California* (Cincinnati: George Conclin, 1845; facsimile repr., Princeton, N.J.: Princeton University Press, 1932), 112–14.

ᴄ

Legends of Mexico (1847)
GEORGE LIPPARD

George Lippard was the most popular American novelist at the time the Mexican War broke out. A former journalist from Philadelphia, Lippard was famous for producing sensationalistic urban fiction, including his best-selling Quaker City; or the Monks of Monk Hall *(1844), a gothic tale of the urban underworld designed to mock the moralist reformers of his day. Lippard then penned two Mexican War novels,* Legends of Mexico *(1847) and* 'Bel of Prairie Eden: A Romance of Mexico *(1848). An ardent Democrat, Lippard aspired to depict the Mexican War as both a heroic romance and a continuation of the American Revolution. On the title page of* Legends of Mexico, *he altered Thomas Paine's statement in* The Crisis *(1776) from "We fight not to enslave, but to set a country free, and to make room upon the earth for honest men to live in" to "We fight not to enslave, nor for conquest . . . ," alluding to the influence of William H. Prescott's* History of the Conquest of Mexico. *Despite the fact that Lippard depicted the Mexican War as "the New Crusade," he felt the need to emphasize that this crusade was somehow different from the Spanish conquest of Mexico.*

PROBLEMS TO CONSIDER

1. How did ideas about nature and the American wilderness shape Lippard's version of "manifest destiny"?
2. Compare and contrast Lippard's characterization of the people of Mexico with William H. Prescott's and Lansford W. Hastings's. For Lippard, what was the connection between race and expansionism?

CHAPTER I: THE CRUSADE OF THE NINETEENTH CENTURY

"Ho! for the New Crusade!"

It was in the spring of 1846, that this cry, thundering from twenty-nine states, aroused a People into arms, and startled Europe, its Kings and Slaves, into shuddering awe....

In the spring of 1846, from the distant south there came echoing in terrible chorus, a Cry, a Groan, a Rumor! That Cry, the earnest voice of two thousand brave men, gathered beneath the Banner of the stars in a far land, encompassed by their foes, with nothing but a bloody vision of Massacre before their eyes. And the Cry, wrung from two thousand manly hearts, said the People of the Union. — We are in danger, but the Banner of the Stars floats above us. An army, twice our number surrounds us, Assassins hung like vultures, in the shadows of our camp, a Plague broods in the poisonous air, of the swamp and chaparral. Come — help us — fight with us! Or if you cannot fight, Come, and behold us die, for the flag of Washington! ...

At once, from the People of twenty-nine states, quivered the Cry —

"To Arms! Ho! for the new crusade!"

Never since the days of Washington, had an excitement, so wild and universal, thrilled in the souls of freemen. From the mountains of Maine — they are yonder, rising ruggedly in their stern grandeur, with snowy mantles, bound about their granite brows — to the prairies of the Texas — blossoming for hundreds of miles, a wilderness of flowers — that cry startled a People into action, and sent the battle-throbs palpitating through fifteen millions hearts.

Long after we are dead, History will tell the children of ages yet to come, how the hosts gathered for the Crusade, in the year 1846....

Yes, the children of Revolutionary veterans, took the rifle of '76 from its resting place, over the hearth, and examined its lock, by the light of the setting sun, and ere another dawn, were on their way to the south, shouting as they extended their hands toward the unseen land — "Mexico!" ...

And while the world wondered, the "PEOPLE" of America rushed to arms, and marched by tens and twenties, by hundreds and thousands, by companies, by legions, by armies, to that golden land, which rose to their vision, rich with the grandeur of past ages.

Standing on the mountain tops, the Crusaders of the Nineteenth Century beheld it — that golden and bloody land of Mexico....

Yes, against this land, so burdened with awful memories, the American People, marched in deadly and determined crusade....

Why this Crusade?

Was it because the Alamo, still cried out for vengeance? That gory Alamo which one day, dripped on its stones and flowers and grass with the blood of five hundred mangled bodies — the bodies of brave Texians cut down by Mexican bayonets and pierced by Mexican balls, and hacked by Mexican knives?

Why this Crusade?

Was it because the American People, having borne for a series of years, the insults and outrages of Mexican Military despots, and seen their brothers in Texas, butchered like dogs, at last resolved, to bear insult and outrage no longer, at last, determined to take from the Tomb of Washington the Banner of the Stars, and swore by his Ghost, never to stay their efforts, until it floated over the City of Mexico! ...

Do you ask the explanation of this mystery? Search the history of the North American People, behold them forsake the shores of Europe, and dare the unknown dangers of the distant wilderness, not for the last of gold or power, but for the sake of a Religion, a Home.

An Exodus like this — the going forth of the oppressed of all nations to a new world — the angels never saw before. All parts of Europe, sent their heart-wounded, their down-trodden thousands to the wilds of North America.

The German and the Frenchman, the Swede and the Irishman, the Scot and the Englishman, met in the wild, and grouped around one altar— Sacred to the majesty of God and the rights of man. From this strangely mingled band of wanderers, a new People sprung into birth.

A vigorous People, rugged as the rocks of the wilderness which sheltered them, free as the forest which gave them shade, bold as the red Indian who forced them to purchase every inch of ground, with the blood of human hearts. To this hardy People—this people created from the pilgrims and wanderers of all nations—this People nursed into full vigor, by long and bloody Indian wars and hardened into iron, by the longest and bloodiest war of all, the Revolution, to this People of Northern America, God Almighty has given the destiny of the entire American Continent.

The handwriting of blood and fire, is upon British America and Southern America.

As the Aztec people, crumbled before the Spaniard, so will the mongrel race, moulded of Indian and Spanish blood, melt into, and be ruled by, the Iron Race of the North. . . .

God Almighty has given the destiny of the Continent, into the hands of the free People of the American Union.

Not the Anglo-Saxon race, for such a race has no existence, save in the brains of certain people, who talk frothily about immense nothings. You might as well call the American People, the Scandinavian race, the Celtic race, the Norman race, as to apply to them, the empty phrase, Anglo-Saxon. This ridiculous word, has been in the mouths of grave men, who should know better, for years: it is high time, that we should discard it for some word, with a slight pretence to a meaning.

WE are no Anglo-Saxon people. No! All Europe sent its exiles to our shores. From all the nations of Northern Europe, we were formed. Germany and Sweden and Ireland and Scotland and Wales and England, aye and glorious France, all sent their oppressed to us, and we grew into a new race.

We are the American People. Our lineage is from that God, who bade us go forth, from the old world, and smiled us into an Empire of Men. Our destiny to possess this Continent, drive from it all shreds of Monarchy, whether British or Spanish or Portuguese, and on the wrecks of shattered empires, built the Altar, second to the BROTHERHOOD OF MAN.

George Lippard, *Legends of Mexico* (Philadelphia: T. B. Peterson, 1847), 11–16.

Manifest Destiny (1855)
AUGUSTINE DUGANNE

Only a minority of northerners ardently opposed the Mexican War; most of this opposition came from the pens of abolitionists and peace activists. William Lloyd Garrison was not much of a poet, but his verse "The War for Slavery" voiced the feelings of many who believed that the war was being fought to extend the realm of the Slave Power of the South. Garrison stated, "If ever war was waged for basest ends, . . . it is the present war with Mexico." Augustine Duganne, like George Lippard, published urban mystery novels prior to the Mexican War. But unlike Lippard's views, Duganne's poem "Manifest Destiny" stands as perhaps the most powerful antiwar poem that exposed the lie behind romantic justifications for continental conquest and racial nationalism.

PROBLEMS TO CONSIDER

1. Who in America would have been most sympathetic, and least sympathetic, to Duganne's sarcastic lampooning of "manifest destiny"?
2. What was the relationship between antiwar and antislavery sentiments in this poem?

Christian men! who lift your hearts
   To Heaven, this day, in prayer—
   And lay your conscience bare,—
KNOW YE not, that War and Wrong
Can never make your temples strong?
   Know ye not that blood and battles
     Are not from the Lord? . . .

DESTINY! Destiny!
Warder! look forth! sound now the warning
   cry—
   Give the alarum-word!
Lo! the Destroyer of Free draws nigh:
Swings the dread balance midway from on
   high—
   The wall with fire is scored:
   AMBITION whets his sword!
War! war! war!
What says this Christian nation to the world?
   Earth with our threats is rife:
Heaven hath beheld our crimson flag unfurled—
In flaming wrath our armies have been hurled
   Against a nation's life!
   War to the bloody knife! . . .

Slaves of the South—arise!
Clang ye your gyves [shackles], to swell the
   cymbals' sound—
   Lift your exulting eyes!
Lo! your white masters have new victims found—
Comrades ye have—in war's red bondage
   bound:

Ye shall hear answering cries,
Swelling your gasping sighs.

   White slaves of Northern gold!
Build ye a Teocalli—where the foes
   Of our ambition bold
May writhe beneath our Anglo-Saxon blows,
And shriek their curses in expiring throes—
   Curses that shall be told
   Till Eternity is old!

   Destiny! Destiny!
Lo! 'tis our *mission* to pour out the tide
   Of our heart-blood, and die,
With foeman's corse [enemy's corpse] stretched
   ghastly by our side;
Or live and trample him in vengeful pride:
   This is our mission high—
   Gospel of Liberty!

   We preach great Freedom's creed?
WE? with our heels upon the writhing necks
   Of millions yet *un*freed,
Whose gasping prayers the soul of Justice vex?
WE! who upon a crumbling nation's wrecks
   Would build a pyramid
   Where millions more might bleed?

––––––––––

A. J. H. Duganne, *Duganne's Poetical Works* ([Philadelphia]: n.p., 1865), 227–30.

↜ *The Arts of Democracy: Commercial Popular Entertainment and Political Culture* ↝

↜ THEATER AND THE ASTOR PLACE RIOT

Popular obsession with theater was inseparably connected to the same democratic nationalism that marked westward expansionism, "manifest destiny," and the racist marginalization of nonwhite residents within the United States. Professional theater enjoyed limited popularity in America before the nineteenth century. During the colonial era, no native-born American ever published or produced a play or sang, danced, or acted professionally on the stage. Theaters were banned or severely restricted during the American Revolution, because the Revolutionary generation considered theatergoing inconsistent with the virtues necessary for the success of a republic.

Opposition to theatrical entertainment waned just as republics and republicanism were supplanted by a new democracy. Masses of Americans began flocking to theaters by the 1820s, not just in the burgeoning cities but in communities of all sizes in every region. Theaters quickly became the first genuine form of mass entertainment in the United States and produced the first set of celebrity entertainers ("stars") in the nation's history. Mass interest grew as more theaters emerged and ticket prices plummeted.

The variety of performances that theaters offered at this time was truly astonishing. Theater managers tried to give their audiences a little bit of everything. American theaters performed classic tragedies alongside comedy skits, farces, carnival acts, equestrian melodramas (featuring horses right on stage), song revues, and clowning songsters in blackface makeup. The most popular productions of all were Shakespeare's plays. For mid-nineteenth-century audiences, Shakespeare seemed a perfect fit within their culture. His plays evoked moral lessons of vices and virtues; his characters stood out as true "actors," responsible for their own destinies; and his plays glorified the spoken word, well suited for a society in which oratory (religious and political) reigned supreme.

American drama drew on a set of stock characters that audiences clamored for at every possible occasion and who represented the mythical images of white manliness and an assumed American cultural superiority. These characters included the honest Yankee farmboy Jonathan; the frontier backwoodsman modeled on the fictional exploits of Davy Crockett; and the working-class hero Mose, the Bowery B'hoy who fought fires and men with equal vigor. By the 1820s, the Indian as noble savage was added to the pantheon of mythical Americans; numerous plays entitled *Pocahontas* became popular successes; and America's most popular actor, Edwin Forrest, commissioned a play—John Augustus Stone's *Metamora*—so that he could play the innocent, independent natural man of the American continent.

Democratic nationalism and emerging class divisions erupted in a violent cultural battle in New York City both at and about the theater. On the evening of May

10, 1849, a crowd of 10,000 gathered outside the Astor Place Opera House to prevent the performance of the British actor William Macready, who was playing the title role of Shakespeare's *Macbeth*. When they began hurling stones through the windows and pushing forward to break open the theater doors, companies of local militia fired directly into the crowd. When order was finally restored, twenty-two persons had been killed, more than 150 wounded, and eighty-six arrested. The documents in this section address the questions: How did a theater performance provoke such intense violence? How was this riot related to a democratic culture in an era of continental expansion and racial nationalism?

Letters of Jonathan Oldstyle, gent. (1824)
WASHINGTON IRVING

Theater audiences reflected the diversity of American society and hence exposed the underlying class tensions present within that society. Theaters maintained a three-tiered division of the audience: in the orchestra boxes sat the fashionable and wealthy classes; in the pit directly in front of the stage, middle-class businessmen mixed with aspiring young "dandies" of the working classes; and in the highest section, the gallery, less affluent workers joined those whom the middle classes described as "undesirables" (prostitutes, gamblers, African Americans, and other "rowdies"). All these groups attended the theater together, although some theaters began to cater exclusively to middle- or working-class audiences.

Theater was not just a spectator event in the early nineteenth century; it was also a participatory activity. Unlike quiet and passive theater and movie audiences in our own era, audiences then made known their physical and vocal presence to performers and spectators alike. Theatergoers often sang along with the performers, recited the well-known speeches, or shouted the punch lines to familiar jokes; they expressed their approval or disapproval with deafening cheers or insults. For many, these participatory actions were the everyday expressions of a democracy, the affirmation of the professed equality espoused in the nation's ideals. For others, such actions represented the signs of an unruly mob, lacking restraint or decorum. Washington Irving gave voice to this latter perspective through the humorous reflections of the fictional Jonathan Oldstyle, whose name evoked a Yankee who was more comfortable in the previous century (much like the Federalist elites that Irving knew quite well). Although fiction, Irving's Letters of Jonathan Oldstyle *still evoked truths about the theater experience in the new democracy.*

PROBLEMS TO CONSIDER

1. What impression of the public in a democracy does Irving want to convey in this satire?
2. Is Irving's portrayal of theater audiences chiefly sympathetic or overly critical?

Sir,
My last communication mentioned my visit to the theatre; the remarks it contained were chiefly confined to the play and the actors; I shall now extend them to the audience, who, I assure you, furnish no inconsiderable part of the entertainment.

As I entered the house some time before the curtain rose, I had sufficient leisure to make some observations. I was much amused with the waggery and humour of the gallery, which, by the way, is kept in *excellent* order by the constables who are stationed here. . . . Somehow or another, the anger of the gods seemed to be aroused all of a sudden, and they commenced a discharge of apples, nuts, and gingerbread, on the heads of the honest folks in the pit, who had no possibility of retreating from this new kind of thunderbolts. I can't say but I was a little irritated at being saluted aside of my head with a rotten pippin; and was going to shake my cane at them, but was prevented by a decent looking man behind me, who informed me that it was useless to threaten or expostulate. They are only *amusing themselves* a little at our expense, said he; sit down quietly and bend your back to it. My kind neighbour was interrupted by a hard green apple that hit him between the shoulders — he made a wry face, but knowing it was all a joke, bore the blow like a philosopher. . . .

I was considerably amused by the queries of the countryman mentioned in my last, who was now making his first visit to the theatre. . . . As this honest man was casting his eye round the house, his attention was suddenly arrested. And pray, who are these? said he, pointing to a cluster of young fellows. These, I suppose, are the critics, of whom I have heard so much. They have, no doubt, got together to communicate their remarks, and compare notes; these are the persons through whom the audience exercise their judgments, and by whom they are told when they are to applaud or to hiss. Critics! ha! ha! my dear sir, they trouble themselves as little about the elements of criticism, as they do about other departments of science and belles-lettres. These are the beaux of the present day, who meet here to lounge away an idle hour, and play off their little impertinencies for the entertainment of the public. They no more regard the merits of the play, nor of the actors, than my cane. . . . I have heard that some have even gone so far in search of amusement, as to propose a game of cards in the theatre, during the performance. . . .

Washington Irving, *Letters of Jonathan Oldstyle, gent.* (New York, 1824; facsimile repr., New York: Columbia University Press, 1941), 18–21.

ॐ

A Card Explaining the Dispute (1848)
EDWIN FORREST

Diary of William Macready (1846–1849)
WILLIAM MACREADY

The controversy that ultimately led to the bloody Astor Place riots began as a protracted quarrel between two leading tragedians — the foremost American actor, Edwin Forrest, and a venerable English actor, William Macready. Forrest, the son of working-class Philadelphia parents, had applied workmanlike tenacity to build his body and craft in order to rival the English actors who dominated the American stage. An imposing figure of a man, with thick and muscular legs and the physique of a laborer, Forrest became an American favorite (especially among the working classes). In the 1840s, he toured England, where he claimed that Macready had conspired with the British papers to ridicule him. In Edinburgh in 1846, Forrest openly hissed at Macready's performance of Hamlet. *When Macready toured the United States in 1848, he was greeted with showers of hisses and assorted debris wherever he performed. Forrest and Macready's conflict occurred at the exact moment of "manifest destiny," when the United States and Britain threatened war over the Oregon Territory, and Americans waged a war against Mexico. Forrest explains his side of the dispute in the following letter to a Philadelphia newspaper. Macready's* Diary *reveals the English actor's views of the quarrel and his growing contempt for an American public that supported Forrest. In May 1849, Macready began a run at the Astor Place Opera House, a newly built theater in New York for well-to-do patrons, while Forrest simultaneously performed before his working-class supporters at the Broadway Theatre.*

PROBLEMS TO CONSIDER

1. What aspects of Forrest's criticisms of Macready are in the spirit of the new democracy in America? How do you explain the nationalist sentiments of each actor?
2. How are Forrest's and Macready's attacks on the English and the Americans rooted in class attitudes or gender conventions?

A CARD EXPLAINING THE DISPUTE

A Card

Mr. Macready, in his speech last night, to the audience assembled at the Arch Street Theatre, made allusion, I understand, to an "American actor," who had the temerity, on one occasion, "openly to hiss him." This is true, and, by the way, the only truth which I have been enabled to gather from the whole scope of his address. But why say "an American actor"? Why not openly charge me with the act? for I did it, and publicly avowed it in the *Times* newspaper, of London, and at the same time asserted my right to do so.

On the occasion alluded to, Mr. Macready introduced a fancy dance into his performance of Hamlet, . . . which I hissed, for I thought it a desecration of the scene, and the audience thought so too, for in a few nights afterwards, when Mr. Macready repeated the part of Hamlet with the

same "tom-foolery," the intelligent audience of Edinburgh greeted it with a universal hiss.

Mr. Macready is stated to have said last night, that up to the time of this act on my part, he "had never entertained towards me a feeling of unkindness." I unhesitatingly pronounce this to be a wilful and unblushing falsehood. I most solemnly aver and do believe that Mr. Macready, instigated by his narrow, envious mind and his selfish fears, did secretly—not openly—suborn several writers for the English press, to write me down. . . .

I assert also, and solemnly believe, that Mr. Macready connived, when his friends went to the theatre in London, to hiss me, and did hiss me, with the purpose of driving me from the stage—and all this happened many months before the affair at Edinburgh, to which Mr. Macready refers, and in relation to which he jesuitically remarks, that "until that act, he never entertained towards me a feeling of unkindness."

Pah! Mr. Macready has no feeling of kindness for any actor who is likely, by his talent, to stand in his way. . . .

EDWIN FORREST
Philadelphia, Nov. 21, 1848

Pennsylvanian (Philadelphia), November 22, 1848. Reprinted in *A Rejoinder to the "Replies from England, etc."*. . . (New York: Stringer and Townsend, 1849), 10–11.

DIARY OF WILLIAM MACREADY

1846

Edinburgh, March 2nd.—Acted Hamlet really with particular care, energy, and discrimination; the audience gave less applause to the first soliloquy than I am in the habit of receiving, but I was bent on acting the part, and I felt, if I can feel at all, that I had strongly excited them, and that their sympathies were cordially, indeed, enthusiastically, with me. On reviewing the performance I can conscientiously pronounce it one of the very best I have given of Hamlet. At the waving of the handkerchief before the play *[a favorite practice of Macready at this particular point in* Hamlet*]*, a man on the right side of the stage—upper boxes or gallery, but said to be upper boxes—hissed! The audience took it up, and I waved the more, and bowed derisively and contemptuously to the individual. The audience carried it, though he was very staunch to his purpose. It discomposed me, and, alas! might have ruined many; but I bore it down. . . .

March 4th.—. . . It is alluded to in the *Scotsman* of to-day with a direct reference to Mr. Forrest. Indeed, it seems placed beyond all doubt. I feel glad that it is not an Englishman—but no Englishman would have done a thing so base; indeed he *dared* not have done it, and that was one argument in my mind for my belief in Mr. Forrest's guilt. I do not think that such an action has its parallel in all theatrical history! The low-minded ruffian! That man would commit a murder, *if he dare*. . . .

March 6th.—Rehearsed. Heard from Mr.

Ryder that Mr. Wyndham, one of the actors, had been told by a bystander that Mr. Forrest justified his act of *hissing* on the plea that he gave applause to actors, and he had an equal right to hiss them! *Mr. Forrest!* . . . Read the *Times*. We shall have war, I think, with America. What charming news to Mr. Forrest! Oh God!—these are *men*! . . .

March 27th.—Saw in a playbill Mr. Forrest's name in the new tragedy of *Aylmere*! I feel I cannot *stomach* the United States as a nation; the good there, I must admit, appears like the quantity of the grains of wheat to the bushel of chaff. . . .

April 4th.—Called on Forster. . . . He showed me the *Times*, in which is a letter of Mr. Edwin Forrest, admitting that he hissed me on my introduction of a "fancy dance" into *Hamlet*; that he had a right to do so; that he was not solitary in the act; and that he often led the applause which he regretted others did not follow. . . . This seems to me . . . to be the seal of his character. . . .

1848

October 16th.—*[Boston]* . . . *This evening has decided me.* It may be a small thing, but it shows to *such an extent* what is partially *admitted* by those who desire me to settle in this country, that I cannot reason against it. The masses, rich and poor, are essentially ignorant and vulgar—utterly deficient in taste and without the modesty to distrust themselves. A crust in England is better than pampering tables here. *"I am for England—God!"* . . .

November 8th.—. . . *I will not live in America*—rather, *if I live to leave it, I will not return to die here*—*I will not.* . . . I acted *against* it all, striving to keep my self-possession, and I acted *well*. The curtain fell, and the audience, who would have cheered on a thick-headed, thick-legged *brute* like Mr. Forrest, took no notice of this, my best performance. This is the civilization—the growing *taste* of the United States!!! . . .

November 22nd.—*[Philadelphia]* . . . Mr. Ryder told me that there was in the *Ledger* a *Card* of

Mr. Forrest's, which I ought to see, asserting the truth of all the statements that had been put forth against me, saying that I had suborned the Press, that I had got people to hiss him, etc. I was staggered and a little alarmed. Having heard so much of the violence of the low rowdies of this place, and seeing clearly that this was a reckless attempt to incite an infuriated spirit against me, I did not feel that *my personal safety* was to be relied on.... *Oh! Mr. Forrest!!!* I felt the blow he had struck upon his own head, but yet was uncertain how far the low class under his influence might be affected by it....

1849

April 11th. — Especially disgusted by a reference to a New York paper, which discusses the *possibility* of certain friends of mine and this blackguard Forrest making the occasion of my appearance a signal for conflict! Are not the vulgar wretches, the stupid, unprincipled dolts of this country, enough to drive a wise man mad? ... There are gentlemen — high-minded, high-hearted, cultivated gentlemen — in the country, but it is a *land of blackguards*. I cannot wonder at Dickens's *aversion* — with me it becomes *loathing*! ...

May 7th. — Rehearsed with much care.... Went to theatre, dressed. My hairdresser told me there would be a good house, for there was — an unusual sight — a great crowd outside.... They *[the audience]* would not let me speak. They hung out placards — "You have been proved a liar," etc.; flung a rotten egg close to me. I pointed it to the audience and smiled with contempt, persisting in my endeavour to be heard. I could not have been less than a quarter of an hour on the stage altogether, with perfect sang-froid and good-humour, reposing in the consciousness of my own truth. At last there was nothing for it, and I said, "Go on," and the play, *Macbeth*, processed in dumb show *[i.e., without voices, in pantomime]*, I hurrying the players on. Copper cents were thrown, some struck me, four or five eggs, a great many apples, nearby —

if not quite — a peck of potatoes, lemons, pieces of wood, a bottle of asafœtida which splashed my own dress, smelling, of course, most horribly.... Behind the scenes some attempted to exhibit sympathy, which I received very loftily, observing, "My concern was for the disgrace such people inflicted on the character of the country."...

May 10th. — I went, gaily, I may say, to the theatre, and on my way, looking down Astor Place, saw one of the Harlem cars on the railroad stop and discharge a full load of policemen; there seemed to be others at the door of the theatre. I observed to myself, "This is good precaution."... My reception was very enthusiastic, but I soon discovered that there was opposition, though less numerously manned than on Monday.... As well as I can remember the bombardment outside now began. Stones were hurled against the windows in Eighth Street, smashing many; the work of destruction became then more systematic; the volleys of stones flew without intermission, battering and smashing all before them; the Gallery and Upper Gallery still kept up the din within, aided by the crashing of glass and boarding without.... The fourth act passed; louder and more fierce waxed the furious noises against the building and from without; for whenever a missile did effectual mischief in its discharge it was hailed with shouts outside.... The death of Macbeth was loudly cheered, and on being lifted up and told that I was called, I went on, and, with action earnestly and most empathically expressive of my sympathy with them and my feelings of gratefulness to them, I quitted the New York stage amid the acclamations of those before me. Going to my room I began without loss of time to undress, but with no feeling of fear or apprehension.... Suddenly we heard a volley of musketry: "Hark! what's that?" I asked. "The soldiers have fired." "My God!" I exclaimed. Another volley, and another! ... News came that several were killed; I was really insensible to the degree of danger in which I stood, and saw at once—there being no avoidance—there was nothing for it but to meet the worst with dignity, and so I stood prepared. . . .

Birmingham, June 26th.—Delighted—constantly did the thought, the sense of *delight* recur to me—to find myself in *England*, to find myself under the security of law and order, and free from the brutal and beastly savages who sought my life in the United States. Thank God! . . .

The Diaries of William Charles Macready, 1833–1851, 2 vols., edited by William Toynbee (New York: G. P. Putnam's Sons, 1912), 2:326–28, 331, 334, 405–7, 410–11, 421–26, 429.

⟿

Placards and Broadsides (MAY 10, 1849)

What began perhaps as the petty jealousies of two self-indulgent actors blossomed into a conflict of larger cultural symbolism. Local newspapers became the vehicle for rallying the faithful to the support of their favorite protagonist, just as they would in the arena of party politics. Newspapers, along with sensationalist writers and orators, helped shape the controversy between Forrest and Macready into a contest between the United States and England, between democrats and aristocrats, or between the rights of equality for working men and the forces of law and order. When Macready's first performance at Astor Place (May 7, 1849) was greeted by such an incredible din that the play could not be heard ("a dumb show") and Macready was driven from the stage under a volley of eggs, produce, and chairs, a group of businessmen and writers (including Washington Irving and Herman Melville) pleaded for Macready to continue his performances in a published appeal in all of the New York newspapers. Their desire for Macready to continue only intensified the determination of the working-class leaders who wished to drive Macready permanently from the stage. These leaders resorted to placards and broadsides posted on walls and poles throughout the city, inciting working men to riot on May 10 at the theatre on Astor Place.

PROBLEMS TO CONSIDER

1. How do these different forms of print express the conflicts of class, even if they do not always describe differences in economic wealth or status? What words in these documents are loaded with class meanings?
2. What is the relationship between class hostility and nationalistic sentiments in these posters?

THE GREAT THEATRICAL WAR.—MACREADY YET IN THE FIELD.—Mr. Macready is a man of pluck. He does not intend to give up the ship, at the occurrence of the first storm. An announcement has been made that he will appear to-night, at the Astor Place theatre. . . . He has been induced to try his strength and luck a second time, by an invitation signed by Washington Irving and a number of other gentlemen, . . . requesting him to finish his farewell engagement on the American stage, and assuring him that they and the friends of order in the country will support him against all rioters. . . .

On the other hand, we perceive that the opposite party, or the "b'hoys," the elementary mob of New York, the rowdies, rioters, or whatever else they may be called, are also determined to dispute this question, and fight the battle of Waterloo over again, or get well licked into the bargain. Here is the *pronunciamento* which was issued yesterday, by those chaps, and posted on vacant places and posts around town:—

☞ WORKING MEN,
SHALL
AMERICANS
OR
ENGLISH RULE
IN THIS CITY?
The Crew of the British steamer have Threatened all Americans who shall dare to express their opinions this night, at the ENGLISH ARISTOCRATIC OPERA HOUSE! We advocate no violence, but a free expression of opinion to all public men.
WORKINGMEN! FREEMEN!
STAND BY YOUR
LAWFUL RIGHTS!
AMERICAN COMMITTEE.

This is certainly a bold and daring step on the part of the rioters. . . . It is, therefore, a very curious question in law and government, as well as theatricals, which is now mooted, and which will be determined to-night at the Astor Place theatre. Shall an organized mob or the public authorities conquer? . . .

The respectable, literary, and philosophical portion of the city are determined that [Macready] shall appear again, and have the decision of Monday reversed to-night. If they are properly supported by the Mayor and police, and if there are courage and capacity in Washington Irving and his associates, to act with as much skill as they write, we rather think that Mr. Macready will succeed, and be permitted to play his engagement, and act before all those who wish to see him in his fine characters.

Under these views, we think that although there may be much excitement around town to-day, and a good deal of threatening about cer-

tain corners, we do not believe there will be any successful attempt to drive Macready from the stage to-night. The conduct of the rioters, on Monday night, has roused the feelings of order and propriety in the community, to such an extent as will render all attempts to riot utterly ineffectual and impracticable. The newspaper press, with some inconsiderable exceptions, is also very strongly in favor of order and justice in the business. Mr. Macready himself has committed no offence against an American audience, not even against Mr. Forrest, notwithstanding all that Forrest has written to the contrary. . . . The rioters will be well licked to-night, or the city again disgraced. Mr. Forrest ought to be satisfied—and so should the "b'hoys."

[Another placard posted around the city on the day of the riot.]

AMERICANS!
AROUSE! THE GREAT CRISIS
HAS COME!!
Decide now whether English
ARISTOCRATS!!!
AND
FOREIGN RULE!
shall triumph in this
AMERICA'S METROPOLIS,
or whether her own
SONS,
whose fathers once compelled the base-born miscreants to succumb, shall meanly lick the hand that strikes, and allow themselves to be deprived of the liberty of opinion
—so dear to every true American heart.
AMERICANS!
come out! and dare to own yourselves sons of the iron hearts of '76!!
AMERICA.

New York Herald, May 10, 1849; May 12, 1849.

⌘

☙ JIM CROW AND ZIP COON:
BLACKFACE MINSTRELSY IN AMERICA

On the night of the Astor Place riot, while Macready and Forrest took the stage at their respective theaters, these two actors were not the only choices for New Yorkers seeking to be entertained. City newspapers reported that a show of "Chinese Curiosities" was playing at the Chinese Museum and that "Mr. McCarthy's Irish Entertainment" was showing at Vauxhall Gardens. But the most widely available commercial entertainment that night was blackface minstrelsy. Three separate blackface minstrel troupes—Christy's Minstrels, New Orleans Serenaders, and Campbell's Minstrels—were playing that evening, featuring white men who performed songs, dances, mock operas, and comedy skits in grossly stereotypical costumes, makeup, and dialects intended to be caricatures of African Americans. At the very moment when rioters were shot in a dispute between Shakespearean actors, a new form of entertainment (the first uniquely American contribution to "show business") was rising to the highest heights of popularity among white working men in the United States.

When blackface minstrel shows emerged in the 1840s, comical or clown figures in face paint (even blackface) were not entirely new to the theater world. Sometime in the early nineteenth century, however, American theater companies began to add a caricatured Black-man to the stock characters of the American stage. In 1828, Thomas D. Rice gave the character a new twist after reportedly watching an old and disfigured black slave in Louisville limp his way through a little dance while singing a catchy tune. Rice's performance of "Jim Crow," with his own rendition of the shuffling dance, became an immediate sensation up and down the East Coast and across the Atlantic in England. "Jumping Jim Crow" made a celebrity out of Rice and stimulated white audiences' demand for more blackfaced performers; still, these performers remained one of many acts on a given night at the theater. In the early 1840s, four veteran blackface performers joined forces and created a show with nothing but blackface entertainment. They called themselves the Virginia Minstrels, and thus was the minstrel show born. Dozens, perhaps hundreds, of different minstrelsy troupes were formed over the next decade, sprouting up in every region of the country. Blackface minstrel shows dominated American commercial entertainment from 1840 to 1870 and stayed alive for many decades thereafter.

The legacy of blackface minstrelsy has pervaded American popular culture since the mid-nineteenth century. Blackface performance, with all of its crude and cruel racism, was at the foundation of the "show business" industry that Americans came to dominate by the twentieth century and export around the world. The seminal events in American movies, for example, were inextricably connected with blackface, including the first feature film to win middle-class favor (*The Birth of a Nation*), the first talking picture (*The Jazz Singer*), and even the most commercialized and universally recognized figure of the American screen, the adorable black rodent with the exaggerated white gloves—Mickey Mouse—who owed part of his conception in the 1920s to blackface caricature.

We should not forget, however, that blackface performers were "players" and that performers and the audience alike had a deeply felt desire to *play* at blackness in ways that ultimately confirmed their shared white racial identity. As such, African American cultural forms—instruments, rhythms, dances, and songs—became the expropriated property of white men. Many minstrel performers admitted that their most popular songs and dances were borrowed ("stolen" might be more accurate) from northern free blacks or southern slaves they had clandestinely observed. This would not be the last time that African American cultural forms were commandeered for the benefit of white performers; the co-opting of jazz into swing, or rhythm and blues into rock-and-roll, offers two of the most obvious examples.

The Autobiography of Mark Twain (1917)
MARK TWAIN

The minstrel show had a simple organization, a formula, that all minstrel troupes followed and audiences expected. It unleashed a comic wildness and improvised spontaneity that white audiences desired from the blackface disguise but which could always be constrained by the standard characters and form of the show. Mark Twain provides us with a lively and accurate portrayal of the typical minstrel show in his Autobiography. *Twain's obsession with the blackface minstrel show can even be glimpsed in his most famous novel,* Huckleberry Finn, *either in the "duke" and the "king" parody of Shakespeare (a frequent comic device within minstrel shows) or in the slave dialect that Twain places in the mouth of the runaway slave, whom he not surprisingly names Jim.*

PROBLEMS TO CONSIDER

1. Analyze how Twain discusses humor: What was such a "laughter-compeller" about the minstrel show? Who was in on the joke, and at whose expense?
2. What does Twain's description of a minstrel show reveal about the cultural and political appeal of this entertainment form?

Where now is Billy Rice? He was a joy to me and so were the other stars of the nigger show—Billy Birch, David Wambold, Backus and a delightful dozen of their brethren who made life a pleasure to me forty years ago. . . . But if I could have the nigger show back again in its pristine purity and perfection I should have but little further use for opera. It seems to me that to the elevated mind and the sensitive spirit the hand organ and the nigger show are a standard and a summit to whose rarefied altitude the other forms of musical art may not hope to reach.

I remember the first negro musical show I ever saw. It must have been in the early forties. It was a new institution. In our village of Hannibal *[Missouri]* we had not heard of it before and it burst upon us as a glad and stunning surprise.

The show remained a week and gave a performance every night. Church members did not attend these performances, but all the world-lings flocked to them and were enchanted. . . . The minstrels appeared with coal-black hands and faces and their clothing was a loud and extravagant burlesque of the clothing worn by the plantation slave of the time; not that the rags of the poor slave were burlesqued, for that would not have been possible; burlesque could have added nothing in the way of extravagance to the sorrowful accumulation of rags and patches which constituted his costume; it was the form and color of his dress that was burlesqued. Standing collars were in fashion in that day and the minstrel appeared in a collar which engulfed and hid half of his head and projected so far forward that he could hardly see sideways over its points. . . . His shoes were rusty and clumsy and cumbersome and five or six sizes too large for him. There were many variations upon this costume and they were all extravagant and were by many believed to be funny.

The minstrel used a very broad negro dialect; he used it competently and with easy facility and it was funny—delightfully and satisfyingly funny. However, there was one member of the minstrel troupe of those early days who was not extravagantly dressed and did not use the negro dialect. He was clothed in the faultless evening costume of the white society gentleman and used a stilted, courtly, artificial and painfully grammatical form of speech, which the innocent villagers took for the real thing as exhibited in high and citified society, and they vastly admired it and envied the man who could frame it on the spot without reflection and deliver it in this easy and fluent and artistic fashion. "Bones" sat at one end of the row of minstrels, "Banjo" sat at the other end, and the dainty gentleman just described sat in the middle. This middleman was the spokesman of the show. The neatness and elegance of his dress, the studied courtliness of his manners and speech and the shapeliness of his undoctored features made him a contrast to the rest of the troupe and particularly to "Bones"

and "Banjo." "Bones" and "Banjo" were the prime jokers and whatever funniness was to be gotten out of paint and exaggerated clothing they utilized to the limit. Their lips were thickened and lengthened with bright red paint to such a degree that their mouths resembled slices cut in a ripe watermelon.

The original ground plan of the minstrel show was maintained without change for a good many years. . . . The minstrels filed in and were received with a wholehearted welcome; they took their seats, each with his musical instrument in his hand; then the aristocrat in the middle began with a remark like this:

"I hope, gentlemen, I have the pleasure of seeing you in your accustomed excellent health and that everything has proceeded prosperously with you since last we had the good fortune to meet."

"Bones" would reply for himself and go on and tell about something in the nature of peculiarly good fortune that had lately fallen to his share; but in the midst of it he would be interrupted by "Banjo," who would throw doubt upon his statement of the matter; then a delightful jangle of assertion and contradiction would break out between the two; the quarrel would gather emphasis, the voices would grow louder and louder and more and more energetic and vindictive, and the two would rise and approach each other, shaking fists and instruments and threatening bloodshed, the courtly middleman meantime imploring them to preserve the peace and observe the proprieties—but all in vain, of course. Sometimes the quarrel would last five minutes, the two contestants shouting deadly threats in each other's faces with their noses not six inches apart, the house shrieking with laughter all the while at this happy and accurate imitation of the usual and familiar negro quarrel, then finally the pair of malignants would gradually back away from each other, each making impressive threats as to what was going to happen the "next time" each should have the misfortune to cross the other's path. . . .

The minstrel troupes had good voices and both their solos and their choruses were a delight to me as long as the negro show continued in existence. In the beginning the songs were rudely comic, such as "Buffalo Gals," "Camptown Races," "Old Dan Tucker," and so on; but a little later sentimental songs were introduced, such as "The Blue Juniata," "Sweet Ellen Bayne," "Nelly Bly," "A Life on the Ocean Wave," "The Larboard Watch," etc.

The minstrel show was born in the early forties and it had a prosperous career for about thirty-five years; then it degenerated into a variety show and was nearly all variety show with a negro act or two thrown in incidentally. The real negro show has been stone dead for thirty years. To my mind it was a thoroughly delightful thing and a most competent laughter-compeller and I am sorry it is gone.

The Autobiography of Mark Twain, edited by Charles Neider (1917; repr., New York: Harper & Brothers, 1959), 58–61.

᎐

Songs: "Jim Crow" (1828) and "Zip Coon" (1834)

Blackface minstrelsy was the popular entertainment during an era characterized as an age of democracy; blackface shows appealed to those sympathetic with democracy in general and the Democratic Party in particular. The vast majority of blackface performers, and the principal base of their audience, came from the northern urban working class and were almost entirely male. This was the entertainment that flourished in factory towns, in the haunts of urban unskilled laborers, and in mining and railroad camps. Blackface singers and their songs were unabashed proponents of western expansionism and "manifest destiny." Stephen Foster's "Oh! Susanna" (written for blackface minstrel shows) glorified westward conquest, was first performed the year that General Winfield Scott conquered Mexico City, and reached its greatest popularity during the California gold rush (also the year of the Astor Place riot). Minstrel performers also associated themselves and their performances with Democratic Party politics and frequently grafted Democratic and anti-Whig lyrics into minstrel songs. Minstrelsy's political viewpoint remained proslavery and anti-abolitionist, much like the northern Democratic Party.

PROBLEMS TO CONSIDER

1. How were democratic political issues introduced into minstrel songs? How did these songs function as politics in this era?
2. Explain what people saw as humorous in these songs. What did laughing at "Jim Crow" or "Zip Coon" do for the white, working-class audiences that flocked to see blackface shows?

"JIM CROW"

1.

Come listen to all you galls and boys,
I'm just from Tuckyhoe;
I'm goin to sing a leetle song,
My name's Jim Crow.

Chorus: Weel about, and turn about,
And do jis so;
Eb'ry time I weel about,
I jump Jim Crow.

2.

I'm a rorer on de fiddle,
An down in ole Virginny;
Dey say I play de skientific,
Like massa Pagganninny.

3.

I cut so many munky shines,
I dance de galloppade;
An wen I done, I res my head,
On shubble, hoe or spade.

4.

I met Miss Dina Scrub one day,
I gib her sich a buss *[kiss]*;
An den she turn an slap my face,
An make a mighty fuss. . . .

12.

O den I go to Washinton,
Wid bank memorial;
But find dey tork sich nonsense,
I spen my time wid Sal. . . .

14.

I teld dem dare be Ole Nick *[Nicholas Biddle,*
president of the Bank of the United States],
Wat wants de bank renew;
He gib me so much mony,
O lor, dey want it too.

15.

I den go to de Presiden *[Andrew Jackson]*.
He ax me wat I do;
I put de veto on de boot,
An nullefy de shoe.

"Jim Crow" (1828), Brown University, Harris Collection of American Poetry and Plays, *Series of Old American Songs*, edited by S. Foster Damon (Providence, R.I.: Brown University Library, 1936), no. 15.

"ZIP COON"

1.

O ole Zip Coon he is a larned skoler,
O ole Zip Coon he is a larned skoler,
O ole Zip Coon he is a larned skoler,
Sings possum up a gum tree an coony in a holler,
Possum up a gum tree, coony on a stump,
Possum up a gum tree, coony on a stump,
Possum up a gum tree, coony on a stump,
Den over dubble trubble, Zip Coon will jump.

. . .

4.

I tell you what will happin den, now bery soon.
De Nited States Bank will be blone to de
moon;
Dare General Jackson will him lampoon,
An de bery nex President will be Zip Coon. . . .

6.

Now mind wat you arter, you tarnel kritter
Crocket,
You shant go head widout old Zip, he is de boy
to block it;
Zip shall be President, *[Davy]* Crocket shall be
vice,
An den dey two togedder, will hab de tings nice.

7.

I hab many tings to tork about, but dont know
wich come first,
So here de toast to old Zip Coon, before he gin
to rust;
May he hab de pretty girls, like de King ob ole,
To sing dis song so many times, 'fore he turn
to mole.

"Zip Coon" (New York: Thomas Birch, 1834). Library of Congress, Music Division, American Nineteenth-Century Sheet Music. Digital ID: sm1834. http://hdl.loc.gov/loc .music/sm1834.360780.

๛

Opposition to Blackfaced Entertainment (1848–1849)
FREDERICK DOUGLASS

Free African Americans in the North could see past the masks of black paint into the racial politics of minstrelsy. Although blackface performers, with a wink of the eye, claimed to be authentically black and their performances based on close observations of African American "character," in reality they and their "authenticity" were elaborate fictions that confirmed the privileges of whiteness and espoused the ideology of a white working man's democracy. Black activists such as Frederick Douglass and Samuel Cornish employed the new technology behind affordable newspapers to get their antislavery message across and to expose the proslavery politics of blackface entertainment to burgeoning numbers of free blacks in northern cities.

PROBLEMS TO CONSIDER

1. On what grounds did Frederick Douglass criticize minstrel shows? What did he see as the biggest harm in blackface performances?
2. In the second document, how did Douglass respond to black actors who perform in blackface minstrel shows? What does this reveal about the nature and power of this entertainment in his day?

THE HUTCHINSON FAMILY. — HUNKERISM

October 27, 1848

The circumstances attending the visit paid last week to our youthful and beautiful city, by these mountain songsters, makes it deserving of special notice. The pro-slavery and narrow-souled demon had preceded them. . . . It had no taste for their soul-enlarging and heart-melting melody. To defeat what it could not enjoy, was its first object. The Hutchinsons were described as poor performers; their popularity was said to be on the wane; abolitionism had ruined them, &c. . . . In this mean work of detraction, we scarcely need say that the miserable dough-face who edits the *[Lewis]* Cass paper in this city . . . took the lead. . . . We believe he does not object to the "Virginia Minstrels," "Christy's Minstrels," the "Ethiopian Serenaders," or any of the filthy scum of white society, who have stolen from us a complexion denied to them by nature, in which to make money, and pander to the corrupt taste of their white fellow-citizens. Those performers are undoubtedly in harmony with his refined and elegant taste! Then those beautiful and highly sentimental songs which they sing, such as "Ole Zip Coon," "Jim Crow," "Ole Dan Tucker," "Jim along Josey," and a few other of such specimens of American musical genius, must spread over his spirit a charm, and awaken in his bosom a rapture only equalled by that celestial transport which thrills his noble heart on witnessing a TREMENDOUS SQUASH!

GAVITT'S ORIGINAL ETHIOPIAN SERENADERS

June 29, 1849

Partly from a love of music, and partly from curiosity to see persons of color exaggerating the peculiarities of their race, we were induced last evening to hear these Serenaders. The Company is said to be composed entirely of colored people; and it may be so. We observed, however, that they, too had recourse to the burnt cork and lamp black, the better to express their characters, and to produce uniformity of complexion. Their lips, too, were evidently painted, and otherwise exaggerated. Their singing generally was but an imitation of white performers, and not even a tolerable representation of the character of colored people. Their attempts at wit showed them to possess a plentiful lack of it, and gave their audience a very low idea of the sharpness and shrewdness of the race to which they belong. With two or three exceptions, they were a poor set, and will make themselves ridiculous wherever they may go. . . . We are not sure that our readers will approve of our mention of those persons, so strong must be their dislike to everything that seems to feed the flame of American prejudice against colored people; and in this they may be right; but we think otherwise. It is something gained, when the colored man in any form can appear before a white audience; and we think that even this company, with industry, application, and a proper cultivation of their taste, may yet be instrumental in removing the prejudice against our race. But they must cease to exaggerate the exaggerations of our enemies; and represent the colored man rather as he is, than as Ethiopian Minstrels usually represent him to be. They will *then* command the respect of both races; whereas *now*, they only shock the taste of the one, and provoke the disgust of the other.

The North Star (Rochester, N.Y.), October 27, 1848; June 29, 1849.

᠀

᠀ PARTISAN POLITICS AS POPULAR ENTERTAINMENT

By the mid-nineteenth century, American politics had assumed a new character. Gone were the deference to local elites and the aversion to organized party politics that had characterized politics in Jefferson's day. By the 1830s, Americans witnessed a full-blown democracy with a new breed of politicians and political campaigning, the centrality of political parties, and mass participation across the classes. In 1856, one Philadelphia newspaper observed that there were "ward meetings and mass meetings and committee meetings every day and every night," almost "every hour in the day and night." No sign offered more telling evidence of this sea change in political behavior than the turnout of voters on election days. Three out of every four eligible voters cast their ballots in presidential elections between the 1840s and 1870s. In contrast, less than half the electorate voted in elections before 1830. Political leaders borrowed the techniques that religious groups and reform societies had invented to get the masses mobilized, and they succeeded in making politics one of the principal forms of popular entertainment in nineteenth-century America. Citizens flocked to mass rallies and meetings, barbecues, picnics, and parades. They sat and listened for three or more hours to stump speeches and debates. Faithful members of political parties formed clubs and musical bands; they sang songs (many of which were written to popular minstrel tunes), marched in parades, gathered for pole raisings and bonfires, and produced an unending stream of written words for their favored party and candidates.

Nonetheless, these new techniques of mass political activity did not necessarily mean that every mid-nineteenth-century American was engaged in party politics or electoral campaigning. By today's standards, the United States at midcentury was not a truly democratic society. Although in general all *white* men could now vote, regardless of their property or wealth, women remained excluded from the privilege of voting and officeholding, slaves continued to be denied political rights, and northern free blacks were systematically stripped of their voting rights. Despite the exclusivity of American politics, and the political indifference that some eligible voters displayed even in that day, politics still became a popular form of entertainment within the public spaces of midcentury American life.

Old Virginia Days and Ways (1916)
SALLY McCARTY PLEASANTS

"What a Shame That Women *Can't Vote!"* (1856)
LYDIA MARIA CHILD

Until recently, historians have written about popular party politics as if the only participants were men. Certainly, only men cast ballots on election day, and no organized mass movement for women's suffrage existed during this era. In fact, the right to vote was not even at the top of the demands of the first woman's rights convention in Seneca Falls in 1848. But women were extremely active in party politics during the so-called age of democracy. Party activists realized that a great deal of excitement and energy could be generated by the inclusion of women in political rallies, meetings, and parades. The Whigs, whose women were more likely to have experience in public affairs from charity and reform societies, moved ahead more quickly in exploiting the resources of politicized women. The Whigs' victory in the presidential election of 1840, the campaign that also brought entertainment into American politics, was the beginning of widespread activism by white women in party politics. Sally McCarty Pleasants recollected the role of local Virginia women in those elections in the 1840s. By the middle of the 1850s, Lydia Maria Child, who was a professional writer and newspaper editor, joined the voices wondering when women would be able not just to participate in political rallies but to step up to the ballot box as well.

PROBLEMS TO CONSIDER

1. How was women's politics similar to and different from men's? What imagery and meanings were attached to the political banners recalled by Pleasants?
2. Are the tone and content of these two women's accounts similar or different? Would you characterize Child's political ideas and language as a reflection of her womanhood, her Republican Party loyalties, or her career as a moral reformer?

OLD VIRGINIA DAYS AND WAYS

My earliest recollections are of endless political discussions. My father was an ardent Whig, and our house was for many years headquarters for the party. Being an only child I was much indulged and was often allowed to sit up with my elders when I should have been in bed. Thus I became tolerantly conversant with the great questions of the day. I remember marching in a torchlight procession with a band of little girls during the Harrison and Van Buren campaign. Never was there device so impressive to a childish mind as the log-cabin with the coon on the roof. Windows were illuminated, every house was thrown open, cold collations were spread and punch and apple-toddy brewed without stint. And the stirring party airs that bands seem to have lost the trick of nowadays! . . .

The subject of a banner for our local delegation was discussed with great excitement. The ladies undertook to prepare it and when completed, all thought it a very splendid affair. . . . A local artist offered to paint upon it the Goddess of Liberty, that most popular of the dramatis personæ of the day, but as our tutelary deity is always depicted in very scant attire, an eminently respectable matron declared firmly that she would have nothing to do with a banner which flaunted the figure of a "nude female." Others were not wanting to echo this praiseworthy sentiment, so the committee decided to turn down the goddess. . . .

In those days as in these, election news was eagerly awaited. A tri-weekly stage plied between Washington and Leesburg, and on the brow of a very high hill which the stage had to cross, the townsfolk used to assemble to greet the messenger of the latest tidings. Local sentiment being strongly Whig, the driver, himself a Whig, would put up a small flag when he bore the news that a State had gone for General Harrison. Great was our excitement on the day when the stage displayed two flags instead of one and the eager throng were greeted with the announcement that New York and Pennsylvania had both declared for the Log-Cabin candidate.

Of Van Buren, the Democratic leader, whose nomination was supposed to be due to the influence of Andrew Jackson, it was said and sung that he had ridden into the White House "On the back of Andrew Jack." Another campaign song had the refrain, "Little Van's a used up man"—a prediction fully justified by the outcome. . . .

In those days the interest in politics was so keen that public events affected people as vitally as their own private affairs. I was only seven years old at the time, but the disappointment and gloom of my elders impressed my youthful

spirits to such a degree that when I was asked to dance that night at the "hop" at the White Sulphur Springs, I declined, giving as my reason that "Tyler had vetoed the Bank Bill." . . .

But the excitement of the Harrison campaign by no means equaled that of the succeeding one in which the opposing candidates were Henry Clay and James K. Polk. Again the little town of Leesburg was the scene of Whig celebrations and again the Loudoun Whigs rallied around the "Tombstone" banner at barbecues, glee clubs and stump speeches. The procession on Barbecue Day was headed by a great wagon containing fourteen girls, thirteen of whom, robed in white and crowned with flowers, bore the insignia of the States which they symbolized, while the fourteenth, the tallest and most beautiful, was dressed in flags and a liberty cap to represent the Union.

. . . Even now, after the lapse of seventy years, my pulses throb and my eyes fill as soon of the strains recur to me:

> Here's to you, Henry Clay,
>   Here's to you, my noble soul,
> Here's to you with right good will,
>   And you shall be the next President,
> The chair of State to fill;
>   Here's to you, Henry Clay!

. . . As glees and songs played a very important part in political campaigns of the day, it was a popular grievance, at the nomination of Clay and Frelinghuysen, that no rhyme could be found for the name of the second party on the ticket. My father overcame this difficulty when rising at a banquet he proposed this toast:

> The cure for Loco-Foco pizen
> ⁄ Is Henry Clay and Frelinghuysen.

Needless to say it was drunk with loud acclaim.

Sally McCarty Pleasants, *Old Virginia Days and Ways: Reminiscences of Mrs. Sally McCarty Pleasants*, edited by Lucy Lee Pleasants (Menasha, Wis.: George Banta Publishing, 1916), 6–13.

"WHAT A SHAME THAT *WOMEN* CAN'T VOTE!"

To Sarah Shaw

Wayland, Aug. 3d, 1856.

My very Dear Friend,

The recent public events have also greatly discouraged me. To have labored so *long* against slavery, and yet to see it always triumphant! The outrage upon Charles Sumner *[In 1856, Sumner, the U.S. Senator from Massachusetts, was beaten over the head with a cane by Rep. Preston Brooks from South Carolina on the floor of the Senate.]* made me literally ill for several days. . . . I *never* was one of those who knew how to serve the Lord by standing and waiting; and to stand and wait *then*! It almost drove me mad. And that miserable Faneuil Hall Meeting! . . . Those Boston respectables, I tell you they are *criminals*. Greater criminals than those who merely destroy *physical* life; for they systematically blind the *minds* of the people, and stagnate their *moral energies*. . . . But I am more hopeful. *Such* a man as Charles Sumner *will* not bleed and suffer in vain! Those noble martyrs of liberty in Kansas will prove missionary ghosts, walking through the land, rousing the nation from its guilty slumbers. Our hopes, like yours, rest on Fremont. I would almost lay down my life to have him elected. There never has been such a crisis since we were a nation. If the Slave-Power is checked *now*, it will *never* regain its strength. If it is *not* checked, civil war is inevitable; and, with all my horror of bloodshed, I could be better resigned to that great calamity, than to endure the tyranny that has so long trampled on us. I do believe the North will not, *this* time, fall asleep again, after shaking her mane and growling a little. . . . I see that Garrison charges Sam J. May with being unfaithful to his peace-principles, in wishing to have Fremont elected. To *me*, it seems otherwise. Because I would *avert* war, I desire to have Fremont victorious. And "our Jessie," *[i.e., Jessie Frémont, wife of John Frémont]* bless her noble soul! Is n't it pleasant to have a woman spontaneously recognized as a moral influence in public affairs? There's *meaning* in that fact.

I saw by the papers that Mr. Curtis was in the field, and I rejoiced to know he was devoting his brilliant talents and generous sympathies to so noble a purpose. I envy him, I want to mount the rostrum myself. I have such a fire burning in my soul, that it seems to me I could pour forth a stream of lava, that would bury all the *respectable* servilities, and all the *mob* servilities, as deep as Pompeii; so that it would be an enormous labor ever to dig up the skeletons of their memories. . . .

We also talk of little else but Kansas and Fremont. Mr. Child thinks his chance of success is great, *provided* fraud can be kept away from the ballot-boxes. Our elections, for some time past, have been systematically managed by bribery and trickery. The idea of *glass* ballot-boxes seems to me a good one. What a shame that *women* can't vote! We'd carry "our Jessie" into the White House on our shoulders; *would* n't we? Never mind! Wait a while! Women-stock's rising in the market. I shall not live to see women vote; but I'll come and *rap* at the ballot-box. Wont *you*? I never was bitten by politics before; but such mighty issues are depending on *this* election, that I cannot be indifferent. Backward or forward the car of human freedom *must* roll. It cannot stand still.

Lydia Maria Child: Selected Letters, 1817–1880, edited by Milton Meltzer and Patricia G. Holland (Amherst: University of Massachusetts Press, 1982), 289–91.

☙

Struggles and Triumphs (1869)

P. T. BARNUM

By the time Abraham Lincoln was put forward as the presidential candidate for the fast-growing Republican Party in 1860, parades were already a common feature of electoral campaigning; but the 1860 campaign brought this form of public display to new heights. Republican Party activists established marching clubs — Wide-Awake associations — to organize torch-light parades to rally Lincoln's supporters. It has been estimated that more than a quarter of a million people witnessed a Republican parade in New York City during the 1860 campaign. The great "humbug" artist, P. T. Barnum, was not above using his unique skills of deception in the realm of politics. In his autobiography, Barnum describes the practical joke he played on a neighbor during a Wide-Awake parade during the campaign of 1860.

PROBLEMS TO CONSIDER

1. What does Barnum's story reveal about the relationship between theatrical performance and American politics? Was deception a positive political value?
2. Was Barnum's humor reminiscent of other expressions of entertainment and politics during this era? Why did the political issues seem less important to Barnum than they were to Lydia Maria Child a few years earlier?

I began my political life as a Democrat, and my newspaper, the "Herald of Freedom," was a Jackson-Democratic journal. . . . The Kansas strifes, in 1854, shook my faith in my party, though I continued to call myself a Democrat, often declaring that if I thought there was a drop of blood in me that was not Democratic, I would let it out if I had to cut the jugular vein. When, however, secession threatened in 1860, I thought it was time for a "new departure," and I identified myself with the Republican party.

During the active and exciting political campaign of 1860, which resulted in Mr. Lincoln's first election to the presidency, it will be remembered that "Wide-Awake" associations, with their uniforms, torches, and processions, were organized in nearly every city, town, and village throughout the North. Arriving at Bridgeport from New York at five o'clock one afternoon, I was informed that the Wide-Awakes were to parade that evening and intended to march out to Lindencroft. So I ordered two boxes of sperm

candles, and prepared for a general illumination of every window in the front of my house. Many of my neighbors, including several Democrats, came to Lindencroft in the evening to witness the illumination and see the Wide-Awake procession. My nearest neighbor, Mr. T., was a strong Democrat, and before he came to my house, he ordered his servants to stay in the basement, and not to show a light above ground, thus intending to prove his Democratic convictions and conclusions by the darkness of his premises; and so, while Lindencroft was all ablaze with a flood of light, the next house was as black as a coal-hole.

My neighbor Mr. James D. Johnson was also a Democrat, but I knew he would not spoil a good joke for the sake of politics, and I asked him to engage the attention of Mr. and Mrs. T., and to keep their faces turned towards Bridgeport and the approaching procession, the light of whose torches could already be seen in the distance, while another Democratic friend, Mr.

George A. Wells, and I, ran over and illuminated Mr. T.'s house. This we did with great success, completing our work five minutes before the procession arrived. As the Wide-Awakes turned into my grounds and saw that the house of Mr. T. was brilliantly illuminated, they concluded that he had become a sudden convert to Republicanism, and gave three rousing cheers for him. Hearing his name thus cheered and wondering at the cause, he happened to turn and see that his house was lighted up from basement to attic, and uttering a single profane ejaculation, he rushed for home. He was not able, however, to put out the lights till the Wide-Awakes had gone on their way rejoicing under the impression that one more Republican had been added to their ranks.

P. T. Barnum, *Struggles and Triumphs: or, The Life of P. T. Barnum, Written by Himself*, 2 vols., edited by George S. Bryan (New York: A. A. Knopf, 1927), 2:565–66.

✌

CHAPTER 9

Sectional Conflict and Civil War: 1850–1865

IN MAY 1861, just weeks after the attack on Fort Sumter that began the Civil War, and while politicians in the North and South predicted a brief and speedy war, Frederick Douglass issued a prophetic warning to the nation. "We have sown the wind, only to reap the whirlwind," he wrote. "The Republic has put one end of the chain upon the ankle of the bondman, and the other end about its own neck. . . . The land is now to weep and howl, amid ten thousand desolations brought upon it by the sins of two centuries." Many Americans shared with Douglass a moral and religious interpretation of this great conflict, yet their definitions of the moral and religious varied widely.

The American Civil War was the nation's great tragedy, its defining moment, a nationalist ending from a separatist beginning. In its time, the Civil War meant different things to different people, much as it still does today. For some, it was a fiery trial or a cleansing tragedy necessary for national regeneration; for others, it signaled the loss of love, youth, body, or family; for still others, it represented a valiant lost cause or the disastrous failings of misguided fanatics. And after 1863, a war to separate from, or to preserve, the Union became a war that would mean freedom for slaves. By anyone's measurement, it was a colossal moment of death and destruction. One of every five soldiers who fought in this war died in it; there were more than 600,000 deaths in all, exceeding the total American deaths in all U.S. wars combined through Vietnam. By the war's end, three-fourths of the white military-aged men of the South had served in the army, and half of those were either wounded, captured, killed, or dead from wartime disease. For more than a generation, an armless or legless veteran could be found in most communities, and nearly every family counted among its kin one of the honored dead.

The Civil War also exposed deep cultural divisions between the sections, and it was fought not only with armaments but with the weapons of cultural expression as well. As one historian recently observed: "Popular culture has played a critical role in preparing for, fighting, and remembering the Civil War; the two were entwined long before the war and long after it." The enormous popularity of battlefield reenactments, the continuing controversies over Confederate flags, and the blockbuster impact of D. W. Griffith's *The Birth of a Nation*, Margaret Mitchell's *Gone with the Wind*, or Ken Burns's *The Civil War*, at different moments in the twentieth century, all attest to the continuing power of popular culture as a means of explaining the Civil War. Americans then and now turned to popular forms of cultural expression, such as novels, songs, sermons, essays, and cartoons, to interpret and explain the meanings of this great national crisis.

∿ Uncle Tom's Cabin *and Anti–Uncle Tom Novels* ∿

"So you're the little lady who started this big war?" Abraham Lincoln supposedly joked when he welcomed Harriet Beecher Stowe to the White House less than a month before he issued the Emancipation Proclamation. Ten years earlier, Stowe's *Uncle Tom's Cabin* had created a firestorm throughout the nation, aggravating the sectional tensions that ultimately rent the nation in two. Within months of its release, *Uncle Tom's Cabin* became the best-selling book of its century. Theatrical productions then made the novel come alive for millions more. Since few northerners by 1850 knew anything firsthand about southern slavery, Stowe's novel offered a powerful imaginary vision of the South and slavery. A white woman, who had herself spent no more than a few hours once in Kentucky, fanned the fires of sectional discord that white politicians, north and south, could not extinguish. "Here was a popular culture with consequences," one historian recently remarked.

Uncle Tom's Cabin was also a sentimental novel, perhaps that genre's quintessential example. Like all sentimental novels, it was written by, for, and about women. Its power for readers lies in shared assumptions about family, religion, and emotions that correspond with already circulating narratives and their meanings. A child's death, for example, might remind readers of the emotional feelings of Christ's death, or perhaps the countless other references in popular writing that present children (and women) as uniquely capable of Christ-like acts of redemption. The novel's immense popularity reminds us again to examine critically the role of women and the conventions of gender when analyzing events prior to and throughout the American Civil War.

Uncle Tom's Cabin (1852)
HARRIET BEECHER STOWE

Stowe penned Uncle Tom's Cabin *as a serial story: after ten months of weekly install-ments in the abolitionist newspaper* The National Era, *the novel was then re-released in 1852 to a larger audience as a book. The novel has two separate plots. The first deals with Uncle Tom, a slave sold away from his wife and children in Kentucky and taken to New Orleans. There he is purchased by Augustine St. Clare after Tom saves the life of St. Clare's daughter, Little Eva, the archetype for all other sentimental characters of child-hood piety and death. Upon Eva's and St. Clare's deaths, Tom is sold to a transplanted New England plantation owner, Simon Legree, who abuses his slaves and eventually murders Tom. The other plot traces the freedom quest of George and Eliza Harris (slaves of mixed, almost white, ancestry), including Eliza's dramatic escape across the ice-covered Ohio River with slave catchers in hot pursuit of her little son Harry. One winter Sunday while awaiting communion in church, Stowe (as her son remembered) had a vision in which she saw the scene of Uncle Tom's death, the defining sentimental moment of the novel. She immediately returned home and wrote that scene; she then read it to her chil-dren, who broke into convulsions of tears. Even southern critics who described the events in the scene as an injustice still insisted they were a distortion of southern plantation life. Reproduced here is Stowe's chapter on Tom's death; Tom knows that Cassy and Emme-line, two of Legree's women slaves (and the objects of Legree's lust), are hiding in the attic of his plantation house, but Tom refuses to betray them.*

PROBLEMS TO CONSIDER

1. What emotions did Stowe wish to evoke from her readers, and what role did race play in appeals to her readers' sympathy? How would those emotional reac-tions have contributed to the sectional conflict?
2. Describe and explain the religious symbolism Stowe employed to represent Tom and his killers. What is the significance of depicting a slave in this way? And how would this reflect on southern slaveholders, northern white readers, or African Americans in general?

CHAPTER 40: THE MARTYR

The escape of Cassy and Emmeline irritated the before surly temper of Legree to the last degree; and his fury, as was to be expected, fell upon the defenceless head of Tom. When he hurriedly announced the tidings among his hands, there was a sudden light in Tom's eye, a sudden up-raising of his hands, that did not escape him. He saw that he did not join the muster of the pur-suers. He thought of forcing him to do it; but, having had, of old, experience of his inflexibility when commanded to take part in any deed of inhumanity, he would not, in his hurry, stop to enter into any conflict with him.

Tom, therefore, remained behind, with a few who had learned of him to pray, and offered up prayers for the escape of the fugitives.

When Legree returned, baffled and disap-pointed, all the long-working hatred of his soul towards his slave began to gather in a deadly and desperate form. Had not this man braved him,—steadily, powerfully, resistlessly,—ever since he bought him? Was there not a spirit in him which, silent as it was, burned on him like the fires of perdition?

"I *hate* him!" said Legree, that night, as he sat up in his bed; "I *hate* him! And isn't he MINE? Can't I do what I like with him? Who's to hinder, I wonder?" And Legree clenched his fist, and shook it, as if he had something in his hands that he could rend in pieces.

But, then, Tom was a faithful, valuable servant; and, although Legree hated him the more for that, yet the consideration was still somewhat of a restraint to him.

The next morning, he determined to say nothing, as yet; to assemble a party, from some neighboring plantations, with dogs and guns; to surround the swamp, and go about the hunt systematically. If it succeeded, well and good; if not, he would summon Tom before him, and—his teeth clenched and his blood boiled—*then* he would break the fellow down, or—there was a dire inward whisper, to which his soul assented.

Ye say that the *interest* of the master is a sufficient safeguard for the slave. In the fury of man's mad will, he will wittingly, and with open eye, sell his own soul to the devil to gain his ends; and will he be more careful of his neighbor's body?

"Well," said Cassy, the next day, from the garret, as she reconnoitred through the knothole, "the hunt's going to begin again, to-day!" . . .

Cassy placed her ear at the knot-hole; and, as the morning air blew directly towards the house, she could overhear a good deal of the conversation. A grave sneer overcast the dark, severe gravity of her face, as she listened, and heard them divide out the ground, discuss the rival merits of the dogs, give orders about firing, and the treatment of each, in case of capture.

Cassy drew back; and, clasping her hands, looked upward, and said, "O, great Almighty God! we are *all* sinners; but what have we done, more than all the rest of the world, that we should be treated so?"

There was a terrible earnestness in her face and voice, as she spoke.

"If it wasn't for *you*, child," she said, looking at Emmeline, "I'd *go* out to them; and I'd thank any one of them that *would* shoot me down; for what use will freedom be to me? Can it give me back my children, or make me what I used to be?"

Emmeline, in her child-like simplicity, was half afraid of the dark moods of Cassy. She looked perplexed, but made no answer. She only took her hand, with a gentle, caressing movement.

"Don't!" said Cassy, trying to draw it away; "you'll get me to loving you; and I never mean to love anything, again!"

"Poor Cassy!" said Emmeline, "don't feel so! If the Lord gives us liberty, perhaps he'll give you back your daughter; at any rate, I'll be like a daughter to you. I know I'll never see my poor old mother again! I shall love you, Cassy, whether you love me or not!"

The gentle, child-like spirit conquered. Cassy sat down by her, put her arm round her neck, stroked her soft, brown hair; and Emmeline then wondered at the beauty of her magnificent eyes, now soft with tears. . . .

The hunt was long, animated, and thorough, but unsuccessful; and, with grave, ironic exultation, Cassy looked down on Legree, as, weary and dispirited, he alighted from his horse.

"Now, Quimbo," said Legree, as he stretched himself down in the sitting-room, "you jest go and walk that Tom up here, right away! The old cuss is at the bottom of this yer whole matter; and I'll have it out of his old black hide, or I'll know the reason why!"

Sambo and Quimbo, both, though hating each other, were joined in one mind by a no less cordial hatred of Tom. . . .

Tom heard the message with a forewarning heart; for he knew all the plan of the fugitives' escape, and the place of their present concealment;—he knew the deadly character of the man he had to deal with, and his despotic power. But he felt strong in God to meet death, rather than betray the helpless.

He sat his basket down by the row, and, looking up, said, "Into thy hands I commend my spirit! Thou hast redeemed me, oh Lord God of truth!"

and then quietly yielded himself to the rough, brutal grasp with which Quimbo seized him.

"Ay, ay!" said the giant, as he dragged him along; "ye'll cotch it, now! I'll boun' Mas'r's back's up *high*! No sneaking out, now! Tell ye, ye'll get it, and no mistake! See how ye'll look, now, helpin' Mas'r's niggers to run away! See what ye'll get!"

The savage words none of them reached that ear!—a higher voice there was saying, "Fear not them that kill the body, and, after that, have no more than they can do." Nerve and bone of that poor man's body vibrated to those words, as if touched by the finger of God; and he felt the strength of a thousand souls in one. . . . His soul throbbed,—his home was in sight,—and the hour of release seemed at hand.

"Well, Tom!" said Legree, walking up, and seizing him grimly by the collar of his coat, and speaking through his teeth, in a paroxysm of determined rage, "do you know I've made up my mind to KILL you?"

"It's very likely, Mas'r," said Tom, calmly.

"I *have*," said Legree, with grim, terrible calmness, "*done—just—that—thing*, Tom, unless you'll tell me what you know about these yer gals!"

Tom stood silent.

"D' ye hear?" said Legree, stamping, with a roar, like that of an incensed lion. "Speak!"

"*I han't got nothing to tell, Mas'r*," said Tom, with a slow, firm, deliberate utterance.

"Do you dare to tell me, ye old black Christian, ye don't *know*?" said Legree.

Tom was silent.

"Speak!" thundered Legree, striking him furiously. "Do you know anything?"

"I know, Mas'r; but I can't tell anything. *I can die!*"

Legree drew in a long breath; and, suppressing his rage, took Tom by the arm, and, approaching his face almost to his, said, in a terrible voice, "Hark 'e, Tom!—ye think, 'cause I've let you off before, I don't mean what I say; but, this time, I've *made up my mind*, and counted the cost. You've always stood it out agin' me: now, I'll *conquer ye, or kill ye!*—one or t' other. I'll count every drop of blood there is in you, and take 'em, one by one, till ye give up!"

Tom looked up to his master, and answered, "Mas'r, if you was sick, or in trouble, or dying, and I could save ye, I'd *give* ye my heart's blood; and, if taking every drop of blood in this poor old body would save your precious soul, I'd give 'em freely, as the Lord gave his for me. O, Mas'r! don't bring this great sin on your soul! It will hurt you more than 't will me! Do the worst you can, my troubles'll be over soon; but, if ye don't repent, yours won't *never* end!"

Like a strange snatch of heavenly music, heard in the lull of a tempest, this burst of feeling made a moment's blank pause. Legree stood aghast, and looked at Tom; and there was such a silence, that the tick of the old clock could be heard, measuring, with silent touch, the last moments of mercy and probation to that hardened heart.

It was but a moment. There was one hesitating pause,—one irresolute, relenting thrill,—and the spirit of evil came back, with seven-fold vehemence; and Legree, foaming with rage, smote his victim to the ground.

Scenes of blood and cruelty are shocking to our ear and heart. What man has nerve to do, man has not nerve to hear. What brother-man and brother-Christian must suffer, cannot be told us, even in our secret chamber, it so harrows up the soul! And yet, oh my country! these things are done under the shadow of thy laws! O, Christ! thy church sees them, almost in silence!

But, of old, there was One whose suffering changed an instrument of torture, degradation and shame, into a symbol of glory, honor, and immortal life; and, where His spirit is, neither degrading stripes, nor blood, nor insults, can make the Christian's last struggle less than glorious.

Was he alone, that long night, whose brave, loving spirit was bearing up, in that old shed, against buffeting and brutal stripes?

Nay! There stood by him ONE,—seen by him alone,—"like unto the Son of God."...

"He's most gone, Mas'r," said Sambo, touched, in spite of himself, by the patience of his victim.

"Pay away, till he gives up! Give it to him!—give it to him!" shouted Legree. "I'll take every drop of blood he has, unless he confesses!"

Tom opened his eyes, and looked upon his master. "Ye poor miserable critter!" he said, "there an't no more ye can do! I forgive ye, with all my soul!" and he fainted entirely away.

"I b'lieve, my soul, he's done for, finally," said Legree, stepping forward, to look at him. "Yes, he is! Well, his mouth's shut up, at last,—that's one comfort!"

Yes, Legree; but who shall shut up that voice in thy soul? that soul, past repentance, past prayer, past hope, in whom the fire that never shall be quenched is already burning!

Yet Tom was not quite gone. His wondrous words and pious prayers had struck upon the hearts of the imbruted blacks, who had been the instruments of cruelty upon him; and, the instant Legree withdrew, they took him down, and, in their ignorance, sought to call him back to life,—as if *that* were any favor to him.

"Sartin, we's been doin' a drefful wicked thing!" said Sambo; "hopes Mas'r 'll have to 'count for it, and not we."...

"O, Tom!" said Quimbo, "we's been awful wicked to ye!"

"I forgive ye, with all my heart!" said Tom, faintly.

"O, Tom! do tell us who is *Jesus*, anyhow?" said Sambo;—"Jesus, that's been a standin' by you so, all this night!—Who is he?"

The word roused the failing, fainting spirit. He poured forth a few energetic sentences of that wondrous One,—his life, his death, his everlasting presence, and power to save.

They wept,—both the two savage men.

"Why didn't I never hear this before?" said Sambo; "but I do believe!—I can't help it! Lord Jesus, have mercy on us!"

"Poor critters!" said Tom, "I'd be willing to bar' all I have, if it'll only bring ye to Christ! O, Lord! give me these two more souls, I pray!"

That prayer was answered!

Harriet Beecher Stowe, *Uncle Tom's Cabin; or, Life Among the Lowly*, 2 vols. (Boston: John P. Jewett & Co., 1852), 2:267–75.

ॐ

North and South; or, Slavery and Its Contrasts (1852)
CAROLINE E. RUSH

Ellen; or, the Fanatic's Daughter (1860)
MRS. V. G. COWDIN

While readers throughout the northern United States and Europe could not stop turning the pages of Uncle Tom's Cabin *and audiences attended sold-out dramatic performances of the novel, many white southerners expressed outrage at this fictional representation of southern life. The attacks on Harriet Beecher Stowe were vicious and personal. She was described as a "vile wretch in petticoats" by one southern reviewer, and a southern clergyman called her "as ugly as Original sin—an abomination in the eyes of civilized people," while branding the novel "a filthy, lying book." Still others thought it necessary to counter Stowe's assault with a fictional rejoinder. With their own literary form, the plantation romance (see chapter 6), at their disposal, southern writers, along with a number of proslavery northerners, tried to mimic the fictional successes of Stowe. Dozens of "anti–Uncle Tom's Cabin" novels were published in both the North and the South between 1852 and the outbreak of the Civil War. These novels could never be described as great fiction. Some of the authors were professional writers, but others had never written before; and all of them abandoned their narratives for long stretches, slipping into passages that resembled the rantings of politicians. The following documents offer two examples of "anti–Uncle Tom" novels penned by white women writers, the first from the North and the second from the South. Caroline Rush's* North and South *illustrates the belligerent railings common in these novels, and Mrs. V. G. Cowdin's* Ellen; or, the Fanatic's Daughter *exhibits the manner in which these novels inverted the representations of slaves and abolitionists that we find in Stowe's fiction.*

PROBLEMS TO CONSIDER

1. Compare the emotions that these authors sought to stimulate in their readers with Stowe's emotional appeals. Did they understand and use race in the same way as Stowe did?
2. Which fictional representation of slaves was more believable, or possessed greater cultural power, *Uncle Tom's Cabin* or the anti–Uncle Tom novels?

NORTH AND SOUTH

I do not for a moment imagine that any thing I can write can equal in style, logic or depth, that far-famed work of Mrs. Stowe, which has aroused a nation's sympathy. "Uncle Tom's Cabin" is a highly wrought fiction, abounding in touching incidents, and clothed with that dangerous sophistry, that indeed looks so much like truth, that it is often mistaken for it. I know not if Mrs. Stowe actually believes what she asserts: I presume she does, but it is very evident she knows little or nothing of Slavery as it really exists in the South, and still less can she comprehend or sympathise with the Slavery of the North. Perhaps she may go so far as to deny its existence in these, our glorious Northern States; she may say there are no slaves around her own home; and in all the great cities of the North, who are born and suffer and die; who toil their weary way from the cradle to the grave, and whose worn, emaciated frames, at last give way in the struggle, and sink into the quiet rest never known in life. . . .

Murder is a very terrible thing. Nothing can excuse it. God gives life, and he alone should take it: but is murder never committed saving and only by such savage creatures as had "Uncle Tom" whipped to death. Have we no cases of murder here at the North, in the midst of our enlightened communities. . . . In a word, oh! free and happy citizens of the North, have you no slaves in your midst. Have you no poor wretched, degraded fellow creatures around you, who drag out a miserable life from day to day; who pine and sicken and starve in loathsome cellars, in filthy courts and vile alleys, and who, work as hard as they may by night as well as day, yet cannot provide themselves with bread. If you will read these pages attentively, I will show you some few pictures of the slavery that exists here. . . .

But to return to the point from which I started: murder! I should like to draw upon the memory of the public a little, and see if they can recall the case which a short time ago appeared in most of our Northern papers; where a so-called lady whipped severely a little bound girl she had living with her, and then, after the whipping, shut her up in a room at the top of the house for many days without food, and when at last she was released with life just remaining in her, she died in a few hours of starvation. What was this but murder, and yet the monster who perpetrated it, was never brought to justice. . . .

Impress this picture on your mind, oh! reader. Compare it with the highly wrought scenes of "Uncle Tom's Cabin." Remember that "Uncle Tom" was a hardy, strong, and powerful negro, while this poor victim was a helpless, defenceless child; of the same colour as yourself, and surely not the less to be pitied on that account. Do you think I have been telling you an idle tale, or repeating an isolated fact. Let the thousands of slender fragile children, in each of our great cities, children covered with the coarsest garments; their little feet bare; their backs bowed over with the weight of the heavy burthens they have to carry; their features sharp and pinched; let these poor children answer for me: let their sorrows plead for my truth. Let their utter wretchedness convince the wonder-working abolitionists, that justice, as well as charity, begins at home. I would never refuse to do a kind action for a person because that person happened to be black, but I would far rather relieve the suffering of my own colour, because I believe they stand far more in need of relief, and are far less apt to be relieved. I find too, in my own race, more honour, honesty, affection, virtue, every thing in fact, that tends to exalt the mind, and purify the character. . . .

I would have you contrast all I have told you of this gentle girl, and her hard fate, her intense sufferings and uncomplaining misery, with the picture of "Uncle Tom," that abused and pious, but imaginary colored individual, for whom a nation's sympathy has been awakened. I do not believe such a being ever existed, save in the realms of fancy, but the poor white slave . . . with all her starving misery, adds to the history of her sufferings, that most charming of all attributes — "truth." We shall see whether "the broad-chested, powerful negro," or the fragile,

delicate girl, with her pure white face, is most entitled to your sympathy and tears. . . . God forbid that you should waste your sympathies on the slaves of the South, and by your indiscreet conduct and mad fanaticism, tighten their chains, and embitter the hearts of their masters against you. . . . Abolish slavery at the North; — the slavery of sewing women, and of the apprentice and bound girl system. . . .

Caroline E. Rush, *North and South; or, Slavery and Its Contrasts* (Philadelphia: Crissy & Markley, 1852; repr., New York: Negro Universities Press, 1968), 9–14, 127–30.

ELLEN

Jack was one of the favorite house servants of Major Wallace. He was verging upon twenty, and was what is usually termed "a proud negro." He was not possessed of much intellect, but an unusual share of self-esteem. . . . He was the son of "Uncle Peter," the oldest and one of the most faithful servants on the plantation. . . .

The fact was, Uncle Peter had once spent some months in New-York city. He had been induced by abolitionists to leave his old master, the father of Major Wallace, who was, at the time, travelling for his health, and had taken Peter, then a young man, along with him. Ever since that period Uncle Peter's opinion of the North and purgatory amounted to much the same thing; and when out of humor with any of his fellow servants, his most vindictive wish was, that his master would send the offenders North and set them free. . . .

One day, when called to his dinner, Jack walked into the room with a very dignified air, and surveying the table, turned off with contempt, saying, there was nothing on it he could eat.

"What's dat you say," cried Uncle Peter. "Well, just get your master to send you North; I guess you will find your appetite there — ha, ha, ha!" and the old man laughed until the tears ran down his cheeks. "Look here, boy," he continued, "look on dis table; here is bread, meat, potatoes, molasses, and buttermilk, yet you can't find nothin' to eat. Well, go North, dat's all de advice I can give you."

"Dat's just where I want to go," said Jack, pertly; "I want to be free, and 'sociate wid de ladies and gentlemen of de North."

"Oh, dat's your notion, is it?" said Uncle Peter. "Well, Jack, I once was as foolish as you is, and tuck a notion to be free, and all dat sort of thing, but bless de Lord for his goodness—he brung me safe through my trials. Set right down here, boy, and let me tell you all about my visit to de great city of New-York."

"You see, Jack," said Uncle Peter, "I went travelling wid old master. . . . We got on to de North widout much trouble, considerin', and I tell you dey has fine things dare sure—but dat don't do de nigger no good. I was mighty well pleased as long as old master stayed, for den I fared fine; but some abolitions and free niggers tuck me in hand, and would hab me free whedder or no. I kep on tellin' dem I was free enough for anybody to be, but dey would keep after me till I guv it up, and stole away one night from old master. Lor! I did feel so mean when I cum to think how kind he had always bin to me. De abolitions treated me right well for a little while, till old master was clean out ob sight—den dey told me to go to work and make a livin'. Well, I 'spected to do dat, but sich work as I had to do! Lor, don't talk! and de little bit of pay—not worth looking at. I tell you, boy, I can sell a pint of pinders here for more dan I could make in a day by my work in dat place. . . . I was hungry all de time, and fell away to skin and bones. I had no good close [*clothes*] to wear, . . . and [they] kept me workin', workin' for dem all day long and half de night. On Chrismus day, for a wonder, dey let me off from workin', and one free black fellow give me a shillin'. 'Now,' says he, 'don't you feel rich? I reckon you neber had so much money to spend in your life!'

"'You is mighty mistaken,' says I. 'Many a time has I had fifty or sixty dollars at a time in my pocket—my own money, made by sellin' my crops.' He just busted out laughin' in my face, 'and,' says he, 'if dat is true, all I have to say, is dat you was a mighty great fool for stayin' here.' . . .

"One day I had walked about till I was tired lookin' for some work; at last I cum to de wharf where de boats was cummin' in and goin' out, jist as fast as could be, so I went aboard a fine steamer, and asked de captin' to set me to work.

"'Why, man,' says he, 'I have taken on my load, and shall start back to New-Orleans in an hour or so.'

"'New-Orleans,' says I, and my heart banged right up into my mouth. 'Old master's place ain't so very far from New-Orleans.'

"'Who was your master?' says he.

"'Mr. Walter Wallace,' says I, 'and if I could get back to him, he should be my master all de days of my life.' 'I know him very well,' said de captin; 'he is a fine man.' 'Dat's de truth,' said I, and I fell to cryin' like a baby; de more I thought about home de worse I felt, till, at last, I just had to set down on de bench, and cry good fashion.

"De captin seemed right sorry for me, and asked if I wanted to go home. . . .

"'Well,' says he, 'go get your goods and chattels, and be here in two hours. I know Mr. Wallace will take you home and forgive you.'

"I told him I had all my goods and chattels on my back, and might as well stay. So, thank de Lord for his goodness to me, I got back home. Old master came out and shook hands with me. 'Peter,' says he, 'I don't think your visit to the North has improved your looks any.'

"'No, master,' says I, 'but I have bin punished mightily for my wrong doin', and I deserved it: but, de Lord willin', I will try to keep de straight road hereafter.'"

Uncle Peter resumed his meal, and Jack also found that he could eat the wholesome food before him. He was very thoughtful for a while, after hearing of his father's troubles, and seemed disposed to be satisfied with his comfortable condition. He did not feel quite so anxious to try his fortune as an independent individual; he was not very courageous, and did not like Uncle Peter's description of abolition hospitality. . . . Jack was not really a bad negro; he had been much indulged, as Southern house servants usually are—was very easily flattered, and of shallow intellect. He was devotedly attached to his master, and usually attentive to his duties.

Mrs. V. G. Cowdin, *Ellen; or, the Fanatic's Daughter* (Mobile, Ala.: S. H. Goetzel, 1860), 16–22.

෴ John Brown's Body: Symbols and Meanings of the Civil War ෴

The American Civil War involved an immense mobilization of men and weaponry, military strategy, and political insight. But it was never fought exclusively on the ground. The war also had to be fought for the hearts and minds of the populace in both regions. The conflict turned on a war of words that rang out from poets, orators, novelists, humorists, preachers, and publishers. Americans on both sides of the conflict produced an enormous popular print culture during the war years. Poetry, sentimental and sensational stories and novels, sermons, folk humor, satire, and war songs—all were made available to male and female audiences, often in new forms of presentation, such as illustrated weeklies, story papers, comic valentines, and illustrated envelopes. Popular print culture gave form to literary sensibilities and rhetorical forms well known since the antebellum years. Yet it also provided an outlet for the beginnings of Confederate nationalism and for a new social and political consciousness in the North.

The vast literary and popular culture creations of the Civil War years played a vital role in building a cultural politics of war. From the opening cannon blasts at Fort Sumter and Manassas, through the appalling deaths at Shiloh and Antietam, to long years of attrition and Sherman's march to the sea, soldiers, civilians, and politicians tried to assign meaning to the course of the war and to the public's daily interaction with its grave and tragic realities. They articulated understandings of the war on personal, local, and national grounds in the sermons, songs, plays, jokes, and essays that poured off the printing presses during the war.

෴ IN SONG AND VERSE

"Arise! Arise! Arise! And gird ye for the fight." As soon as the Civil War began, someone was ready with a song or poem about it. Copies of George F. Root's song "The First Gun Is Fired" were already in print three days after the attack on Fort Sumter. Both sides of the battle lines, Confederate and Union, witnessed a deluge of songs and poetry during the war years, with more than 10,000 songs making it into print. Oliver Wendell Holmes, later a Supreme Court justice, remembered that popular war songs were "dinned in our ears by all manner of voices until they have made spots on our ear-drums like those the drumsticks made on the drum-head."

Songwriters touched on all of the themes that resonated elsewhere in wartime popular culture—nationalism, patriotism, recruitment, salvation, romance, love, family, death, disloyalty, humor, and race. The most popular songs reveal how participants wished to explain the war to themselves and their communities. These songs gave vent to common emotions, they inspired patriotism and loyalty, and they prescribed appropriate wartime behavior. Many of the songs, such as the sentimental ballads of dying soldiers, won audiences in both the North and the South. Although Confederates often sang "Yankee" songs without knowing that these songs were, in the words of one southern magazine, "palmed off upon the people as Southern productions," place of origin made little difference in how each side sang about the war.

John Brown's Song (1861)

Battle Hymn of the Republic (1862)

At the onset of the Civil War, the Confederate States urgently needed the ritual foundations of a new nationalism. Repeated calls for a national song of the Confederacy echoed from southern magazines, but to no avail. Instead, it was Union soldiers who first adopted a marching song that spread rapidly throughout their ranks (and on the home front as well), losing little of its popularity from the beginning to the end of the conflict. Ironically, "John Brown's Song" was not even written about the volatile abolitionist John Brown, who led a failed raid on the arsenal at Harpers Ferry, Virginia, hoping to spark a violent slave insurrection. The song began among a Boston volunteer infantry battalion, one of whose members (and company singers) was named John Brown and thus became the object of the regiment's ribbing. But after years of horrendous slaughter, associations with the abolitionist martyr resonated in the song's performance as well as its meaning. Julia Ward Howe, a female poet and Unitarian whose reformer husband never approved of her public writings, then reinterpreted this song during the devastating early years of the war and gave it an even more pronounced apocalyptic tone. After attending a bungled review of Union troops outside Washington, Howe took a minister friend's words to heart and wrote "some new words to that tune." "Battle Hymn of the Republic" was published a few months later in the Atlantic Monthly.

PROBLEMS TO CONSIDER

1. What factors likely contributed to the immense popularity of "John Brown's Song" as a war song? Which aspects of this song might have reminded northern audiences of the radical abolitionist John Brown?
2. How do the subject of the song and the position of the singer change once Howe transformed the original into her "Battle Hymn"? What did it imply when northerners sang this song in musters and parades?

"JOHN BROWN'S SONG"

John Brown's body lies a-mouldering in the grave;
John Brown's body lies a-mouldering in the grave;
John Brown's body lies a-mouldering in the grave;
  His soul is marching on!

Chorus
Glory, halle — hallelujah!
Glory, halle — hallelujah!
Glory, halle — hallelujah!
  His soul is marching on!

He's gone to be a soldier in the army of the Lord! [repeat 2 times]
  His soul is marching on! (Chorus)

John Brown's knapsack is strapped upon his back! [repeat 2 times]
  His soul is marching on! (Chorus)

The pet lambs and angels will meet him on the way, [repeat 2 times]
  As they go marching on! (Chorus)

We'll hang Jeff Davis to a sour apple-tree! [repeat 2 times]
  As we go marching on! (Chorus)

Now, three rousing cheers for the Union! [repeat 2 times]
  As we are marching on! (Chorus)

The Civil War in Song and Story, edited by Frank Moore (New York: P. F. Collier, 1889), 509.

"BATTLE HYMN OF THE REPUBLIC"

Mine eyes have seen the glory of the coming of the Lord:
He is trampling out the vintage where the grapes of wrath are stored;
He hath loosed the fateful lightning of His terrible swift sword:
  His truth is marching on.

Chorus
Glory, Glory, Hallelujah
Glory, Glory, Hallelujah
Glory, Glory, Hallelujah
His truth is marching on.

I have seen Him in the watch-fires of a hundred circling camps;
They have builded Him an altar in the evening dews and damps;
I can read His righteous sentence by the dim and flaring lamps:
  His day is marching on. (Chorus)

I have read a fiery gospel writ in burnished rows of steel;
"As ye deal with my contemners, so with you my grace shall deal;
Let the Hero, born of woman, crush the serpent with his heel,
  Since God is marching on." (Chorus)

He has sounded forth the trumpet that shall never call retreat;
He is sifting out the hearts of men before His judgment-seat:
Oh, be swift, my soul, to answer Him! be jubilant, my feet!
  Our God is marching on. (Chorus)

In the beauty of the lilies Christ was born across the sea,
With a glory in his bosom that transfigures you and me:
As he died to make men holy, let us die to make men free,
  While God is marching on. (Chorus)

"Battle Hymn of the Republic," *Atlantic Monthly* 9 (February 1862), 145.

Who Will Care for Mother Now? (1863)

Kiss Me Before I Die, Mother! (1864)

Few songs of battlefield heroics ever gained real popularity during the Civil War, but not so the sentimental songs of dying soldiers whispering their last words to the lovers and mothers they had left behind. In the North and South, no songs were more widely sung than those involving a dying soldier's mother. "Mother Can This Glory Be?," "Mother, Is the Battle Over?," "Mother, Oh! Sing Me to Rest," and "Dear Mother, I'll Come Home Again" were just some of the dozens of motherhood war songs. These verses paralleled popular wartime literature, which was filled with tales of loss and separation from loved ones. Songs about mothers, then, gave voice to the deep anxieties felt on both sides about the suffering and death of ordinary soldiers. These songs also expose the gender and family dramas brought on by a war amidst a Victorian culture that glorified the home. But for all the popularity of songs about mothers, fathers were virtually absent from wartime poetry and song.

PROBLEMS TO CONSIDER

1. What comfort or reassurance might come from singing about a mother's grief? How would you explain the fear that a soldier's sacrifice might go unrecognized or his dying words unrecorded? Why sing about mothers, but not fathers?
2. Did these sentimental songs share any similarities with marching songs such as the "Battle Hymn" or "John Brown's Song"? Can you compare them to family dramas such as *Uncle Tom's Cabin*?

"WHO WILL CARE FOR MOTHER NOW?"

Why am I so weak and weary?
See how faint my heated breath;
All around to me seems darkness;
Tell me, comrades, is this death?
Ah! how well I know your answer,
To my fate I meekly bow,
If you'll only tell me truly
Who will care for mother now?

Chorus
Soon with angels I'll be marching,
With bright laurels on my brow;
I have for my country fallen,
Who will care for mother now?

Who will comfort her in sorrow?
Who will dry the falling tear,
Gently smooth her wrinkled forehead?
Who will whisper words of cheer?
Even now I think I see her
Kneeling, praying for me! how
Can I leave her in anguish?
Who will care for mother now? (Chorus)

Let this knapsack be my pillow;
And my mantle be the sky;
Hasten, comrades, to the battle!
I will like a soldier die.
Soon with angels I'll be marching,
With bright laurels on my brow;
I have for my country fallen,
Who will care for mother now? (Chorus)

Charles C. Sawyer, *Who Will Care for Mother Now?* (Brooklyn, N.Y.: Sawyer and Thompson, 1863).

"KISS ME BEFORE I DIE, MOTHER!"

Kiss me before I die, Mother—oh! press thy
lips to mine.
And twine thy loved arms round me, ere life's
bright day decline.
I feel death's shadows thicken—see, see them
on my brow,
Kiss me before I die, Mother, oh! kiss thy darling now!
Kiss me before I die, Mother, oh! kiss thy darling now!

Kiss me before I die, Mother!—stoop low, that
I may bless
The hand that trained my footsteps with so
much tenderness.
Around our hearthside, Mother, will stand an
empty chair;

There is one beyond the stars, Mother—I go
to claim it there!
There is one beyond the stars, Mother—I go
to claim it there!

Kiss me before I die, Mother!—I would have
lived to see
Our fair land free, my mother, from this base
tyranny.
But hark! Death's angel cometh! Dear Mother,
do not sigh,
But meet thy boy in Heaven; Mother, oh! kiss
me before I die!
But meet thy boy in Heaven; Mother, oh! kiss
me before I die!

———

The Army Songster (Richmond, Va.: George L. Bidgood,
1864), 18.

ꝏ

A Hint to Poets: Showing How to Make a War Song (1862)

*Marching songs appeared in print alongside songs of inspiration, sentiment, sensational-
ism, or humor, and side by side with hymns, spirituals, and minstrel ditties. By 1862, the
editors of* Vanity Fair *recognized the humor inherent in parodying the many conventions
of Civil War songwriters, so they published a facetious how-to guide for prospective new
songsmiths.*

PROBLEMS TO CONSIDER

1. In poking fun at the songwriters, was the poet also questioning the Union
cause?
2. Was this song mere cynicism, or pointed political satire?

The air is glad with bannered life
And gay with pomp of stripes and stars!
(Here, for the rhyme, you'll mention "strife,"
And happily allude to "Mars.")
A nation musters to the field,
Truth to maintain and wrong to right!
(Here promise that the foe shall yield,
And promise it with all your might.)

Rebellion rears its rampant head,
And Hate lets loose the dogs of war,
(Here speak about the "gory bed"
Where heroes are provided for.)
But while the hearts of freemen beat,
And while their hands can wield the sword—
(Describe them pouring "leaden sleet,"
And falling on the "traitor horde.")

GOD's lightning rifts the battle's gloom!
The souls of heroes lead us on!
(Here touch on Vernon's sacred tomb,
And bones of glorious WASHINGTON.)
The listening nations hold their breath,
And guardian angels throng the sky—
(Here talk of "Liberty or Death,"
And say "we conquer or we die.")

The destinies of all the race
Hang on the issue of the hour;
(Here give considerable space
To sneers at royal pomp and power.)
For in the West is Freedom's star,
And in the West is Freedom's crown
(Here say that sceptres near and far,
As also thrones, must tumble down.)

For, face to face and hand to hand,
We'll beat the dastard traitors back;

(Allude here to "our native land,"
And, by the way, to "glory's track.")
Till once again from sea to sea
Our starry Flag shall proudly fly!
(Here swell "the anthem of the free,"
And don't forget to swell it high.)

And when at last the foot of Truth
Has crushed Rebellion's serpent head,
(Here someway you must speak of "youth,"
Though any rhyme will do instead.)
She'll hurl her lightning from the sun
And break the chains of all the world!
(And that will do—for all is done
When once the lightning's safely hurled.)

"A Hint to Poets: Showing How to Make a War Song," *Vanity Fair*, March 8, 1862, 123.

⌇

⌇ GENDER AND THE CIVIL WAR

War songs about motherhood exposed the concerns prevalent in both regions about a woman's role in the conflict, and they illustrate the importance of gender in the Civil War. The wartime crisis raised again the question of women's rights, which had divided the antebellum populace, but it was now disguised as the dilemma of how to win the war. For some women (northern or southern, white or black), the Civil War prompted them to transgress gender constraints, disguise themselves as soldiers, and fight in the army. Others lamented their status at this moment of crisis: "How I wish I was a man," "Would God I were a man," and similar sentiments found their way into women's diaries and letters. By the time Union soldiers had marched on Baton Rouge, Louisiana, one woman had hidden a pistol and carving knife in her clothing and replied, "There are *no* women here! We are *all* men!" The war shook the foundations of sexual difference and hence provoked an equally forceful reassertion of those differences.

For white men, the Civil War became a defining point of one's manhood. Both Confederate and Union sides looked to volunteering as a sign of the transition from boyhood to manhood. One white woman in Alabama broke off her engagement when her fiancé failed to enlist. She sent him a skirt and women's undergarments, with a note saying "wear these or volunteer." Ironically, as soon as soldiers were in an army camp, they needed to perform the acts of cooking, cleaning, and comfort that were defined as women's work. For African American men, once they were permitted to join the army, the conflict represented an even more pronounced struggle to acquire both manhood and freedom.

White women in the North and South played both a symbolic and a real role in defining the sacrifice and patriotism that were the very essence of the war. They were not just bystanders in a discourse that praised courage and sacrifice; rather, women writers created much of the popular wartime print culture that claimed for women a stake in the cultural politics of war.

Soldiers' Wives (1862)
FANNY FERN

A Call to My Country-Women (1863)
GAIL HAMILTON

Fanny Fern and Gail Hamilton were two of the North's most important writers of the Civil War era. Both women wrote under pen names (their real names were Sara Willis Parton and Mary Dodge respectively); both wrote with such a bold style that their writing was commonly mistaken for a man's; and both produced work that was consciously and emphatically political. But these similarities ended with their backgrounds and intended audiences. Fanny Fern wrote compelling editorials on the conditions of working women and commentaries on the relations between husbands and wives. By 1855, she was earning $100 per weekly newspaper column for the New York Ledger, *more than any other contemporary columnist, man or woman. Gail Hamilton wrote for middle-class and mainstream religious magazines, but during the Civil War era she declared, "I shall not confine myself to my sphere. I hate my sphere. I like everything that is outside of it. . . . I was born into the whole world." Fern and Hamilton used their pens to convince other northern women that they had an important stake in the national ordeal of the Civil War.*

PROBLEMS TO CONSIDER

1. How do Fern's and Hamilton's perspectives on the sufferings and sacrifices of women compare with the sentimental songs of a dying soldier and a comforting mother? How did concepts of class influence their gendered interpretation of the war?
2. What are the implications of stating that the outcome of the Civil War "depends quite as much upon American women as upon American men"?

SOLDIERS' WIVES

What an immense amount of heroism among this class passes unnoticed, or is taken as a matter of course; not only in this most righteous war we are at present waging, but in those of all past time. For the soldier, he has his comrades about him, shoulder to shoulder; he has excitement; he has praise if he do well; he has honorable mention, and pitying tears, if he fall nobly striving. But alas! for the soldier's *wife*! Even an officer's wife, who has sympathizing friends, who has the comforts and many of the luxuries of life; whose children's future is provided for if their father fall; what hours of dreadful suspense and anxiety must *she* pass, even in these favorable circumstances! How hard for *her*! But for the wife of the *poor* soldier, who in giving her husband to her country, has given everything; who knows not whether the meal she and her little ones are eating, may not be the last for many a hungry—desolate—day: who has no friend to say "well done" as the lagging weeks of suspense creep on, and she stands bravely at her post, keeping want and starvation at bay; imagination busy among the heaps of dead and wounded, or traversing the wretched prison dens, and shuddering at the thought of their demoniac keepers; keeping down her sobs, as the little daughter trustfully offers up her nightly prayers "for dear papa to come home;" or when her little son, just old enough to read, traces slowly with his forefinger the long list of killed and wounded, "to see if father's name is there;" shrouding her eyes from the possible future of her children, should *her* strength give out under the pressure of want and anxiety; no friend to turn to, when her hand is palsied for labor. Nor waving banners, nor martial music, nor long processions to chronicle *her* valorous deeds; none but God and her own brave heart the witnesses of her noble unaided struggle; when I think of these solitary women scattered through the length and breadth of the land, my heart warms toward them; and I would fain hold them up in their silent heroism, for all the world to admire.

When the history of this war shall be written, (and *that* cannot be *now*,) let the historian, what else soever he may forget, forget not to chronicle the sublime valor of the hearthstone all over our struggling land.

———

Fanny Fern, "Soldiers' Wives," *New York Ledger*, November 8, 1862.

A CALL TO MY COUNTRY-WOMEN

. . . True, women cannot fight, and there is no call for any great number of female nurses; notwithstanding this, I believe, that, to-day, the issue of this war depends quite as much upon American women as upon American men,—and depends, too, not upon the few who write, but upon the many who do not. The women of the Revolution were not only Mrs. Adams, Mrs. Reed, and Mrs. Schuyler, but the wives of the farmers and shoemakers and blacksmiths everywhere. It is not Mrs. Stowe, or Mrs. Howe, or Miss Stevenson, or Miss Dix, alone, who is to save the country, but the thousands upon thousands who are at this moment darning stockings, tending babies, sweeping floors. It is to them I speak. It is they whom I wish to get hold of; for in their hands lies slumbering the future of this nation.

The women of to-day have not come up to the level of to-day. They do not stand abreast with its issues. They do not rise to the height of its great argument. I do not forget what you have done. I have beheld, O Dorcases, with admiration and gratitude, the coats and garments, the lint and bandages, which you have made. Tender hearts, if you could have finished the war with your needles, it would have been finished long ago; but stitching does not crush rebellion, does not annihilate treason, or hew traitors in pieces before the Lord. Excellent as far as it goes, it stops fearfully short of the goal. This ought ye to do, but there are other things which you ought not to leave undone. The war cannot be finished by sheets and pillow-cases. Sometimes I am tempted to believe that it cannot be finished till we have flung them all away. When I read of the Rebels fighting bare-headed, bare-footed, haggard, and unshorn, in rags and filth, — fighting bravely, heroically, successfully, — I am ready to make a burnt-offering of our stacks of clothing. I feel and fear that we must come down, as they have done, to a recklessness of all incidentals, down to the rough and rugged fastnesses of life, down to the very gates of death itself, before we shall be ready and worthy to win victories. . . .

This soul of fire is what I wish to see kindled in our women, — burning white and strong and steady, through all weakness, timidity, vacillation, treachery in Church or State or press or parlor, scorching, blasting, annihilating whatsoever loveth and maketh a lie, — extinguished by no tempest of defeat, no drizzle of delay, but glowing on its steadfast path till it shall have cleared through the abomination of our desolation a highway for the Prince of Peace.

O my country-women, I long to see you stand under the time and bear it up in your strong hearts, and not need to be borne up through it. I wish you to stimulate, and not crave stimulants from others. I wish you to be the consolers, the encouragers, the sustainers, and not tremble in perpetual need of consolation and encouragement. . . . Go farther than this. Consecrate to a holy cause not only the incidentals of life, but life itself. Father, husband, child, — I do not say, Give them up to toil, exposure, suffering, death, without a murmur; — that implies reluctance. I rather say, Urge them to the offering; fill them with sacred fury; fire them with irresistible desire; strengthen them to heroic will. . . . Count it all joy that you are reckoned worthy to suffer in a grand and righteous cause. Give thanks evermore that you were born in this time; and *because* it is dark, be you the light of the world.

And follow the soldier to the battlefield with your spirit. The great army of letters that marches Southward with every morning sun is a powerful engine of war. Fill them with tears and sighs, lament separation and suffering, dwell on your loneliness and fears, mourn over the dishonesty of contractors and the incompetency of leaders, doubt if the South will ever be conquered, and foresee financial ruin, and you will damp the powder and dull the swords that ought to deal death upon the foe. . . . In camp, the roughest man idealizes his far-off home, and every word of love uplifts him to a lover. But let your tenderness unfold its sunny side, and keep the shadows for His pity who knows the end from the beginning, and whom no foreboding can dishearten. Glory in your tribulation. Show your soldier that his unflinching courage, his undying fortitude, are your crown of rejoicing. Incite him to enthusiasm by your inspiration. Make a mock of your discomforts. Be unwearying in details of the little interests of home. Fill your letters with kittens and Canaries, with baby's shoes, and Johnny's sled, and the old cloak which you have turned into a handsome gown. Keep him posted in all the village-gossip, the lectures, the courtings, the sleigh-rides, and the singing-schools. Bring out the good points of the world in strong relief. Tell every sweet and brave and pleasant and funny story you can think of. Show him that you clearly apprehend that all this warfare means peace, and that a dastardly peace would pave the way for speedy, incessant, and more appalling warfare. Help him to bear his burdens by showing him how elastic you are under yours. Hearten him, enliven him, tone him up to the true hero-pitch. . . .

Under God, the only question, as to whether this war shall be conducted to a shameful or an honorable close, is not of men or money or material resource. In these our superiority is unquestioned. . . . Women need not beat their pewter spoons into bullets, for there are plenty of bullets without them. It is not whether our soldiers shall fight a good fight; they have played the man on a hundred battle-fields. It is not whether officers are or are not competent; generals have blundered nations into victory since the world began. It is whether this people shall have virtue to endure to the end,—to endure, not starving, not cold, but the pangs of hope deferred, of disappointment and uncertainty, of commerce deranged and outward prosperity checked. Will our vigilance to detect treachery and our perseverance to punish it hold out? If we stand firm, we shall be saved, though so as by fire. If we do not, we shall fall, and shall richly deserve to fall; and may God sweep us off from the face of the earth, and plant in our stead a nation with the hearts of men, and not of chickens! . . .

. . . Failure will write disgrace upon the brow of this generation, and shame will outlast the age. It is not with us as with the South. She can surrender without dishonor. She is the weaker power, and her success will be against the nature of things. Her dishonor lay in her attempt, not in its relinquishment. But we shall fail, not because of mechanics and mathematics, but because our manhood and womanhood weighed in the balance are found wanting. There are few who will not share in the sin. There are none who will not share in the shame. . . .

Gail Hamilton, "A Call to My Country-Women," *Atlantic Monthly* 11 (March 1863): 345–49.

⫸

Comic Valentines: "Home Guard" and "Dodging the Draft"

Harriet Beecher Stowe's only record of her White House meeting with Abraham Lincoln was a letter to her sister. She did not mention Lincoln's statement about a little lady and a great war but wrote instead, "I will only say now that it was all very funny—and we were ready to explode with laughter all the while." Laughter and the Civil War? Not what we expect from dour Victorians during the nation's greatest crisis. Yet Lincoln's cabinet members often noted that he read to them from humor books, and a sizable portion of Civil War–era print culture was devoted to humor. Comic songs, cartoons, and the writings of war humorists were published independently or in joke almanacs and humor journals, such as Phunny Phellow *and* Frank Leslie's Budget of Fun *in the North or* Southern Punch *in the South. These writers especially targeted the sentimental songs of dying soldiers; "Mother Would Comfort Me," for example, was parodied as "Mother Would Wallop Me." One popular form of jocularity was the comic valentine, the era's equivalent of today's funny greeting card; they could be purchased individually or in sets and circulated among frontline soldiers as well as back home.*

PROBLEMS TO CONSIDER

1. Investigate all of the synonyms and antonyms of manhood used in these valentines. Which are the strongest critiques of these "slackers"—the visual images or the words?
2. What was serious about this humor? That is, how did humor work to prescribe the boundaries of patriotism?

"Home Guard."

(Comic Valentine Collection, The Library Company
of Philadelphia.)

"Dodging the Draft."

(Comic Valentine Collection, The Library Company
of Philadelphia.)

ᴔ GOD'S MISSION, BUT FOR WHOM?

A century after the Civil War, folksinger Bob Dylan tried to make Vietnam
War–era Americans think about their country's militarism. The protagonist in
Dylan's song "With God on Our Side" recalls being forced to memorize the heroes
of the Civil War, who had marched off with the assurance of God's favor. But
whose side was God's side? Julia Ward Howe's "Battle Hymn of the Republic"
defined the march of the Union's armies as the marching of God, while E. K.
Blunt's song "The Southern Cross" reminded Confederates that "On our side,
Southern men, / The God of battles fights!" Both sections of the United States
shared a revivalist heritage as well as deeply held assumptions about the nation's

special mission guided by divine Providence. It was not a difficult leap, then, to interpret the nation's most cataclysmic event as something more than a mere political or military conflict. The hundreds of thousands of men and women who died each year must be dying for a greater purpose. To proclaim and believe that "on our side, God fights," ordinary soldiers, clergymen, and politicians needed to articulate their visions of the particular mission of the war. As they did, they fused together ideas about nationalism, civil religion, progress, warnings of God's wrath, and a providential view of history. Orators and writers on all sides spoke of the redeeming power derived from the tremendous sacrifice of human lives, calling it the "baptism of blood." And yet African Americans, Confederate clergymen, and white northern ministers saw different divine missions at work in the war. Whose side was God's side?

The Mission of the War (1864)
FREDERICK DOUGLASS

W. E. B. Du Bois wrote in the early twentieth century that when the Civil War commenced, the 4 million African Americans in bondage knew that "God was real." "To these black folk," Du Bois maintained, the war "was the Apocalypse." For black Americans, the Civil War was the culmination of their long struggle for freedom. To Frederick Douglass, the best-known former slave in the North, this war needed to be fought for the minds and hearts in the North, as well as for the emancipation of the millions enslaved. By 1864, Douglass was determined to keep a moral definition of the war ever present before the northern public, best illustrated in his lecture "The Mission of the War." This lecture marked the beginning of Douglass's decades–long quest to keep alive an alternative memory and interpretation of the meaning of the Civil War.

PROBLEMS TO CONSIDER

1. One historian has argued that Douglass wanted "a new definition of American nationality." How did Douglass's understanding of the mission of the war reflect his thinking about the nation and nationalism? What part did religious ideas play in his thinking?
2. What did Douglass wish his audiences to understand about the relationship of both slavery and abolition to the Civil War?

Ladies and Gentlemen:
By the mission of the war I mean nothing occult, arbitrary or difficult to be understood, but simply those great moral changes in the fundamental condition of the people, demanded by the situation of the country, plainly involved in the nature of the war, and which if the war is conducted in accordance with its true character, it is naturally and logically fitted to accomplish.

. . . The war looms before me simply as a great national opportunity, which may be improved to national salvation, or neglected to national ruin. I hope much from the bravery of our soldiers, but in vain is the might of armies if our rulers fail to profit by experience, and refuse to listen to the suggestions of wisdom and justice. The most hopeful fact of the hour is that we are now in a salutary school—the school of affliction. If sharp and signal retribution, long protracted, wide-sweeping and overwhelming, can teach a great nation respect for the long-despised claims of justice, surely we shall be taught now and for all time to come. But if, on the other hand, this potent teacher, whose lessons are written in characters of blood, and thundered to us from a hundred battle-fields shall fail, we shall go down, as we shall deserve to go down, as a warning to all other nations which shall come after us. . . .

Now, for what is all this desolation, ruin, shame, suffering, and sorrow? Can anybody want the answer? Can anybody be ignorant of the answer? It has been given a thousand times from this and other platforms. We all know it is Slavery. Less than a half a million of Southern slaveholders—holding in bondage four million slaves—finding themselves outvoted in the effort to get possession of the United States Government, in order to serve the interests of Slavery, have madly resorted to the sword—have undertaken to accomplish by bullets what they failed to accomplish by ballots. That is the answer. . . .

Whence came the guilty ambition equal to this atrocious crime. A peculiar education was necessary to this bold wickedness. Here all is plain again. Slavery—the peculiar institution—is aptly fitted to produce just such patriots, who first plunder, and then seek to destroy their country. A system which rewards labor with stripes and chains!—which robs the slave of his manhood, and the master of all just consideration for the rights of his fellow-man—has prepared the characters—male and female—that figure in this Rebellion—and for all its cold-blooded and hellish atrocities. In all the most horrid details of torture, starvation and murder, in the treatment of our prisoners, I behold the features of the monster in whose presence I was born, and that is Slavery. . . . Looking at the matter from no higher ground than patriotism—setting aside the high considerations of justice, liberty, progress, and civilization—the American people should resolve that this shall be the

last slave-holding Rebellion that shall ever curse this continent. Let the War cost more or cost little—let it be long or short—the work now begun should suffer no pause, no abatement, until it is done and done forever. . . .

The blow we strike is not merely to free a country or continent—but the whole world from Slavery—for when Slavery falls here—it will fall everywhere. We have no business to mourn over our mission. We are writing the statutes of eternal justice and liberty in the blood of the worst of tyrants as a warning to all after-comers. We should rejoice that there was moral life and health enough in us to stand in our appointed place, and do this great service for mankind. . . .

Why is this war fiercely denounced as an Abolition war? I answer, because the nation has long and bitterly hated Abolition, and the enemies of the war confidently rely upon this hatred to serve the ends of treason. Why do the loyal people deny the charge? I answer, because they know that Abolition, though now a vast power, is still odious. Both the charge and the denial tell how the people hate and despise the only measure that can save the country.

An Abolition war! Well, let us thank the Democracy for teaching us this word. The charge in a comprehensive sense is most true, and it is a pity that it is true, but it would be a vast pity if it were not true. Would that it were more true than it is. When our Government and people shall bravely avow this to be an Abolition war, then the country will be safe. Then our work will be fairly mapped out. Then the uplifted arm of the nation will swing unfettered to its work, and the spirit and power of the rebellion will be broken. . . .

The abolition of Slavery is the comprehensive and logical object of the war, for it includes everything else which the struggle involves. It is a war for the Union, a war for the Constitution, I admit; but it is logically such a war only in the sense that the greater includes the lesser. Slavery has proved itself the strong man of our national house. In every Rebel State it proved itself stronger than the Union, stronger than the

Constitution, and stronger than Republican Institutions. It overrode majorities, made no account of the ballot-box, and had everything its own way. It is plain that this strong man must be bound and cast out of our house before Union, Constitution and Republican institutions can become possible. . . .

Here is a part of the platform of principles upon which it seems to me every loyal man should take his stand at this hour:

First: That this war, which we are compelled to wage against slave-holding Rebels and traitors, at untold cost of blood and treasure, shall be, and of right ought to be, an Abolition War.

Secondly: That we, the loyal people of the North and of the whole country, while determined to make this a short and final war, will offer no peace, accept no peace, consent to no peace, which shall not be to all intents and purposes an Abolition peace.

Thirdly: That we regard the whole colored population of the country, in the loyal as well as in the disloyal States, as our *countrymen*—valuable in peace as laborers, valuable in war as soldiers—entitled to all the rights, protection, and opportunities for achieving distinction enjoyed by any other class of our countrymen.

Fourthly: Believing that the white race has nothing to fear from fair competition with the black race, and that the freedom and elevation of one race are not to be purchased or in any manner rightfully subserved by the disfranchisement of another, we shall favor immediate and unconditional emancipation in all the States, invest the black man everywhere with the right to vote and to be voted for, and remove all discriminations against his rights on account of his color, whether as a citizen or a soldier. . . .

What we now want is a country—a free country—a country not saddened by the foot-prints of a single slave—and nowhere cursed by the presence of a slaveholder. We want a country, and we are fighting for a country, which shall not brand the Declaration of Independence as a lie. We want a country whose fundamental institutions we can proudly defend before the highest intelligence and civilization of the age. . . . We are in fact, and from absolute necessity, transplanting the whole South with the higher civilization of the North. The New-England schoolhouse is bound to take the place of the Southern whipping-post. Not because we love the Negro, but the nation; not because we prefer to do this, because we must or give up the contest, and give up the country. . . .

You and I know that the mission of this war is National regeneration. We know and consider that a nation is not born in a day. We know that large bodies move slowly—and often seem to move thus—when, could we perceive their actual velocity, we should be astonished at its greatness. A great battle lost or won is easily described, understood and appreciated, but the moral growth of a great nation requires reflection, as well as observation, to appreciate it. . . .

I end where I began—no war but an Abolition war; no peace but an Abolition peace; liberty for all, chains for none; the black man a soldier in war, a laborer in peace; a voter at the South as well as at the North; America his permanent home, and all Americans his fellow-countrymen. Such, fellow-citizens, is my idea of the mission of the war. If accomplished, our glory as a nation will be complete, our peace will flow like a river, and our foundations will be the everlasting rocks.

Frederick Douglass, "The Mission of the War: A Lecture by Frederick Douglass," *New York Tribune,* January 14, 1864.

☙

Gideon's Water-Lappers (1864)

STEPHEN ELLIOTT

Interpreting the Confederate cause as God's own began even before secession. Clergymen rivaled "fire-eating" politicians in their efforts to persuade southerners that secession was part of a divine plan. By the time the war started, they had developed a discourse that likened the Confederate nation to God's people. Among the most prolific Confederate spokespersons for defining the "mission" of the war was Stephen Elliott, the Episcopal bishop of Savannah, Georgia. Elliott shared with other Confederate clergy this assumption of divine purpose. To Elliott, the initial victory at Fort Sumter was an answer to a prayer. Subsequent battlefield successes led him to compose a sermon entitled "Our Cause in Harmony with the Purposes of God in Christ Jesus." And when the military momentum turned against the Confederacy with Union victories at Vicksburg and Gettysburg, Elliott joined other ministers in preaching against the sins of the Confederate people, reminding them that "final success depends altogether upon [God's] presence and his favor." After three years of war, on a national day of fasting, Elliott still did not budge from his contention that behind the war was a set of divinely approved principles.

PROBLEMS TO CONSIDER

1. How did Elliott define the "moral power" of the Confederacy? Did he expect that all southerners would agree with this "mission"? What makes his northern adversaries the enemies of God?
2. What similarities can you discern between Frederick Douglass's lecture and Elliott's sermon? What are their most important disagreements about the terms of the "mission"?

Upon such a critical occasion, it becomes us to prelude our solemn fast, and the observations which arise naturally out of it, with a song of thanksgiving for the favours which have crowned us in the past, and for the position which we yet maintain in the face of our enemies and of the world. "It is of God's mercies that we have not been consumed," for we have assuredly had everything against us; numbers overwhelming, hate bitter and cruel, resources without stint, the command by our enemies of the ocean and the rivers, the ear of the world shut to us, the cry put upon us of slavery and barbarism. With all these things have we been contending for three weary years, through storm and sunshine, in cold and hunger and nakedness, creating as we fought, weeping while we labored, reaping courage and endurance from the fields sown with the blood of our children, and yet through the mercy of God, we stand this day unconquered and defiant, looking to final success with as full assurance, as upon the day when we threw down the gauntlet under the walls of the ocean girdled Sumter. Army after army has been hurled back from its desperate advances. . . .

But it may be said, this is a one-sided view of the case. The enemy has been steadily gaining upon us, and every year finds him in possession of some new territory which weakens us and gives him confidence of final success. Admitting this to be so, we must remember the cost at which these advantages, such as they are, have been achieved. Already has the United States government accumulated a permanent dent of Fifteen hundred millions of Dollars, besides a floating debt, which it dares not look in the face, of several hundred millions more, amounting together to one half the national debt of Great Britain, already have their military drafts exceeded a million of men, some hundreds of thousands of whom have been disabled, or whose bones he scattered over the debateable ground of Virginia and Tennessee. . . . Can they at this rate continue this expenditure long enough to finish their work? Will the people of the United States consent to be maimed and slaughtered through an indefinite series of years for the annual honor of marching from Washington to the Rappahannock, and from Nashville to Chattanooga? Impossible! for it would require, according to their present rate of progress, at least two more Presidential terms and the accumulation of a debt unheard of in the annals of the world, before they could overrun territory, even supposing that they should meet no such crushing defeats as they have encountered in the past. Truly their prospect is not a bright one, even when admitting their own pretensions. . . .

One of the great mistakes which our enemies have made throughout this war, has been in supposing that mere numbers and material power were to decide this conflict—that right was nothing—that moral power was nothing—that the defence of a great trust was nothing—that the maintenance of a mighty principle was nothing. How grandly Carlyle strikes down this wretched materialism when he says, "One man that has a higher wisdom, a hitherto unknown spiritual truth in him is stronger, not than ten men that have it not, or than ten thousand, but than all men that have it not. . . ." And so with a cause which has in it all the inspiration of a great moral truth. Its success can never be measured by the mere numbers who defend it. It has in itself a spirit which can never be crushed. . . .

The only purpose which makes a struggle for independence worth the cost of blood and feeling which it always demands, is that it should bring out of its fermenting and convulsed elements an earnest people; a people worthy to live, because sensible of the great trusts and responsibilities which will rest upon it. To shed such blood, as we have spilled in this contest, for the mere name of independence, for the vanity or the pride of having a separate national existence, would be unjustifiable before God and man. We must have higher aims than these, and sublimer views, ere we can stand before the judgment seat of God with clean hands and clear consciences. And I think that we can confidently say, that we have in view objects entirely worthy of any struggle we may be summoned to pass through. We have been entrusted with the moral and religious education of an inferior race, made more sacred to us by the events of this war, because we have been made to see what will be their miserable fate should they pass out of our nurturing hands. We have been appointed to preserve upon this continent all that is valuable in morals and legislation and religion. We have been selected to be a bulwark against the worst developments of human nature, fanaticism, democracy, license, atheism. For such purposes God is disciplining and refining us in the fires of affliction, and when he shall perceive that we have been ennobled by our struggle, purified by our sacrifices, exalted by our self-denial—that we have learned to put at their true value wealth, and luxury, and show—to distinguish between false pretension and genuine merit—to understand the infinite, absolute, immutable character of virtue—to worship the honest and the true, and the good, and the beautiful—to keep in our eye the religion of Jesus, as we find it revealed in the Scriptures and exemplified in his pure and holy and self-sacrificing life—He will give us our deliverance and establish us in this land flowing with milk and honey, as a nation consecrated for His own mysterious yet all-wise purposes.

To produce such a result, earnest, single-minded, self-sacrificing men are demanded; men who, when they are called to the battle, will not turn back from timidity, or fearfulness, or envy, or weariness; who, when the trumpet sounds to conflict, will not bow down upon their knees to drink, but will lap water as a dog lappeth, in their haste to press forward to their duty; who will follow in faith of God and of their leader, even though their numbers be reduced to a mere handful. Such men will God ever bless with his presence; by such men will God conquer, because they will never say, "Mine own hand hath saved me.". . . Let us, my hearers, offer ourselves willingly to the Lord, for indeed his honor and glory are most deeply concerned. Our maddened adversaries are warring not only against us, but against God—warring against his arrangements, against his purposes, against his moral law, against his holy religion. . . .

_____

Stephen Elliott, *Gideon's Water-Lappers: A Sermon Preached in Christ Church, Savannah, on Friday, the 8th day of April, 1864, the Day Set Apart by the Congress of the Confederate States, as a Day of Humiliation, Fasting and Prayer* (Macon, Ga.: Burke, Boykin & Co., 1864), 6, 8–9, 12–13, 20–22.

✌

Our Obligations to the Dead (1865)
HORACE BUSHNELL

A few months after the Civil War's end, Connecticut minister Horace Bushnell told a commencement audience at Yale College that "we are not the same people that we were, and never can be again." Several times during the war, Bushnell tried to articulate its meaning and purpose. Following the Union army's humbling defeat at Bull Run (Manassas), he thought the nation needed "reverses and losses, and times of deep concern" to test its vigor. By the time of Lincoln's reelection, Bushnell spoke of a theocratic government and the rule of "divine right" as preferable to the dangers of democracy. Yet, like so many other Americans at the war's end, Bushnell returned again to the question of what these hundreds of thousands of deaths meant for those who survived and needed to rebuild a nation.

PROBLEMS TO CONSIDER

1. Compare and contrast how Douglass, Elliott, and Bushnell expressed the "mission" of the Civil War. How do you account for the similarities in their rhetoric?
2. Does Bushnell's interpretation of the meaning of the war foretell the conflicts that would follow during the reconstruction of the Union? How important will memories of the dead be in that newly constructed unity?

Reserving it therefore as my privilege . . . . . . I propose a more general subject in which due honors may be paid to all, viz., *The obligations we owe to the dead*,—all the dead who have fallen in this gigantic and fearfully bloody war. . . .

These grim heroes therefore, dead and dumb, that have strewed so many fields with their bodies,—these are the price and purchase-money of our triumph. A great many of us were ready to live, but these offered themselves, in a sense, to die, and by their cost the victory is won. . . .

For the life is in the blood,—all life; and it is put flowing within, partly for the serving of a nobler use in flowing out on fit occasion, to quicken and consecrate whatever it touches. God could not plan a Peace-Society world, to live in the sweet amenities, and grow great and happy by simply thriving and feeding. There must be bleeding also. Sentiments must be born that are children of thunder; there must be heroes and heroic nationalities, and martyr testimonies, else there will be only mediocrities, insipidities, common-place men, and common-place writings,—a sordid and mean peace, liberties without a pulse, and epics that are only eclogues.

And here it is that the dead of our war have done for us a work so precious, which is all their own,—they have bled for us; and by this simple sacrifice of blood they have opened for us a new great chapter of life. We were living before in trade and commerce, bragging of our new cities and our census reports, and our liberties that were also consciously mocked by our hypocrisies. . . . But the blood of our dead has touched our souls with thoughts more serious and deeper, and begotten, as I trust, somewhat of that high-bred inspiration which is itself the possibility of genius, and of a true public greatness. . . .

In this view, we are not the same people that we were, and never can be again. Our young scholars, . . . [t]he pitch of their life is raised. The tragic blood of the war is a kind of new capacity for them. They perceive what it is to have a country and a public devotion. Great aims are close at hand, and in such aims a finer type of manners. And what shall follow, but that, in their more invigorated, nobler life, they are seen hereafter to be manlier in thought and scholarship, and closer to genius in action.

I must also speak of the new great history sanctified by this war, and the blood of its fearfully bloody sacrifices. . . . We had a little very beautiful history before, which we were beginning to cherish and fondly cultivate. But we had not enough of it to beget a full historic consciousness. As was just now intimated in a different way, no people ever become vigorously conscious, till they mightily do, and heroically suffer. The historic sense is close akin to tragedy. We say it accusingly often,—and foolishly,—that history cannot live on peace, but must feed itself on blood. The reason is that, without the blood, there is really nothing great enough in motive and action, taking the world as it is, to create a great people or story. If a gospel can be executed only in blood, if there is no power of salvation strong enough to carry the world's feeling which is not gained by dying for it, how shall a selfish race get far enough above itself, to be kindled by the story of its action in the dull routine of its common arts of peace? . . . The great cause must be great as in the clashing of evil; and heroic inspirations, and the bleeding of heroic worth must be the zest of the story. Nations can sufficiently live only as they find how to energetically die. In this view, some of us have felt, for a long time, the want of a more historic life, to make us a truly great people. This want is now supplied; for now, at last, we may be said to have gotten a history. The story of this four years' war is the grandest chapter, I think, of heroic fact, and tragic devotion, and spontaneous public sacrifice, that has ever been made in our world. . . . There was never a better, and never so great a cause; order against faction, law against conspiracy, liberty and right against the madness and defiant wrong of slavery, the unity and salvation of the greatest future nationality and freest government of the world, a perpetual state of war to be averted, and the preservation for mankind of an example of popular government and free society that is a token of promise for true manhood, and an omen of death to old abuse and prescriptive wrong the world over; this has been our cause, and it is something to say that we have borne ourselves worthily in it. Our noblest and best sons have given their life to it. We have dotted whole regions with battlefields. We have stained how many rivers, and bays, and how many hundred leagues of railroad, with our blood! . . .

But we have duties upon us that are closer at hand; viz., to wind up and settle this great tragedy in a way to exactly justify every drop of blood that has been shed in it. . . .

First of all we are sworn to see that no vestige of state sovereignty is left, and the perpetual, supreme sovereignty of the nation established. For what but this have our heroes died? Not one of them would have died for a government of mere optional continuance; not one for a government fit to be rebelled against. But they volunteered for a government in perfect right, and one to be perpetual as the stars, and they went to the death as against the crime of hell. . . .

One thing more we are also sworn upon the dead to do; viz., to see that every vestige of slavery is swept clean. We did not begin the war to extirpate slavery; but the war itself took hold of slavery on its way, and as this had been the gangrene

of our wound from the first, we shortly put ourselves heartily to the cleansing, and shall not, as good surgeons, leave a part of the virus in it. We are not to extirpate the form and leave the fact. The whole black code must go; the law of passes, and the law of evidence, and the unequal laws of suit and impeachment for crime. We are bound, if possible, to make the emancipation work well. . . . And this kind relationship never can be secured, till the dejected and despised race are put upon the footing of men, and allowed to assert themselves somehow in the laws. Putting aside all theoretic notions of equality, and regarding nothing but the practical want of the emancipation, negro suffrage appears to be indispensable. . . . I remember too, that we have taken more than a hundred thousand of these freedmen of the war to fight our common battle. I remember the massacre of Fort Pillow. I remember the fatal assault of Fort Wagner and the gallant Shaw sleeping there in the pile of his black followers. . . . Ah, there is a debt of honor here! And honor is never so sacred as when it is due to the weak. Blasted and accursed be the soul that will forget these dead! If they had no offices or honors, if they fought and died in the plane of their humility, — Thou just God, forbid that we suffer them now to be robbed of the hope that inspired them!

Horace Bushnell, "Our Obligations to the Dead" (1865), in Horace Bushnell, *Building Eras in Religion* (New York: Charles Scribner's Sons, 1881), 320, 322, 326–27, 331–33, 350, 352–54.

CHAPTER 10

A Second American Revolution: 1865–1877

THE CIVIL WAR was a seismic event in the social and political landscape of the United States. It produced catastrophic destruction as well as triumphant emancipation. With slavery's demise, the familiar world for the South's white and black population was gone forever. Four million black men, women, and children were now free, ushering in a time of exhilarating promise of education, landownership, political participation, and self-determination. The war also permanently reconfigured the economic and political map of both the North and the South. White southern planters found their political dominance challenged by the increased political consciousness of black freedmen and poorer whites. An unrivaled era of large-scale consolidated industrial capitalism ("big business") was born out of wartime profits in the North. And the unprecedented empowerment of the national state meant that ultimate authority rested with the federal government. *The Nation*, a magazine founded by antislavery activists in 1865, proclaimed that the war confirmed "by the blood of thousands of her sons" the triumph of "the consolidation of nationality under democratic forms."

Not since 1776 had the political universe in America been turned on its head. As the New York *Herald* stated, the nation had to recognize that "we have passed through the fiery ordeal of a mighty revolution, and that the pre-existing order of things is gone and we can return no more." Beginning with the Freedmen's Bureau and Civil Rights Acts of 1866, followed by the Fourteenth Amendment and the Reconstruction Acts of 1867, Congress divided the former Confederacy into five military districts; established that readmission to the Union depended on the recognition of black citizenship rights, or else former Confederates would be barred from political officeholding; and gave the federal Freedmen's Bureau the authority to void labor contracts that forced former slaves into work situations that resembled slavery. Senator Lott Morrill of

Maine called these acts of legislation "absolutely revolutionary." But then, Morrill noted, "are we not in the midst of a revolution?" It is these seismic shifts in the political landscape that have led historians to consider the Reconstruction era as the "second American Revolution." Ironically, the last veteran of the first American Revolution died during the same months that Congress was deliberating the Reconstruction Acts of 1867.

This revolution focused on the identity of the nation's citizenry. For the first time since the nation's founding, the United States grappled with the question, as abolitionist Wendell Phillips phrased it, of "what makes or constitutes a citizen." The battle would continue for years after the war's end. Neither the Emancipation Proclamation, the North's victory, nor the Thirteenth Amendment, which abolished slavery, guaranteed the rights of citizenship for former slaves. Yet the emancipation of slaves prompted protests by other Americans — white women in the North, white southerners, and native-born laborers in the West — who felt that the new revolution had omitted them from the promise of liberation and citizenship.

❧ *Free at Last! The Black Man's Vote and Woman's Suffrage* ❧

Like the first American Revolution, Reconstruction proved more revolutionary for men than for women. Its overriding concerns focused on landownership and voting, both of which were privileges extended principally to men and denied entirely to married women under existing laws. Freed slaves immediately demanded the right to vote as one of their essential rights as new citizens. A delegate to North Carolina's Freedmen's Convention in 1865 outlined the rights new black citizens expected: "First, *the right to testify in courts of justice*, in order that we may defend our property and our rights. Secondly, *representation in the jury box*. . . . Thirdly and finally, *the black man should have the right to carry his ballot to the ballot box*." Not without difficulty, the Republican Party gradually tied its future to the citizenship and voting rights of black men in the South. Republicans were caught in a dilemma on this issue. First, only a few Radical Republicans wanted to extend voting rights to the North's free black residents. Second, even the Radicals in the party were divided between those who wanted to use black suffrage to change "the whole fabric of southern society" and those who thought black suffrage would be the quickest and least painful method for northerners to avoid any long-term national responsibility for governing race relations in the South. As *Harper's Weekly* explained, once blacks had the vote, "the 'Negro Question' will take care of itself." When Radical Republicans took control of reconstructing the South, black voting became their political goal and their tool for social reform.

The enfranchising of black men created a dilemma of its own for women's rights activists such as Elizabeth Cady Stanton and Susan B. Anthony. After all, these women began their careers in the abolitionist movement and for years had understood that the enslavement of African Americans was equivalent to their own subjugation under male-dominated laws and social conventions. With emancipation, women's rights activists pursued a strategy of demanding universal suffrage, an inseparable and simultaneous appeal for voting rights for both blacks and women. However, northern antislavery politicians, who were now wedded to the fortunes of the Republican Party, dismissed women's demands as a distraction from their first concern—votes for black men. In August 1865, Stanton wrote to Anthony describing her continual arguments with abolitionist-Republicans: "I fear one and all will favor enfranchising the negro without us. Woman's cause is in deep water." In response to abolitionist Wendell Phillips's declaration before the American Anti-Slavery Society that "this hour belongs to the negro," women suffrage activists girded for a fight.

Letter to the Editor (1865)
FRANCES D. GAGE

This Is the Negro's Hour (1865)
ELIZABETH CADY STANTON

Frances Gage was the first to respond to this impending abandonment of white women's suffrage in favor of black men's voting rights in a letter she wrote to a national abolitionist newspaper. Gage was strongly committed to racial equality. She had volunteered for the first efforts to assist slaves' transition into freedom on South Carolina's Sea Islands during the Civil War, and after the war she became a chief agent of the Freedmen's Bureau. (Gage is perhaps most famous for penning the words "Ar'n't I a Woman," attributed to former slave Sojourner Truth.) A month after Gage's letter, Elizabeth Cady Stanton wrote her own response to Wendell Phillips's declaration that it was "the negro's hour." At this moment, Gage and Stanton were still firmly behind the strategy of universal suffrage, and both insisted that African American women would be denied full emancipation under the Republicans' strategy of black male suffrage. Stanton summarized her position in an acerbic letter to Phillips, asking that he answer one question: "Do you believe the African race is composed entirely of males?"

PROBLEMS TO CONSIDER

1. On what grounds did women suffrage activists assert a woman's right to vote? Can you also discern the arguments against women's suffrage that activists such as Gage and Stanton needed to confront?
2. What was the case these women made for universal, as opposed to just male, citizenship rights?

LETTER TO THE EDITOR

Sir, . . . Can any one tell us why the great advocates of Human Equality, such men as Wendell Phillips and Wm. L. Garrison, who a few years ago were bold champions for equality before the law for women, and gave eloquent lectures in behalf of the sex—more than one-half of the people of the United States, oppressed by unjust laws and partial legislation—now wholly ignore that part of the subject, and forget that once when they were a weak party and needed all the womanly strength of the nation to help them on, they always united the words, "without regard to sex, race, or color"? Who ever hears of sex now from any of these champions of freedom?

Are the four or five millions of hard working women at the North, whose half-priced labor reduces them almost to the dead line of starvation, of no account? Will the two millions of emancipated women of the South be fully protected against the cruel practices of their old tyrants by giving a vote only to male citizens?

Every day we hear arguments in favor of negro suffrage, urged on the ground that he has held the bayonet during this last war. Have the women of the North done nothing to help the nation forward to its present position? Have they who gave husbands and sons[,] time, money, strength, health—all that makes life desirable for their country, no claim to broader privilege? Is it so unjust for a colored man to work for poor wages, such as voting landowners or capitalists may compel, and yet no injustice to women? Is taxation without representation tyranny to them and not to us? . . . And please tell us, while you are about it, why justice to *all* is not better for a nation and a people than injustice to the majority. . . .

N.B.—My sense is *too short* to see the justice of some of the arguments I read in these days of majestic enthusiasm for liberty with woman left out.

FRANCES D. GAGE

National Anti-Slavery Standard, November 29, 1865.

THIS IS THE NEGRO'S HOUR

Sir:—By an amendment of the Constitution, ratified by three-fourths of the loyal States, the black man is declared free. The largest and most influential political party is demanding suffrage for him throughout the Union, which right in many of the States is already conceded. Although this may remain a question for politicians to wrangle over for five or ten years, the black man is still, in a political point of view, far above the educated women of the country. The representative women of the nation have done their uttermost for the last thirty years to secure freedom for the negro, and so long as he was lowest in the scale of being we were willing to press *his* claims; but now, as the celestial gate to civil rights is slowly moving on its hinges, it becomes a serious question whether we had better stand aside and see "Sambo" walk into the kingdom first. As self-preservation is the first law of nature, would it not be wiser to keep our lamps trimmed and burning, and when the constitutional door is open, avail ourselves of the strong arm and blue uniform of the black soldier to walk in by his side, and thus make the gap so wide that no privileged class could ever again close it against the humblest citizen in the republic?

"This is the negro's hour." Are we sure that he, once entrenched in all his inalienable rights, may not be an added power to hold us at bay? Have not "black male citizens" been heard to say they doubted the wisdom of extending the right of suffrage to women? Why should the African prove more just and generous than his Saxon compeers? If the two millions of Southern black women are not to be secured in their rights of person, property, wages, and children, their emancipation is but another form of slavery. In fact, it is better to be the slave of an educated white man, than of a degraded, ignorant black one. We who know what absolute power the statute laws of most of the States give man, in all his civil, political, and social relations, demand that in changing the status of the four millions of Africans, the women as well as the men shall be secured in all the rights, privileges, and immunities of citizens.

It is all very well for the privileged order to look down complacently and tell us, "This is the negro's hour; do not clog his way; do not embarrass the Republican party with any new issue; be generous and magnanimous; the negro once safe, the woman comes next." Now, if our prayer involved a new set of measures, or a new train of thought, it would be cruel to tax "white male citizens" with even two simple questions at a time; but the disfranchised all make the same demand, and the same logic and justice that secures suffrage to one class gives it to all. . . . This is our opportunity to retrieve the errors of the past and mould anew the elements of Democracy. The nation is ready for a long step in the right direction; party lines are obliterated, and all men are thinking for themselves. If our rulers have the justice to give the black man suffrage, woman should avail herself of that new-born virtue to secure her rights; if not, she should begin with renewed earnestness to educate the people into the idea of universal suffrage.

ELIZABETH CADY STANTON

Elizabeth Cady Stanton, "This Is the Negro's Hour," *National Anti-Slavery Standard*, December 26, 1865, in *History of Woman Suffrage*, 6 vols., edited by Elizabeth Cady Stanton et al. (Rochester, N.Y.: Susan B. Anthony, 1881–1922), 2:94–95.

ஃ

Speech Before the National Woman Suffrage Convention (1869)
ELIZABETH CADY STANTON

The Republicans succeeded in passing the Fourteenth Amendment to the Constitution in 1866, as women's rights activists anticipated. It not only defined freedmen as citizens and guaranteed them equal protection under the law but also reduced a state's representation in Congress if it denied any of its "male inhabitants" the right to vote. For the first time, the Constitution defined a voting citizen as "male" and inscribed sexual discrimination into the fundamental law of the land. Abolitionist and feminist women felt betrayed. Supporters of women's suffrage became increasingly critical of the Republican Party, which shunned their demands in favor of black suffrage. By 1869, Radical Republicans in Congress succeeded in passing the Fifteenth Amendment, which committed the federal government to prohibiting any state from disfranchising its citizens on the basis of race. Democrats called the Fifteenth Amendment "the most revolutionary measure" ever conceived by Congress.

The Fifteenth Amendment created a permanent rift in the white female constituency of the suffragist movement. Elizabeth Cady Stanton and Susan B. Anthony severed the historic ties of women's suffrage to abolitionism and the Republican Party and formed an independent political movement, the National Woman Suffrage Association (NWSA). They called their newspaper the Revolution. *Another faction, led by Lucy Stone, Julia Ward Howe, and abolitionist-Republican men, remained loyal to the Republican Party and formed the American Woman Suffrage Association. (This division among suffragists would not be healed until 1890.) During the debates over the passage of the Fifteenth Amendment, the NWSA began to petition for the adoption of a sixteenth amendment, penned by Anthony, calling for the right of suffrage to all citizens regardless of their sex. This turn of events led Stanton and Anthony further from the position of universal suffrage and racial equity, as evidenced in Stanton's address before the National Woman Suffrage Convention in 1869.*

PROBLEMS TO CONSIDER

1. Compare Stanton's 1869 speech to her 1865 essay: Did her position on the interdependence of black and woman suffrage change during these four years?
2. How and why did Stanton build her argument for women's equality on the basis of the supposed sexual differences between women and men?

Those who represent what is called "the Woman's Rights Movement," have argued their right to political equality from every standpoint of justice, religion, and logic, for the last twenty years. . . . There are no new arguments to be made on human rights, our work to-day is to apply to ourselves those so familiar to all; to teach man that woman is not an anomalous being, outside all laws and constitutions, but one whose rights are to be established by the same process of reason as that by which he demands his own.

. . . The same arguments . . . used by the great Republican party to enfranchise a million black men in the South, all these arguments we have to-day to offer for woman, and one, in addition, stronger than all besides, the difference in man and woman. Because man and woman are the complement of one another, we need woman's thought in national affairs to make a safe and stable government.

The Republican party to-day congratulates itself on having carried the Fifteenth Amendment of the Constitution, thus securing "manhood suffrage" and establishing an aristocracy of sex on this continent. . . .

This fundamental principle of our government—the equality of all the citizens of the republic—should be incorporated in the Federal Constitution, there to remain forever. To leave this question to the States and partial acts of Congress, is to defer indefinitely its settlement. . . . Hence, we appeal to the party now in power, everywhere to end this protracted debate on suffrage, and declare it the inalienable right of every citizen who is amenable to the laws of the land, who pays taxes and the penalty of crime. We have a splendid theory of a genuine republic, why not realize it and make our government homogeneous, from Maine to California. The Republican party has the power to do this, and now is its only opportunity. . . .

I urge a speedy adoption of a Sixteenth Amendment for the following reasons:

1. A government, based on the principle of caste and class, can not stand. The aristocratic idea, in any form, is opposed to the genius of our free institutions. . . . While all men, everywhere, are rejoicing in new-found liberties, shall woman alone be denied the rights, privileges, and immunities of citizenship? . . . While here, in our own land, slaves, but just rejoicing in the proclamation of emancipation, ignorant alike of its power and significance, have the ballot unasked, unsought, already laid at their feet—think you the daughters of Adams, Jefferson, and Patrick Henry, in whose veins flows the blood of two Revolutions, will forever linger round the campfires of an old barbarism, with no longings to join this grand army of freedom in its onward march to roll back the golden gates of a higher and better civilization? Of all kinds of aristocracy, that of sex is the most odious and unnatural; invading, as it does, our homes, desecrating our family altars, dividing those whom God has joined together, exalting the son above the mother who bore him, and subjugating, everywhere, moral power to brute force. Such a government would not be worth the blood and treasure so freely poured out in its long struggles for freedom. . . .

2. I urge a Sixteenth Amendment, because "manhood suffrage" or a man's government, is civil, religious, and social disorganization. The male element is a destructive force, stern, selfish, aggrandizing, loving war, violence, conquest, acquisition, breeding in the material and

moral world alike discord, disorder, disease, and death. . . . The male element has held high carnival thus far, it has fairly run riot from the beginning, overpowering the feminine element everywhere, crushing out all the diviner qualities in human nature, until we know but little of true manhood and womanhood. . . .

People object to the demands of those whom they choose to call the strong-minded, because they say, "the right of suffrage will make the women masculine." That is just the difficulty in which we are involved to-day. Though disfranchised we have few women in the best sense, we have simply so many reflections, varieties, and dilutions of the masculine gender. The strong, natural characteristics of womanhood are repressed and ignored in dependence, for so long as man feeds woman she will try to please the giver and adapt herself to his condition. To keep a foothold in society woman must be as near like man as possible, reflect his ideas, opinions, virtues, motives, prejudices, and vices. . . .

We ask woman's enfranchisement, as the first step toward the recognition of that essential element in government that can only secure the health, strength, and prosperity of the nation. Whatever is done to lift woman to her true position will help to usher in a new day of peace and perfection for the race. . . . But government gains no new element of strength in admitting all men to the ballot-box, for we have too much of the man-power there already. We see this in every department of legislation, and it is a common remark, that unless some new virtue is infused into our public life the nation is doomed to destruction. Will the foreign element, the dregs of China, Germany, England, Ireland, and Africa supply this needed force, or the nobler types of American womanhood who have taught our presidents, senators, and congressmen the rudiments of all they know?

3. I urge a Sixteenth Amendment because, when "manhood suffrage" is established from Maine to California, woman has reached the lowest depths of political degradation. So long as there is a disfranchised class in this country, and that class its women, a man's government is worse than a white man's government with suffrage limited by property and educational qualifications. . . . If American women find it hard to bear the oppressions of their own Saxon fathers, the best orders of manhood, what may they not be called to endure when all the lower orders of foreigners now crowding our shores legislate for them and their daughters. Think of Patrick and Sambo and Hans and Yung Tung, who do not know the difference between a monarchy and a republic, who can not read the Declaration of Independence or Webster's spelling-book, making laws for Lucretia Mott, Ernestine L. Rose, and Anna E. Dickinson. . . . This manhood suffrage is an appalling question, and it would be well for thinking women, who seem to consider it so magnanimous to hold their own claims in abeyance until all men are crowned with citizenship, to remember that the most ignorant men are ever the most hostile to the equality of women, as they have known them only in slavery and degradation. . . .

It is a startling assertion, but nevertheless true, that in none of the nations of modern Europe are the higher classes of women politically so degraded as are the women of this Republic to-day. . . . In our Southern States even, before the war, women were not degraded below the working population. They were not humiliated in seeing their coachmen, gardeners, and waiters go to the polls to legislate for them; but here, in this boasted Northern civilization, women of wealth and education, who pay taxes and obey the laws, who in morals and intellect are the peers of their proudest rulers, are thrust outside the pale of political consideration with minors, paupers, lunatics, traitors, idiots, with those guilty of bribery, larceny, and infamous crimes.

History of Woman Suffrage, 6 vols., edited by Elizabeth Cady Stanton et al. (Rochester, N.Y.: Susan B. Anthony, 1881–1922), 2:349–55.

❧

The First Vote (1867)

Frederick Douglass Addresses the American Equal Rights Association (1868 and 1869)

"Slavery is not abolished," Frederick Douglass told a group of abolitionists in 1865, "until the black man has the ballot." Black demands for suffrage affirmed traditional American principles that equated manhood and military service with citizenship and voting rights. Since the nation's founding, one's claim to have fought for the nation gave one the right to deliberate in the nation's political decision making. Douglass phrased it in this way: "To say that I am a citizen to pay taxes . . . obey laws . . . and fight the battles of the country, but in all that respects voting and representation, I am but as so much inert matter, is to insult my manhood." Many black Civil War veterans shared those sentiments. An illustration, entitled "The First Vote," for a cover of Harper's Weekly *in 1867, captured that perspective. However, Douglass did not rest his arguments for black suffrage on sexual difference alone, nor did he oppose the right of women to vote. For almost two decades prior to Reconstruction, Douglass could be heard speaking out at women's rights conventions when few other men (white or black) were anywhere to be found. So there was nothing unusual about Douglass addressing the annual meeting of the American Equal Rights Association in 1868 and 1869; but at that moment, he articulated his reasons for insisting that the right to vote for black men was a more urgent demand than suffrage for white women.*

PROBLEMS TO CONSIDER

1. What do the various men in "The First Vote" illustration symbolize? And what does the image reveal about the thinking of some white northerners about black men's suffrage?
2. Explain why Frederick Douglass thought that black suffrage was more urgently needed than women's voting rights. Is his an argument about race, human rights, or class?

ADDRESS (1868)

The call upon me for a speech on this occasion has been unexpected, and unsought, and I have no lengthy or elaborate remarks to offer. But I must say that I know of no argument that can be adduced in favor of the right of man to suffrage which is not equally forcible, and equally applicable to woman. If it be essential to the dignity of man; if it be necessary to protect the rights of man, it must be equally essential and necessary to woman. If it have the effect to elevate a man,

to inspire within him higher ideas of duty, and of honor, it will necessarily have the same influence upon woman.

I am sorry to say that the race to which I belong have not generally taken the right ground on this question. The idea of obtaining their own rights has so occupied their minds as to exclude the thought of what justice demanded for others. Or if they thought of it, they were not ready to acknowledge the right in the case of women. But, after all, there is a great deal of human nature exhibited in this feeling. It is

"THE FIRST VOTE."—Drawn by A. R. Waud.—[See next page.]

"The First Vote," *Harper's Weekly*, November 16, 1867.

(The Granger Collection, New York.)

eminently natural and habitual in men and women too to be clamorous for their own rights while they ignore or deny the existence of the same rights in others.

What our Government now needs is more honesty, more goodness, more virtue in its coun-cils, and for this reason I advocate the admission of the votes of the women of the land. . . . I pre-sume that woman is about like man in these respects—that is, the instincts of the human heart in woman are substantially the same as those in man. And I see no better way than to take in the women, in order to make our government pure. . . .

Since the termination of the war the popular sentiment is crying, "Down with the Rebellion!" and advocating the freedom of the slave, but they do not want them *quite* so free as themselves, they are willing to leave upon their limbs a few links of their chains to remind them of the rock out of which they have been hewn. There is no such thing as instantaneous emancipation; true, the links of the chain may be broken in an instant, but it will take not less than a century to obliterate all traces of the institution. Our Government must be the best and strongest in the world if it be only made consistent with genuine Republicanism, the principle of deriving its power from the consent of a people governed, taxation and representation going side by side. No man should be excluded from the Government on account of his color, no woman on account of her sex; there should be no shoulder that does not bear its burden of the Government, and no individual conscience debarred of chance to exercise its influence for good on the National councils. Then will our Government be the strongest ever seen, and be lasting until the end of the world. I do not expect that the extension of the franchise to my race and to woman is going to suddenly accomplish all this good, but it will accomplish in the end some great results. To the race to which I belong the ballot means something more than a mere abstract idea. It means the right to live and to protect itself by honest industry. You women have representatives. Your brothers, and your husbands, and your fathers vote for you, but the black wife has no husband who can vote for her. . . . The impeachment of the President *[Andrew Johnson]* will be a hopeful indication of the triumph of our right to vote. It will mean the negro's right to vote, and mean that the fair South shall no longer be governed by the Regulators and the Ku-Klux Klan, but by fair and impartial law.

New York Daily Tribune, May 15, 1868.

ADDRESS (1869)

Mr. Douglass:—I came here more as a listener than to speak, and I have listened with a great deal of pleasure. . . . There is no name greater than that of Elizabeth Cady Stanton in the matter of woman's rights and equal rights, but my sentiments are tinged a little against *The Revolution.* There was in the address to which I allude the employment of certain names, such as "Sambo," and the gardener, and the bootblack, and the daughters of Jefferson and Washington, and all the rest that I can not coincide with. I have asked what difference there is between the daughters of Jefferson and Washington and other daughters. (Laughter.) I must say that I do not see how any one can pretend that there is the same urgency in giving the ballot to woman as to the negro. With us, the matter is a question of life and death, at least, in fifteen States of the Union. When women, because they are women, are hunted down through the cities of New York and New Orleans; when they are dragged from their houses and hung upon lamp-posts; when their children are torn from their arms, and their brains dashed out upon the pavement; when they are objects of insult and outrage at every turn; when they are in danger of having their homes burnt down over their heads; when their children are not allowed to enter schools; then they will have an urgency to obtain the ballot equal to our own. (Great applause.)

A voice:—Is that not all true about black women?

Mr. Douglass:—Yes, yes, yes; it is true of the black woman, but not because she is a woman, but because she is black. (Applause.) Julia Ward Howe at the conclusion of her great speech delivered at the convention in Boston last year, said: "I am willing that the negro shall get the ballot before me." (Applause.) . . . I am in favor of woman's suffrage in order that we shall have all the virtue and vice confronted. . . .

Miss Anthony:—The old anti-slavery school say women must stand back and wait until the negroes shall be recognized. But we say, if you will not give the whole loaf of suffrage to the entire people, give it to the most intelligent first. (Applause.) If intelligence, justice, and morality are to have precedence in the Government, let the question of woman be brought up first and that of the negro last. (Applause.) . . . When Mr. Douglass mentioned the black man first and the woman last, if he had noticed he would have seen that it was the men that clapped and not the women. There is not the woman born who desires to eat the bread of dependence, no matter whether it be from the hand of father, hus-

band, or brother. . . . (Applause.) Mr. Douglass talks about the wrongs of the negro; but with all the outrages that he to-day suffers, he would not exchange his sex and take the place of Elizabeth Cady Stanton. (Laughter and applause.)

Mr. Douglass: —I want to know if granting you the right of suffrage will change the nature of our sexes? (Great laughter.)

History of Woman Suffrage, 6 vols., edited by Elizabeth Cady Stanton et al. (Rochester, N.Y.: Susan B. Anthony, 1881–1922), 2:382–83.

ᕽ

ᕽ White Terror and Racial Violence ᕽ

Black voting in the South was truly revolutionary. After the Reconstruction Acts of 1867, more than 700,000 black voters were registered in ten southern states; four-fifths of them voted in the elections of 1867 and 1868. African Americans were elected to every state legislature and even constituted a majority in the South Carolina legislature. Between 1868 and 1876, southern states elected fourteen black U.S. congressmen, two U.S. senators, and six lieutenant governors. Even if these numbers did not constitute parity (keep in mind that in five states blacks actually constituted a majority of the electorate), these were extraordinary gains, especially compared with the complete denial of political rights to African Americans under slavery.

A counterrevolutionary movement emerged in the South during Reconstruction. It manifested itself as a loosely organized, but ruthlessly violent, domestic terrorist campaign. White southerners who refused to acquiesce to the new social and political order of Radical Reconstruction turned to the Ku Klux Klan and similar organizations, such as the Knights of the White Camellia or the White Brotherhood, to try to reverse the revolutionary changes in their midst.

The Ku Klux Klan was a vigilante, paramilitary force dedicated to using violence and intimidation (under the cover of night and disguise) to overturn Republican Party rule and restore white supremacy. Violence now became the new reality of politics, and the Klan emerged as the violent arm of the Democratic Party. Klansmen targeted not only blacks who voted Republican or won elections to political office but also so-called "uppity" blacks, who taught in schools, refused to accept unfair labor contracts, acquired land or livestock, or rejected the deferential behavior demanded under slavery. In Camilla, Georgia, four hundred armed whites opened fire on a black election parade, killing and wounding more than twenty. In two separate massacres, in Saint Landry Parish (1868) and Colfax (1873) in Louisiana, Klan mobs killed more than 200 and 280 blacks respectively.

The Ku Klux Klan was founded in Pulaski, Tennessee, in 1866, but as the Reconstruction Acts of 1867 took effect in the spring of 1868 and a presidential election neared, Klan organizations and violence sprang up in nearly every southern state. Some areas of the former Confederacy remained largely untouched by the Klan. Its activity tended to flourish in the piedmont regions where small farms and nearly equal racial populations and political party strength made white violence an effective weapon for intimidating freedmen and Republicans. Night riding and violence effectively broke up the Republican Party in Georgia and Louisiana, but the party's presidential candidate, Ulysses S. Grant, still carried all of the other southern states in the 1868 election.

Klansmen and their sympathizers created a culture of terror in the Reconstruction South. Night-riding terrorist episodes spilled over into popular racial ideologies, which found their way into print as folktales, off-color jokes, and political oratory. Newspapers and books have too rarely been examined for their role in developing a popular consumer culture of white terror. By examining this culture, we can discover the powerful legacy of minstrelsy humor as an instrument of terror. Moreover, we also expose the new ways that white supremacists sexualized political discourse and created a counterrevolutionary ideology that justified violence against blacks as a safeguard against an alleged sexual threat of black men's political freedom in the South.

❧ THE KLAN AS MINSTRELSY: HUMOR AND TERROR

The Klan's own origin legend states that it began as a social club for young Confederate veterans returning home only to find no prospects for business and a complete absence of "amusements and social diversions." Klansmen maintained that their original purpose was to "have fun, make mischief, and play pranks on the public." Of course, by "the public" they meant their white Republican enemies and a newly freed black population. In light of the violence that followed, we should not lose sight of the cultural significance of how the Klan entwined humor with terror to accomplish its goals. Agents of white terror exploited forms of comic discourse for the consumption of a white public, offering them a palatable ideology for reasserting racial dominance once legalized slavery—the foundation of their earlier domination—had been abolished. We need not psychoanalyze this phenomenon to affirm Freud's observation that jokes can often express "brutal hostility, forbidden by law."

Southern newspapers and humorists combined to create a receptive climate for acts of Klan violence. The staple of their humor involved comic tales of black fright and flight. White folktales of pranks and scares were placed side by side with depictions of disfigured black bodies and performances of Klan night riders who donned outrageous costumes and posed as the wartime dead. Americans already had an indigenous form of humorous entertainment designed to reinforce a racial hierarchy—the popular shows of blackface minstrel performers (see chapter 8)—and minstrelsy played an important role in the reception of the Klan. In the years before the Civil War, minstrel companies regularly visited southern towns, and their popularity continued after the war. Black fright and cowardice, as we have seen, were typical comic ploys of minstrel shows, as were slapstick routines that made scares and violence part of the jokes that audiences and performers shared. During Reconstruction, a sympathetic print culture turned racial cruelty into popular comedy whose significance was apparent to all southern people, whether white or black.

A Terrified Negro (1868)

Ku-Klux in a Safe (1868)

K.K.K.K. (1868)

As they had been throughout the nineteenth century, newspapers during Reconstruction were published to advance the interests of a political party. Thus, it was Republican papers that recorded most of the atrocities committed by the Klan, while Democratic papers encouraged more lighthearted attitudes toward Klan activity. For instance, the Pulaski Citizen, *published in the Klan's birthplace, circulated legends of Klansmen consuming human flesh, advertised for a local "Ku Klux Soda Fount," and even jokingly threatened to send the Klan after readers who failed to pay their subscriptions. Even more common, Democratic newspapers such as the* Nashville Union and Dispatch *published tales depicting Klansmen frightening blacks with practical jokes that combined humor with terror, drawing on stereotypes of African American superstitions about ghosts, as well as comic slapstick routines from minstrel shows.*

PROBLEMS TO CONSIDER

1. How might this humor have shaped the way white southerners discussed black politics? Why was it important that readers laugh at these episodes of terror?
2. What does the emerging market for Klan commodities suggest about the relationship between politics and the consumer economy in the South?

A TERRIFIED NEGRO

A negro was met by one of the Ku-Klux near Franklin a few days ago, and the cowled knight of the black cross and scarlet robe cordially offered to shake hands. The negro grasped the extended palm, but no sooner had he touched it than it dropped off, leaving nothing but the bleeding stump of a gory wrist. Sambo, with a mingled shriek and yell of horror and fright, took to his heels and never once stopped until he had reached home, a distance of some five miles, where he curled up on his cabin floor, remaining in that position several hours before he could recover sufficiently to relate what had occurred.

"A Terrified Negro," *Nashville Union and American*, March 1, 1868.

KU-KLUX IN A SAFE

Night before last, the clerks at the Chattanooga Depot perpetrated a fearful joke upon a darkie employed there, who goes by the name of General Butler. One of them, wrapping himself in a newly washed sheet, and donning a tall hat constructed of blotting paper, placed himself inside of a big safe, and at a late hour the negro was sent to the safe with two books, which he had orders to deposit. As he slowly swung the door on its hinges, a deep groan that seemed to come from the door itself in complaint at being disturbed, nearly lifted poor Butler from his boots. Almost simultaneously, a shriek, as from some yawning grave, fell upon his ear, and a ghostly figure rushed toward him. With a loud yell of horror and dismay, the darkie sank upon the floor, where he doubled himself as if of India rubber, and lay till the graceless scamps who had imposed upon him could bring to bear the proper restoratives, and lay the mischievous ghost who had come so near being the death of him.

"Ku-Klux in a Safe," *Nashville Union and Dispatch*, April 3, 1868.

K.K.K.K.

The genius and enterprise of some people is truly astonishing. Since the "Ku Klux fever" was at its highest pitch in our midst, we have had "Ku Klux Music" from the Music houses, "Ku Klux hats" from Furnishing emporiums, "Ku Klux Cocktails" from the different saloons, together with the many little "Ku Klux etceteras" not in mind. And to cap the climax we now have the genuine "Ku Klux Klan Knife," with cabalistic letters and the terrible symbols of the order on its blade. That sterling firm, Craighead, Breast & Gibson, Exclusive Wholesale Hardware Merchants, 45 Public Square, conceived the happy idea some weeks since and yesterday a large invoice of *their express designings* from their trans-Atlantic manufacturers, Frederick Ware & Co., Sheffield, England, was received at their warerooms in this city.

"K.K.K.K.," *Nashville Union and Dispatch*, June 26, 1868.

ᵔ

Testimony Taken by the Sub-Committee of Elections in Louisiana (1870)

Members of the Ku Klux Klan were sworn to secrecy and waged most of their acts of terror after nightfall in rural areas, where the only witnesses were the victims of violence, who lacked printing presses to tell their stories. Fortunately, the Klan's terrorist campaign forced northern Republicans to intervene. A series of Enforcement Acts, followed by the Ku Klux Klan Act of 1871, brought the federal courts into action and led to lengthy investigations of Klan activity by congressional committees. These congressional testimonies gave voice to black perspectives on the Klan, even as they confirmed the Klan's intertwining of practical jokes and terror. Some former slaves likened the Klan to antebellum slave patrols, but many others knew that Klan violence far exceeded the ferocity of slave patrols and that it stemmed from the new social and political circumstances that followed emancipation.

PROBLEMS TO CONSIDER

1. How does this testimony help us understand the reasons that Klansmen terrorized black southerners?
2. How did black men and women in the South understand the actions and performances of the Klan?

George Washington (colored) sworn and examined.
. . .

Question. Where were you during the late election?—*Answer.* I was home, but I did not go to the polls.

Q. Why didn't you go?—*A.* Because it was too dangerous.

Q. Why was it considered too dangerous?—*A.* Because there were so many threats out against the republican party.

Q. Who made those threats?—*A.* The white people. Just before the election, Mr. Don Williams told me he heard fifty men in Mansfield swear they would kill me if I made my appearance. . . .

Q. Did you run on the republican ticket for any office?—*A.* I was on the republican ticket in the election previous to the last election, but was not a candidate at the last election.

Q. Why did these men say they would kill you?—*A.* Because I was in a party opposite against them.

Q. Because you were a republican?—*A.* Yes, sir.

Q. Had you done anything to make them angry with you personally?—*A.* Not at all. . . .

Q. How is it with the parties up there on the question of suffrage? Are the democrats up there satisfied to let the colored people vote?—*A.* I believe they are perfectly willing for them to vote, provided they vote as they want them to vote. . . .

Q. Were there any threats of violence?—*A.* There was plenty of that from time to time. One thing that was frequently said was, that you could not vote against a man and eat out of his smoke-house: another, that you could not vote against a man and expect to receive justice from him at all. This has been pretty much the talk; and against me as the leader, they made mighty heavy threats.

Q. Was there anything said up there amongst the colored people about the Ku-Klux?—*A.* Oh, yes, sir; there was Ku-Klux up there.

Q. What was said about them?—*A.* The Ku Klux went to some of their houses once or twice. They had not got to killing at that time, but they were so disguised you could not state whether they were men or not. They passed as spirits, and pretended to raise the dead rebel soldiers. They went to the graveyard and frightened one woman very bad. They charged right through the graveyard on horseback.

Q. How did the Ku-Klux appear when they came?—*A.* I never got my "eye-sight" on them, but I saw people that did. They passed for ghosts—for men raised from the dead. They would come round and tell a man "Hold my head till I fix my backbone right"; and the colored people didn't know whether they were ghosts or not, because one of them went to a man's house and called for a drink of water. He drew three buckets of water and carried to him, and he drank every drop of it. He had to go to the pump and start it fresh three times, and when he came back the bucket each time was empty. I never saw them, but there were some of the worst disguised people you ever saw. Some of them had sheets round them. . . .

Q. What did they do when they first came out?—*A.* One man saw one of the Ku-Klux and though he was a spirit, and raised his gun and was going to shoot at him when the man said "Look out; don't shoot me, sir;" and then he knew he was a man, and rode off. They had not commenced killing people when they first came out. I took it for a sort of fun, and didn't believe they would hurt anybody.

Q. Afterwards what did they do?—*A.* Afterwards they came to a man's house and killed him. They didn't play with him then. . . .

Q. Were they afraid of them?—*A.* Yes, sir; and I don't blame them for being afraid.

Q. Did they understand that this had anything to do with politics?—*A.* They very well knew that it all arose from politics, because we never heard of such a thing before.

Isham Buckhalter (black man) sworn and examined on behalf of Mr. Sypher.

I live in Franklintown, Washington Parish, I am working a farm on shares. I have lived there for twenty-three or twenty-four years. . . . I voted the democratic ticket at the November election. I am not a democrat. That is not my principles. I was bound to vote the democratic ticket or to do worse.

Question. How did you expect to do worse?—*Answer.* I expected to be flung out of employment into the woods.

Q. Why did you think so?—*A.* I had reason to think so. I tried all I could to vote my way, and could not do it. I had to vote the other way. I had republican tickets but I was afraid to distribute them. I was afraid of the whole democratic party of the parish.

Q. Did they ever threaten you?—*A.* Yes; they Ku-Kluxed my house and knocked down one leaf of the door. I got away out of the house. They came in and inquired for the radical tickets that I had. They happened to be in my purse, and I had it in the pocket of my pants. There were some old tickets there, which they took and burned up. I cannot tell you who these men were. They were disguised. They were dressed in sheets, and wore false faces. They fired off a gun and pistol while they were in my house.

Q. Are you a leading man up there among the colored people?—*A.* They call me a leading man among them. . . .

Question. How many Ku-Klux came to your house?—*Answer.* About fifteen or twenty, not less than fifteen. My father-in-law was there, but he was disabled; he could not get up without crutches. My family were all in the house; my little boy got frightened, and every now and then since he has spasms, and will cry out, "Look, papa, Ku-Klux!" When I hear that, I tell you it hurts me through. The Ku-Klux looked like people. Some had hats, and some caps. They had false faces and white sheets all over their horses.

. . . I heard the Sunday evening before that they had killed John Kemp and another colored man. I thought to myself that they would kill me, too, as they called me a leading colored man. I believe to-day that they would have killed me if they had caught me. . . .

Q. Were the colored people much afraid of them?—*A.* They were bound to be afraid of them. What could they do but be afraid? Certainly they were afraid. If it had not been for them, they would have voted as they wanted to vote. They did not think they were ghosts. Any sensible human would know that they were not ghosts. I never heard of ghosts jumping off their horses and knocking down doors, and taking such shapes as that. We knew they were men. . . .

Q. What did you colored men understand by their doings?—*A.* That they were going around scaring us to make us vote their way.

41st Congress, 2d Session, House of Representatives, *Testimony Taken by the Sub-Committee of Elections in Louisiana* (Washington, D.C.: Government Printing Office, 1870), Part 1, 150, 153–54, 400–401.

⁊

Sut Lovingood's Allegory (1868)
GEORGE WASHINGTON HARRIS

One of the South's most popular humor writers, George Washington Harris, a Tennessee native, rose to prominence and produced most of his best-known work at the same time as the Klan's insurgency. Harris's collection of comic sketches entitled Yarns Spun by a Nat'ral Durn'd Fool *featured the country bumpkin Sut Lovingood. The tales were published just as Congress was passing the Reconstruction Acts and the Klan's popularity was spreading throughout those areas most receptive to Harris's sketches. Sut Lovingood stories appeared in Klan-sympathizing newspapers, including those that capitalized on the Klan sensation, such as the* Ku Klux Kaleidoscope *(Goldsboro, N.C.). Literary critics and other scholars, however, have usually dismissed Harris's humor as a regional folk genre, a form of rowdy frontier humor. Too little attention has been focused on the interrelationship between Harris's comic sketches of racial violence and the Reconstruction counterrevolution during which the Klan flourished. White southern readers were apt to consume Harris's Sut Lovingood tales as part of a print culture that included comic newspaper stories, such as the ones reproduced earlier in the chapter. An example of a Sut Lovingood yarn is this brief allegory in which Harris uses a black goat (goats were a common folk symbol for sexual disorder and adultery) to represent the black Republican social order brought on by Reconstruction. Most of Harris's tales involve Sut's violent pranks against actual freed slaves, rather than an animal allegory, and contain graphically offensive racist language.*

PROBLEMS TO CONSIDER

1. How might Harris's tales be seen as part of a culture war during Reconstruction?
2. How do Harris's tales relate to "The First Vote" illustration at the beginning of this chapter, or to other aspects of the South's social and political revolution?

I was just thinking boys, while Sut was speaking, whether we are the gainer by the discoveries—inventions—innovations, and prayers, of the last forty years. Whether the railway—telegraph—chloroform—moral reform, and other advancements, as they are termed, have really advanced us any, in the right direction or—

"Stop right thar, George, an' take my idear ove the thing, fresh from water. I know powerful well that I is a durn'd fool, an' all that—but I can *see*, by golly! Don't the Bible tell about them seekin' out many strange inventions?" . . .

"No, boys, we aint as *good* as we wer forty years ago. We am too dam artifichul, interprizin an' *sharp*—we know too much. We ought to be sarved like Old Brakebill sarved his black billy goat. We desarve hit, mos' all ove us." . . .

Well! Sut if you will not let me talk, suppose you tell us how Brakebill served his black billy goat. And let us draw no comparisons between the lost past and the present, which we must endure.

"Oh! I dont know much about hit. Only hearsay, from the old folks, you know. Hit seems that he had, what would be call'd now a days, a progressive billy goat—a regular, walkin insult to man, an' beast; he strutted, with his hine laigs, and munched, like a fool gall with hir fore ones. An' then his tail—hit said, 'you-be-dam,' all day long, an' him as black as a coal cellar, at midnight at that. He would a suited our day to a dot tho', an' our day would a suited him. He could a hilt his own, ever agin the 'business men.' . . .

"But, he wer altogether too dam smart for Brakebill, or Brakebill's day, an' generashun beyant all sort of doubt. That ar meterfistickal, free will, billy goat wer forty years ahead ove *his* day. As they say in praise ove some cussed raskil, when he gets a million in a week, when at the gineril rate ove fortin makin, hit had orter took him sixty days. He had been showin many marks ove progress, an' higher law, for a good while, without attractin much notice anyway. Sich as buttin old misses Brakebill, bucket an' all, belly down, clean thru onder the cow, as she stoop'd to milk her. An' then buttin the cow herself out ove her slop tub, so that he could wet his own beard in her supper. That wer 'higher law,' warnt hit? Or he'd watch for the old man to go from the crib to the hog pen, with thirty big ears of corn, piled on his arm. When he'd make a de-monstrashun in the rear, that would send the old feller, spread eagle fashion, plowin gravel with his snout, while he impudently munch'd the hog's corn. That were financeerin, I s'pose. . . .

"But at last Mister Benny overdid the thing; he got to be a little too durn'd progressive for old Brakebill and his times. His sin foun' him out, an' he wer made to simmer down to a level sur-face with the loss ove all, that makes life whole-some to a goat. The fac' is, like mos' ove these yere human progress humbugs, he jis' played h—l with hissef.

"Old Brakebill got to noticin that thar was something wrong with his sheep. The ewes butted at the ram, spiteful like, butted one an-other an' behaved powerful bad ginerally. Arter a while, on 'zaminin he foun' that some ove the lambs had patches ove coarse har in their wool, an' wer sproutin' beards. Nex' he found' his young pigs behavin' curious to be dutch hog's children. Rarin' up strait on thar hine laigs, clost fornint one another. Walkin' on top ove the fences—climbin' onto the shed roof ove the milk house, an' then buttin' another off agin. An' every now an' then, one would hist his tail as strait up as a stack pole, an' put on a stiff strut. . . . Misses Brakebill left the plantation, an' the very devil was to pay generally. If you had a wanted

to a bought the farm, you would a axed that dam goat the price ove hit, from his airs an' impudent ways, while the owner looked like a scared dorg, or a stepchild on the out aidge ove sufferance. Now, all this troubled the poor old Dutchman a power. He know'd that at the rate things were gwine on, his stock, very soon, wouldent be worth a tinker's durn. . . . You must bar in mind that the poor feller dident know the fust durn'd thing about 'progress.' At last, by the livin' jingo! the *true* idear struck him, as hit mus *us* some time. So one mornin' arter drams, he come acrost a bran new, curious, little cuss, lookin' like a cross atwixt the devil an' a cookin' stove, stand-in' on hit's hine laigs, a suckin' the muley cow. Arter brainin' hit with a wagon standard, he jist sot down, an' whetted his knife, ontil it would shave the har off his arm. Now, boys, that's about all that anybody now livin' knows ove the matter. Only this much was noticed thararter: That Mister Benny, billy goat, instid ove chawin his cud, with a short, quick, sassey nip, nip, nip, arter that mornin', an' plum on, ontil he dried up, an' died in a sink-hole, he chaw'd hit arter the fashion ove an old, lazy cow, when she is standin' onder the shade ove the willers, belly-full, an' bellydeep in the creek. His tail never agin flauntd the sky, surjestin 'youbedam.' He wer the very last one that you'd a thought ove axin about the price ove the farm. An *he dident raise any more family.*"

George Washington Harris, *Sut Lovingood's Yarns*, edited by M. Thomas Inge (New Haven: College and University Press, 1966), 315–20.

ᘒ

ᘒ THE SEXUALIZATION OF POLITICS AND THE WORK OF WHITE SUPREMACY

As "Sut Lovingood's Allegory" reveals, white southerners expressed their fears of the new freedoms and independence of African Americans in the language of height-ened anxiety about the sexual agency of black men. Southerners, white and black, admitted that black men associated voting with an assertion of their manhood. Joseph H. Rainey, a black congressman from South Carolina, declared on the floor of the U.S. House of Representatives that southern white men wished to deny suffrage to black men because they knew it "had a tendency to make him feel his manhood." "Just as soon as we begin to assert our manhood and demand our rights," Rainey concluded, "we become objectionable, we become obnoxious, and we hear this howl about social equality." In the face of the rapid dismantling of centuries of restraint over every aspect of former slaves' lives, many white southerners latched onto the phrase "social equality" to express their hostility to black and white people intermingling in public and private spaces. For many, that phrase was meant to hoist up a warning flag against sexual encounters between black men and white women.

If we conjure images of white southerners' responses to sex between white women and black men, a picture of unflinching hostility and immediate violence, typified by lynchings or Klan raids, commonly appears. But this was not a timeless phenomenon; rather, it sprang from the unique social and political developments that shaped the history of the South after the Civil War. Before the war, southern communities tolerated a variety of liaisons between black men and white women, and only rarely did such relationships result in violent or extralegal retribution. The legal institution of slavery prevented that. The bodies of slave men belonged to their master, and their property status guaranteed a certain degree of toleration. But once the bulwarks of white supremacy were swept away by slavery's demise, those who wished to maintain a system of racial dominance needed to build a new foundation for it in the South.

In the nineteenth-century South, power, politics, freedom, and citizenship rights were tied intimately to the racial constructions of gender and sexuality. White patriarchs of the slave South could measure their dominance by the freedom with which they could sexually abuse black women with impunity. Not surprisingly, they exploited fears that manhood rights for black men might now include access to white women, and they tied those fears to the violent counterrevolution against Reconstruction politics.

U.S. Senate Investigation of the Ku Klux Klan, Testimony of Thomas Tate and J. R. Smith (1872)

The U.S. Senate's investigation of Klan activities in the early 1870s brought together the voices of white and black southerners, Republicans and Democrats, Klan supporters and its opponents. Frequently, witnesses testified to the connections between politics and gender and sexuality. Reproduced here are excerpts of the testimonies of Thomas Tate, a former member of the Klan in North Carolina, and J. R. Smith, a white Republican postmaster in Meridian, Mississippi.

PROBLEMS TO CONSIDER

1. Explain all of the references to both politics and gender in the Klan's oath read at the beginning of Tate's testimony. What does it reveal about the social order that opponents of Reconstruction desired?
2. What do these testimonies reveal about the role of race or class in constructing the meaning of the term "social equality"?

TESTIMONY OF THOMAS TATE
Raleigh, North Carolina, January 1872

COUNSEL. Mr. Tate, listen to this:

"I, before the great immaculate God of heaven and earth, do take and subscribe to the following sacred binding oath and obligation: I promise and swear that I will uphold and defend the Constitution of the United States as it was handed down by our forefathers, in its original purity. I promise and swear that I will reject and oppose the principles of the radical party in all its forms, and forever maintain and contend that intelligent white men shall govern this country. I promise and pledge myself to assist, according to my pecuniary circumstances, all brothers in distress. Females, widows, and their households shall ever be specially in my care and protection. I promise and swear that I will obey all instructions given me by my chief; and should I ever divulge, or cause to be divulged, any secret, signs, or passwords of the Invisible Empire, I must meet with the fearful and the just penalty of the traitor, which is death, death, death, at the hands of the brethren."

Did you ever hear that before?

Answer. Yes, sir.

Question. Where did you hear this?

Answer. At our meetings.

Question. The Invisible Empire?

Answer. Yes, sir; at Horse Creek Den. . . .

Question. How did you come to have disguises, any way?

Answer. It was ordered by the chief to have them. . . .

Question. Did you ever go on any raid?

Answer. Yes, sir; three of them.

Question. Where?

Answer. The first on some colored man, Robert McKinney, and Widow Bridges.

Question. What did you understand it was for?

Answer. That was the orders. I was not at the meeting and didn't know why. I didn't help to whip them. . . .

Question. What was the purpose of the society?

Answer. It was to keep down the colored un's from mixing with the whites.

Question. How?

Answer. To keep them from marrying, &c., and to keep them from voting.

TESTIMONY OF J. R. SMITH
Washington, D.C., June 27, 1871

J. R. SMITH sworn and examined. . . .

Question. Is there not considerable apprehension on the part of the poor white people of that region in regard to negro equality and social equality? . . .

Answer. No, sir; there are remarkably few negroes that show a disposition to—

Question. Is not that the point upon which the democratic leaders always try to stir up the white people?

Answer. That is the means adopted by the leaders of the democratic party.

Question. That is what I mean.

Answer. Oh, yes; they talk much of that idea, and endeavor to instill it into the minds of the white people generally, and are successful to a very great extent.

Question. I want to get at the method by which they arouse the feelings of the poorer white men.

Answer. That is the burden of their argument; this question of equality that they say is endeavored to be forced upon them by the republican party, putting the negro everywhere, and putting him into position.

Question. How do they talk about this subject?

Answer. They put it in very plain terms. They say that the object of the republican party and of the Government is to put the negro in control, to make a sort of negro supremacy, to give him the control of the affairs of the Government, to put him in office, and gradually to force him into social relations with the white people. That is the argument they make use of, to the exclusion of almost every other argument, when they come before the poorer classes of the white people. That has been the case for the last three years, and it does affect the opinions of a large number of the poor white men who are really and honestly republicans, and friends of the Government. But that thing is pressed upon them so strenuously by these leaders that it has had its effect.

Question. Not only political but social equality?

Answer. Yes, sir.

Question. Marrying the whites to blacks?

Answer. Yes, sir; they take the position that putting colored men into office, in positions of prominence, will gradually lead them to demand social equality, and to intermingle by marriage with the whites.

Question. Do the negroes themselves attempt anything of this kind?

Answer. They do not; not in my section of the State. There has been very little, if any, effort on the part of any negro to force himself forward, socially, upon the whites.

U.S. Congress, Joint Select Committee on the Condition of Affairs in the Late Insurrectionary States, *Testimony Taken by the Joint Select Committee to Inquire into the Condition of Affairs in the Late Insurrectionary States*, 13 vols. (Washington, D.C.: Government Printing Office, 1872), 2:434; 11:63, 76.

ᷧ

U.S. Senate Investigation of the Ku Klux Klan, Testimony Regarding Jourdan Ware (1871)

The following Senate testimony revolves around a successful former slave, Jourdan Ware, who lived near Rome, Georgia. Ware was severely beaten by "disguised men" and forced to move off his farm. And although these witnesses were not aware at the time, Ware would be beaten to death in a later encounter with the Klan.

PROBLEMS TO CONSIDER

1. What is the connection between politics, Ware's economic success, and accusations of inappropriate sexual remarks by Ware in these testimonies?
2. How did class influence the way politics became sexualized?

TESTIMONY OF P. M. SHEIBLEY
Washington, D.C., July 10, 1871

[Sheibley was the white Republican postmaster at Rome, Georgia.]

P. M. SHEIBLEY sworn and examined. . . .

Answer. . . . At present, disturbances are still greater and violence occurs. This violence is done by disguised men, and generally toward the colored people, threatening them that they shall not vote; shall not interfere in the elections; that they must not vote the radical ticket. In several instances where I have known outrages to be committed, the parties have come to me; I did not myself see the outrages committed, because I was not with the band. But two different negroes have come to me and asked what they should do—what could be done for them. One of these negroes was named Jourdan Ware, and lived about two and a half miles from Rome. He was taken out of his house, and beaten and abused; he came to my office with his head mangled. . . .

Question. How long had you known him?

Answer. Ever since he registered. The registration took place in 1867, I believe. . . .

Question. What is his reputation and character?

Answer. So far as I know, his reputation was good.

Question. Did you ever hear him charged with any offense or violation of law?

Answer. No, sir; I never did. . . .

Question. Was he to any extent a leading man, a prominent man among the colored people?

Answer. Rather so. The Ware family is one of some prominence; old Mr. Ware, the old man of all, had owned a great many slaves. . . .

Question. What did he tell you in reference to the particulars of that transaction?

Answer. I have stated that it was on account of his politics.

Question. Was this assault committed upon him by a band of disguised men?

Answer. Yes, sir; by disguised men.

Question. Did he say that they told him it was on account of his politics?

Answer. Yes, sir; and then an additional reason, which he mentioned, was to get possession of his place; that is, "to break him up," as the common phrase is. He was fixed very comfortably there. He had rented a place from a lady living in town, and was cultivating about thirty acres of land, and was taking care of the place for her at a specified rate.

Question. Was it because somebody else wanted to get possession of that property, or did they merely want to break him up and drive him off?

Answer. This band wanted to break him up. In connection with telling him that he was a radical, and should not vote the radical ticket any more, they told him that he must go away from there.

Question. What became of this man Ware?

Answer. I have not seen him more than once or twice since, and I do not know what has become of him. He has left the place, however, and is not in possession of it. . . .

Question. Did you ever hear from anybody that there was any allegation against this man Ware, that he had committed any offense against anybody?

Answer. No, sir.

TESTIMONY OF B. F. SAWYER
Atlanta, Georgia, November 1, 1871

[Sawyer was a Democratic newspaper editor in Rome.]

B. F. SAWYER sworn and examined. . . .

Question. What was the case of the negro Jordan [Ware] to which you allude here?

Answer. The case as reported to me by an ex-Federal soldier, a gentleman by the name of Helmcamp, was this: I asked him why they whipped Jordan. It was done on the premises where he was. He said Jordan had insulted a white lady a few days before, and they had whipped him for that. That is all I know about it. . . . I asked him what he would have done. He said, "I should not have waited until night to have whipped him, but I would have blowed his brains out that day."

Question. What was the insult given?

Answer. He had made lecherous advances to the lady.

Question. In what way?

Answer. By speaking to her, and also by his acts.

Question. What had he said to her?

Answer. He called her "wife," and thrust out his tongue at her. The lady ran away very much frightened.

Question. That was the information you had?

Answer. That was the information Mr. Helmcamp gave me.

Question. You spoke of him as an ex-Federal soldier. Why did you mention that fact in connection with what you say was his statement to you?

Answer. I thought that you would regard him as good authority, at any rate as one who would not be apt to be biased.

Question. What are his politics?

Answer. He was a republican, I think, until the last election; at the last election he voted the democratic ticket.

TESTIMONY OF Z. B. HARGROVE
Washington, D.C., July 12, 1871

[Hargrove was a white attorney in Rome.] . . .

Z. B. HARGROVE sworn and examined. . . .

Question. What were you during the war?

Answer. I was an officer in the confederate army for nearly two and a half years. I was a rebel, and a true one, I reckon, if there ever was one. . . .

Question. What have been your political opinions since the war?

Answer. My antecedents are all democratic. . . . I was a reconstruction man, though that was rather in antagonism to my party. . . . I will say that the reason they gave for beating Jourdan Ware was that he had made some insulting remark to a white lady—a lady with whom I am well acquainted. Previous to that time he had borne the reputation of being an humble and obedient negro. He had a little farm, and was doing well, and was comfortable, though in a neighborhood surrounded by the poorer class of white people, who did not like his residence there. He may or may not have made some insulting remark to a white lady; I do not say whether he did or did not, though, from my knowledge of him, my opinion is that he did not.

Question. Let me understand the character of the allegation against him. You say that he made some insulting proposal to a white lady?

Answer. O, no; that he had just made some insulting remark. He remarked, "How d'ye, sis," or something of that kind, as the young lady passed down the road. She was a sister of the lady of whom he had rented the place on which he was living. He was driven away from his home, and came very near being killed. . . .

U.S. Congress, Joint Select Committee on the Condition of Affairs in the Late Insurrectionary States, *Testimony Taken by the Joint Select Committee to Inquire into the Condition of Affairs in the Late Insurrectionary States*, 13 vols. (Washington, D.C.: Government Printing Office, 1872), 6:43–45, 73–75; 7:878, 885.

ॐ

ॐ Tracks of Conflict: Railroads and Chinese Immigration ॐ

The contested question that Wendell Phillips raised—"what makes or constitutes a citizen"—was not limited to conflicts between the North and South or between whites and blacks after the Civil War. The identity and privileges of citizenship also reared its head in heated battles between industrial capitalists and American laborers, and between white native-born workers and Chinese immigrant laborers, as the North's economic culture was crowned the victor after the war.

Perhaps the most significant development after the Civil War was the rapid expansion of railroads in the United States. In the eight years after the war ended (1865–1873), railroad companies in America laid 31,000 miles of track and capped that achievement with the completion of a transcontinental railroad in 1869. Its western road (the Central Pacific) was built almost entirely by the labor of 12,000 Chinese immigrant workers. Chinese immigrants were welcomed when their labor was needed, but even their employers balked at the idea of admitting them into the body politic. Central Pacific executive Charles Crocker, who probably hired more Chinese immigrants than anyone else, told a legislative committee in 1877, "I do not believe they are going to remain here long enough to become good citizens, and I would not admit them to citizenship." Even if they so desired, Chinese immigrants could not become citizens because the federal Naturalization Act of 1790 restricted naturalized citizenship to "white persons." That racial restriction certainly posed no problems to Americans before the Civil War, given that Indians had been forcibly removed and the vast majority of blacks were enslaved. But with Reconstruction, the possibility of nonwhite citizenship became a more pressing concern for white Americans.

The documents in this section reveal the transformative power of the railroads in American culture and expose the hostilities directed against Chinese immigrants in the years leading up to the Chinese Exclusion Act of 1882, as well as the growing cleavage between labor and big business during the great railroad strike of 1877.

Humors of Railroad Travel (1873)

THOMAS WORTH

Railroads transformed American life in the nineteenth century. Everything suddenly moved faster. The sounds, smells, and smoke of railroad engines became an indelible feature of the American landscape. Railroads represented the enormous energy of progress, and as John Gast's painting reveals (see chapter 8), they also became symbols of racial "manifest destiny." When a delegation of Americans led by Commodore Matthew C. Perry visited Japan in 1854 to open its ports for trade, they transported and built a quarter-scale model railroad on a circular track to demonstrate the irresistible strength of American technology. Railroads were also the source of repeated conflicts in the United States. As early as the 1840s, Ralph Waldo Emerson called the railroad "that work of art which agitates and drives mad the whole people." In his 1873 cartoon entitled "Humors of Railroad Travel," the illustrator Thomas Worth captured the bumps, bustles, and confusions that went along with railroad travel. By the 1870s, populists and labor activists also came to see railroads as the country's greatest source of corruption, exploitation, and monopoly privilege.

PROBLEMS TO CONSIDER

1. Is this cartoon an endorsement or a criticism of railroad travel?
2. What are the principal themes of the humor in this cartoon?

Thomas Worth, "Humors of Railroad Travel," *Harper's Weekly*, September 20, 1873.
(The Granger Collection, New York.)

The Chinese in California (1869)

HENRY GEORGE

Many years after the transcontinental railroad had been built, Henry George liked to recall that during the 1850s he went to a theater in San Francisco, and at a climax in the performance a curtain was dropped with a bold painting depicting the overland railroad wending its way to the Pacific. The audience sprang to their feet with thunderous applause. But George recalled that he stopped and wondered whether the railroad would actually improve the lives of laborers. "As the country grows, people come in, wages will go down," were his thoughts. George was a young newspaper editor when the railroad neared completion. In 1868, he published an essay entitled "What the Railroad Will Bring Us." A year later, he focused his concerns on the "Chinese problem" caused by industrialists' desire for cheap Chinese immigrant labor and wondered what would be the consequences when thousands of Chinese workers had completed their work on the railroads. A decade later, George published Progress and Poverty *(1879), the most widely read radical book of the nineteenth century. In it he devised a scheme—the "single tax"—to strip the wealthy of their monopoly on land, make laborers into farmers, drive up wages, and end unemployment and periodic industrial depressions.*

PROBLEMS TO CONSIDER

1. Unlike other racist anti-immigrant sentiments, George offers a fairly positive appraisal of Chinese immigrants. In his opinion, why does this make them even more dangerous?
2. Whom does George blame for the "Chinese problem"?

CHARACTER OF THE ASIATIC IMMIGRATION—THE PROBLEM OF THE PACIFIC COAST

Look at the swarming that is possible from this vast human hive! Consider that if all humanity were marshaled, every third man in the line would wear the queue and the blouse of a Chinaman: that this half billion people could throw off annually six, ten, twenty millions of emigrants, and this not merely without feeling the loss, but without there being any loss. . . .

According to the count of the six great Chinese Companies—to one or the other of which all, or nearly all of the Chinese upon the Pacific Coast belong—there are some 65,000 Chinamen in California and adjacent States and Territories. Knowing the jealousy with which they

are regarded, the Chinese are disposed to understate their numbers, and it is probable that the true figures are nearer 100,000 than those given. Speaking roughly, they may be said to constitute at least one-fourth of the adult male population. . . .

But it would be easier to recount the industries in which Chinamen are not yet to some extent engaged than to mention those in which they are, and every day their employment is extending, as employers in one branch of production after another, discover that they can avail themselves of this cheap labor. They are not only grading railways and opening roads (work for which they are now altogether relied on) cutting wood, picking fruit, tending stock, weaving cloth, and running sewing machines; but acting as firemen upon steamers, running stationary engines, painting carriages, upholstering furniture, making boots, shoes, clothing, cigars, tin and wooden-ware. . . .

The great characteristics of the Chinese as laborers are patience and economy—the first makes them efficient laborers, the second cheap laborers. As a rule they have not the physical strength of Europeans, but their steadiness makes up for this. They take less earth at a spadefull than an Irishman; but in a day's work take up more spadesfull. This patient steadiness peculiarly adapts the Chinese for tending machinery and for manufacturing. The tendency of modern production is to a greater and greater subdivision of labor—to confine the operative to one part of the process, and to require of him close attention, patience, and manual dexterity, rather than knowledge, judgment, and skill. It is in these qualities that the Chinese excel. . . .

CHEAPNESS OF CHINESE LABOR

But the great recommendation of Chinese labor is its cheapness. There are no people in the world who are such close economists as the Chinese. They will live, and live well, according to their notions, where an American or European would starve. A little rice suffices them for food, a little piece of pork cooked with it constitutes high living, an occasional chicken makes it luxurious. Their clothes cost but little and last for a long while. Go into a Chinese habitation and you will see that every inch of space is utilized. . . . Their standard of comfort is very much lower than that of our own people—very much lower than that of any European immigrants who come among us. This fact enables them to underbid all competitors in the labor market. Reduce wages to the starvation point for our mechanics, and the Chinaman will not merely be able to work for less, but to live better than at home, and to save money from his earnings. And thus in every case in which Chinese comes into fair competition with white labor, the whites

must either retire from the field or come down to the Chinese standard of living. . . .

HOSTILITY TO THE CHINESE—UNEQUAL TAXATION

. . . But though the Chinese in many parts of the Pacific coast have been treated badly enough, a most exaggerated idea upon this subject prevails in the East. It is not true, as is sometimes asserted, that a Chinamen cannot walk the streets of a Pacific town without being insulted or assailed. One cannot walk half a block in these towns without meeting a Chinaman, and in any part of San Francisco, at any time, day or night, Chinamen (though boys occasionally shy stones at them) are much safer than are strangers in New-York.

As the competition of Chinese labor with white labor has become more general and threatening, the feeling against them has become correspondingly intense. But a counteracting feeling in their favor has also been developed. While making enemies of the workmen with whom they come into competition, they have made friends of the employers, who found a profit in their labor, and as they have become massed in the employ of great corporations, and in the cities, they are more easily protected.

There is now more reason for an anti-Chinese feeling in California than at any time before; and that feeling, though less general, may be more intense, but it certainly is not as powerful as it has been, and it is doubtful if it could at present secure the prohibition of Chinese immigration, even were there no Constitutional obstacles in the way. . . . There are too many interests becoming involved in the employment of Chinese labor to make this feasible, unless by some sudden awakening to their danger the working classes should be led to such thorough union as should make numbers count for more than capital. . . . A very large and powerful class, rapidly becoming larger and more powerful, is directly interested in maintaining their right to avail themselves of Chinese labor; and this class is further reinforced by those who will prospectively profit by the cheapening of wages, and those whom political sentiment has led to an acceptance in all its fullness of the doctrine of the equality of the races. . . .

CHARACTER OF THE CHINESE

. . . The Mongolians, who are now coming among us on the other side of the continent, differ from our own race by as strongly marked characteristics as do the negroes, while they will not as readily fall into our ways as the negroes. The difference between the two races in this respect is as the difference between an ignorant but docile child and a grown man, sharp but narrow-minded, opinionated and set in character. The negro when brought to this country was a simple barbarian with nothing to unlearn; the Chinese have a civilization and history of their own; a vanity which causes them to look down on all other races, habits of thought rendered permanent by being stamped upon countless generations. . . . A population born in China, reared in China, expecting to return to China, living while here in a little China of its own, and without the slightest attachment to this country—utter heathens, treacherous, sensual, cowardly, and cruel. They bring no women with them . . . except those intended for purposes of prostitution. . . .

WHAT SHALL WE DO WITH THEM?

Take it in any aspect, does not this Chinese question merit more attention than it has received? A little cloud now on the far Western horizon, does it not bid fair to overshadow the whole future of the Republic? . . . Give him fair play and this quality enables him to drive out stronger races. One hundred thousand Mongolians on the Pacific coast means so many less of our race now and hereafter to be. . . .

In truth it is not to be wondered at that Chinese immigration should find so many advocates in the Pacific States. With their unparalleled natural resources, an unlimited supply of this cheap labor will make them beyond all question the most remunerative field in the world for the employment of capital, where the rich will get richer with unexampled rapidity. California will not only become a great mining and a great agricultural State, but a great manufacturing State; controlling by virtue of her cheap labor the immense market opening in the heart of the continent, and competing successfully with New and Old England almost to their doors. Let but the introduction of Chinese labor go a little further and the same change which was wrought in Southern sentiment regarding Slavery by the invention of the cotton-gin will be completed on the Pacific in the feeling toward Chinese labor.

Henry George, "The Chinese in California," *New York Daily Tribune*, May 1, 1869.

⟋

Chinese Immigrants Challenge Nativist Discrimination: California State Senate Investigation (1876)

As we might expect, the voices of Chinese immigrants never were heard as loudly in the public sphere as were the anti-immigration voices of native-born laborers. The docility of Chinese workers, however, was a myth that suited nativist aggression. When facing discrimination or exploitation, Chinese immigrants did rise up and resist, although with mixed results. In the spring of 1867, thousands of Chinese workers went on strike against the Central Pacific Railroad, demanding an eight-hour workday and wages of forty-five dollars a month. Charles Crocker flirted with the idea of transporting 10,000 black men from the South to replace the striking Chinese workers but instead settled on a plan of cutting off their food supplies and literally starving them back to work. In 1876, the California legislature initiated hearings on the problem of Chinese immigration. Although the legislature concluded that such immigration was "an unmitigated evil" and they successfully lobbied Congress to eventually pass the Chinese Exclusion Act in 1882, these hearings gave Chinese immigrants a chance to raise their voices against the daily discrimination they faced. Legislators tried to get most Chinese witnesses to confirm their presumed stereotypes (for example, that the Chinese were dirty or that they exploited women as prostitutes), but occasionally an independent immigrant would confound their efforts.

PROBLEMS TO CONSIDER

1. How did these immigrants challenge the hostile questioning they encountered from state legislators?
2. What do these testimonies reveal about the way Chinese immigrants understood the era's labor and citizenship issues? Compare their perspectives with Henry George's.

TESTIMONY OF HONG CHUNG (1876)

Hong Chung sworn.

Mr. Donovan—How long have you been in this country?

A.—Twenty-four years.

Q.—Are you in business here?

A.—I am Inspector for the Sam-yup Company.

Q.—Have you declared your intention of becoming an American citizen?

A.—Yes, sir. . . .

Q.—Are many other Chinamen going to become citizens?

A.—Yes, sir.

Q.—A great many?

A.—Yes, sir.

Q.—Will all become American citizens?

A.—Yes, sir.

Q.—And stay here?

A.—Yes, sir.

Q.—Will they become candidates for the office of Governor of the State as soon as they are citizens?

A.—May be; I don't know. They are going to become citizens. I like to be citizen. American man make no good laws for Chinaman. We make good laws for Chinaman citizens.

Q.—Would you like to be Governor of the State of California?

A.—Of course. I like the State of California a long time; I like a free country.

Q.—Would you like to be Governor?

A.—I cannot be Governor. I like the State of California, and I like to be a citizen of the American man's people.

Q.—Would you like to hold office under the free American Government?

A.—No, I wouldn't do it.

TESTIMONY OF LEM SCHAUM (1876)

LEM SCHAUM sworn.

Mr. Haymond—How long have you resided in California?

A.—About fourteen years, sir.

Q.—From what part of China did you come?

A.—One hundred and fifty miles from Canton. . . .

Q.—Are you a Christian Chinaman?

A.—Yes, sir.

Q.—How long since you believed in the Christian religion?

A.—Since about eighteen hundred and seventy.

Q.—Have you tried to make Christians out of your countrymen here?

A.—I tried that; but it is very hard work to do it.

Q.—Do some of them pretend to be Christians when they are not?

A.—Only those grown-up fellows; the young boys do not. Boys working around see the American customs, and we can instruct them in no time; but the old ones think Confucius' is the only good religion, and with them it is very hard work. . . .

Q.—How many Christian Chinamen do you think there are in California altogether?

A.—About four years ago we formed a Chinese Young Men's Christian Association at the Rev. Dr. Loomis' place. There were twenty-eight of us when we formed that society, but the number has grown up to about five hundred.

Q.—Do you think that many are Christians?

A.—I think about half are real Christians. . . .

Q.—You have seen the Chinese quarters? Do you think that it is good for the Chinese, or for the Americans, to have those people living as they do?

A.—I think it is very bad for both Chinese and Americans.

Q.—As a general rule, taking the one hundred and fifty thousand of them in California, they don't learn much good after they come here, do they? Don't they learn the vices of the country?

A.—That is your own fault. No Chinaman can take a walk up and down the street unless you find an Irishman or a Dutchman to strike them down. They struck one down and I told them I would have them arrested and put in the County Jail for six months. A great many Chinamen desire to learn to read and write English, and then also our methods of business, or any kind of work; perhaps the arts or sciences.

Q.—They live very cheaply, don't they?

A.—They must live cheaply, sir. They have got to live cheaply because they only get about fifteen dollars a month, or three or four dollars a week.

Q.—A great many live in the same house?

A.—Yes; a great many live together, because they have not got money enough to have rooms as you have. . . .

Q.—Suppose the mass of that immigration was stopped, do you think it would have any influence on our commercial relations with other parts of China?

A.—No. I think this immigration must stop. I say it is not only ruining Americans, but it ruins the Chinese. Their wages, we notice, come down every day. A short time ago Chinamen got thirty-six dollars a month working on the railroad. What do they get now? Twenty-six dollars per month—one dollar a day. This immigration must be stopped in some way. . . .

Q.—What is the general opinion of Christian Chinamen with whom you associate in this State as to the policy or impolicy of having this Chinese immigration continue without any limits?

A.—We think that this immigration must be stopped. It must be stopped in some way, and then we can look after those Christians educated in this country. We want to stretch forth our hand as far as we can so as instruct them about a better world than this. That is our object, and a good many of them are going back to preach at home. Looking at this thing from a Christian standpoint, I think that christianity is not advanced by this immigration, and I would give anything in the world to have it stopped.

Q.—In the Eastern States, when we proposed to check this immigration, or to limit it to the better class of Chinese, we were met with this proposition: that Chinese immigration to this country would have the result of christianizing China. I understand you to say that the immigration, such as is coming here now, don't tend to the advancement of christianity?

A. —It does not.

Q.—So it would be better, then, from your standpoint as a Chinaman, to stop it, for by stopping it you would make more Christians?

A. —Yes, sir.

_____

Chinese Immigration: The Social, Moral, and Political Effect of Chinese Immigration. *Testimony Taken Before a Committee of the Senate of the State of California* (Sacramento: State Printing Office, 1876), 114, 135–39.

ᔜ

Every Dog (No Distinction of Color) Has His Day (1879)
THOMAS NAST

Thomas Nast was the most prolific and best-known political cartoonist in nineteenth-century America. He was also a first-generation immigrant, born in Landau in the Rhineland (a region claimed at different times by Prussia, Bavaria, France, and Germany), and emigrated to the United States at age six. By the time he was fifteen, Nast had been hired as a cartoonist for the top illustrated newspaper in New York. He is responsible for the image of the Republican elephant and the Democratic donkey, icons that are still in use today. Nast was also a Radical Republican, and his editorial cartoons advocated civil rights for former slaves, although his images often reinforced rather than challenged American racial stereotypes. At the height of anti-Chinese politics in the 1870s, Nast produced the following cartoon for the cover of Harper's Weekly. *In it, he caricatures the slogans of postwar nativist politics, giving it the caption "Red Gentleman to Yellow Gentleman: 'Pale face 'fraid you crowd him out, as he did me.'" In the background is a freedman, sitting on a cotton bale, with the caption "My day is coming."*

PROBLEMS TO CONSIDER

1. What are the various messages embedded in Nast's cartoon?
2. Was Nast's cartoon directed at any particular group of Americans?

Thomas Nast, "Every Dog (No Distinction of Color) Has His Day," *Harper's Weekly*, February 8, 1879.

(The Granger Collection, New York.)

Fair Wages (1877)
A "STRIKER"

The Recent Strikes (1877)
THOMAS A. SCOTT

Railroad corporations were the vanguard of the rise of "big business" in the United States. They leaped to adopt modern management methods, stimulating additional manufacturing sectors such as the iron and coal industries and creating a national market for the products of American manufacturers. Yet despite tremendous industrial growth after the Civil War, in 1873 the nation entered the worst depression in its history, a four-year-long stagnation that left as many as a million workers unemployed. Railroad workers endured repeated wage reductions throughout the depression, prompting railroad strikes in 1873 and 1874, but none compared to the "Great Uprising" in 1877. In March 1877, the presidents of four railroads agreed to cut wages again. Workers had reached their breaking point. Simultaneous work stoppages occurred in fourteen states that July; and in Pittsburgh, the Pennsylvania state militia opened fire on strikers, killing forty people and prompting strikers to burn, loot, and destroy tracks, locomotives, and other railroad property. Railroad lines were disrupted throughout the Northeast and Midwest, and sympathetic strikes of other industrial workers broke out everywhere. In Chicago, 20,000 workers took to the streets. The 1877 railroad strike was the first nationwide strike in American history, and the first in which the federal government directed its considerable resources (the army) to support big business. Soon after the strike, the North American Review *published separately a letter from a striking railway worker and a letter from Thomas Scott, president of the Pennsylvania Railroad. Their statements illustrate the sharp differences between capital and labor during an era of unprecedented industrial expansion in America.*

PROBLEMS TO CONSIDER

1. How do the values and ideals of this railroad worker and the president of the Pennsylvania Railroad differ? Both men appear fearful for the future; what does each anticipate the future will bring?
2. What were the repercussions of using a slavery analogy to describe capital versus labor at the end of Reconstruction?

FAIR WAGES

Forty years ago my father came over to this country from Sweden. . . . He heard that North America was peopled and governed by working-men, and the care of the States was mainly engaged in the welfare and prosperity of labor. That moved him, and so I came to be born here.

He, and millions like him, made this country their home, and their homes have mainly made this country what it is. . . .

[Since the Civil War,] it seems to me, the power has got fixed so long in one set of hands that things are settling down into a condition like what my father left behind in Europe forty years ago, and what stands there still. I mean the slavery of labor. The landed aristocracy over there made the feudal system, just as the mon-eyed men of this continent are now making a ruling class. As the aristocracy used to make war on each other, so in our time the millionnaires live on each other's ruin. As the feudal lords hired mercenary soldiers to garrison their strong-holds and to prey on the common people, so the railway lords and stock-exchange barons hire a mercenary press to defend power, the object of both being the same: the spoils of labor. . . .

That government has been regarded by the laboring classes of Europe and by our people as the stronghold of the workingman, and in this our present difficulty we are referred to its Con-stitution which should afford us a remedy for our grievances, the ballot-box is the panacea for all and every complaint. It is not so; and those who point to the remedy know it to be a sham, — they know they can buy idlers and vagabonds enough to swell the ranks of wealth and run up a majority whenever a show of hands is required. They recruit the very men that wrecked Pittsburgh, and would pillage New York if they dared to face us, the workingmen, that fill the ranks of the militia.

We are sick of this game, we are soul-weary of looking around for some sympathy or spirit of justice, and, finding none, we turn to each other and form brotherhoods and unions, depots of the army of labor, officered by the skilled mechanic.

This organized force is now in process of for-mation, and prepared to meet the great ques-tions of the age: Has labor any rights? If so, what are they? Our claim is simple. We demand *fair wages.*

We say that the man able and willing to work, and for whom there is work to do, is entitled to wages sufficient to provide him with enough food, shelter, and clothing to sustain and pre-serve his health and strength. We contend that the employer has no right to speculate on star-vation when he reduces wages below a living fig-ure, saying, if we refuse that remuneration, there are plenty of starving men out of work that will gladly accept half a loaf instead of no bread.

We contend that to regard the laboring class in this manner is to consider them as the captain of a slave-ship regards his cargo, who throws overboard those unable to stand their sufferings. Let those who knew the South before the war go now amongst the mining districts of Penn-sylvania, and compare the home of the white la-borer with the quarters of the slave; let them compare the fruits of freedom with the produce of slavery!

But we know the question is a difficult one to settle, — we do not want to force it on with threats. The late strike was not intended to break out as it did; things broke loose and took a direction we regretted. We find ourselves an-swerable for results we had no share in or con-trol over. Nevertheless we accept the event as a symptom of the disorder that is consuming our body and pray the country to look to it, — it is not a passing complaint. . . .

When folks say that labor and capital must find, by the laws of demand and supply, their natural relations to each other in all commercial enterprises, and neither one has any rights it can enforce on the other, they take for granted that the labor "market" is like the produce market, li-able to natural fluctuations. If that were so, we should not complain. But it is not. The labor market has got to be like the stock and share market; a few large capitalists control it and make what prices they please. This sort of game may ruin the gamblers in stocks, and injure those who invest, but the trouble is confined mostly to those who deserve to lose or those who can afford it.

But not so when the same practice operates in the labor market. The capitalist must not gamble with the bread of the workingman, or if he does, let him regard where that speculation led France one hundred years ago, when the fin-anciers made a corner in flour, and the people broke the ring with the axe of the guillotine.

A "STRIKER"

A "Striker," "Fair Wages," *North American Review* 125 (Sep-tember 1877): 322–25.

THE RECENT STRIKES

I do not wish, and happily it is not necessary, to fill your pages with the mere recital of the distressing cases of violence and outrage which marked the course of these riots unexampled in American history. Suffice it to say that the conduct of the rioters is entirely inconsistent with the idea that this movement could have been directed by serious, right-minded men bent on improving the condition of the laboring classes. How wages could be improved by destroying property, the existence of which alone made the payment of any wages at all possible, it is difficult to understand. Nothing but the insanity of passion, played upon by designing and mischievous leaders, can explain the destruction of vast quantities of railroad equipment absolutely necessary to the transaction of its business, by men whose complaint was that the business done by the full equipment in possession of the railways did not pay them sufficient compensation for their labor.

During the greater part of our century of national existence we have enjoyed such unbroken prosperity that we had perhaps come to expect exemption from many of the worst problems which perplex other and older civilizations. The vast area of public land open to cultivation and settlement had steadily drained off not only our own surplus population, but that of other countries, and the rapid extension of our railway system, by furnishing markets for the productions of all parts of the country, had increased the national wealth and built up a general prosperity. But for the Civil War [*followed by the panic of 1873*] this state of things might have continued to exist. . . . Every important industry in the country has been compelled to practise the closest and most rigid economies, in order to escape marketing its products at an absolute loss. . . . In every manufacturing State in the country it is perfectly well known that many establishments have been kept in operation simply that the men

might be employed. This has been done often without one iota of profit to the owners. . . .

With the falling off of revenue from traffic, the question was presented at once to railway managers, . . . whether it would not be both wiser and kinder to retain as many men as possible in the service, by so allotting the work as to permit all to earn a sum, smaller indeed than in the past, yet it was hoped sufficient to support themselves and their families during the severe period of depression. . . .

This insurrection, which extended through fourteen States, and in many cases successfully defied the local authorities, presents a state of acts almost as serious as that which prevailed at the outbreak of the Civil War. Unless our own experience is to differ entirely from other countries,—and it is not easy to see why it should, with the increasing population of our large cities and business centres, and the inevitable assemblage at such points of the vicious and evil-disposed,—the late troubles may be but the prelude to other manifestations of mob violence, with this added peril, that now, for the first time in American history, has an organized mob learned its power to terrorize the law-abiding citizens of great communities. . . .

If the government of the United States is to exercise its power of protection or of remedy, it perhaps can do so only through an adequate exhibition of the military force that may be given it for such purposes by Congress. The important question is to ascertain in what way the government can so exhibit its military force as to secure the utmost possible efficiency in the enforcement of law and order without jarring or disturbing the general framework of our institutions and our laws. It seems to be indispensable, in the light of recent events, that whatever force is to be used by the government in such emergencies should be so distributed and controlled that it may be concentrated upon any point or points that may be threatened within a few hours of any outbreak. . . .

The magnitude of the evil to be met and dealt with can hardly be overstated. The remedy to be provided should be equally prompt and effective. It must be discussed and adopted in the interest of the whole country, and not of any particular class; for the interests of all classes of our citizens are the same in the maintenance of domestic peace and civil order.

But to no one class in the community is an absolute assurance of peace so important as to the men who have no capital but their labor. When the accumulations of labor are put in peril by lawlessness, capital may always protect itself by suspending the enterprises which give labor its value and insure it its reward. Anarchy not only deprives the laboring man of his present subsistence, but puts in jeopardy all his hopes of improvement for his own future and the future of his family.

THOMAS A. SCOTT

Thomas A. Scott, "The Recent Strikes," *North American Review* 125 (September 1877): 352–62.

✌

ᵔ TEXT CREDITS